I0094799

August V.T. Spies

In the Supreme Court of Illinois

August V.T. Spies

In the Supreme Court of Illinois

ISBN/EAN: 9783744794046

Printed in Europe, USA, Canada, Australia, Japan

Cover: Foto ©Suzi / pixelio.de

More available books at **www.hansebooks.com**

IN THE

Supreme Court of Illinois,

NORTHERN GRAND DIVISION.

March Term, A. D. 1887.

AUGUST SPIES et al.,
Plaintiffs in Error,

vs.

THE PEOPLE OF THE STATE OF
ILLINOIS,
Defendant in Error.

Error to the
Criminal Court of
Cook County.

Hon. Jos. E. Gary,
Presiding.

INDICTMENT FOR MURDER.

BRIEF AND ARGUMENT FOR PLAINTIFFS IN ERROR.

W. P. BLACK AND
SALOMON & ZEISLER,

Attorneys for Plaintiffs in Error.

CHICAGO:
BARNARD & GUNTHORP, LAW PRINTERS, 44 & 46 LASALLE STREET.
1887.

INDEX.

	Page.
STATEMENT OF CHARGE	1

A. THE PLAINTIFFS IN ERROR ARE NOT GUILTY.

EVIDENCE LEGITIMATELY BEFORE THE JURY	2
Oscar Neebe	2
Samuel Fielden	3
a.) The claim that he made threats	7
b.) The claim that he fired from the wagon	10
c.) The claim that he fired from behind the wagon	13
Albert R. Parsons	20
Michael Schwab	27
a.) His movements	29
b.) Spies' movements	32
c.) Improbability of Thompson's story	38
August Spies	40
a.) The McCormick meeting	40
b.) The Revenge circular	45
c.) The circular calling the Haymarket meeting	49
d.) The signal " Ruhe,"	50
e.) Spies' Haymarket speech	53
f.) Gilmer's testimony	57
1.) Schnaubelt's height	60
2.) Spies did not enter the alley	60
3.) Fischer at Zepf's Hall	66
4.) Bomb not thrown from alley	68
5.) Gilmer's impeachment	74
Adolph Fischer	82
The W. Lake St. meeting conspiracy	83
1.) Six accused no parties to it	91
2.) Bomb-throwing foreign to it	91
3.) Bomb not thrown by a member thereof	93

EVIDENCE LEGITIMATELY BEFORE THE JURY (*Continued*):   Page.

George Engel 96

Louis Lingg 99

The Haymarket Meeting 112

OUR POSITIONS UPON THE LEGITIMATE EVIDENCE 123

   I. Mere participation in an unlawful assembly does not make responsible for the independent crime of a participant 123

  II. To hold the accused as accessories on the ground of conspiracy, the principal must be identified as co-conspirator 138

 III. And the crime must have been within its purview 141

ILLEGITIMATE EVIDENCE 145

   I. Newspaper literature 155

  II. Johann Most's book 161

 III. Various objects 164

     1.) Bloody clothes 164

     2.) Fragments resulting from dynamite experiments 165

     3.) Tin cans 166

     4.) Blasting furnace 168

     5.) Flags and mottoes 169

     6.) Dynamite at Arbeiter Zeitung 169

     7.) Weapons found on Fischer 172

     8.) Bombs found after May 4, 1886 172

 IV. Evidence extorted from accused 173

     1.) Improper cross-examination 174

     2.) Objects unlawfully seized 179

  V. Speeches and private utterances 184

     a.) The Board of Trade demonstration 185

     b.) West 12th street meeting 189

     c.) The American Group 190

     d.) Private conversations of Spies 193

     e.) Eight-hour agitation meeting 195

     f.) General tendency of utterances 197

 VI. Other illegitimate evidence 198

     Injuries of officers 198

     Schnaubelt's disguise 198

Page.

OUR POSITIONS UPON THE ILLEGITIMATE EVIDENCE.................. 203

I. No responsibilty for the act of an associate in purpose, but not in action... 203

II. Evidence of distinct substantive offenses inadmissible... 207

III. Prima facie conspiracy must first be established, before acts or declarations of one are evidence against another 212

IV. Such acts and declarations must be in prosecution of conspiracy.. 213

REFUSAL OF MOTIONS AT CLOSE OF STATE'S CASE..................... 219

I. Motion for Neebe............ 219

II. Motion for other accused except Spies and Fischer....... 226

B. ERRORS COMPLAINED OF:

SUMMARY OF ERRORS CONSIDERED BEFORE 231

AA. ERRORS IN THE MATTER OF INSTRUCTIONS...................... 232

Summary of our complaints... 232
I. Necessity of identifying principal....................... 234
II. Instructions at variance with proof.................... 248
III. Hypothesis unwarranted by evidence.................... 255
IV. Mere general advice does not constitute accessoryship.. 256
V. Instruction 5½ contains no reference to evidence......... 269
VI. Erroneous instructions on reasonable doubt................ 272
VII. Instruction limiting right of jury to judge of the law... 276
VIII. Instructions refused. 279
IX. The court's instruction *sua motu*............................ 286
X. The instruction as to form of verdict....................... 290
XI. The instructions as a whole................................. 291

BB. ERRORS ON IMPANELING OF JURY.............................. 299

I. The law relating to qualifications of jurors................. 299
a.) Constitutional Provisions.................. 299
b.) Their construction by the U. S. Supreme Court.......... 300
c.) Their Interpretation by our own Supreme Court........ 305
d.) The Statute of 1874 and its Judicial Construction....... 311
e.) Construction of similar statutes in other States.......... 318
f.) Propriety of Questions in reference to Peremptory Challenges 330

BB. Errors on Impaneling of Jury (*Continued*):   Page.

  II. Judge Gary's Rulings.. 332

    His Positions. 332

    Our Contentions 335

  III. Examinations of jurors illustrative of Judge Gary's rulings 338

  IV. The twelve who tried the case.. 380

  V. The conduct of the special bailiff.................................. 391

  VI. Misconduct of jury... 393

  VII. Number of peremptory challenges allowed the state....... 394

  VIII. Manner of impaneling the jury 397

CC. Improper Remarks by the Court................................... 399

DD. Improprieties of Closing Argument of State's Attorney 408

  I. The objectionable remarks.. 409

  II. Decisions relating thereto... 415

EE. Refusing to Arrest Judgment....................................... 420

  Conclusion 422

On the night of the 4th of May, 1886, in the city of Chicago, a meeting of citizens was being held on Desplaines street, between Randolph and Lake, commonly called the Haymarket meeting. Some of the plaintiffs in error were present at that meeting during a part or the whole of the time. Others were not there at all while the meeting was being held. As it was approaching a close, a large body of police, some 180 in number, under the command of Inspector John Bonfield, came from the Desplaines street police station, situate about half a block south of Randolph street, on Desplaines, to the meeting, approaching it from the south, and on reaching a line about six or eight feet south of the wagon, from which the crowd was being addressed, commanded its immediate dispersion. Directly after this command was given, a dynamite bomb was thrown, which exploded among the policemen, resulting in the killing of several of them, among whom was Mathias J. Degan.

The indictment in this case, stripped of legal verbiage, so far as it was attempted to be supported by evidence, charged the plaintiffs in error, together with William Seliger and Rudolph Schnaubelt, with having thrown the bomb which killed Mathias J. Degan, or with having aided, abetted, assisted, advised or encouraged some person in the throwing of that bomb.

The provisions of the statute applicable to the latter charge, and which must be considered in the determination of this question, are Secs. 2 and 3 of Div. 2 of Chap. 38, Rev. Stat. of Ill., 1874, found as Secs. 274 and 275 of our Criminal Code, which are as follows:

" SEC. 2. An accessory is he who stands by and aids,

" abets or assists, or who, not being present aiding, abet-
" ting or assisting, hath advised, encouraged, aided or
" abetted the perpetration of the crime. He who thus
" aids, abets, assists, advises or encourages, shall be con-
" sidered as principal, and punished accordingly."

" Sec. 3. Every such accessory, when a crime is
" committed, within or without this state, by his aid or
" procurement in this state, may be indicted and convicted
" at the same time as the principal, or before or after his
" conviction, and whether the principal is convicted or
" amenable to justice or not, and punished as principal."

We claim that the evidence in this case fails to
establish the above charge against any of the plaintiffs
in error, and therefore we maintain that

A. THE PLAINTIFFS IN ERROR ARE NOT GUILTY.

In support of this contention, we shall consider, separately, the cases of the eight plaintiffs in error, so far as
the charge was attempted to be supported by

EVIDENCE LEGITIMATELY BEFORE THE JURY.

Oscar Neebe.

The verdict of the jury adjudged Oscar W. Neebe to
be " guilty of murder in manner and form as charged in
" the indictment," and the court sentenced him to fifteen
years in the penitentiary. As to Mr. Neebe, we contend that there is no pretense finding support in the
evidence that he was present at this meeting, or knew
of the purpose of holding it, or was consulted as to
calling it, or knew that the same would be held; and
that there is no testimony that shows, or tends to show,

that he advised, aided, encouraged, abetted or assisted the throwing of the bomb. We find ourselves at a loss to argue the case of Mr. Neebe. There is absolutely nothing in the record to support his conviction; and in presenting this case in the first instance, to the consideration of this honorable court, we will rest as to Mr. Neebe and wait to see what the representatives of the prosecution can say upon this record in support of a verdict and judgment against him under the above indictment.

SAMUEL FIELDEN.

It is admitted that he was present at the Haymarket meeting and was one of its speakers, his address being interrupted by the appearance of the police and the order for its dispersion; and that he was on the ground at the time of the explosion of the bomb.

But there is evidence uncontradicted which shows, in reference to his prior movements, and his connection with this meeting, the following state of facts: On Sunday night, May 2d, he had made an engagement to speak at a labor meeting, to be held at either 368 or 378 West 12th street, on Tuesday night, May 4th (Vol. M, 340; A, 272);* on May 4th, on arriving home in the evening, from his work of teaming, he saw in the Evening News an announcement of a meeting of the American group of the International Working People's Association, of which group he was a member, and at that time the treasurer. The notice called the meeting to be held at 107 5th avenue at 8 o'clock that night, and the announcement said " Important business." Seeing this announcement, Fielden determined to attend that meeting, because of his

---

*A. means Vol. 2 of the abstract. Vol. 1 of the abstract will be cited by " 1A." We cite the record by the letter of the volume.

official relation to the group, instead of going to his appointment on West 12th street. He arrived at 107 5th avenue about 8 p. m. (Vol. M, 306, 307; A, 265). The meeting, which was attended by about fifteen members, among whom was A. R. Parsons, considered the matter of the organization of the sewing women of Chicago, with reference to the eight-hour movement, and some money was paid out by Fielden, upon the order of the meeting, for that purpose. The meeting lasted until about 9 p. m. During the progress of the meeting, Balthazar Rau called, and said that speakers were wanted at the Haymarket meeting. Pursuant to this notification (the business for which the American group meeting was called having been substantially transacted), the group meeting adjourned, and Fielden Parsons and nearly all of the others present went over to the Haymarket meeting. All this appears from the testimony of the witnesses, Patterson (Vol. M, 42, 44; A, 228), Snyder (Vol. M, 101; A, 235), Brown (Vol. M, 120, 123; A, 238), Waldo (Vol. M, 168; A, 245), Mrs. Holmes (Vol. M, 279, 281; A, 261), Parsons (Vol. M, 110; A, 313), and other witnesses.

It nowhere appears in the record that this meeting of the American group considered anything else, or transacted any other business, or was called for any other purpose except as above suggested. The first knowledge that Fielden had that the Haymarket meeting was to be held was acquired by him at this meeting of the American group. (Vol. M, 321; A, 269.) When Fielden reached the Haymarket meeting he went on the speakers' wagon with Parsons, Brown and Snyder. At that time Spies was still speaking, but stopped shortly after their appearance, and introduced Mr. Parsons as the next speaker. (Vol. M, 102, 340, 341; A, 235, 272.)

Parsons made a speech of about an hour, after which Fielden spoke for about twenty minutes. Probably the most reliable account of his speech that was presented by the prosecution is found in the testimony of Mr. English, who attended the meeting as a reporter for the Chicago Tribune, and took shorthand notes at intervals of the proceedings, and the speeches made. (A, 129.) It is to be observed, however, that Mr. English himself says his instructions from the Tribune office were to take *only the most incendiary part of the speeches* (K, 286; A, 134), and that his testimony presents *only an abstract* of what the speakers said (A, 130; K, 277, 278); while Fielden claims that English's report was *garbled*, and does not give the connections, and therefore *does not make sense.* (M, 346, 347; A, 273.) In Fielden's speech, even as reported by English, however (A, 132, 133), not one word can be found which has the least reference to the bomb-throwing, or contains any proposition or suggestion for the use of violence that night, or in the immediate future. Fielden took for his text an utterance of Congressman Foran of Ohio, to the effect that the laborer can get no relief from legislation, and tried to deduce from the facts stated by him, that the law protected only the employer, affording no protection to the workingmen, if they were injured in their interests. Speaking of the so-called McCormick riot on the afternoon of May 3d, the day preceding the Haymarket meeting, to which we shall have occasion to refer hereafter, he said, " Men, in their blind rage, attacked McCormick's factory," etc. (K, 282; A, 132.)

" Men in their *blind rage* "—that was the characterization by Fielden of the persons who threw stones at McCormick's factory and employes. True, Fielden said, as a conclusion from the facts stated by him, "You have "nothing more to do with the law, except to lay hands on "it and throttle it until it makes its last kick. It turns your "brothers out on the wayside, and has degraded them "until they have lost the last vestige of humanity, and "they are mere things and animals. Keep your eye "upon it, throttle it, kill it, stab it, do everything you can "to wound it or impede its progress." (K, 282; A, 132.) This is foolish talk, but what man in his right senses will claim that this or any other remark testified to as having been made by Fielden is anything more than a rhetorical flourish or theoretical statement in regard to the law in the abstract as affecting the working classes? How can it be seriously maintained that such language constituted advice to the throwing of a bomb into the ranks of the police, who had not yet made their appearance on the scene, who were not then expected by anybody, last of all by Fielden, who swears he had no idea of there being a superior number of police at the station near by? (M, 358; A, 275.) As well argue that the excited politician who proposes to "knife" an obnoxious candidate, or to "lay him out," or "put a "head" on him, or to "destroy" the opposite party, or to "throttle" the opposition, in these expressions counsels personal violence as against the individuals involved in the suggestion. It seems to us that the suggestion that these words of Mr. Fielden imported advice to personal violence against the officers of the law, or that *they* should be stabbed, throttled, impeded, wounded, killed, is without foundation. He was talking of a system, and not of any class of men, of an abstraction, and not of individuals.

A strenuous effort was made on the part of the prose-cution, to involve Mr. Fielden personally with the matters occurring at this meeting in connection with and immediately following the throwing of the bomb, and we propose briefly to' review the testimony adduced in this effort. It consists of three parts.

(*a.*) *The claim that Fielden made threats.*

Officer Quinn and Officer Haas swear that they heard Fielden, the speaker, upon the wagon, who was speaking at the time the police force approached, cry out in a loud voice, "Here come the blood-hounds of the police! Men, do your duty and I will do mine," or similar words.

Quinn testifies (A, 14) that he heard that remark when within about *fifty feet* of where the speaker was, while Haas (A, 128; K, 251) says, he heard it when the first company of the police got north of Randolph street, within *ten or fifteen feet* of the wagon. Haas was then pretty near the middle of the street and within five or six feet, yet Haas admits on cross-examination that he was a *witness at the coroner's inquest,* on which occasion *he said nothing of having heard Fielden utter these words.* (A, 128; K, 268.) These two are the only witnesses who positively swear that it was Fielden who made that utterance.

Lieut. Steele (A, 13) testifies that his and Quinn's companies constituted the front line; that shortly prior to the halt being called, he heard somebody say, "Here "comes the blood-hounds. You do your duty and we "will do ours;" but he says distinctly that *he cannot tell who made the remark,* the sound coming from in front, while they were marching. It appears that Lieut. Steele was on the east side of the street, and was therefore nearer to the wagon than Quinn, whose company was to the left of Steele's. (A., 13; I, 183.) Besides, Quinn says he is not positive whether it was Ward or Bonfield who commanded the meeting to disperse, although he admits that he has known Ward for fourteen years, Bonfield for eight or ten years. (A., 15; I, 202, 203.) This witness therefore confesses that he could not distinguish the voice of the officer, who admittedly gave the command to disperse in a *very loud* tone of voice (A., 3; I, 46), who stood at the time not more than *twenty or twenty-five feet* distant from him (A., 15; I, 195), and whom he had *known for fourteen years;* but still he claims to positively recognize the voice of Fielden, who was a *stranger to him* and was *fifty feet distant* from him at the time of the alleged remark.

Officer Krueger says (A, 17) he stood number one, front rank of the column, and that when he got up *within twenty-five or thirty feet* of the wagon, he heard something like this: " Here they are now, the blood-" hounds." *He does not claim to have heard the second part of the alleged remark :* he says that he would judge it was the speaker on the wagon that made the remark, but would not be positive.

Officer Wessler (A, 18) says he was in Lieut. Bowler's company, which was the second of the column, and when he got about as far as the *Randolph street car-track* (a distance of about *one hundred feet*), he heard the remark: " Here comes the blood-hounds," but does not state who made it.

Lieut. Bowler testifies (A, 22) that while they were marching to the scene, he heard the words: " Here come " the blood-hounds," said by somebody close to the wagon, but does not pretend that it was said by any one on the wagon; while Officer Doyle says (A, 25) that he was in Bowler's company and heard the words: " Now is your " time, now is your time," said by some one looking like

Fielden. But he further says that the man who said " Now is your time " did not shoot in the wagon or going from it.

This is the whole of the state's case as to this particular utterance; and it will be observed that of all the witnesses called by the state, only a few policemen pretend to have heard those significant words; further, that they claim to have heard it from all possible distances and in all possible forms.

On the other hand, neither Bonfield nor Ward, who were a little in advance of the front rank of the column, claim to have heard any such remark; while Freeman, a reporter for the Inter Ocean, says that he was at the time some eight or ten feet from Fielden (Vol. K, 47; A, 107), that he did not hear that remark and that he knows of nothing to prevent his hearing it if Fielden had said it. Hull, a reporter for the News, also a witness for the prosecution, stated (Vol. K, 132; A, 118) that he heard Fielden remark, as he was approaching the end of his speech: "In conclusion," but that he did not hear the remark testified to by Quinn.

Besides these witnesses for the state, the following witnesses introduced by the defendants testified positively that no such remark was made, and they were all in a position, where, if such a remark had been made in a tone of voice loud enough to have been heard at a distance of from 50 to 100 feet, they could not but have heard it, and from the nature of the remark it could not but have attracted their attention, namely: Simonson (A., 178; L, 69); Richter (A., 187; L, 183); Liebel (A., 189; L, 201); Taylor (A., 191; L, 229); Gutscher (A., 198; L, 302); Urban (A., 202; L, 350); Lindinger (A., 215; L, 474); Heidekrueger (A., 222; L, 546); Holloway (A., 230; M, 61); Snyder (A., 237; M, 111);

Murphy (A., 256; M, 243); Bach (A., 281; M, 406);
Ingram (A., 288; M. 452); Spies (A., 303; N, 55):
and Fielden himself (A., 269; N, 321).

Mr. English, although he was upon the scene with instructions to report *the most incendiary utterances*, and
although he distinctly heard the order for dispersion given
by Capt. Ward, says positively that he did not hear the
remark testified to by Quinn and his supporters. (A.,
134; K, 287.) It is further to be observed, that not
one of the many witnesses put upon the stand by the state,
who were reporters for the various papers, and who testified that they wrote up reports for publication in the
issue of the following day, pretended to testify to any
such remark as is attributed to Fielden.

When to this we add the fact that this particular remark is one of the heirlooms of the detectives and the
police, having served on duty on previous occasions, as,
for instance, in the trial of Thomas Reynolds, reported in
Morgan's " Trials in Ireland," page 53, where in the attempt to procure a conviction upon a charge of riot and
assault, precisely the same remark was attributed by the
police swearers to the accused, we think we are justified
in saying that this particular charge against Mr. Fielden
is absolutely exploded, and the respective statements of
the witnesses in that behalf are shown by the whole evidence, if taken together, to be mere creations of the
fancy.

(b.) *The claim that Fielden fired from the wagon.*

Lieut. Quinn swore with absolute positiveness that
after the order for the dispersing of the meeting was
given by Capt. Ward, Fielden, while still standing upon
the wagon, drew a revolver from his hip pocket and fired

a shot in a downward direction, aimed at Capt. Ward, Capt. Bonfield and Lieut. Steele, who at the time were grouped together, not more than four to six feet from Fielden. (A., 14.) This testimony is en-entirely unsupported, no other witness in the case corroborating him or attempting to do so, while his contradiction is so overwhelming that we have some question as to whether we are justified in going into an argument to show that upon this point he was strangely and totally mistaken. There is no pretense, except this testimony of Quinn, that a shot was fired by anybody upon or from the wagon at the time and in the manner detailed by him, but both the witnesses for the prosecution and for the defense agree that *no shot was fired by anybody prior to the explosion of the bomb.*

Quinn in his testimony (A., 13 to 15) claims that while Capt. Ward gave the order to disperse and before he finished, Fielden said, " We are peaceable," and at the same time, while getting down from the wagon, fired a shot from the wagon in a downward direction right into Capt. Ward, Capt. Bonfield and Lieut. Steele; that upon seeing Fielden shoot, he dropped his club, took his pistol and returned the fire, discharging his own revolver. Then he looked back and saw the explosion of the bomb in the shape of a bunch of fire-crackers. Upon cross-examination, he states that when Capt. Ward, in his command, had got as far as " In the name of the people of the State of Illinois, I command, etc., to disperse, and I command you and you," he heard the command— " Halt! " Immediately he turned around and repeated the halt to his company, facing his men, with his back and side to the wagon. He had *no time to dress up his line before the bomb exploded.* The bomb exploded two or three seconds after he repeated the order to halt.

When he heard the halt Fielden had not started to leave the wagon.

As to Quinn's testimony, we feel justified in asking the court to observe its absolute and repeated self-contradictions. When did Quinn see Fielden shoot? Before Quinn turned to repeat the halt and dress up his line Fielden had not started to leave the wagon, therefore had not shot yet, because Quinn says he shot while getting off the wagon. After Quinn had turned, and *before he had time to dress up his line, while he was standing with his back and side to the wagon, the bomb exploded.* Quinn could not see Fielden, while thus turned to his company, therefore could not see him shoot before the explosion of the bomb. Again, Quinn says Fielden shot before Ward had finished his command to disperse; but Quinn turned when Ward had got so far as " you and you," so that only the words " to assist " lacked to complete the command. The two words " to assist " must have been spoken within a second after Quinn turned to repeat the halt and dress up his line. The command must have been finished before Quinn faced the wagon again. Now, if Fielden shot before the command was finished, how, we ask again, could Quinn see it? Again, Quinn says, when he turned to his company to repeat the halt, before he could dress up his line, the bomb exploded; then he turns, he sees Fielden shoot and thereupon discharges his pistol; then he looks back again and sees the explosion in the shape of a bunch of fire-crackers. This is a physical impossibility, for the bomb did not explode twice.

Furthermore, Capt. Bonfield, Capt. Ward and Lieut. Steele, at whom, according to Quinn, that shot of Fielden was aimed, did not see it. Capt. Bonfield describes the movements of Fielden after the com-

mand to disperse was given (Vol. I, 24; A. 2),
but does not pretend in one word to have seen Fielden
shoot. Capt. Ward, who says he was so near to the
wagon he could have touched it with his club (Vol.
I, 434; A, 37), says Fielden was facing him until he had
finished his command. Then he saw Fielden get off
the truck (Vol. I, 436; A, 37). He does not claim to have
seen Fielden shoot, and says there was no pistol firing of
any kind by anybody before the explosion of the bomb.
(Vol. I, 437; A, 37.) Lieut. Steele says Fielden stepped
off the wagon, turned to the sidewalk, and he lost sight
of him (Vol. I, 174, A 13), and that Fielden was on the
sidewalk when the bomb exploded. (Vol. I, 180) No
pretense that he saw Fielden shoot or aim at him. Lieut.
Bowler says (A, 22; Vol. I, 293-4) that he saw firing
close by the wagon after the explosion, but not from in
the wagon; that he saw Fielden coming off the wagon
very plainly, yet saw no one either in the wagon or getting out of it do any firing. Edgar E. Owen, a reporter
for the Times and witness for the prosecution, says, he
noticed Fielden jump off the wagon, but is silent about
having seen him shoot at that time. (A., 125, Vol. K, 206.)

There is no possibility of harmonizing these conflicting
statements of Quinn; while his whole story in this respect
is demonstrated by the evidence in the record to be absolutely untrue; and whether that untruth be wilful, or
whether it be the result of some mental aberration, the
entire testimony of this witness is in our judgment thereby
discredited.

(c.) *The claim that Fielden fired from behind the wagon.*

It was next attempted to be shown in the attack,
upon Mr. Fielden that he fired at least two shots after the
explosion of the bomb from a position on the sidewalk,

behind the wagon. The testimony upon this subject presented by the state was in brief as follows:

Officer Krueger testified that Fielden stepped just one step north of the south end of the wagon, took cover behind it (Vol. I, 245; A, 17) and then fired two shots directly at the column of police; then he *saw Fielden in the crowd and shot at him.* (A., 17; I, 234, 235.)

Officer Wessler says that after the explosion of the bomb he drew his revolver and ran north on the sidewalk next to Crane's building, probably twenty or thirty feet north of the alley. There he shot twice, then he heard the order, " Fall in," in his rear. He ran back and saw Fielden, behind the wagon, get up and get down twice and shoot twice into the police. Then Wessler shot him and *Fielden fell under the wagon.* (Vol. I, 251, 252; A, 18.) It may have been two minutes after the explosion of the bomb that Wessler started on his charge to the north, together with Officer Foley. (Vol. I, 260; A, 19.)

Officer Foley testified that he went north on the sidewalk after the explosion of the bomb, and while searching some fellows near the steps of Crane Bros.' building, saw Officer Wessler *shoot at a man who was lying under the body of the wagon,* between the fore and hind wheels. Going by the wagon, Foley picked up a revolver that was lying on the sidewalk. It was a five-chamber Harrington. Three chambers were empty, two cartridges remained. (Vol. I, 268 to 275; A, 19, 20.)

Officer Baumann swears he saw Fielden shoot once from east to west, while standing on the sidewalk. He admits that he saw Fielden that night for the first time, that he did not see him since then until he testified, and that he asked *some of the officers* who that man was that fired the shot, and they *told him it was Fielden.* (Vol. I, 296, 302, 303; A, 22, 23.)

Officer Hanley swears he saw Fielden fire one shot and then *run with the crowd toward the alley.* (Vol. I, 307, 308; A, 23.)

Officer Spierling (Vol. L, 341 to 343; A, 26) swears that after the bomb exploded he saw Fielden get off the wagon and fire one shot; Fielden was standing behind the wagon, on the sidewalk. He shot west; Spierling thinks it was a little before the explosion of the bomb that Fielden shot. But upon cross-examination, he says that the man he identifies as Fielden, and who fired this shot, *got off the wagon to the sidewalk, between the two wheels of the wagon.* It is evident, therefore, that Mr. Spierling did not see Mr. Fielden at all fire any shot: for the testimony is without contradiction that Fielden got off the wagon at the south end, stepping down to the street next to Ward and Bonfield, and from there stepping upon the sidewalk.

This is the entire testimony offered by the state in support of this charge. It is shown by the overwhelming preponderance of the testimony to be untrue.

We call attention first to the absolutely contradictory character of the testimony of these witnesses introduced by the state. Krueger swears that Fielden fired twice and then ran away with the crowd, and that he (Krueger) shot Fielden as he ran, staggering him, but not causing him to fall (A, 17; Vol. I, 235), and Hanley swears that he saw Fielden fire one shot, then run with the crowd toward the alley; but Wessler swears that after his excursion up the street, firing upon the crowd, on his return to the wagon, he found Fielden still there, shooting at the police, and thereupon, from immediately behind him, he shot him, and Fielden fell under the wagon. If Fielden ran towards the alley, as claimed by Krueger and Hanley, which was in a direction south from

the wagon, how is it possible that he should at the same
time have stepped north between the side wheels of the
wagon? And how can you reconcile Wessler's testimony,
that he shot Fielden and that Fielden fell under the
wagon, with the positive statement of Foley, that Wessler
shot at a man who was already lying under the body of
the wagon between the wheels? Of course these stories
cannot all be true and apply to the one man, Samuel
Fielden. Their contradictions are absolutely irreconcilable. But we go beyond this to call attention to positive testimony, which absolutely refutes this story.

Of the witnesses for the state we desire to call particular attention upon this point to the testimony of William
H. Freeman, a reporter for the Inter Ocean. He says,
(A, 106, 107; K, 41, 42, 48-50) that he stood on the
sidewalk between the speaker's wagon and Crane Bros.'
building, within three or four feet of the wagon, and when
the pistol firing commenced, crouched down behind the
wagon; that there was *no shooting between him and the
wagon*, although two police officers stood by the wagon
with their pistols pointed dangerously close at him; that
*he did not see Fielden shoot as he jumped down from the
wagon, nor see him shoot at all.* That after remaining a
moment or two in his position between the wagon and the
building, he went toward the alley and went into it, there
being no firing from the alley. He says positively that he
does not think that any one was between himself and the
wagon firing or anything of that kind.

William Snyder (A, 236), testifies that he was on
the wagon while Fielden was speaking, and when the order to disperse was given; that he then stepped down
and called Fielden to get down, who immediately assented,
and that he assisted Fielden in dismounting. That the
explosion of the bomb came while they were in the act

of getting off the wagon; that *Fielden did not shoot when getting off the wagon;* had he done so he would have shot Snyder; that Fielden had no revolver, and *did not fire at the police officers* or at anybody else; that he remained with Fielden, and with his hand upon him, until they *both reached the mouth of the alley,* when they separated, Snyder making his escape into the alley.

Frank Stenner (A., 196) says that when the shooting commenced he was on the east side of the wagon, close to the Crane Brothers building; that he was arrested himself by Foley while lying down on the steps of the Crane Brothers building to avoid being shot. That Foley *picked up a revolver about fifty feet south of the wagon,* as he was leading him to the station, after the firing was through; that there was *no shot fired from the wagon* before the bomb exploded; that he was looking at Fielden when he dismounted from the wagon and did not see him shoot, and that he *did not see Fielden or anybody else stand behind the wagon and fire.*

Dr. James D. Taylor (A., 190) testified that he stood but a few feet distant from the wagon; saw Fielden on the wagon; remained in his position until after the explosion of the bomb and the pistol firing, and that *he did not see Fielden draw a revolver and shoot in the direction of the police, or use a pistol on or off the wagon;* that he watched him as long as he could see him. (A. 191, K 230, 231.)

Conrad Messer testifies (A., 208) that he stood by the south-east corner of the wagon at the time the police arrived; that at the time of the explosion of the bomb Fielden was down off the wagon near the sidewalk; that he saw Fielden during all that time, and that *Fielden had no pistol in his hand, and he did not see him fire one shot;*

that Fielden stepped on to the sidewalk, and after that the witness saw him no more.

John Holloway (A., 229, 230) testifies that he stood during the speaking and the firing that followed, near the lamp-post on the southeast corner of the alley and the street; that he saw *no firing coming from the direction of the wagon*, and did not see Fielden shoot.

Sleeper T. Ingram testifies (A., 287, 288) that he stood on the sidewalk near the steps of the Crane Brothers building, just east of the wagon; that he saw Fielden when the police came up and when the bomb exploded; that he *did not see Fielden have any revolver or fire any shot*.

Mr. Fielden's own testimony is positive, unequivocal and clear. He says he *never carried a revolver* in his life, did not have one that night, and *did not fire* on that occasion at all; *never fired at any person in his life;* that he did not, after leaving the wagon, step back between the wheels of the wagon and fire from behind the wagon; did not stay there at all (A., 268; M, 319); that he got down from the south end of the wagon after the order to the meeting to disperse was given by Capt. Ward, and started in a slightly south-east direction (A., 267): that just as he got upon the sidewalk the explosion of the bomb came, and he rushed with the crowd trying to get behind some protection, unavailingly, and made a dash for the north-east corner of Randolph and Desplaines, turned the corner and ran until he got to Jefferson street. Just after the explosion of the bomb he was struck with a ball and wounded above the knee; that his whole course was from the wagon south, without stopping except for an instant when startled by the explosion.

Of course, in the confusion following such an event as the explosion of this bomb, and the immediate opening of fire by the police, particularly in the night-time with no light except a single street lamp upon the corner of the alley (and some of the witnesses testified that that was extinguished about the moment of the explosion), it was not to be expected that to any great extent the people in the crowd would be watching each other's movements; on the contrary, they were engaged in looking out each for his own safety. It happened fortunately, however, that owing to the position which Mr. Fielden occupied he was subject to more observation than would otherwise have been fixed upon him; and that from the lips of these witnesses we are enabled to disprove this story as to his stepping behind the wagon and opening fire upon the police.

The attack made by the police officers upon Mr. Fielden, attempting to implicate him by describing his alleged personal conduct that evening, in our judgment utterly fails. On this point we think it not improper to call attention to the fact that when an effort was made to show by the testimony of Mr. Fielden, that he was present at the examination of the various officers, *upon the coroner's inquest*, and that *not a word was there testified as to his having fired at any time that night*, the going into that subject was objected to by the state's attorney, and the proposed testimony was excluded by the court over the exception of defendants (A., 277); while Mr. Knox, a reporter for the News, put upon the stand for the prosecution, testifying of an interview with Fielden on the night of the 5th of May, in the presence of one or more of the police officers, after the coroner's inquest had recommended that Mr. Fielden be held for the murder of Degan, says that *he does not think anything was asked of Fielden as to his having fired any shots at the Haymarket;* that he did not know of such a

charge at the time, and *had never heard of such a claim*
advanced up to that time by anybody (A., 89; Vol. J,
333, 334); while Hugh Hume, a reporter for the
Inter Ocean, also testifying on behalf of the people
of an interview had by him near midnight of that
same May 5th, with Fielden, says that he *don't remember asking Fielden anything about firing*, or that any
question of that sort was suggested by any one. We
think we are warranted, in view of these statements, in
asserting that it sufficiently appears from the evidence in
this record that the charge that Samuel Fielden fired any
shots on the night of May 4th was never advanced by
any human being until, certainly, after the 5th day of
May, and after the investigation by the coroner's jury of
the facts connected with the death of Officer Degan.

As to Mr. Fielden, therefore, we affirm upon this record that the testimony shows that he had nothing whatever to do with the calling of the Haymarket meeting,
and no notice or knowledge that such a meeting was to
be held until it was already in progress. That his presence at the Haymarket and his speaking there resulted
simply from the request for speakers sent to the meeting
of the American group; that he had no knowledge of the
throwing of a bomb on that night, nor did he contemplate
any violence whatever as likely to occur; that he had no
knowledge of the bomb-thrower, nor ever advised or
planned for the throwing of that bomb; that in fact the
throwing of that bomb was as much a surprise to him
as to any other person.

ALBERT R. PARSONS.

The testimony shows, without any contradiction, that
on Sunday, May 2, 1886, Albert R. Parsons was
in the city of Cincinnati, Ohio, and came back from

there to Chicago on the morning of Tuesday, May 4th
(A., 313; N, 109); that he caused a notice calling for
a meeting of the American group at 107 5th avenue
on the evening of May 4th, to be inserted in the Daily
News of that afternoon. That in the evening he left his
house *in company with his wife, Mrs. Holmes, a lady
friend, and his two little children:* that on their way down
they walked as far as the corner of Randolph and Halsted streets, where he met two reporters, Mr. Heineman
and Mr. Owen. There Mr. Parsons and his party took a
car and rode directly up to 107 5th avenue, where they
arrived about half past 8 o'clock and remained about half
an hour. Concerning this meeting at the corner of Halsted
and Randolph streets, Mr. Owen (a witness for the state)
testified (A., 124; K, 200, 201): "I saw Parsons at
" the corner of Halsted and Randolph streets shortly be-
" fore 8 o'clock. I asked him where the meeting was
" to be held; he said *he didn't know anything about the
" meeting.* I asked him whether he was going to speak.
" He said, '*No, he was going over to the south side.*'
" Mrs. Parsons and some children came up just then, and
" Parsons stopped an Indiana street car, slapped me fa-
" miliarly upon the back, and asked me if I was armed,
" and I said ' No; have you any dynamite about you?' He
" laughed, and Mrs. Parsons said, ' He is a very danger-
" ous looking man, isn't he? ' and they got on the car and
" went east. I believe Mr. Heineman was with me."
Mr. Heineman also testified as to that meeting (A., 126;
K, 233).

Pursuant to the request for speakers mentioned above,
Parsons, with others, went to the Haymarket meeting; he
reached the same sometime after 9 o'clock, when Spies was
speaking, and directly afterward he himself spoke, his
speech occupying from three-quarters of an hour to an hour.

It is concurred in by all the witnesses who testify in reference to Parsons' speech, that it was largely statistical in its nature, and a review of the disturbed condition of the labor world; and it is conceded by all that when, in the course of his remarks, he mentioned the name of Jay Gould, in connection with the south-western railway troubles, and some one in his audience proposed the hanging of the railway magnate, Parsons immediately replied deprecating such utterance, saying in effect: *No! this is not a conflict between individuals, but for a change of system,* and socialism desires to remove the causes which produced the pauper and the millionaire, but *does not aim at the life of the individual.* That in that connection he made use of the figure that if Jay Gould were killed, another or a hundred others would come up in his place like a Jack in a box; and that he also used the figure that to kill the individual millionaire or capitalist would be like killing a flea upon a dog, whereas the purpose of socialism was the destruction of the dog himself—the change of the present system. (A., 320; N, 136.) This utterance, or the substance of it, is also testified to by the following witnesses: Simonson (A., 177; L, 65), Ferguson (A., 182; L, 130, 131), Gleason (A., 203; L, 361), Snyder (A., 236; M, 109), Bach (A., 281; M, 410), Freeman (A., 105; K, 40).

Some of the witnesses for the state testified that at some point in his discourse he used the expression, " To " arms! to arms! to arms!" This is the only incendiary utterance claimed to have been made use of by him. Upon this point Mr. English's testimony, based upon his notes taken at the time, is substantially as follows (A., 131; K. 281): " It behooves you, as you love " your wife and children, if you do not want to see them " perish with hunger, killed, or cut down like dogs on the

" street, Americans, in the interest of your liberty and
" your independence, to arm, to arm yourselves (ap-
" plause, and cries of ' We will do it; we are ready now ').
" You are not." And Mr. English says positively in this
connection that when Parsons said " to arm " he said it
in his ordinary tone of voice. He says further, that this
expression shortly followed an utterance of Parsons in the
following language: " *I am not here for the purpose of in-*
" *citing anybody*, but to speak out, to tell the facts as they
" exist, even though it shall cost me my life before morn-
" ing."

It was a very natural mistake for persons in the audience, not listening closely, and not taking notes of the
speech, to have received the impression that Parsons said
" To arms! to arms! to arms!" But a mistake it clearly
is. For the short-hand notes of Mr. English are surely
more reliable than the testimony of the other witnesses
testifying merely from recollection. It will further be observed that Mr. English's entire testimony as to Parsons'
speech occupies but a little more than one page of the record, and the evidence shows that he took but very little of
it out of matter which occupied nearly an hour in its deliv-
ery; which is explained, as we understand it, by the fact that
Mr. English was under instructions to report only " the
" most inflammatory utterances;" and that in point of fact
he found in Mr. Parsons' speech scarcely anything to
report under these instructions. Mr. Parsons, upon
the witness stand, gave in detail, as near as he
could repeat it, his speech at the Haymarket (A., 315
to 320; N., 118 to 136), and we invite the attention
of the court to that speech as there detailed, in connection with the testimony of Mr. English and also the
testimony of the other witnesses as to the character of his
speech, in support of our assertion that it was an

unusually moderate utterance for such an occasion. Certainly, there was nothing in that speech which in the remotest degree incited immediate violence, or indicated in any manner that the speaker contemplated any immediate outbreak upon the part of his audience or any portion of it. Mayor Harrison, who heard Parsons' speech, and attended the meeting for the purpose of dispersing it, if anything should occur to require interference, left the meeting at the end of that speech, and told Capt. Bonfield at the station that "*nothing had occurred yet or* "*looked likely to occur to require interference,* and that " he had better issue orders to his reserves at the other " stations to go home"; whereupon Mr. Harrison himself went home. (A., 174, 175; L., 29-31, 47.)

After Parsons, Mr. Fielden spoke in all about twenty minutes. After Mr. Fielden had been speaking some ten minutes or so, it is admitted by all the witnesses that a cloud accompanied by a very cold wind swept up in the northern sky, threatening rain; and that thereupon Parsons interrupted Fielden and *suggested an adjournment* of the meeting to Zepf's Hall, a hall in a building situate on the north-east corner of Lake and Desplaines streets, and consequently about a half a block from the location of the Haymarket meeting. To this somebody in the crowd responded that the hall was occupied by a meeting of the furniture-workers' union, and *Fielden suggested that he would be through in a few minutes, and then they could all go home;* and Fielden proceeded with his remarks. (A., 314; N, 113.) Besides the testimony of Mr. Parsons, this fact is further established by a large number of witnesses, both for the State and the defendants, among whom we will mention the following: Freeman (A., 108; K, 51, 52), Heineman (A., 127; K, 246), English (A., 132. 133; K, 282), Simonson (A., 178; L,

66, 67), Richter (A., 187; L, 184), Urban (A., 201; L, 343), Ingram (A., 287; M, 447). But it is established without contradiction, that a very large portion of the audience, fully one-half, as estimated by substantially all of the witnesses, and more than that as estimated by many, scattered upon Parsons' motion and Fielden's suggestion, and that Mr. Parsons himself went from the speakers' wagon to a wagon located a few feet north of it, in which sat his wife and Mrs. Holmes, who had accompanied him to the Haymarket; and that he then *proposed to them that they should all go to Zepf's Hall, which they accordingly did.* It is proved incontestably also that at the time of the explosion of the bomb, Parsons, together with his wife, Mrs. Holmes, and others, was in Zepf's saloon, and not at the Haymarket meeting. This is substantiated by the testimony of the following witnesses, viz.: Michael D. Malkoff (A., 224), Thomas Brown (A., 238; M, 125), Otto Wandray (A., 248; M, 192), Lizzie May Holmes (A., 261, M. 284, 285), S. I. Ingram (A., 287; Vol. M, 448); besides the testimony of Mr. Parsons himself (A., 314, 315; N, 114-116). No effort was made to meet or refute this testimony, or to show, by a single witness, that Mr. Parsons was at the Haymarket at the time of the explosion of the bomb. A review of the evidence touching Parsons' attendance, presence and utterances at the Haymarket meeting, accompanied, as he was, by his wife and Mrs. Holmes, proposing an adjournment of the meeting before the police had moved upon them, and himself thereupon leaving the theater of action, must satisfy any rational mind that Mr. Parsons had no idea that any violence was contemplated, proposed, arranged for, or likely to occur at the Haymarket meeting, of which his first notice was received from Mr. Owen, about 8 o'clock that evening, as appears from the testimony of that gentleman.

It is not, therefore, to be wondered at that when the
trial came on, involving Mr. Parsons in a charge of participation in the murder of Mathias J. Degan, he should
have *voluntarily come to the bar of the court*, as he did,
and presented himself for trial, strong in his consciousness
of innocence, and convinced of his power to successfully
meet any charge in that behalf that might be brought
against him.   And we respectfully submit that no jury
dispassionate, unprejudiced and governed by the testimony in the case, could rationally have reached the conclusion which was reached in this case; and that such
conclusion is explicable alone by the fact that he was
compelled to submit his cause, under the rulings of the
trial court, to a jury who had prejudged him, and who
forced the result into conformity with the opinion with
which they entered the jury box.

MICHAEL SCHWAB.

The incriminatory evidence adduced by the state
against Michael Schwab, in connection with the tragedy
of the Haymarket, is alone that of M. M. Thompson. No
other witness on behalf of the state attempts to connect
Schwab with the throwing of the bomb.   It is, therefore,
proper, in this connection, to consider critically the testimony of Mr. Thompson.   (A., 134-137.)   Thompson's
story is, that on the evening of May 4th, he attended at
the Haymarket, reaching the corner of Desplaines and
Randolph streets, about twenty-five minutes of 8.   That
he there met Mr. Brazleton, a reporter of the Inter Ocean,
and talked with him about fifteen minutes; then asked the
time, and Brazleton replied it was then ten minutes of 8;
that while talking with Brazleton, Brazleton pointed out
Schwab, whom Thompson had never seen before, who

was rushing along Desplaines street, apparently in a great hurry. That Thompson then walked to the east side of Desplaines street, up Desplaines, near to the corner of Lake, and back again to the alley by Crane Bros.', standing just by the alley. That he saw Spies get up on the wagon, and heard him ask for Parsons, who did not respond, and that Spies then got down, and Schwab and Spies walked into the alley, south of Crane Bros.' (K, 288.) That when he saw Spies and Schwab go into the alley, *there was a crowd there.* (K, 291.) Thompson was standing *within three feet north of the alley*, up against the building. (K, 292.) From this position he heard a conversation between Schwab and Spies, in the alley. He admits that *he had never before seen either of these parties*, and had *never heard either of them speak*, save that he heard Spies inquire from the wagon for Parsons. (K, 295.) He states that he *could not see down the alley, unless he turned his face to it, and did not look into the alley to see who were the parties holding the conversation* testified of (K, 292, 293), but that he heard in a conversation between them, the word "pistols" and the word "police," the latter word twice; that *the first remark he heard was about a minute and a half after Spies and Schwab went into the alley and out of sight.* (K, 295.) That he drew up within a foot of the alley, when Spies said: "Do you think one is enough, or hadn't "we better go and get more?" (K, 294.) To which he heard no response. That Spies and Schwab then came out of the alley, walked south on Desplaines street to Randolph, west on the north side of Randolph to Halsted, crossed Halsted diagonally to the south-west corner of the street intersection, remained there about three minutes; then left the crowd and came back; that on the way back, as the pair neared Union street, he heard the word "police" again. At that moment he passed the pair, and Schwab said: "Now, if they come, we will "give it to them," to which Spies replied that he thought they were afraid to bother with them. On the north-west corner of Desplaines and Randolph he halted and they passed him, going diagonally across Desplaines street in a north-eastern direction, and striking the side-walk about fifteen or twenty feet south of the alley. Then he followed them across Desplaines street, but a little more to the south, striking the sidewalk some ten or fifteen feet south of them, when a third party stepped from the wall of the building towards the center of the sidewalk, and that the group of three then stood, *Spies facing south and directly toward Thompson*, Schwab facing north, and *the third man facing west*. (K, 305–310.) The group appeared to get in a huddle, and there was something passed between Spies and the third man—he could not tell what; that the third man took this something and put it in his right-hand coat pocket. That they then went to the wagon, Spies got up and the third man mounted after him. That he no-ticed this third man afterwards sitting on the wagon, and that he kept his hand in his pocket. He attempted to identify this man by means of a photograph of Schnau-belt, shown to him, and said that he thought that was the picture of the third man. That he remained on the Hay-market until Mr. Fielden commenced to speak and then left. (K, 289, 290.)

Thompson admitted that *he did not understand German*, and said that the conversation which he heard was carried on in English. (K, 293, 301.) He could not give the connection of the conversation which he related.

If any such occurrence between anybody took place as he describes, then it is evident from his whole testimony that it must have been somewhere between 8 and half-past 8 o'clock.

There is incontestable evidence in this record, we undertake to say, which demonstrates conclusively the utter untruth of this testimony, as attempted to be applied to Michael Schwab and August Spies; for Michael Schwab was not walking around the Haymarket at the time alleged, and did not see Spies there at all, nor take with him the journey detailed, nor did he or Spies have the conversation either with one another or with anybody else. To this testimony we now beg to call the attention of the court in detail.

(*a.*)   *Schwab's movements.*

Schwab's account of himself, which is in every particular confirmed by unimpeachable testimony to which we shall call attention later on, is as follows (A., 294–96):

That, on the evening of May 4th, he left his home, 51 Florimond street, at twenty minutes to 8 o'clock, and went to the Arbeiter Zeitung office, reaching there about 8 o'clock, where he remained about ten minutes. That while he was there, a telephone message was received, asking Mr. Spies to speak at Deering, and that Schwab's purpose in going to the Haymarket was to get Spies to respond to that call. That he went to the Haymarket, looked hurriedly through the crowd for Spies, *failed to find him*, and then *took a car for Deering* himself, to speak at that point. As to his course, he says that he went over on Washington street, turned north on Desplaines, across Randolph, and that north of Randolph, on Desplaines, he met Schnaubelt, and talked with him about the Deering meeting; then took an east-bound car to the court-house, and at the court-house, a Cly-

bourne avenue car, going out to Deering's factory. That at
the car stables he was met by a Mr. Preusser. That the
time required to go from the Haymarket to the court-
house by the car was about ten minutes, and from forty
to forty-five minutes were required to go from the court-
house to Fullerton avenue. That he went with Mr.
Preusser to 888 Clybourn avenue to see the committee,
but not finding them, went out on the prairie, corner of
Fullerton and Clybourn avenues, where he met the committee, talked with them a few minutes, mounted the
stand, and made a speech of twenty or twenty-five
minutes' duration about the eight-hour movement,
to the men there gathered, who had struck that day,
demanding eight hours work' and ten hours' pay. That
after the meeting was over, he returned with Preusser to
a saloon, took a glass of beer and some lunch, and then
took a car going south, leaving the car at Willow street and
walking home, this occupying him about twenty minutes,
and reached home at about 11 o'clock that night.

He says that he did not, while at the Haymarket, enter
Crane's alley, or any other alley, with Mr. Spies—had no
conversation with him near the mouth of any alley; did
not walk that night in company with Spies on Randolph
street west to Halsted street, and back again to the wagon
—did not, in company with Spies, meet Schnaubelt, and
*did not see or speak to Spies at all that night at the
Haymarket.* That he did not say anything to Spies or
anybody else, in the mouth of Crane's alley, about pistols
or police, or whether one would be enough. Had no
such conversation with anybody at the Haymarket, or
anywhere else, and did not say to Spies, or anybody else, at
any time, that if the police came we were ready for them,
or would give it to them, or words to that effect. About
the middle of Randolph street he met Mr. Heinemann;

he made some inquiry for Spies, and directly thereafter,—
it was then about half-past 8 o'clock—he took the car
on Randolph street, returning to the court house, and
about twenty minutes of 9 he took the Clybourn avenue
car.

That Mr. Schwab was at 107 5th avenue, and there
received a telephone call to Deering, Spies being first
called for, and that he left that place after receiving that
telephone message is evidenced as follows: By the positive testimony of Patterson (A., 228; M., 42), Waldo
(A., 245; M., 168), Bach (A., 279; M., 398, 399), and
Fielden (A., 265; M., 307). That the telephone message was sent from Deering to the Arbeiter Zeitung, is
evidenced by the testimony of Preusser (A., 248, 249;
M., 197-200). That he was seen on the corner of Randolph and Desplaines at the time stated by him is evidenced by the witnesses of the prosecution, Heinemann,
a reporter of the Tribune (A., 126; K., 232), and Owen,
a reporter of the Times (A., 124; K., 202). *No other
witness, except Mr. Thompson, claims to have seen Schwab
upon this alleged journey from the alley, on Desplaines
and Randolph streets, and back again.* That something
after 8 o'clock, Schwab came south on Desplaines street
and took an east-bound car on Randolph, is evidenced by
the testimony of Hermann Becker (A., 250).

That he, in fact, went to Deering and spoke there, is
historic, and will not be questioned by the representatives
of the state. Concerning his arrival, etc., we desire, however, to call attention to the testimony of Edward Preusser (A., 249; M., 200), Fritz Stettler (A., 250), William
Radtke (A., 221) and Dietrich Behrens (A., 222). These
witnesses confirm Schwab's testimony in every material
particular; their testimony conclusively shows that he
remained at Deering, all told, at least three-quarters

of an hour, and from that to an hour, having reached there at half-past 9 to twenty minutes to 10. It is demonstrated, therefore, that he *did not leave Deering until in the neighborhood of half-past 10 o'clock* and that it was nearly an hour's journey from there to the Haymarket. It will not be pretended by the representatives of the state that Mr. Schwab was at the Haymarket during the meeting that night, although certain of the state's witnesses early in the case stated that they thought they saw him there during the speaking; nor will it be pretended that he was present at the time of the explosion of the bomb.

(*b.*) *Spies' movements.*

In order to further demonstrate the error of Mr. Thompson, we now call attention to the testimony of Mr. Spies and of other parties accounting for his movement that night, and absolutely refuting this story.

August Spies testifies in reference to this matter (A., 299, N, 33 *et seq.*), that he arrived at the Haymarket about twenty to twenty-five minutes after 8, in company with his brother Henry; that when he reached there no meeting was in progress, but there were crowds standing about the corners; that he looked about for a speakers' stand and selected the wagon, without moving it; that after some moments he called the crowd together, mounted the wagon and inquired for Parsons. That some one replied that Parsons was speaking at the corner of Halsted and Randolph streets, and that thereupon he descended from the wagon, and, in company with his brother Henry, with Ernest Legner and with Rudolph Schnaubelt, whom he had just met, he started to find Parsons; that *Schwab was not with him* at that time nor at any time during that evening, and that Schnaubelt told him that Schwab had gone to Deering. That *he did not go, on leaving the wagon, to the mouth of Crane's alley, and did not enter it* or have any conversation there with Schwab or any one else in which he referred to pistols and police, nor any other matter, and never had any such conversation with anybody. That on leaving the wagon he *moved in a south-westerly direction obliquely across* Desplaines street to the corner of the Haymarket, and from there went west on Randolph a little beyond Union, when, seeing only some small groups of people, and not seeing Parsons, he returned and again walked diagonally across Desplaines street to the wagon; that he had no conversation with Schwab at the corner of Union street, nor with anybody else, in which there was any suggestion about being ready for them, or giving it to them, or anything of that kind. That he did not meet Schnaubelt on the sidewalk south of the alley on Desplaines street, but that Schnaubelt was with him in, walking from the wagon to Randolph, west on Randolph and back to the wagon. That there was no truth whatever in the testimony of Thompson upon the stand in regard to this.

This testimony of Spies is corroborated in every material particular by the testimony of Henry W. Spies (A., 240, 241), and finds corroboration in the testimony of other witnesses, as follows:

That after inquiring for Parsons from the wagon, and then dismounting therefrom, he *walked in a south-westerly direction in a group of three or four men* toward the north-west corner of Desplaines and Randolph, and did not go in the direction of the Crane Bros. alley, or into it, is evidenced by Wilhelm Sahl (A., 205), who swears that he stood about the middle of Desplaines street in a south-westerly direction from the wagon, and this group passed him. Sahl also says that *he knows Schwab*, and that *he did not see Schwab with Spies* on the wagon, or afterwards, and that he was not in the group of men who accompanied Spies.

Carl Richter (A., 186, 187) says that he had been slightly acquainted with Spies for a year or more prior to the Haymarket meeting; that he attended that meeting, standing in the mouth of Crane's alley when the meeting was opened; that Spies, after having asked for Parsons, left the wagon, but the witness *did not see him enter the alley*, although there was nothing to have prevented his seeing him, had he in fact gone in there. That he went to the meeting with Robert Lindinger, who remained with him during the entire evening.

Robert Lindinger (A., 215), testifies that he was with Richter, standing at the mouth of Crane's alley, about midway between the two sidewalks, and midway between the curbstone and the building line, and that he *did not see Spies or anybody else pass into the alley*—had never seen Schwab in his life before the time of his testifying; saw Spies leave the wagon after asking for Parsons, and return in about five or ten minutes, and then open the meeting.

Frederick Liebel (A., 188) testifies that he was standing by the lamp-post on the corner of the alley, when Spies inquired for Parsons and then left the wagon: that *he knew Schwab by sight, but did not see him on or near the wagon when Spies made his inquiry; didn't see Schwab there that night*, and *didn't see Spies go towards the alley*; that the lamp was lighted at the time and light enough for him to notice faces. It is evident, that if Spies and Schwab had entered the alley and had the conversation detailed by Thompson, the witnesses last named, from their respective positions with reference to that locality, could not have failed to observe the parties attempted to be involved.

Besides this, the testimony of August Spies and of Henry Spies, as to the direction taken by them when August Spies left the wagon in search of Parsons, and that he did not go into the alley, as testified by Thompson, is positively corroborated by at least two of the witnesses for the state, who were on the stand before Mr. Thompson testified. Officer Cosgrove (A., 120, 121; K, 167), testifies that "when Spies got on the wagon first, he called out "twice if Parsons was there, and told somebody in the "crowd to go and find Parsons, and he said Fielden "would be here later. Then he said he would get down "from the wagon and go and find Parsons, himself. *He* "*got down and went in a south-westerly direction.* He came "back in a short time and commenced speaking."

Still stronger is the testimony of Officer McKeough, who, like Cosgrove, was detailed on detective service at that meeting. His testimony is as follows (A., 122; K, 176): "Spies got on the wagon and called out twice, 'Is "Parsons here?' He received no answer, and said, 'Never "mind, I will go and find him myself.' Somebody "said, 'Let's pull the wagon around on Randolph street "and hold the meeting there.' Mr. Spies said, 'We may "stop the street cars.' *He started away then, and Officer* "*Meyers and myself followed him as far as the corner.* "There was a man with him, who I think was Schwab, but "I am not very sure about that, and in about five minutes "he returned, and when I got back he was addressing "the meeting, and talking about what had happened to "their brethren the day before at McCormick's."

If it is true, as Officer Cosgrove says, that Spies got down from the wagon and *went in a south-westerly direction* (and this is confirmed by the witness Sahl, as

above stated), and if Officer McKeough with Officer
Meyers *followed him as far as the corner* (the corner of
Randolph and Desplaines streets), then the statement
of Mr. Thompson that August Spies and Schwab
passed from the wagon in a *southeasterly* direction into
the alley, and had there the conversation which he
narrates, is shown to be absolutely without foundation in fact. This position finds further corroboration,
though not so much in detail, from the testimony of
Mr. English, who says (A., 129; K., 274), that he
was present when Spies got up on the wagon, and that
he got down off the wagon *and went over towards Randolph street.* He says further that he was gone perhaps
some five or ten minutes, and adds: " As he passed me
" in coming back, I asked him if Parsons was going to
" speak. I understood him to say, yes. Then he got up
" on the wagon and said, ' Gentlemen, please come to
" order." How is it, that Mr. English, who knew the
parties, had heard them make speeches for years (A.,
133; K. 284), who, as appears from his testimony, did
not only see Spies on his way back to the wagon, but
even spoke with him, did not observe that ' getting into
a hudde ' of the group, as described so vividly by Mr.
Thompson? How is it that Mr. English is so absolutely
silent about the presence of Mr. Schwab on that occasion?
True, these facts only appear negatively, but it must not
be forgotten, that at the time Mr. English was cross-
examined, Mr. Thompson had not yet been called upon
the stand.

We feel justified in this connection in calling attention
to another matter. Brazleton, the reporter of the Inter
Ocean, was named by Mr. Thompson, as the man who
pointed out Schwab to him upon the Haymarket some
time before 8 o'clock. Brazleton's name was endorsed

on the back of the indictment as one of the witnesses for the State (Record, Vol. 1, p. 21, 22), yet Brazleton was not produced by the State as a witness, even when the State was notified by the defendants to produce him.

Ernest Legner, the young man mentioned in the testimony of August Spies and Henry Spies, as accompanying them and Schnaubelt on this trip, was also one of the witnesses for the State, whose name was indorsed upon the indictment (Record, Vol. 1, p. 21, 22); but who was not produced as a witness, although his production was demanded by the defendants by formal notice. The omission to produce Legner and put him on the stand, was, in our view, extremely significant in this case, and that significance will become more apparent when we consider another feature of the testimony in connection with the case of Mr. Spies. The fact is, that Legner's presence was very much desired by the defendants, and that every effort, as the record shows was made by them to procure his attendance after it became known that the State would not call him as a witness, but unavailingly. Legner had gone out of the state, and his whereabouts could not be ascertained by the defendants, nor his attendance procured. The State chose to offer Mr. Thompson's testimony without attempting to corroborate it by Brazleton; and did not produce Mr. Legner, although they had him as a witness before the grand jury (1 A., 4), and his name was upon the indictment, when they could have easily taken the steps under the provisions of the law which would have compelled his presence and testimony.

(c.) *Inherent improbability of Thompson's story.*

As to Thompson's entire story, we have to choose
between his uncorroborated statement on the one side,
and the testimony of all of the witnesses above reviewed
both on behalf of the State and the defendants on the
other. No one can hesitate one moment in saying that Mr-
Thompson's testimony is refuted by an overwhelming
preponderance of the evidence. But beyond this, we desire to call attention to certain inherent improbabilities,
which characterize this testimony, and which, in our judgment, stamp it as unquestionably false. The testimony
shows without contradiction that *Spies and Schwab were
both German born.* (A., 296; N, 8, 18.) It was offered
by the defendants to prove that they were *in the habit of
carrying on their personal conversations in their mother
tongue*, but the offer was rejected by the judge, to which
ruling the defendants excepted. (N, 56; A., 303.) In our
judgment, this ruling of the court was clearly erroneous, as
the fact, if proved, was certainly material to be considered
in connection with this issue.

When a man in Mr. Thompson's position admits that
he had *never before seen either of these parties ;* that
he never had heard Schwab speak at all and *did not
know his voice ;* that he *never had heard Spies speak*
save the single question from the wagon " Is Parsons
here? " — probably spoken in a loud tone of voice,
while it is not probable that he shouted in the alley when
speaking about police and revolvers, with a crowd of
people around him—undertakes to swear positively that
standing with his back to a wall he heard a conversation,
and claims that it was held between *Spies* and *Schwab*,
though he admits *he did not turn around to see who the*

parties were, though he *could not recognize them by their voices*, and though *the first remark occurred about a minute and a half after Spies and Schwab had disappeared in the alley*, he is making a statement which he has no right to ask any one to believe. But aside from this, can it be conceived that these two Germans, if engaged in plotting a direful conspiracy, would have carried on their conversation in the English language rather than their mother tongue? Is it reasonable to believe that they would have arranged the details for its execution and for the throwing of that bomb, while they were surrounded by a crowd, as Thompson admits (A., 135, K, 291)? Would conspirators planning street murder, attempt to discuss the details of their plan publicly and openly, in a tone of voice which could be heard by an eaves-dropper standing several feet around the corner of the building, or, as was claimed by Thompson as to the alleged conversation at the crossing of Union street, in a tone of voice loud enough for the audience of passers-by?

Still another suggestion. Mr. Thompson admits that he had not seen ever before that night either Schwab or Schnaubelt (K, 291, 307); and Schnaubelt he has certainly never seen since. Yet he undertakes to identify both. Is such identification worthy of consideration? As to Schnaubelt, he saw him only *at a distance of eight or ten feet*, and then *his back was turned to Thompson* (K, 308); while when Schnaubelt was on the wagon his back was substantially toward where Thompson stood. On that day, as is evidenced by reference to any standard almanac, the moon was in full dark, and the sun set at 6:59 P. M.; so that at 8 o'clock there was no light, save artificial. As to this, the evidence shows conclusively that there was no light on the wagon, and the only street lamp near was that on the corner of the alley, fully twenty feet from the south end of the wagon. Besides this, there was the electric light from the front of a theater located on Desplaines street, more than a block to the south. The faces of the persons on the wagon, therefore, when they faced west toward their audience, were in the shadow; or, at most, were only in the light in profile. Besides, Schnaubelt had on a hat, which could not but partially shade his face—while his photograph was taken bare-headed. What shall be said of a witness who, after the lapse of more than two months, attempts to identify by a photograph under such conditions, a man whom he was never near enough to master the details of form, color and expression so essential to reliable identification, in the absence of personal acquaintance?

Mr. Thompson's testimony thus utterly discredited, there remains not a shadow of proof connecting Mr. Schwab with the Haymarket meeting or the throwing of the bomb thereat.

August Spies.

(a.) *The McCormick Meeting.*

On the afternoon of May 3d, Mr. Spies attended the so-called McCormick meeting. The testimony introduced by the state as to that meeting is as follows: On the afternoon of that day a meeting of the Lumber Shovers' Union was held in the vicinity of McCormick's factory, whose object was to receive the report of a committee that had been sent to the bosses of the lumber yards to get the eight-hour concession. There were from five to six thousand men in the crowd. The meeting was addressed from the top of a freight car first by one Fehling, afterwards by Spies, the plaintiff in error.

Haraster, the president of the Bohemian section of the
Lumber Shovers' Union, tried to prevent the speakers
from speaking, and told the people not to listen to them.
(A., 34, 35.) Spies addressed the crowd in German
for about ten or fifteen minutes; he was rather excited,
and very earnest; the crowd patiently listened to him until the bell of McCormick's factory rung (A., 33; I,
402), when all of a sudden somebody on the opposite
end of the car from which Spies was speaking (A.,
33; I, 398, 402) shouted, "Now, boys, let us go for them
"damn scabs." At that moment a portion of the crowd
which was near McCormick's factory commenced to
move towards McCormick's. (A., 33; I, 403.) Spies
did not go with the crowd. (A., 32; I, 395, 396.)
The crowd pitched into McCormick's men going home
from work, threw bricks, stones and sticks into them and
into the windows of the factory. Officer West (A.,
31), who was stationed at the factory, was himself attacked; he turned in the alarm for the police, who arrived
within a few minutes and scattered the crowd (A., 32;
I, 392), firing into them, and using their clubs. Officer
Enright (A., 35) claims that he heard shots from the
crowd, but he cannot say whether the police had fired
before he heard those shots. However, none of the police were shot, though some of them were hit with
stones. (A., 35; I, 420.) Immediately after the patrol
wagon, containing eleven policemen, had arrived (A.,
35; I, 416), a couple of hundred other policemen came
upon the ground (A., 36; I, 421); at that time, however, the firing was over. The crowd scattered as soon
as they saw the additional force approaching. (A.,
36; I, 422.) Officer Shane testified (A., 36) that he
was detailed to look up the injured citizens, and admits
that he found, as a result of the police firing, one who

died, and two or three others who were injured. As to the contents of Spies' speech, the *only* testimony offered by the state is that of Mr. Baker, who says (A., 33; I, 402) he heard him speak *of wives and children and homes, and appealing for their protection.*

In connection with the foregoing testimony the state was permitted to introduce in evidence an account of the McCormick meeting, written by Spies and published in the Arbeiter Zeitung the following day. (People's Exhibit 63; 1 A., 179).

The testimony introduced in behalf of the plaintiff in error, Spies, as to the McCormick meeting, so called, was in brief as follows: That on Sunday morning, May 2d, at a meeting of the Central Labor Union, which is a body composed of delegates from about twenty-five or thirty different labor unions in Chicago (A., 185; L, 156), the delegates of the Lumber Shovers' Union, then on a strike for the shortening of the hours of labor, suggested that a meeting of the lumber shovers had been called for Monday afternoon at the Black road, and requested that a good speaker, who could keep the meeting quiet and orderly, be sent to that meeting. In the afternoon, at another meeting of the Central Labor Union, which Mr. Spies attended in the capacity of a reporter, Mr. Zeller, of the agitation committee of the Central Labor Union, requested Mr. Spies to go out the next day and address the lumber shovers' meeting. All this is uncontradicted and appears from the testimony of Zeller (A., 184, 185; L, 155, 156), Urban (A., 201; L, 340-342), Witt (A., 251), and Spies (A., 297; N, 20).

On the following day Spies went out to the appointed place of meeting, and found there gathered a crowd of over six thousand men. Other speakers were present,

some of whom preceded him upon the platform. He was
introduced by Mr. Breest, secretary of the Lumber Shovers' Union. Objection to his speaking was made by some
persons present, on the ground that he was a socialist, but
Breest stated that Spies had been invited to address the
audience and was sent by the Central Labor Union. Mr.
Spies then proceeded to speak. (A., 297; A., 253.) The
substance of his speech was to the effect that he advised
the workingmen to stand together and to enforce their
demands at all hazards, otherwise the bosses would, one
by one, defeat them. Nothing was said by him of an
incendiary nature; no suggestion of violence was made,
not one word was said in regard to the use of force or
arms. (A., 297; N, 23.) Besides the testimony of
Spies, this appears from the testimony of Witt (A., 252;
M, 220), Breest (A., 253; M, 229), Schlavin (A., 254;
M, 233), Pfeiffer (A., 254; M, 236).

Spies swears that he had no idea, when he was invited,
of any relationship of McCormick's employes to that
meeting, or that the locality of the proposed meeting was
in the proximity of the McCormick works. (A., 297:
N, 21.) Besides, it is shown, without contradiction, that
the lumber shovers whom Spies was addressing had
*absolutely no connection with the factory or employes of
McCormick.* (A., 252; M, 221; A., 255, M, 237.)

While Spies was speaking and when McCormick's bell
rang, a part of the crowd on the outskirts, some 500
people, detached themselves and ran towards where the
men were coming out of McCormick's works, distant
some three or four blocks from the meeting. Spies
beckoned to the crowd to remain, saying, in the course of
his remarks, that they had nothing to do with McCormick's. He went on with his speech to a conclusion,
speaking some five or ten minutes after the interruption,

and was thereupon elected by the Lumber Shovers' Union as a member of a committee appointed to wait upon the lumber bosses. (A., 252; M, 223; A., 298; N, 24.)

Meantime the sound of shots was heard at the meeting, and at the same time the police drove up in a patrol wagon towards McCormick's, followed immediately by a large number of police on foot. Then only, Mr. Spies, who to his duties as editor of the Arbeiter Zeitung added those of a reporter for the same paper, went up to McCormick's, and, coming into the neighborhood of the meeting, discovered that the police were chasing people who were unarmed and fleeing in every direction, pursuing them behind cars and in various localities, and firing upon them indiscriminately.

At that moment he was advised by one whom he met coming from the direction of McCormick's, a stranger to him, that *two men had been carried away dead*, and at least twenty-five had been shot, adding words of contempt for the union men, assembled there who would let those men be shot down like dogs.

Mr. Spies admits that his blood was boiling over what he heard and witnessed, and that he thereupon went back to the meeting that he had been addressing, and made an appeal to them that they should proceed to the relief of the parties who were under the fire of the police, near the McCormick works, but they were unconcerned and went home. Seeing that nothing could be done, Spies returned to the Arbeiter Zeitung office, and under the excitement of the hour, and what he had seen and heard, wrote the Revenge circular, so-called.

It is evident from the foregoing review of the testimony that the claim made by the state, that Spies incited the violence against McCormick's property and employes, is without any foundation in fact. For this reason, the whole evidence relating to the McCormick meeting was immaterial; besides, it was wholly irrelevant, as bearing no relation to the Haymarket meeting. *A fortiori* we claim it was incompetent as against any of the other plaintiffs who are in no wise connected with this affair. Therefore, it was error for the court to admit it over the objection and exception of the plaintiffs in error, particularly those other than Spies.

(*b.*) *The Revenge Circular.*

We have, however, considered the details of the McCormick meeting, because it explains the circumstances under which Spies wrote the Revenge circular, the English part of which is as follows: (1 A., 141.) "Revenge! "Workingmen! To arms! Your masters sent out their "blood-hounds — the police — they killed six of your "brothers at McCormick's this afternoon. They killed "the poor wretches, because they, like you, had courage "to disobey the supreme will of your bosses. They killed "them because they dared ask for the shortening of the "hours of toil. They killed them to show you 'free "American citizens' that you must be satisfied and con-"tented with whatever your bosses condescend to allow "you, or you will get killed!

"You have for years endured the most abject humili-"ations; you have for years suffered immeasurable "iniquities; you have worked yourselves to death; you "have endured the pangs of want and hunger; your "children you have sacrificed to the factory lords—in "short, you have been miserable and obedient slaves all "these years. Why? To satisfy the insatiable greed "and fill the coffers of your lazy, thieving master! When

" you ask him now to lessen your burden, he sends his
" blood-hounds out to shoot you, kill you!

" If you are men, if you are the sons of your grand-
" sires, who have shed their blood to free you, then you
" will rise in your might, Hercules, and destroy the hideous
" monster that seeks to destroy you.

" To arms, we call you, to arms!

" YOUR BROTHERS."

The German part of the circular, which followed the
above, expresses the same ideas in substance, and may be
found incorporated in the report of the McCormick meeting published in the Arbeiter Zeitung of May 4th (1 A.,
179–182).

As to the assertion in this circular that six workingmen
had been killed, it appears from the testimony of Mr.
Spies that he wrote at first that *two* had been killed, according to the information received by him before leaving the vicinity of McCormick's; but upon seeing a report about
the occurrence in the 5 o'clock News, in which it was
stated that *six* men had been killed by the police, Spies
changed the figure accordingly. (A., 298; N, 27.) This
is not contradicted, and if it were not correct it would have
been very easy for the state to prove that the 5 o'oclock
edition of the Daily News of that day did not contain any
such information.

The testimony shows that on the same afternoon Mr.
Spies detained six compositors in the Arbeiter Zeitung
office after the regular hour for quitting work, which was
5 o'clock, and had the Revenge circular put in type by
them. This was done in about half an hour or an hour.
Then the form was sent over to Burgess' printing
establishment, where, from time to time, different parties
called to get copies of that circular.

The testimony further shows that this circular was distributed that night, principally at different labor meetings,
among them a meeting of the metal workers at Seamen's
Hall, a meeting of the Carpenters' Union at Zepf's Hall, a
meeting of the brewers at the north side Turner Hall, and
at meetings at 54 West Lake street.

H. C. Smythe, a Tribune reporter, testifies that *a few
minutes after 6 o'clock* on Monday afternoon, while standing in the entrance of 54 West Lake street, talking with
the proprietor, Mr. Greif, his attention was attracted by
seeing a few of the circulars flying through the air. He
picked up one. Just at that moment he saw a horseman
(A., 92, 93), but he did not see the man on horseback
distributing the bills, and is not positive that the man who
rode the horse brought the circulars. This testimony is
entirely uncorroborated by any other evidence in the
record. As to the time fixed by Mr. Smythe, he is directly contradicted by Riechel, also a witness for the state,
who says *it was after 7 o'clock when he took the galley of
the Revenge circular over to Burgess* (A., 94; J, 384).

There were printed about twenty-five hundred of those
circulars (A., 84; J, 280), but not more than half of
them were actually distributed (A., 298; N, 27).

In regard to his motives in publishing this circular, Mr.
Spies gives the following explanation (A., 311; N, 99 *et
seq.*): " When I wrote it, I thought it was proper; I
" don't think so now. I wrote it to arouse the working
" people, who are stupid and ignorant, to a consciousness
" of the condition that they were in, not to submit
" to such brutal treatment as that by which they
" had been shot down at McCormick's. I wanted
" them not to attend meetings under such circumstances
" unless they could resist. I didn't want them to do any-
" thing in particular; I didn't want them to do anything.

" That I called them to arms is a phrase, probably an
" extravagance. I did intend that they should arm them-
" selves. I have called upon the workingmen for years
" and years, and others have done the same thing before
" me, to arm themselves; they have a right under the
" constitution to arm themselves, and it would be well for
" them if they were all armed. I called on them to arm
" themselves, not for the purpose of resisting the lawfully
" constituted authorities of the city and county, in case
" they should meet with opposition from them, but for
" the purpose of resisting the unlawful attacks of the
" police, or the unconstitutional or unlawful demands of
" any organization, whether police, militia or any other."

There is also evidence tending to show that this circular was read before a meeting of the armed sections of
different socialistic organizations held on the night of May
3, 1886, in the basement of 54 West Lake street, of
which meeting we shall speak more fully hereafter ; that
the McCormick meeting and the action of the police
thereat were discussed by that meeting, and as a result
the Haymarket meeting was called for the next evening,
for the express purpose of denouncing the atrocious act
of the police.

But there is no evidence whatever tending to show
that Mr. Spies had any knowledge of, connection with,
or relation to that meeting of the armed groups; there is
no evidence that he knew that such a meeting would
be held or that the circular written by him would
be read by that meeting. Not one word can be found
in the circular itself which in anywise relates to the
Haymarket meeting, or the throwing of the bomb thereat.
There is no evidence whatever that the party who threw
the bomb ever read the circular, ever heard of it or ever
was influenced or induced by it to commit the crime

charged in the indictment. Its being permitted to be introduced in evidence and read to the jury as evidence against *all* plaintiffs (A., 27; O, 348-9) was palpable error.

(c.) *The circular calling the Haymarket meeting.*

On the morning of May 4, 1886, August Spies was asked by Adolph Fischer to address a meeting of workingmen on the Haymarket square that evening. (A., 299; N., 29, 30.) To this request Mr. Spies gave a favorable answer. Shortly thereafter, there came under his observation, for the first time, the circular calling the meeting, in the preparation of which circular he had had no part. The English portion of the circular, as presented to him, was in the words and figures following:

" Attention, Workingmen! Great mass-meeting to-
" night, at 7:30 o'clock, at the Haymarket, Randolph St.,
" bet. Desplaines and Halsted. Good speakers will be
" present to denounce the latest atrocious act of the police,
" the shooting of our fellow-workmen yesterday afternoon.
' Workingmen, arm yourselves, and appear in full force!
                    " THE EXECUTIVE COMMITTEE."

Immediately upon reading the circular over, Mr. Spies stated that the line, " Workingmen arm yourselves and " appear in full force," must be stricken out of the circular, or he would not attend the meeting or speak thereat. (A., 299; N, 31, 32.) His reasons for doing this Mr. Spies states as follows (A., 311; N, 97, 98):
" I objected to that principally because I thought it was
" ridiculous to put a phrase in which would prevent peo-
" ple from attending the meeting; another reason was
" that there was some excitement at that time, and a call
" for arms like that might have caused trouble between

" the police and the attendants of that meeting." At that time the circulars had not been distributed, and but a few of them had been printed. It is possible that a few of those that had been printed had theretofore been or were thereafter carried away by unknown parties, but there was no general distribution of that circular. Mr. Fischer at once acquiesced in the proposal that that line should be stricken out and sent over to the printers, Wehrer & Klein, and had the line taken out; and thereafter about 20,000 circulars were printed with this line omitted, otherwise the same as above, and distributed generally throughout the city. (A., 299, N, 32; A., 257, M, 251-253; A., 138, K, 319, 320.) This circular called the Haymarket meeting, and the foregoing is August Spies' connection and his entire connection therewith. He had, personally, nothing whatever to do with the calling of the meeting, and no instrumentality in procuring it to be called. He knew nothing of any purpose to hold the meeting until, on the morning of May 4th, he was requested by Mr. Fischer to address it. (A., 299, N, 30.) That afternoon, in the issue of the Arbeiter Zeitung, this circular was reprinted in the announcement column, in the same form in which it was distributed, namely: with the line, " Workingmen, arm your-" selves," etc., omitted. (N, 32.)

(d.) *The signal "Ruhe."*

It appears that the meeting of the armed sections at 54 West Lake street, on Monday night, resolved that in certain contingencies, the word " Ruhe " should be published in the Arbeiter Zeitung under the heading " Briefkasten" (Letter-box), as a signal for certain action by the members there present. This we shall consider more

particularly in the review of the case made against
Adolph Fischer. It also appears that in the Arbeiter
Zeitung of May 4th the word " Ruhe " actually did
appear under the heading " Briefkasten." " Ruhe " is
a German word, meaning quiet, rest. (A., 4; J, 59.)
Mr. Spies wrote the word " Ruhe " for insertion in the
Arbeiter Zeitung on May 4th, as he himself admits; but
there is no evidence showing or tending to show that Mr.
Spies at the time knew of any special import attached to
that word. In fact, there was no evidence introduced by
the state as to how Mr. Spies came to write that word
for publication. Mr. Spies himself gives the following
account, which is entirely uncontradicted (A., 306; N,
63 et seq.): "It happened just the same as with any
" other announcement that would come in. I received a
" batch of announcements from a number of labor or-
" ganizations and societies a little after 11 o'clock in my
" editorial room, and went over them. Among them was
" one which read, ' Mr. Editor, please insert in the letter-
" box the word "Ruhe " in prominent letters.' This was
" in German. There is an announcement column of
" meetings in the Arbeiter Zeitung, and a single word, or
" something like that, would be lost sight of in the an-
" nouncements. In such cases, people generally ask to
" have that inserted under the heading of letter-box.
" Upon reading that request, I just took a piece of paper
" and marked on it ' Brief-kasten ' and the word ' Ruhe.'
" The manuscript which is in evidence is in my hand-
" writing. At the time I wrote that word, and sent it up to
" be put in the paper, I did not know of any import what-
" ever attached to it."

This explanation finds corroboration in the testimony of
Fricke, a witness for the prosecution, and formerly book-
keeper for the Arbeiter Zeitung, who says (A., 43, I, 487,

et seq.): " About the 1st of May there was sometimes
" almost a whole column in the Arbeiter Zeitung occupied
" by notices of meetings of workingmen at different
" places and halls. They would bring such notices to the
" Arbeiter Zeitung and say to Mr. Spies, ' put so and so
" under the column of meetings.' It was a common thing
" for postal cards to be received at the office of the Ar-
" beiter Zeitung, and that Spies or Schwab would take it
" and read it over, and then revise it or alter it, and send
" it up for publication in the letter-box, or in this column
" where notices were published."

Mr. Spies further says in regard to the same subject
(A., 306, 165): " My attention was next called to the
" word *Ruhe*, a little after 3 o'clock in the afternoon.
" Balthazar Rau, an advertising agent of the Arbeiter
" Zeitung, came and asked me if the word *Ruhe* was
" in the Arbeiter Zeitung. I had myself forgotten about
" it, and took a copy of the paper and found it there.
" He asked me if I knew what it meant and I said I did
" not. He said there was a rumor that the armed sections
" had held a meeting the night before and had resolved to
" put in that word as a signal for the armed sections to keep
" themselves in readiness, in case the police should precipi-
" tate a riot, to go to the assistance of the attacked. I sent
" for Fischer, who had invited me to speak at the meeting
" that evening, and asked him if that word had any refer-
" ence to that meeting.] He said none whatever, that it was
" merely a signal for the boys, for those who were armed
" to keep their powder dry in case they might be called
" upon to fight within the next days. I told Rau it was a
" very silly thing, or at least there was not much rational
" sense in that, and asked him if he knew how it could be
" managed that this nonsense would be stopped, how it
" could be undone, and Rau said he knew some persons who

" had something to say in the armed organizations, and I
" told him *to go and tell them that the word was put in by*
" *mistake*. Rau went, pursuant to the suggestion, and re-
" turned to me at 5 o'clock. I was not a member of any
" armed section; I have not been for six years."

That the signal, *Ruhe*, had no relation whatever to the
Haymarket meeting will appear conclusively when we
come to consider the Monday night meeting. That Mr.
Spies had no knowledge of its meaning at the time he
wrote it for insertion in the Arbeiter Zeitung, there is no
reason to doubt; that he did not consent to any action to
be taken pursuant to such signal, and that, in fact, he did
all he could to prevent its being acted upon by those who
knew its meaning, appears from his own testimony,
which is not contradicted.

(*c*.)   *Spies' Haymarket speech.*

On the evening of May 4th, Mr. Spies attended the Haymarket meeting, was the first of the speakers on the ground,
although he did not arrive until about half-past 8; he
explained the tardiness of his appearance by saying that he
understood he was to address the meeting in German,
and expected that English speakers would precede him
(A., 299; N, 33). After Mr. Spies had mounted the
truck wagon near the Crane Bros. factory, somebody
suggested to draw the wagon into the Haymarket, to
which Spies replied that the crowd will interfere with the
street traffic. (A., 300, N, 36; A., 129, K, 275.) Then,
after inquiring for Mr. Parsons, Mr. Spies went in search
of him, as already detailed in the review of the testimony
in Mr. Schwab's case. About ten minutes thereafter,
returning to the wagon, not having found Parsons, he
commenced speaking and spoke for about twenty min-

utes. Directly after Parsons' arrival, he brought his remarks to a close, and introduced Parsons.

Concerning the speech itself, Mr. English read his
short-hand notes, taken on a tablet in his coat pocket.
There are occasional breaks in Mr. English's notes, which
he could not supply; but to give the connection as fully as
may be we will simply quote the testimony of Mr. English as it stands in the record (A., 129; K, 276):

" Gentlemen and fellow-workmen, Mr. Parsons and
" Mr. Fielden will be here in a very short time to address
" you. I will say, however, first, this meeting was called
" for the purpose of discussing the general situation of the
" eight-hour strike, and the events which have taken
" place during the last forty-eight hours. It seems to
" have been the opinion of the authorities that this meet-
" ing has been called for the purpose of raising a little
" row and disturbance. *This, however, was not the inten-*
" *tion of the committee that called the meeting.* The
" committee that called the meeting wanted to tell you
" certain facts of which you are probably aware. The
" capitalistic press has been misleading, misrepresenting
" the cause of labor for the last few weeks, so much so "—
" there is something here unintelligible that I cannot
" read; some of it went off on the side of my pocket;
" the next is: " Whenever strikes have taken place;
" whenever people have been driven to violence by the
" oppression of their "—something unintelligible—" Then
" the police "—a few unintelligible words, then there were
" cheers—" But I want to tell you, gentlemen, that these
" acts of violence are the natural outcome of the degra-
" dation and subjection to which working people are sub-
" jected. I was addressing a meeting of ten thousand
" wage slaves, yesterday afternoon, in the neighborhood
" of McCormick's. They did not want me to speak.

" The most of them were good, church-going people.
" They didn't want me to speak because I was a socialist.
" They wanted to tear me down from the cars, but I
" spoke to them and tola them that they must stick to-
" gether,"—some more that is unintelligible—" and he
" would have to submit to them if they would stick to-
" gether." The next I have is, " They were not anar-
" chists, but good, church-going people; they were good
" Christians. The patrol wagons came and blood was
" shed." Some one in the crowd said, " Shame on them!"
The next thing I have is, " Throwing stones at the facto-
" ry; most harmless sport." Then Spies said, " What
" did the police do?" (Some one in the crowd said,
" Murdered them.") Then he went on, "They only came
" to the meeting there as if attending church." * * *
" Such things tell you of the agitation." * * *
" Couldn't help themselves any more. It was then when
" they resorted to violence." * * * " Before you
" starve." * * * " This fight that is going on now is
" simply a struggle for the existence of the oppressed
" classes." My pocket got fuller and fuller of paper, my
" notes got more unintelligible, *the meeting seemed to be*
" *orderly; I took another position in the face of the*
" *speaker, took out my paper, and reported openly during*
" *all the rest of the meeting.* The balance of my notes I
" have not got. From what appears in my report in the
" Tribune I can give you part of what Spies, Fielden and
" Parsons said. It is, however, *only an abstract* of what
" they said. So far as it goes it is verbatim, except the
" pronouns and the verbs are changed."

The balance of Spies' speech is as follows (reading):
" It was said that I inspired the attack on McCormick's.
" That is a lie. The fight is going on. Now is the
" chance to strike for the existence of the oppressed

" classes. The oppressors want us to be content. They
" will kill us. The thought of liberty which inspired
" your sires to fight for their freedom ought to animate
" you to-day. The day is not far distant when we will
" resort to hanging these men." (Applause and cries of
" Hang them now.") " McCormick is the man who
" created the row Monday, and he must be held responsi-
" ble for the murder of our brothers." (Cries of " Hang
" him.") " Don't make any threats--they are of no
" avail. Whenever you get ready to do something do it,
" and don't make any threats beforehand. There are in
" the city to-day between forty and fifty thousand men
" locked out because they refuse to obey the supreme will
" or dictation of a small number of men. The families of
" twenty-five or thirty thousand men are starving because
" their husbands and fathers are not men enough to with-
" stand and resist the dictation of a few thieves on a grand
" scale, to take it out of the power of a few men to say
" whether they should work or not. You place your
" lives, your happiness—everything, under the arbitrary
" power of a few rascals who have been raised in idle-
" ness and luxury upon the fruits of your labor. Will
" you stand that?" (Cries of " No.") " The press say
" we are Bohemians, Poles, Russians, Germans—that
" there are no Americans among us. That is a lie; every
" honest American is with us. Those who are not are
" unworthy of their traditions and their forefathers."

" Spies spoke fifteen or twenty minutes. What I have
" given here would not represent more than five or six
" minutes of actual talking."

We submit, with great confidence, to this court, that
the reading of Mr. Spies' speech, as above reported, demonstrates the position that he was not counseling, nor
even contemplating, any act of violence for that occasion.

That so far from making a speech in furtherance of a conspiracy to cause the throwing of a bomb that night at that meeting for purposes of violence, he was in fact simply commenting upon the then existing situation, and the probable outcome thereof, with no thought of any attack either by or upon the police then and there. In other words, there is in this speech nothing in the nature of an incitement to violence. The facts that occurred after the making of this speech, and up to the time when the meeting was interrupted by the descent of the police, we have already presented, in connection with our observations as to the cases of Mr. Schwab, Mr. Fielden and Mr. Parsons.

(*f.*)   *Gilmer's testimony.*

At this point in their attempted case the state introduced as a witness Harry L. Gilmer. The character of the testimony of this witness demands a careful scrutiny thereof, and we shall not need to apologize to this court for any length to which we may carry our criticism.

Mr. Gilmer testified in effect (A., 141–147; K, 362– 412), that he went to the Haymarket meeting, reaching there about a quarter to 10 o'clock, on his way home from the Palmer House, where he says he went expecting to meet Governor Merrill and Judge Cole, of Iowa. He stood near the lamp-post on the corner of Crane Bros.' alley, between the lamp-post and the wagon and up near the east side of the wagon for a few minutes; Fielden was speaking when he came to the meeting; he stood there for a few minutes looking for a party whom he expected to find there, and then stepped back in the alley between the Crane Bros. building and the building immediately south of it;

standing in the alley and looking around, he noticed
parties in conversation directly across the alley on the
south side thereof; some one on the edge of the sidewalk said: "Here comes the police"! and there was
a sort of a rush to see the police come up; *a man
thereupon came from the wagon down to the parties*
on the south side of the alley, lit a match and touched
off something, a fuse which commenced to fizzle, and
the party who held it took two steps forward and tossed
it into the street; he knew by sight the man who threw
"the fizzing thing into the street," but did not know his
name; he was a man about five feet ten inches high,
somewhat full-chested, with a light sandy beard, full
faced, with an eye set somewhat back in the head, and
probably weighing 180 pounds; he had on a brown or
black hat; the photograph of Schnaubelt, presented to
the witness, is the man who threw the bomb out of the
alley; Spies was the man who came from the wagon
toward the group; and Fischer was one of the group;
after the bomb was thrown these parties immediately left
through the alley; witness stood still until the firing
ceased.

Upon *cross-examination* he stated that he made no out-
cry at that time, and did not for some time afterwards
communicate to any person whatever what he had seen
and heard upon that night, although he had different
conversations about the meeting in which he had stated
that he had been there. On the afternoon of the
next day at the city hall he did state *to a Times
reporter* and another man, that he believed he could
identify the man who threw the bomb if he ever saw him
again, but did not at that time detail the occurrence;
from the position which he occupied in the alley, he could
not see the wagon, and therefore *did not see Spies get off*

the wagon, but that he came from the direction of the
wagon, and that *he had seen Spies before standing on
the sidewalk* and talking with somebody; he was inclined
to think it was Schwab; he did not run at the time of the
shooting, but stood perfectly still; there were no bullets
coming in around his locality in the alley; and after it
was all over, he backed out of the alley, took a car and
went home; there was much excitement and talking about
the meeting upon the car and elsewhere, but he communicated to nobody what he had seen or heard; his
interview as to these occurrences had been mostly with
detective James Bonfield, but he would not be positive that
he had ever told Mr. Bonfield that he saw the man light
the match (K, 392); he had seen Spies and knew him
by sight for a year and a half, but not by name,
had frequently seen and heard him speak at public
meetings, but never inquired what his name was,
though he had heard him once at a meeting on Market
street, a year ago last spring, and had seen from the
paper afterwards that Spies had been one of the speakers
at that meeting. Witness was in the city at the time of
the proceedings before the different coroner's juries, who
investigated the cause of the death of the officers killed
at the Haymarket; that the officers then knew his name
and address, but that they never called upon him to go
either before the grand jury or the coroner's jury. He
stated that he detailed his experiences at the Haymarket
to Mr. Grinnell on the Sunday after the Haymarket meeting,
but that he only told Mr. Grinnell that he believed he could
identify the person who threw the bomb if he saw him;
he thought, however, that he told him he saw one
man strike the match and light the fuse, and another man
throw the bomb; he had received money from time to
time in small sums from Bonfield, but he had not told

any one except the officers named that he saw the act of lighting the bomb accomplished; witness was six feet three inches in height and could nearly see right over the head of the man who threw the bomb.

This is substantially Gilmer's testimony. We believe we can demonstrate that it is absolutely untrue.

We will demonstrate from the record (1) that Gilmer's description of the bomb-thrower does not fit Schnaubelt; (2) that August Spies did not enter the Crane Bros. alley at the time sworn to; (3) that at that very time Adolph Fischer was in Zepf's Hall, more than half a block distant; (4) that the bomb was not thrown out of the alley at all, but from the sidewalk on Desplaines street from a point variously estimated from fifteen to forty feet south of the alley line, from behind a lot of boxes that were piled on the outer edge of the sidewalk next south of the lamp-post which stood on the south-east corner of the alley; (5) that Gilmer's character for truth and veracity and his testimony are impeached.

1. SCHNAUBELT'S HEIGHT.

The record shows without contradiction that Schnaubelt was a man about six feet three inches high (A., 303, N, 56), and therefore it would have been a physical impossibility for Mr. Gilmer to see over his head.

2. SPIES DID NOT ENTER THE ALLEY.

That Spies did not enter the alley at all at the time testified by Gilmer, but in fact remained upon the wagon until the order to disperse had been given, and then dismounted therefrom and turned immediately north, proceeding in the direction of Zepf's Hall, is proved by the following testimony:

(1.) August Spies himself so testifies. He says that when Capt. Ward commanded the dispersal of the audience, he, Spies, was upon the wagon (A., 303; N, 53), and that his brother Henry, together with Ernst Legner, stood by the side of the wagon and reached their hands out and helped him to dismount; that just as he reached the sidewalk he heard the explosion; that when the firing commenced, he pushed or was carried along with the people towards the north, going into Zepf's Hall in the confusion, and afterwards making his way home; *that he did not go to the alley at all, nor in the direction of the alley.*

(2.) Henry Spies (A., 241, 242; M, 148, 150) testifies that when the police commanded the meeting to disperse, his brother Angust was *still upon the wagon*, that he was standing by the side of the wagon and told August to get off, and he reached out his hand and helped him down; that just as August dismounted from the wagon some one jumped behind him with a pistol which Henry Spies grabbed, and in warding off the pistol shot from August received it in his own person, the ball passing through the testicle in a downward oblique direction. The direction of the ball, it may here be stated, was demonstrated by the production of the clothing worn by Henry Spies, showing where the ball went in and where it came out, and by the positive testimony of Dr. Thilo, who attended Henry Spies for this wound. (A., 275.) It is true that Henry Spies, directly after the Haymarket meeting, stated to the police officers that he received this wound while standing in the door of Zepf's saloon, and that it was a stray shot from the direction of the Haymarket meeting; but he says frankly that the statement was not true, and was resorted to by him to prevent his own arrest, his brothers August and Chris having been already arrested. That it was not true is physically demonstrated by the direction of the wound itself.

(3.) In this connection we deem it proper to call attention to the fact that when August Spies was first arrested, he gave to the police officials this same account of his movements on the night of that meeting, and told them that Legner was with him, as testified by Officer James Bonfield (A., 27; I, 349, 350); except that Bonfield says that Spies stated that he went through the alley and came out on Randolph street, after the explosion of the bomb.

It further appears in the record (1 A., 4), that Ernst Legner was a witness before the grand jury; and that his name was indorsed as one of the witnesses for the state on the indictment, but was not used as a witness by the prosecution. We claim, therefore, that it follows as an irresistible conclusion that Ernst Legner, when under oath, gave substantially the same account as to Spies being on the wagon when the police came up, and his helping Spies to dismount from the wagon at the time of the explosion, that was given by Spies to Bonfield; or the state would have had Legner present and put him upon the stand to contradict this testimony of Mr. Spies and his brother Henry. We argue that Legner's testimony would have fully corroborated the testimony of August Spies and his brother Henry throughout, or he would have been upon the stand to contradict them.

But, in addition to this testimony of August and Henry Spies, that August Spies remained upon the wagon until the order of dispersal was given, and until the very instant preceding the explosion of the bomb, and that therefore it was a physical impossibility that he should have gone from the wagon into the alley, struck a match, and with it lighted the fuse of the bomb, we call attention to the following testimony:

(4.) Joseph Bach testifies (A., 280, 281; M, 404, 405) that he and Mitlacher were standing upon a platform by the door of the building south of the alley, on the Desplaines street east sidewalk, their position being some six feet or more from the alley; from this elevation they could look over the heads of the crowd standing upon the sidewalk and in the alley space, and have a distinct view of the wagon and its occupants, and those immediately about it; when the police came up he looked at them and then at the wagon; that he saw Henry Spies (to whom he had shortly before spoken, when he himself went up near the wagon, and then returned to his point of observation), and noticed August Spies attempt to get from the wagon to the sidewalk; that immediately thereafter he turned to go away, and had taken but one or two steps when the bomb exploded; *it was at the instant before the explosion of the bomb that he noticed August Spies getting off the wagon*, and Henry standing with his arm up to help him down; that he did not see August Spies, shortly before the explosion of the bomb, dismount from the wagon and go to the alley near which he stood.

(5.) Max Mitlacher, a brother-in-law of Bach, who was with him at the time (A, 284-85), corroborates Bach in every particular. He says (Vol. M, 430) that he saw, *after the police came up, Fielden and Spies standing upon the wagon*, and saw Spies jump down from the wagon, on the east side, to the sidewalk, and that he saw Henry Spies reach up and help August dismount, though Henry's back was towards him and he did not see his face, but saw his hat; and that he did not see August Spies leave the wagon in advance and come to the alley.

(6.) John Holloway (A., 229 *et seq.*) says he stood on the corner of the alley, against the lamp-post, when the police came (M, 58); he looked at the wagon, when the command to disperse was given (M, 61); he *did not observe anybody leaving the wagon prior to the appearance of the police.*

(7.) Sleeper T. Ingram, a workingman in the employ of Crane Bros., living at home with his parents (A., 286, 287), says he was upon the steps of Crane Bros.' establishment, immediately east of the wagon and but a few feet from it, when the police came up; Fielden and Spies were on the wagon at that time (M, 449); *as Fielden made the remark that they were peaceable, Spies turned around and started to go off the wagon;* he reached his left hand down to be assisted, stooped and jumped, and had no more than got to the sidewalk when the bomb exploded. (M, 451.)

(8.) Conrad Messer (A., 208) testified that when the police came up and the command to disperse was given, he saw both Fielden and Spies on the wagon (L, 400), and that *Spies left the wagon about the same time that Fielden* did, perhaps two or three seconds before; that he saw *Spies on the wagon after the captain commenced to give the command* for the dispersing of the meeting (L, 401).

(9.) August Krumm testifies (A., 210; L, 414, 416) that he and a friend of his, named Albright, were in the alley, near the mouth of it, and near the building to the south, at the time the police came up; a short while before the police came up he himself struck a match and lighted his pipe, and held it while Albright also lighted his pipe; that no other match was lighted nor was any fuse lighted in that alley at that time; that he *did not see Spies come toward that alley nor into it* at any time that evening.

(10) William Albright (A., 217, 218) corroborates this testimony of Krumm in every particular.

(11.) William Murphy (A., 255) says that, five or ten

minutes before the police arrived, he climbed upon the
wagon to look for a friend whom he supposed to be in the
crowd, and remained on the wagon until he heard the word
" disperse "; there were about six persons in the wagon
when he got up; *no one got down from the wagon before
he himself dismounted.*

(12.) Adolph Tennes (A., 259; M, 269) says that at
the time the officers came upon the meeting, he stood about
four or five feet south of the wagon; that as soon as he
heard the order to disperse given, he started to run; and
that at the the time he started to run *August Spies was
still on the wagon.*

(13.) Mr. Fielden testifies that Spies was at his side
on the wagon when Ward was talking with him. (A., 268;
M, 318.)

It is thus demonstrated, by a conclusive preponderance
of testimony, that *Mr. Spies did not leave the wagon
until the order to disperse had been given;* it is therefore
impossible that he should have stood on the sidewalk at
the side of the wagon in conversation with somebody
before Gilmer went into the alley. The fact is, Gilmer
said on his direct examination that Spies came down from
the wagon into the alley and lighted the bomb (A., 141;
K, 363). But upon cross-examination, he stated that
at the time Spies came into the alley, he, Gilmer, was
standing about twelve or fourteen feet from the mouth of
the alley, and was forced to admit that it was physically
impossible for him to have seen the wagon from that
point; finding himself thus cornered, he said Spies did
not get down off of the wagon, but came from towards
the wagon, where he had seen him standing on the sidewalk, before he, Gilmer, went into the alley (A., 144; K,
378-380). It is further conclusively shown by the testimony of the above witnesses that *Spies did not enter the*

alley at all, did not there light a match and with that match light a bomb or the fuse, and that the story of Mr. Gilmer, so far as it attempts to implicate Spies in that occurrence, is absolutely untrue.

3. FISCHER WAS AT ZEPF'S HALL.

But neither was Fischer there. Fischer was at that moment in Zepf's Hall, to which point he had gone some little time before. In support of this assertion, we call attention to the following testimony:

(1.) Otto Wandray testifies (A, 247, 248; Vol. M, 190, 196) that he met Fischer at the Haymarket meeting between 9 and 10 o'clock; that after listening to the speaking for about half an hour they went to Zepf's Hall, where they had a glass of beer, sitting at a table close behind and a little north of the stove. *At the time of the explosion of the bomb, Fischer was at Wandray's side at Zepf's Hall:* when he and Fischer entered Zepf's saloon, he looked at the clock and it was then a little after 10 o'clock.

(2.) As to Wandray's testimony, we cite, as a matter of confirmation, that Lieut. John D. Shea, of the police force, a witness for the State (A., 60; J, 72), admitted that he had a conversation with Fischer while under arrest at police headquarters, wherein Fischer stated to him that on the evening of May 4th he was at Zepf's Hall at the time of the explosion of the bomb, in company with Wandray; that directly thereafter *Wandray was sent for by Shea* and examined, *and stated that Fischer was in the hall* with him at the time of the explosion.

(3.) Mrs. Lizzie May Holmes (A., 262; M, 287, 288) swears that she went in company with Mrs. Parsons, Mr.

Parsons and Mr. Brown, from the Haymarket meeting to
Zepf's Hall shortly before the explosion of the bomb, and
was in Zepf's Hall with those parties when the bomb
exploded; that after entering the hall, she *saw Fischer
sitting at the table further north*, and saw him there from
time to time thereafter, *up to the explosion of the bomb*,
and does not think that he left the building at all in that
interval.

(4.) Thos. Brown testifies (A., 238, 239; M, 124, 125)
that he went to Zepf's Hall on the night of the Haymarket meeting, while Fielden was speaking, in company with Mr. and Mrs. Parsons and Mrs. Holmes;
when the party went into the saloon, witness *saw Fischer
there;* this was about four or five minutes before the
bomb exploded; witness did not see Fischer go out of
the room in that interval.

(5.) Albert R. Parsons testifies (A., 314, 315; N, 115)
that, after moving the adjournment of the Haymarket
meeting, he went, in company with Mr. Brown, Mrs.
Parsons and Mrs. Holmes, to Zepf's saloon, as before
stated; that after entering the saloon, he *noticed Mr.
Fischer sitting at one of the tables*, and spoke to him,
sitting at the table himself a few moments, and then went
around to where the ladies were; that almost instantly
thereafter he saw the flash of the explosion of the bomb,
followed by the roar of that explosion, and almost simul-
tanously saw and heard the volley of revolvers.

By the testimony of these witnesses, therefore, Mr.
Gilmer's statement that he was almost certain, in fact,
quite sure, that Fischer was one of the group in the
alley connected with the bomb-throwing, is completely
refuted, and the fact that Fischer was at the time of the
explosion in Zepf's Hall, and not in Crane Bros.' alley, is
established, without other contradiction than this opinion
of Gilmer.

4. THE BOMB WAS NOT THROWN FROM THE ALLEY.

We further maintain that the evidence overwhelmingly shows, without other contradiction than that of Gilmer himself, that this bomb was in fact not thrown out of the alley at all. We call attention in support of this position to the following testimony:

(1.) Officer Louis Haas, one of the witnesses of the state (A., 128; K, 252, 253), testified that he was attending the meeting in citizen's clothes, and that at the time of the throwing of the bomb he was standing in the center of the street, but within five or six feet of the wagon; that he saw the bomb, which came from *about five or six feet south of the corner of the alley.*

(2.) Paul C. Hull, a reporter of the Daily News, also a witness of the state (A., 116), testifies that he was standing, at the time of the explosion of the bomb, upon the landing at the head of the stairway on the brick building at the north-west corner of Randolph and Desplaines streets; that directly opposite to where he stood was the pile of boxes testified of as south of the lamp-post, on the east side of Desplaines street; that he saw the bomb in its progress through the air before its explosion, and, according to his recollection (K, 124), it seemed to come from *about fifteen to twenty feet south of Crane's alley,* flying over the heads of the police. On cross-examination he further testified (A., 118; K, 141) that his recollection is that the bomb struck the ground about on a line with the south line of the alley, and that it apparently fell north from the point where he first saw it in the air.

(3.) H. E. O. Heinemann, a reporter for the Chicago Tribune, another witness for the State, testifies (A.,

126; K, 235), that at the time of the explosion of the bomb he was on the east side of the sidewalk of Desplaines street, about half way between Crane Bros.' alley and Randolph street. That he saw the bomb or burning fuse rise out of the crowd, and that it rose very near the south-east corner of the alley.

On behalf of the defendants, the testimony as to the point from which the bomb was thrown was as follows:

(4.) Barton Simonson (A., 178, 179; L, 71 *et seq.*) testified that at the time the police came up, and in fact during substantially the entire meeting, he stood upon the stairway of the building at the north-west corner of Randolph and Desplaines, about half way up the stairs, which brought his head probably twenty feet from the ground, and gave him a clear view over the heads of the audience; that directly after the command to disperse had been given he saw the bomb come up from *a point nearly twenty feet south of the south line of Crane's alley,* from about the center of the sidewalk, on the east side of the street, from behind some boxes.

(5.) Ludwig Zeller testified (A., 184; L, 149, 150), that he stood near the lamp-post on the alley, and after the order to disperse was given, turned to walk south to Randolph street. As he turned and started south he saw the lighted fuse go through the air *from six, eight or ten feet south of the lamp;* that it went in a north-westerly direction in the midst of the police, and was followed immediately by the explosion. Upon cross-examination (A., 185; L, 159) he stated more particularly that he *was standing at the moment the bomb was thrown some five or six feet south of the alley, and saw the lighted fuse about eight or ten feet south of him.*

(6.) Fredk. Liebel (A., 188, 189; L, 201–203) says that he also was standing near the lamp-post, and when the police came up and the order to disperse was given turned to go south and get out of the crowd, and as he was proceeding south saw the lighted fuse, which at the time he took to be the stump of a lighted cigar, thrown from the sidewalk, at a point which he took to be *near midway between the alley and Randolph street.* And he says that the bomb went in a north-westerly direction, and then exploded.

(7.) Dr. James D. Taylor (A., 191, 192; L, 230, *et seq.*), after stating that he stood over the curbstone at the intersection of the street and alley on the north side of Crane Bros.' alley, says that after the police and the order to disperse was given, he saw the bomb thrown. He says he saw the bomb in the air, *somewhere between twenty and forty feet south of the alley, and the man who threw it stood beyond a number of boxes which stood south of the lamp-post;* that he revisited the ground the next morning after the occurrence, and saw the boxes still there; that he did not see the man who threw the bomb, and when the bomb was thrown could see nothing but his head; that when he first saw the bomb he took it to be a boy's fire-cracker; that it circled through the air in a north-westerly direction, and alighted between the first and second lines of police, a little west of the center of the street, and perhaps a little south of the line of the alley.

(8.) William Urban (A., 201; L, 344, *et seq.*) states that he saw something like a fire-cracker in the air, followed by the explosion, and then the pistol firing: that what looked to him like a fire-cracker must have started *from fifteen to eighteen feet south of the lamp-post at Crane's alley;* that it went very fast, made a kind of a circle, going north-westerly, and about one or two seconds after he first observed it he heard the explosion.

(9.) August Krumm (A, 210; L, 415), after explaining that he stood near the mouth of the alley and next the building on the south, states that he saw something looking like an extinguished match go through the air and drop about the middle of the street, which he says must have started from *about twenty feet south of the alley;* was about twelve feet up in the air when he saw it, and that it did not start and could not have started out of the alley; that he saw the streak of fire, and right after that heard the explosion of the bomb.

(10.) William Albright (A., 217; L, 493) swears that he was with Krumm, as detailed by the latter, and that the bomb was *not lighted in nor thrown from the alley where they stood.*

(11.) Joseph Bach and (12) Max Mitlacher whose testimony we have already considered upon another point, both testify that immediately before the explosion they were looking towards the wagon, *and that they did not see any object thrown out of the alley* into the street. (A., 281, M, 407, 408; A., 285; M, 433.)

(13.) John Holloway (A., 230, 231), who stood against the lamp-post at Crane's alley (M, 58), and was looking at the speaker's wagon at the time of the dispersal and until the explosion of the bomb (M, 59, 60), says he is sure nothing came out of the alley while he stood there. (M, 63.) In the nature of things, if the bomb had been thrown from out of the alley it could not have escaped his attention.

(14.) George Koehler testifies (A., 218; Vol. L, 508–518) that *he stood on the north-west corner of Randolp* *and Desplaines* streets when the police came up, and saw the bomb come from the east side of the street *from opposite where he stood from the middle of the sidewalk and flying in a north-westerly direction.*

(15.) Edward Lehnert (A, 234; Vol. M, 89, 90), after

stating that he stood on the west side of Desplaines street, about thirty paces north from Randolph, and twenty paces south from opposite the wagon, states that from that point he saw a streak of fire which looked like a stump of cigar in the air, which he learned later was the bomb, and that it came *from about twenty paces south of the alley*, according to his best judgment, and went north-west, and struck the ground in the middle of the street, a little south of the alley.

(16.) Finally, John Bernett (A., 292; M, 483, *et seq.*) testifies as follows: That he is not acquainted with any of the defendants, although he had heard some of them speak; was not a socialist, communist or anarchist; was at the Haymarket meeting at the time the bomb exploded; that at the time of the explosion he stood about thirty-eight feet south of Crane's alley; that on the Wednesday preceding his testimony he had made a careful examination of the ground to find out the locality where he stood; *that he saw the man who threw the bomb, and saw the bomb go through the air; that its direction was west and a little north; that the man who threw the bomb was right in front of Bernett at the time, and was about Bernett's size, having a mustache with no chin beard.* (We would here observe, that Bernett was a man of about five feet nine inches in height.) When shown Mr. *Schnaubelt's photograph* and asked if he recognized that as being the man who threw the bomb, he said that the photograph had been shown him by Mr. Furthman about two weeks before his testifying, and that *it was not the picture of the bomb-thrower*, and that he had so told Mr. Furthman. On *cross-examination* (A., 293) he stated that he had had different interviews with the representatives of the prose-cution and had told Capt. Schaack and Mr. Grinnell that the man who threw the bomb was in front of the witness, and he could not tell how he did look; that he told Mr. Furthman that he thought the bomb was thrown *from about fifteen steps south of the alley*, counting a step at about two and a half feet; that on that night there was a pile of boxes south of the lamp-post which was on the corner of the alley; that he went to the central station on the 7th day of May, and talked to Officer Bonfield in the presence of Mr. Grinnell; that he did not think that at that time he said the bomb was thrown from behind the boxes, nor did he think that some weeks ago he stated it was thrown from a point twenty to twenty-five feet south of the alley; did not remember how many feet he did state the distance was, but thinks he has it right in his present testimony. On re-direct examination (A., 294), he stated that he told Capt. Schaack that the man that threw the bomb was but little larger than himself, *had a mustache and no chin whiskers*, and that he has said so all the time; that he had never measured the distance from the alley to the place where he stood on that night until the Wednesday preceding his testimony; that when the bomb was thrown he saw the motion of throwing; saw the fire right from the hand; followed the light with his eye, and saw the light where the bomb exploded, heard the explosion, saw the flash of the bomb, and then ran away.

Here we have Bernett, an absolutely disinterested and unimpeachable witness. We say unimpeachable, because it developed upon the cross-examination of this witness that he had made substantially the same statement over and again to the representatives of the state -to Mr. Grinnell, Capt. Schaack and Officer Bonfield; and if it had been possible to impeach Mr. Bernett, we assume that the state would have made that attempt, knowing

as long in advance as they did substantially what his
testimony would be. No such attempt was made.
There was an effort made to show that he had estimated the distance south from the alley of the bomb-
thrower differently at different times; but this very evidence shows that he had always located the bomb-
thrower south of the alley, and on the east sidewalk of
Desplaines street.

But in this direct issue of veracity between Bernett on
the one side and Gilmer on the other, we find Gilmer absolutely unsupported by a single other witness in the
record; while Bernett is conclusively corroborated by *fifteen witnesses*, directly by three of the state's witnesses,
Haas, Hull and Heinemann, and nine witnesses for the
defendants, namely, Simonson, Zeller, Liebel, Taylor, Urban, Krumm, Lehnert, Albright and Koehler, and inferen-
tially by the testimony of Bach, Mitlacher and Holloway.
As between the two, therefore, no man who is not wilfully
determined to disregard all the rules of evidence can hesitate in according credence to the statement of Mr. Bernett, and in rejecting absolutely the story of Gilmer.

5. GILMER'S IMPEACHMENT.

But in addition to all this Gilmer was successfully impeached. Nine citizens of Chicago, called to the witness
stand in behalf of the defendants, testified unequivocally
that they knew Harry L. Gilmer, were acquainted with
his general reputation for truth and veracity in the neighborhood where he resided, and among his neighbors and
acquaintances, that that reputation was bad, and that *they
would not believe him under oath*. These witnesses were
as follows:

(1.) Lucius M. Moses (A., 194, 195; L, 268 273),
a grocer, sixty-four years old, residing at 301 West
Randolph street, in which neighborhood Gilmer had been
living for a number of months.

(2.) Mrs. B. P. Lee (A., 195, 196; L, 279), residing
at 295 West Randolph street, and keeping a boarding-
house.

(3.) John G. Brixey (A., 199), living at 297 West
Randolph street, to whom for a time Gilmer lived as next-
door neighbor. Mr. Brixey had known Mr. Gilmer for
a considerable period of time, and on two occasions had
lived adjacent to him. And on cross-examination he gave
the names of a number of parties whom he had heard
speak of Gilmer's reputation for veracity.

(4.) John Garrick (A., 200), residing at 279 Fulton
street, formerly chief deputy sheriff under Sheriff Kern,
and a man of property, in whose house and in whose
neighborhood Gilmer lived at one time.

(5.) Mrs. Mary Grubb (A., 227), residing at 22 North
Ann street, and in whose house Gilmer at one time lived
for a number of weeks.

(6.) Phineas H. Adams (A., 250), a machinist, engaged in business with his brother at 31 South Canal
street, who at one time lived in the same block with
Gilmer.

(7.) Edward H. Castle (A., 258) residing at 51 Wal-
nut street, seventy-five years old, who had been a resident of Cook county since 1839, of whom Gilmer had
one time been a tenant, and who is a man of large
property, as appears from the testimony.

(8.) H. S. Howe (A., 259), sixty-two years old, and
in the undertaking business.

(9.) John W. Gage (A., 292), residing at 216 S.
Paulina street, in the painting and wall paper business,

forty-five years of age, employing all the way up to forty men in his business. On cross-examination Gage stated that Gilmer lived next door to him about four months.

It is true that an effort was made to meet this impeachment of the reputation of Mr. Gilmer by the introduction of various witnesses by the state. The witnesses introduced included eight brought from Des Moines, Iowa, to testify as to Mr. Gilmer's reputation while he lived in that city, about ten years ago, which had not been attacked; and about an equal number of citizens of Chicago. Concerning this attempt to sustain Mr. Gilmer's reputation, we have a few suggestions to submit.

First. Judge Cole and Governor Merrill, of Iowa, were among the witnesses produced by the state. Both of them testified that *they were not in Chicago on the evening of May 4th at the Palmer House or elsewhere: that they were not expecting to be in Chicago at that time*; that they had no appointment in Chicago at or about that time to meet Mr. Gilmer, or to meet anybody else; and that *they had never communicated with Mr. Gilmer;* that they had never had any correspondence with him, nor made any such appointment with him; thus establishing conclusively that when Mr. Gilmer stated upon the stand, that he went to the Palmer House on the night of May 4th expecting there to meet Mr. Merrill and Judge Cole, he was stating an invention instead of a fact; the purpose doubtless being to impress the jury with his supposed consequence and the dignity of his relations among men.

Second. Concerning these witnesses, and all of the witnesses from Iowa, we beg further to suggest that they were substantially all of them *occupying a different walk of life* from that in which Mr. Gilmer moved, and who, substantially, all of them, admitted that they *did not know his reputation while living in Iowa among his imme-diate neighbors and acquaintances* for truth and veracity, but simply that they had been residents of the same city where they had known him slightly, and where they had heard no special question about his reputation. Judge Cole, for example, simply lived in the same city, and had had Gilmer do a little painting for him; but beyond that practically knew nothing about him.

Third. So as to the witnesses called from Chicago to testify as to his reputation. They were in the main worthy citizens, but they were men who confessedly, as brought out on their respective cross-examinations, did not commingle in the society of which Mr. Gilmer was a member, did not move in the same walk of life, *had never lived in the same neighborhood in which he lived;* and *most of them admitted that in fact they never had known where Gilmer did live at any time.* Not one of them knew him in the intimacy of daily association in a neigh-borly way, these parties at the most being able, as they were forced to admit on their respective cross-examinations, to state that they were members of the Union Veteran Club along with Mr. Gilmer, or members of Battery D, and *had casually met him in those associations and nowhere else,* and talked with others in those associations who had met him in like manner; associations in which he would naturally seek to be esteemed, and where he would naturally be upon his good behavior for purely selfish considerations. When, however, we enter the circle of his neighbors, daily acquaintances and associates in work and business, living near where he lived, sometimes in the same house or under the same roof, we find that he was a man whose reputation could be most suc-cessfully impeached; while not a single witness was produced by the State out of the list of the man's neigh-

bors and acquaintances to speak a word in his behalf.
Was there any design on the part of the representatives
of the State in thus limiting their investigation as to Mr.
Gilmer's reputation? And was there, likewise, any. design upon their part to possibly impose upon the jury by
the dignity of the men whom they would produce, who
were ready to swear that they considered his reputation
good, *although they did not know what it was?*

We understand the correct rule in reference to attempts
to impeach or support testimony of witnesses to be that
laid down by this court in the case of *Frye* v. *The Bank
of Illinois*, 11 Ill., 367, as found in the opinion of the
court at page 379, where it is said: " The proper ques-
" tion to be put to a witness to impeach another is, *whether*
" *he knows the general reputation* of the person sought
" to be impeached *among his neighbors* for truth and ve-
" racity. If this question be answered affirmatively, the
" witness may then be inquired of as to what that reputa-
" tion is, and whether from that reputation he would be-
" lieve him on oath." And a number of authorities are
cited in support of the rule thus announced.

In the light of this rule of law, we insist that the effort
thus made to sustain Mr. Gilmer utterly failed, for the
reason that not a single neighbor, not a single acquaintance accustomed to associate with him in daily life, and
commingle with his neighbors and daily associates, was
produced; that the cross-examination of every witness
called by the state in this behalf conclusively shows that
they knew nothing of the *general reputation* of Gilmer
for truth and veracity, and that the reputation to which
those witnesses pretended to testify did not come from
Gilmer's *neighbors and associates*, and that it was error
for the court to admit the testimony of such witnesses
over the objection and exception of the defendants.

But further than that, the defendants called to the
stand as a witness W. A. S. Graham, a reporter for the
Chicago Times (Abst., 321, 322, Vol. N, 144, 149). He
said that he had occupied the position of reporter upon
the Times for twenty-five months, and had been a newspaper man for eight years; that he knew Harry L.
Gilmer since the 5th day of May, the day following the
Haymarket riot; that on that day he saw Gilmer in the
corridor of the basement in the City Hall, just outside
the police headquarters; that he had a conversation with
Gilmer on that occasion in regard to what he saw at the
Haymarket, and who threw the bomb.

At this point Mr. Gilmer was recalled by the defendants
for further cross-examination, which developed the fact
(A., 321, 322; M, 145-47) that Mr. Graham was the
reporter whom Gilmer mentions in his cross-examination
(A., 143; K, 370) as one of the parties to whom he stated,
on May 5th or 6th, at the central station, that he believed
he could identify the man who threw the bomb if he ever
saw him again. He further stated that he did not say to
Mr. Graham in that conversation that he saw the man
throw the bomb, but his back was toward Gilmer, and
he could not see him very well, and that he *believed* he
had whiskers; he did not think that he said at that
time and place that he saw the man light the fuse *and*
throw the bomb—did not say it was a man of medium
size, and that he saw him light the fuse *and* throw the
bomb; that he had no such conversation with Mr. Graham.

Mr. Graham then, further examined, testified that in
the conversation referred to Gilmer stated to Graham that
he (Gilmer) saw the man light the fuse *and* throw the
bomb, and added, " I think I could identify him if I saw
" him." Graham proceeded substantially as follows: " I

" asked him what kind of a looking man he was, and
" Gilmer said ' he was a man of *medium height*, and I
" *think he had whiskers*, and wore a soft, black slouch
" hat, *but his back was turned towards me.*' And to the
" best of my recollection, Gilmer said the man had dark
" clothes. *He said nothing about anybody else in that con-*
" *nection.*"

Upon cross-examination Mr. Graham stated: " I had
" this conversation about 4 o'clock in the afternoon
" of May 5th. I talked with him about three or four
" minutes. *He said nothing about there being more than*
' *one man at that location*, a knot of men, or any-
" thing of that kind; he said that *one man lighted the*
" *fuse and threw the bomb;* he did not say anything about
" how it was lighted, whether with a match or a cigar; I
" did not ask him that; he said he was standing in Crane's
" alley when it was done."

Mr. Graham is an unimpeached witness; it cannot be
conceived that he had any interest—particularly when his
relations to the newspaper and the condition of public
opinion and sentiment at the time he testified are considered—to pervert his testimony in the service of the accused. If his testimony is true, then Gilmer's is false.
Not only does Graham contradict Gilmer as to the substance of the conversation at the central station, on the afternoon of May 4th, but if Graham tells the truth, then the
version of affairs which Gilmer gave at the time, when the
events were fresh in his mind, is absolutely irreconcilable
with the version given by him as a witness upon the stand.
Upon the stand he swears that the man *had whiskers*, and
he pretended to recognize a photograph. To Graham he
stated that the man *had his back toward him*, and would
only say that *he thought he had whiskers*, and he believed he could recognize him if he saw him again. Upon

the witness stand he stated that he saw August Spies light the fuse, and a totally different man throw the bomb, while still another of the defendants stood by, watching the operation. To Graham he stated that he saw *the man light the fuse and throw the bomb*, speaking of a single transaction by one individual, and making no pretense whatever that other parties were at the time present or interested in this operation. He stated to Graham that he could identify the man who threw the bomb, but did not mention anything about the man who lighted the fuse of the bomb, although he claimed (A., 146; K, 394) that *he had known Spies by sight for a year and a half, and had very frequently seen and heard him* speak at public meetings. If the story told by Gilmer upon the stand were true, could he have given to Graham the version of the affair to which Graham testifies?

If corroboration of Graham upon this point is needed, it is to be found in the fact that in his opening statement to the jury, after having had repeated interviews with Gilmer, as the record shows, and having advised himself thoroughly of the story which Gilmer was prepared to tell, Mr. Grinnell, in reference to the bomb-throwing, did not give the detail of this story as told by Gilmer upon the stand. (1 A., 32; O, 91.) Is it creditable that Mr. Grinnell willfully suppressed matters within his knowledge in reference to the details attending the throwing of the bomb? If Mr. Grinnell knew, at the time he made his opening statement, that Mr. Gilmer would testify that August Spies lighted the fuse of the bomb, that Rudolph Schnaubelt threw the bomb, and that Adolph Fischer stood by while this was being done, he certainly would, as in fairness bound to do, have so stated in his opening.

The effort of the state, therefore, to show that the Haymarket bomb was thrown by Rudolph Schnaubelt, the fuse thereof lighted by August Spies, and that Adolph Fischer stood by while the bomb was lighted and thrown, rests upon the unsupported testimony of a single witness, whose subsequent conduct in keeping this information to himself cannot be explained consistently with any theory of honesty of purpose or sincerity of utterance; who stands impeached upon this record as to his general reputation for truth and veracity, and who is contradicted by a score of unimpeached witnesses as to the most vital and material points in his statement. We think we might safely dismiss this branch of the case as absolutely and finally disposed of.

Taking it altogether, there is an absolute want of credible evidence, which connects Mr. Spies with the act of throwing the bomb at the Haymarket, which shows or tends to show that he had any knowledge of, or gave his aid or assistance to any plan for using violence at that or any other meeting by or against anybody.

ADOLPH FISCHER.

The testimony shows that Adolph Fischer was a compositor on the Arbeiter Zeitung, of which Spies and Schwab were the editors. On the morning of May 4th, he caused the printing and distribution of the circular calling the Haymarket meeting for that evening, and requested Mr. Spies to speak. As before stated, when Spies' attention was called to the form of the circular, he insisted that the line "Workingmen, Arm Yourselves," etc., should be stricken out, and Fischer caused this to be done. Fischer was at the Haymarket during a part of the time as an auditor, but took no part in the meeting itself, and as shown by the evidence heretofore considered in connection with the case of Mr. Spies and the testimony of Harry L. Gilmer, he was, in fact, in Zepf's Hall at the time of the explosion of the bomb. No utterance of Fischer's suggesting or urging violence upon that evening, either in speech or print, is in this record. The evidence not only shows that he was not present when the act which resulted in the death of Mathias J. Degan was committed, but it absolutely fails to show that he did or said anything by way of aiding, encouraging, advising, abetting or assisting the performance of that act.

There is but little that remains to be said about this branch of the case as to Mr. Fischer, the evidence upon these points having been already so fully considered in presenting our views as to the cases attempted to be made against others of the plaintiffs in error.

But it is proper that we should here enter upon the consideration of another fact proved in this case, upon which the state relies as entitling it to claim that this conviction of Adolph Fischer shall be sustained.

The West Lake Street Meeting Conspiracy.

It is claimed that on the night of Monday, May 3, 1886, there was a meeting held at 54 West Lake street, attended by Fischer and Engel of the plaintiffs in error, at which a conspiracy was entered into, and at which the calling of the Haymarket meeting was resolved upon. In our view, the testimony as to this meeting was irrelevant to the issue to be determined in this case; and when the testimony of the witnesses who speak as to that meeting was introduced, it came in subject to our objection, and was retained in the record as against our motion to exclude. We shall present briefly an outline of that testimony, and then suggest to the court the grounds of our objection to it and our motion for its exclusion.

The State introduced as witnesses, who testified in regard to this Monday night meeting, Godfried Waller, who presided at the meeting, Bernard Schrade and Gustave Lehmann, who were present, and Greif, the proprietor of the hall. The leading witness was the informer, Godfried Waller. He says (A., 4; I, 52, *et seq.*) he went to the meeting pursuant to an advertisement which he saw in the Fackel (the Sunday issue of the Arbeiter Zeitung) of May 2d. A translation into English of that advertisement is as follows: " Y---Come Monday night;" which notice he says meant a call for the armed men of the various groups to meet at 54 West Lake street, Greif's Hall. Reaching the building about 8 P. M., it was found that the halls were all fully occupied with workingmen's meetings, and that the only place where a meeting could be held pursuant to this notice was in the basement. He says he called the meeting to order at about half-past eight, and that there were some seventy or eighty present, while the testimony of Schrade, Lehmann and Greif shows that there were in attendance not more than about thirty to forty.

Describing the occurrences of the meeting, this witness says that there was first some talk about six men supposed to have been killed at McCormick's; that there were present circulars headed " Revenge," and treating about that occurrence; then Mr. Engel stated a resolution passed by a prior meeting of the north-west side group, and it was afterwards resolved by the meeting there present to adopt the plan of action reported, which was to the effect, that if the word " Ruhe " should be published under the heading Briefkasten (letter-box), of the Arbeiter Zeitung, it should be a signal for the armed men to meet.

The north-west side group had determined upon Wicker park as their meeting place in that case. A committee should observe the movement in the city, and if a conflict should occur, the committee should report to the armed men, who should then storm the police stations by throwing a bomb, and should shoot down everything that would come out or in their way. The police station on North avenue was referred to, but no other, the action beyond that to be determined by circumstances.

This program having been agreed upon, as this witness states, he himself then suggested that there ought to be a meeting of workingmen called for Tuesday morning on Market square. Fischer said that would be a mouse trap and that the meeting should be on the Haymarket in the evening. It was then resolved that the meeting should be held at 8 P. M. at the Haymarket; and it was stated that the purpose of the meeting was to cheer up the workingmen so that they should be prepared in case a conflict would happen. Fischer was commissioned to call the meeting through hand-bills; he went away to order them, but came back after half an hour and said the printing establishment was closed. It was said that the armed men should not participate in the meeting on the Haymarket. Asked in direct examination, " What was " said, if anything, as to what should be done in case " the police should attempt to disperse the Haymarket " meeting ?" he replied, " *There was nothing said about* " *the Haymarket. There was nothing expected that the* " *police would get to the Haymarket.*" Those present were representatives from the west, south and north side groups. A committee, composed of one or two from each group, was to be sent to the Haymarket; but this committee was not only to observe the movement on the Haymarket square, but in different parts of the city; he only knew one member of the proposed committee, named Kraemer; if a conflict happened in the daytime, the committee was to cause the publication of the word *Ruhe;* while if it happened at night, they were to report to the members, personally, at their homes. He did not, himself, on the 4th of May, understand why the word *Ruhe* was published, as it was to be inserted only in the event that a revolution had broken out. Fischer first mentioned the word *Ruhe.* Schnaubelt was present at the Lake street meeting, and said that the resolution adopted should be communicated to members of the organization in other localities, so that the movement should commence in other places also. This same witness further stated that this plan of operations introduced at the meeting at 54 West Lake street, by Mr. Engel, was a plan which Engel had proposed at a meeting of the north-west side group on Sunday morning, May 2d, at its meeting-place on Emma street, at which meeting he says both Fischer and Engel were present.

On cross-examination this witness states that, at the meeting at Emma street and at that meeting at Greif's Hall, Mr. Engel stated that the plan proposed by him was to be followed only in the event of a police attack, and that the workingmen *should only defend themselves if thus attacked by the police.* He repeated positively that nothing was said as to any action to be taken at the Haymarket; that *they were not to do anything at the Haymarket square;* that the plan was that they were not to be present there at all. *They did not think the police would come to the Haymarket; no preparations were made for meeting any police attack there.* He further stated that on the night of May 4th he was with Fischer, walking about the streets in the neigborhood of the Haymarket for a time, and then went to a meeting of the fur-

niture-workers' union at Zepf's Hall, and was there when
the bomb exploded; that Fischer and himself walked together over to the Desplaines station, where the police were
mounting five or six patrol wagons, upon which the witness said, "I suppose they are getting ready to drive out
" to McCormick's, so that they might be out there early
" in the morning;" to which Mr. Fischer assented. He
stated that the principal purpose of the Haymarket meeting was to protest against the action of the police at the
riot at McCormick's factory, and that while he was with
Fischer at the Haymarket nothing was said between
them about preparations to meet an attack by the police,
and Fischer did not ask him why he was not at Wicker
park. He admitted that he had received various sums of
money from Capt. Schaack, and that his wife also had
received moneys.

Bernard Schrade, testifying as to the same meeting
(A., 9 to 12) says, when he reached the meeting
in the basement, Waller was presiding, and explained
what had been spoken of prior to his coming; Waller
stated that so many men had been shot at McCormick's
by the police, and that a mass-meeting was to be held at
Haymarket square, and that they should be prepared in
case the police should go beyond their bounds and attack
them; that he heard nothing about assembling in other
parts of the city; that circulars headed " Revenge "
were distributed; that he was present at the meeting on
Emma street on the Sunday previous, and that in that
meeting it was suggested in effect that there might be
trouble after the 1st of May, in which event they were to
help one another—that if they should get into a conflict
with the police they should mutually aid one another, and
that the north-western group should meet at Wicker
park in the event of a police attack, to defend themselves

as well as they could; but that *nothing was said about dynamite, and the word "stuff" was not used*, and that nothing was said about telegraph wires; that it was suggested that in case of an outbreak, it would be desirable to cripple the effectiveness of the firemen by cutting their hose. He says further, that he heard nothing whatever about the word *Ruhe* in the meeting at 54 West Lake street, and that he did not see it in the Arbeiter Zeitung. Upon cross-examination he stated that *nothing was said at any of the meetings about dynamite or bombs*, and nothing was said about a meeting at any particular time to throw bombs; that it was not agreed to throw bombs at the Haymarket meeting; that while at that meeting he, himself, had no bomb, and didn't know dynamite if he should see it; that he knew of no one who was going to take a bomb to that meeting; that he was at the meeting, and when he left it everything was quiet; *that he did not anticipate any trouble there, and that he left the Haymarket only on account of the approach of the storm.*

Thomas Greif, the proprietor of Greif's hall, 54 West Lake street, says (A., 24, 25) that on Monday evening, May 3d, a man rented the basement for a meeting, and told Greif, " if the Y folks come, to tell them to go down-stairs." Witness had to go down-stairs once to tap the beer. There were two men standing on the stairs talking together; there were twenty-five or thirty men present when he was down there at about 9 o'clock.

Gustaf Lehmann (A., 73), testified that he attended this meeting at 54 West Lake street, on the evening of May 3d, reaching there at a quarter of 9; but Lehmann could give no account of the occurrences in the meeting, for the reason, as he states, that he was deputed to step outside and see that there was no eavesdropping by persons going down the front way to the water-closet, who had to pass by from the door opening into the area way from the basement. He said, however, that he went into the meeting twice, and on one occasion heard Fischer say that he was going to have some handbills printed.

This is the entire testimony of the state as to the Monday night meeting. Our position in reference to it is this: that if it establishes a conspiracy at all, it was not a conspiracy which contemplated or provided for the throwing of a bomb or the use of any violence by any of the co-conspirators at the Haymarket meeting on the night of May 4th; and that, therefore, the introduction of this testimony was improper, as not being relevant to the issue which was under consideration; and that it was erroneous, as having a manifest tendency to prejudice the jury and thus injure the plaintiffs in error.

This testimony moreover was allowed to come in and to have full force as against *all of the plaintiffs in error*, although no effort was made to show that any of them, other than Fischer and Engel, were present at either the Emma street meeting or the West Lake street meeting, save possibly a slight attempt in that direction as to Lingg, which we shall consider hereafter. In other words, the plaintiffs in error, other than Fischer and Engel, were compelled to meet, in the minds of the jury, the full impression of this testimony over their objection and exception (A., 4; I, 57), and a motion to exclude the same was likewise overruled (A., 8; I, 106).

Our understanding of the law is, that when a conspiracy to do an unlawful act is proved and an unlawful act within the purview of the conspiracy is subsequently done by one of the conspirators in pursuance of the common design, then all of the conspirators who are parties to the original design are equally liable with the doer of the deed.

If this be a correct statement of the rule of law as applicable to such cases, and we think it will not be seriously questioned, then it is incumbent upon the state, when attempting to establish the guilt of a conspirator not engaged in the very act itself as an accessory before the fact, to show, in addition to the fact that there was a conspiracy to do an unlawful act:

First. That the accused was a party to such conspiracy.

Second. That the unlawful act charged was committed " in furtherance of the original design," and " in the attempt to execute the common purpose."

Third. That such act was done by one identified as a party to the conspiracy, or by the procurement of one of such parties, " in prosecution of the common object."

As to each of these points, we understand the burden is upon the prosecution to make a case beyond any reasonable doubt by competent testimony. Even if a conspiracy were proved and an unlawful act were done by one of the conspirators, yet the conspirators would not be responsible unless that act was done in pursuance of the conspiracy, and " in the attempt to execute the common purpose," and was within the " natural and probable consequences that may arise from" such execution. In other words, if a co-conspirator should, after the formation of the conspiracy, commit a different crime, acting in that behalf upon his own responsibility, and without consultation with his associates, he alone must bear the consequences of his evil deed, and cannot involve his associates in the penalty.

Let us test the evidence now under consideration by these rules.

I. *Six of the plaintiffs in error were not parties to the conspiracy.*

Only two, or at the very most, three, of the plaintiffs in error, are shown to have had any knowledge of, or to have yielded any acquiescence to, the program or plan of operations agreed upon at the meeting at 54 West Lake street. Before the testimony concerning that meeting could be competent as against plaintiffs in error, other than those present, it was incumbent upon the state to show, by legal evidence, some actual connection between the other plaintiffs in error and that meeting, either by pre-arrangement and consent to the proposed scheme, or by subsequent acquiescence and participation in the design. Not only had no such evidence been introduced in this case up to the time the testimony of Waller and Schrade was introduced, and received over the objection of the plaintiffs in error, but in fact no legal evidence was adduced in the entire trial, which connects the plaintiffs in error other than Fischer and Engel, save perhaps Lingg, with the West Lake street meeting, or the designs then and there adopted. The state failed to show, and certainly it failed to show beyond a reasonable doubt, that the accused other than Fischer and Engel were parties to the conspiracy, and as to them one of the essential requirements of guilt on the ground of the West Lake street conspiracy fails.

II. *The throwing of the bomb at the Haymarket was absolutely foreign to the original design.*

The design itself was absolutely foreign, in legal contemplation, to the Haymarket tragedy. Whatever may be said of the idea of the parties associated in the

West Lake street meeting, it is evident that they did not have in view the throwing of bombs by individual members of their groups, upon their individual judgment, but that they were providing for concerted action in the contingency of an unlawful attack by the police upon workingmen, and that in the event of such contingency the conspirators were to be notified in a certain manner.

The evidence further shows that the meeting of Tuesday night was not at all within the general scope of the plan agreed upon. In fact, that date was too near at hand to allow of the carrying out of the details of their own plan, which contemplated, according to the testimony, the communication with bodies outside of Chicago. The witnesses further swear that *after* this general plan of operations had been discussed, adopted and *disposed* of, the suggestion was *then* made that there ought to be a meeting of laboring men to protest against the conduct of the police at the McCormick riot; it was distinctly agreed that *the members of this association should not be present;* there was no expectation at the Monday night meeting that there would be any police disturbance or interference at the proposed Tuesday night meeting. There was *no plan or arrangement for any act to be done by the conspirators or any of them on Tuesday night at the proposed meeting.*

On the contrary, it appears that only a committee should observe the movements *in the city generally*, and that when trouble should arise in the daytime they should cause the publication of the word "Ruhe"; if at night, they should notify the conspirators at their homes. If thus notified, then they should meet in certain places and proceed by concerted action.

Nothing of the kind was done. Though the word "Ruhe" appeared in the Arbeiter Zeitung, as above shown, still there is *no evidence that any of the conspirators acted upon it*, that they met pursuant thereto in their appointed meeting places: Wicker park, etc.; or that they proceeded to attack any station or march down to the heart of the city to come to the rescue of a body of attacked strikers. According to the arrangement at the West Lake street meeting, the conspirators ought to have been notified at once, when the police attacked the Haymarket meeting. *This was not done; no part of the design alleged to have been agreed upon on Monday night was carried out.* But *somebody* threw a bomb into the ranks of the police. If he was a member of that conspiracy—of which we claim there is no proof in the record---then he acted *in direct opposition to the plan agreed upon, he disregarded the directions of his associates, he defeated their objects,* and his act was as much *his individual act, as if he had been a total stranger to the conspiracy.*

As it appears from the testimony of the informers, that there was no expectation of violence at the Haymarket meeting, and no provision therefor, as, on the contrary, it was expressly agreed, that the conspirators should not attend or do anything at the same, it cannot be maintained that the crime charged was within the " natural and probable consequences" that might arise from the carrying into execution of the original design.

III. *There is no credible evidence that the bomb was thrown by a party to the conspiracy.*

The only attempt made by the state to show that the bomb was thrown by a member of the conspiracy is the testimony of Harry L. Gilmer. We have demonstrated in the preceding pages that the overwhelming preponderance of the evidence absolutely refutes Gilmer's testimony; that the bomb was not thrown out of the alley at all, but from a point variously estimated as between fifteen and thirty-five feet south of the alley; that Gilmer's description of the bomb-thrower as a man of five feet eight, nine or ten inches in height, does not apply to Rudolph Schnaubelt, a man six feet and three inches tall; that the whole story of the group in the alley is without foundation, evidently an afterthought of Gilmer, and contradicted by the incontestable evidence as to Spies' and Fischer's movements, and finally that Gilmer was successfully impeached as to his character for truth and veracity.

Aside from this we have upon the part of the defendants the following testimony to show that Schnaubelt had left the Haymarket meeting five or ten minutes prior to the explosion of the bomb, evidently with the intention of going home.

Edward Lehnert (A., 233, 234; M, 82 *et seq.*) says he knew Schnaubelt, and that he met him on the west side of Desplaines street, opposite the speakers' wagon, about the time that the dark cloud came up, and before the explosion of the bomb; that August Krueger was present, and that Krueger spoke to Schnaubelt, when the two went away toward Randolph street.

It was further offered to prove by this witness that in the conversation which he then and there had with Schnaubelt, Schnaubelt stated to Lehnert that he did not understand English, had expected that German speakers would address the meeting; that he did not wish to stay any longer and *was going home,* and asked Lehnert if he would go along. Lehnert stated that he did not go in the same direction, whereupon Schnaubelt went away with Krueger.

We respectfully submit that this testimony was competent as part of the *res gestae*, in connection with evidence as to the movements of Rudolph Schnaubelt, who, at that time, upon the testimony of the state, stood charged with throwing the bomb, and that its exclusion by the court, to which the defendants excepted (A., 234; M, 89), was error.

Krueger testifies in reference to this same occurrence (A., 243; M, 157), that he met Schnaubelt at the Haymarket meeting, standing with Mr. Lehnert on the west side of Desplaines street, a little north of Randolph, about ten o'clock; that Schnaubelt stayed there about five minutes. *Witness went with Schnaubelt down Randolph street up to Clinton, a distance of over two blocks*, where he turned north on Clinton street, while Schnaubelt proceeded east on Randolph, but how much further no testimony discloses. We were denied the privilege of putting in the evidence which would have shown affirmatively to the jury the reason of Schnaubelt's leaving the meeting, and that he was leaving it finally, and with no thought of returning to it. On the other hand, there is no evidence that Schnaubelt was at the meeting at the time of the explosion, except the impeached and contradictory testimony of Gilmer, who attempts to identify him from a photograph.

The evidence is conclusive that Schnaubelt did not throw the bomb. It is perhaps enough to say in regard to the testimony of Gilmer, that so completely and overwhelmingly was he impeached, contradicted and discredited, that *the state did not ask a single instruction to the jury based upon the belief by them that Rudolph Schnaubelt threw that bomb as detailed by Gilmer.* The testimony of Gilmer was abandoned by the representatives of the state as unworthy of credence or consideration, in the instructions asked by them.

There is no other evidence as to who did that act. Our claim, therefore, is that *the state failed to establish that the bomb was thrown by a member of the conspiracy, or by the procurement of one of the conspirators in prosecution of the common object.*

The result of the foregoing investigation shows the testimony as to the West Lake street meeting conspiracy to have been incompetent as against all the plaintiffs in error, even Fischer and Engel, and therefore it cannot affect any of them.

Taking the testimony as a whole, we maintain that there is an entire absence of credible evidence showing that Adolph Fischer was present at, or ever agreed to the throwing of a bomb at the Haymarket meeting, ever expected any such act, ever did anything toward providing for such violence, ever entered into any conspiracy having that act as an object, or even as an incident of its consummation. The testimony in regard to the Sunday and the Monday night meetings, as given by the state's own witnesses, absolutely refutes the theory that the Haymarket bomb was thrown as the result of a conspiracy to which Fischer, Engel and others were parties, and for which they can be held upon the principle of accessoryship before the fact.

GEORGE ENGEL.

The case attempted by the state to be made against George Engel in connection with the Haymarket meeting has already been considered in a large measure in the preceding pages. One additional matter requires brief consideration.

There was no pretense that Engel was present at the

Haymarket meeting at the time that the bomb was thrown, nor for some considerable time prior thereto though there is evidence tending to show that he was at the locality of the meeting early in the evening. Waller testifies (A., 6; I, 73) that after the bomb was exploded, and after he had left Zepf's Hall, he proceeded immediately home, by way of Engel's house, stopping in there; that he found Engel at home with several friends, as he expresses it, " around a jovial glass of beer," to whom he told what had occurred at the Haymarket.

He says that upon this announcement being made, he told the party there gathered that he thought they had better go home; to which Engel assented in effect, saying yes, they should all go home; and that nothing else occurred.

Concerning this meeting at Engel's house after the bomb-throwing, one other witness testifies, namely August Krueger (A., 243). Krueger says that he was at the Haymarket meeting, and remained there until about 10 o'clock; that he then left the meeting and went to Engel's house, reaching it about a quarter past 10 o'clock; that Mr. and Mrs. Engel were there, and the witness drank a pint of beer with them; that later, Waller came in, said that he came from the Haymarket, and that three hundred men had been shot by the police, and that " we ought to go down there and do something." To this Engel responded that *whoever threw that bomb did a foolish thing*, it was nonsense, and *he did not sympathize with such a butchery*, and he told Waller he had better go home as quick as possible; he said the policemen were just as good people, and that the revolution must grow out of the people, then the police and militia would throw away their arms and go with the people.

From the concurring testimony of these two witnesses,

it appears beyond question that at the time the bomb was thrown Engel was quietly at home with a little party of friends, not anticipating any violence or any unlawful conduct; and that when he was advised of what had occurred at the Haymarket, he immediately deprecated such conduct as unwise, denouncing it as a butchery to which he was opposed. Krueger swears that to Waller's proposition that something should be done by the parties there gathered, Mr. Engel responded that they should all go home. Waller denies that he made the suggestion of which Krueger speaks, but admits that Engel concurred in the suggestion that they should go to their homes quietly.

If the Haymarket meeting had been planned with reference to carrying out the programme of action discussed and alleged to have been agreed upon at the Monday night meeting, then the natural thing for Engel and his associates, when the news was brought to them of the outbreak at the Haymarket, would have been to have gathered themselves together and inaugurated their movement against the police. The fact that no such suggestion came from Engel; and that if such a suggestion was made from any source, it found no entertainment with him, is evidence to our mind, along with all the other testimony in the case, that the event of the Haymarket was a matter of absolute surprise to Mr. Engel.

Nothing in his conduct, as testified to by these witnesses, gives color for a moment to the suggestion that he considered the event of the Haymarket as a matter growing out of any purpose or enterprise entertained by him, or as within the purview of any understanding or agreement, to which he was a party. The bomb was thrown in his absence, by some party acting without any reference whatever to Mr. Engel's attitude, views or utterances. In other words, Mr. Engel never aided, advised, assisted, encouraged or abetted the perpetration of the crime at the Haymarket.

Louis Lingg.

The evidence introduced by the state shows that Louis Lingg did not attend the Haymarket meeting, nor was within a distance of about two miles thereof during the entire evening. The incriminatory evidence against Lingg is chiefly that of William Seliger, coupled with the fact that Lingg manufactured a number of dynamite bombs. But there is no evidence in the record to show that Lingg knew that a bomb would be thrown at the Haymarket, or that he gave a bomb of his manufacture to any person for the purpose of having it there thrown, or had any knowledge or intimation that any bomb made by him might or would be thrown by any person whatever on that occasion.

Seliger testifies (A., 44, *et seq.*) substantially as follows: "On Tuesday I rose at half-past 7, and after "I got up Lingg came. I had previously told him "that I wanted those things (bomb and bomb material) "removed from my dwelling. He told me to work dili- "gently at those bombs, and they would be taken away "that day; I took some coffee and after a time I worked "at some shells—at some loaded shells. I drilled holes "through which the bolt went, a shell like this (indicat- "ing shell introduced in evidence). I worked on the "shells half an hour. Lingg went to the west side to a "meeting; got back probably after 1 o'clock. He said "I didn't do much; I ought to have worked more dili- "gently. I said: 'I hadn't any pleasure at the work.' "Lingg said: 'Well we will have to work very dili- "gently this afternoon.' During the afternoon I did dif-

" ferent work at the shells. In the morning I had a con-
" versation about the bolts. He told me he had not
" enough of them. He gave me one and told me to go
" to Clybourne avenue and get some that he had already
" spoken to the man about. I got about fifty. I worked
" at the bombs during the whole of the afternoon, at dif-
" ferent times. Huebner, Munsenberg and Heuman
" were helping. I worked in the front room, also in
" Lingg's room and the rear room. Lingg first worked
" at gas or water pipes, such as these (indicating).
" There were probably thirty or forty or fifty bombs
" made that afternoon. The round bombs had been
" cast once before by Lingg, in the rear room on my
" stove, probably six weeks previous to the 4th of May.
" The first bomb I ever saw was in Lingg's room; that
" was still before that; at that time he told me he
" was going to make bombs; I saw dynamite for the first
" time in Lingg's room, about five or six weeks previous
" to the 4th of May; Lingg said every working man
" should get some dynamite, that there should be consider-
" able agitation; that every working man should learn to
" handle these things; during that Tuesday afternoon
" Lingg said those bombs were going to be good fodder
" for the capitalists and the police when they came to
" protect the capitalists; nothing was said about when
" they wanted the bombs completed or ready; I only told
" him that I wanted these things out of my room; there
" was only a remark that they were to be used that even-
" ing, but nothing positive as to time. I left the house at
" half-past 8 that evening. Huebner was at the house
" probably from 4 to 6 o'clock; I did not see what he
" did; he worked in the front room with Lingg; I was
" in Lingg's room; Munsenberg was there as long as
" Huebner; Thielen was there half an hour—quite that;

" I did not see what he was doing. The Lehmanns were
" at the house for a little while. I did not see what they
" were doing; they were in the front room. Heumann
" also worked at the bombs. I left that house in the
" evening with Lingg. We had a little trunk with
" bombs in. The trunk was probably two feet long, one
" foot high and one foot wide. It was covered with
" coarse linen. There were round and pipe bombs in it.
" They were loaded with dynamite and caps fixed to
" them. I don't know how many there were. The
" trunk might have weighed from thirty to fifty pounds.
" We pulled a stick, which Lingg had broken,
" through the handle. That is the way we
" carried the trunk, which was taken to Neff's Hall,
" 58 Clybourn avenue. On the way to Neff's Hall,
" Munsenberg met us. We took the package into the
" building, and through the saloon on the side into the
" hallway that led to the rear. After the bombs were
" put down in the passage way, there were different
" ones there, three or four, who took bombs out for them-
" selves. I took two pipe bombs myself. Carried them
" in my pocket. We went away from Neff's Hall and
" left that package in the passage. The hall back of
" Neff's Hall is known under the name of the " Shanty of
" the Communists.' Different socialistic and anarchistic
" organizations met there. The north side group met
" there; I heard that the Saxon Bund met there. I don't
" know any others that met there. When I left Neff's Hall,
" Thielen and Gustav Lehmann were with me. Later,
" two large men of the Lehr und Wehr Verein came to
" us; I believe they all had bombs. We went on to Cly-
" bourn avenue, north, toward Lincoln avenue, to the
" Larrabee street station, where we halted. Lingg and
" myself halted there. I don't know what had become of

" the others. Some went ahead of us. Lingg and I had
" a conversation, that there should be made a disturb-
" ance everywhere on the north side, and keep the police
" from going over to the west side. In front of the
" Larrabee street station Lingg said it might be a beau-
" tiful thing if we would walk over and throw one or
" two bombs into the station. There were two police-
" men sitting in front of the station, and Lingg said
" if the others came out these two could not do much.
" We would shoot these two down. Then we went
" further north to Lincoln avenue and Larrabee street,
" where we took a glass of beer. Webster avenue sta-
" tion is near there. After we left the saloon we went
" a few blocks north, then turned about and came back to
" North avenue and Larrabee street. While we stood
" there the patrol wagon passed. We were standing
" south of North avenue and Larrabee street. Lingg said
" that he was going to throw a bomb; that was the best
" opportunity to throw the bomb, and I said: ' It would
" not have any purpose.' Then he became quite wild,
" excited; said I should give him a light. I was smoking
" a cigar, and I jumped into the front opening before a
" store and lighted a match, as if I intended to light
" a cigar, so I could not give him a light. When I had
" lighted my cigar, the patrol wagon was just passing.
" Lingg said he was going to go after the wagon to see
" what had happened, saying that something had certainly
" happened on the west side, some trouble; the patrol
" wagon was completely manned, going south on Larra-
" bee street; we were four or five houses distant from
" the station; then I went into a boarding house between
" Mohawk and Larrabee streets and lighted a cigar; then
" we went towards home. First Lingg wanted to wait
" until the patrol wagon would come back, but I impor-

" tuned him to go home with me. We got home proba-
" bly shortly before 11, I cannot tell exactly. On the
" way home Lingg asked me whether I had seen a no-
" tice that a meeting of the armed men should be held on
" the west side; I said I had seen nothing; Lingg
" wanted to go out; I took the Arbeiter Zeitung, tore it
" in two parts, he took one and I one: thereupon he said:
" ' Here it is!' and called my attention to the word *Ruhe*.
" This here (paper marked People's Exhibit No. 4),
" is the same that I saw in my house. I didn't know
" the meaning of the word *Ruhe* until the time I saw
" it. Lingg said there was to have been a meeting
" on the west side that night, and he was going to go at
" once to it—that *Ruhe* meant that everything was to go
" topsy-turvy; that there was to be trouble; he said that
" a meeting had been held at which it was determined that
" the word *Ruhe* should go into the paper, when all the
" armed men should appear at 54 West Lake street; that
" there should be trouble. After that talk we went
" away; Lingg wanted to go to the west side, and I
" talked with him to go with me to 58 Clybourn ave-
" nue. Lingg and I went there; there were several per-
" sons present at Neff's Hall. I did not speak with
" Lingg at Neff's Hall; a certain Hermann said to him
" in an energetic tone of voice: ' You are the fault of all
" of it.' I did not hear what Lingg said to that; they
" spoke in a subdued tone; somebody said a bomb had
" fallen which had killed many and wounded many; I did
" not hear what Lingg said to that. On the way home
" Lingg said that he was even now scolded, chided for
" the work he had done; we got home shortly after
" twelve. We laid the bombs off on our way on Sigel
" street between Sedgwick and Hurlbut, under an ele-
" vated sidewalk. I laid two pipe bombs there: I saw

" Lingg put some bombs there; I don't know what
" kind."

On cross-examination this witness admitted that he had
been under arrest, had himself been indicted for murder
in this same matter, that he had been furnished money
from time to time by Capt. Schaack, and that he had
from time to time, at the instance of the officers, signed
different written statements as to the occurrences testified
of, statements that differed from one another, but had
finally made substantially the same statement as he had
testified to.   He also stated that Schaack had from time
to time paid his wife money, since his arrest, and stated
(A., 50) that the agreement on Tuesday afternoon
was that they were to go that evening with the bombs
they were manufacturing. to Clybourn avenue; that
there was no agreement that the bombs were to be taken
anywhere else, nor what was to be done with them after
they were taken there; that *he had never heard of any
agreement that any of the bombs manufactured on May 4th
were to be taken by anybody to the Haymarket; that
they were not on that occasion making bombs to take to
the Haymarket and destroy the police;* they were to be
taken to Clybourn avenue that evening, and the witness
stated that he could not say that a single bomb was made
for use at the Haymarket meeting.

Mrs. Seliger's testimony (A., 51-53) substantially corroborates the testimony of her husband as to the fact that
Lingg was making bombs, and as to the fact that the
bomb-making was carried on at her house on the 4th day
of May, 1886.

Concerning these matters, Gustaf Lehmann testifies
(A., 73; J, 198, *et seq.*) that he went to Lingg's room on
the afternoon of May 4th, reaching there about 5 o'clock:
that he there saw Lingg, Seliger, Huebner and a black-

smith whose name he could not remember; he remained there about ten minutes; they did some work in the bed-room which the witness did not understand; Lingg and Huebner had a cloth tied around their faces; later, after going away for a time, witness returned to Lingg's room about 7 o'clock, and remained there a few minutes; that at that time Huebner was cutting a coil of fuse into pieces; during the afternoon, Lingg gave to the witness a small hand satchel, with a tin box in it, three round bombs, two coils of fuse and some caps. Lingg said to the witness that he wanted him to keep these things so that no one could find them; witness took them home with him to the wood shed, and that night carried them away to the prairie, near Clybourn avenue, behind Ogden's Grove; about half-past nine he went to Neff's Hall, because Lingg had told him on Monday night that, if he wanted to know something, he should come to 58 Clybourn avenue on Tuesday evening; he stayed about ten minutes at Neff's Hall; he did not see anybody there whom he knew except the barkeeper; later that night, witness met Seliger and Lingg on the sidewalk on Lar-rabee street near Clybourn avenue, and conversed with them for a few minutes; either Lingg or Seliger sug-gested that they should not all keep together, and there-upon they separated.

Moriz Neff, (A., 82, 83,) testifies that he is the pro-prietor of the saloon at 58 Clybourn avenue, and that on the night when the bomb was thrown, Lingg, Seliger and a stranger came to his saloon, bringing a satchel, arriving about a quarter past 8; they went out of the side door of the saloon with the satchel or bag; Lingg asked him if somebody had asked for him; he saw Lingg and Seliger again that night about 11 o'clock; during the whole even-ing nobody had inquired for Lingg. After Lingg went

away upon his first visit, a number of persons came into
the saloon, among them the Hermanns, the Lehmanns,
the Hagemanns and Hirschberger; shortly after these
Lingg and Seliger came in, and all talked together. Witness did not pay much attention to the conversation, but
heard some one of the party speak out very loud: "That
"is all your fault." Some of the parties stated that a
bomb had been thrown among the police, and some of
them had been killed, but he could not tell whether any
of the parties to the conversation had been at the Haymarket meeting, whether they were speaking from knowledge or from hearsay.

All this testimony came in under objection, and particularly under objection in behalf of the defendants other
than Lingg.

One of the witnesses for the State, namely Capt.
Schaack, said that Lingg had admitted to him that
he was present at the meeting at No. 54 West Lake
street on the night of May 3d. But that he was present at
that meeting, was conclusively disproved by the testimony
of Ernst Niendorf (A., 276), who had been called as a
witness by the state, and that of Jacob Sherman (A., 276),
both of whom swear that Lingg was present at a meeting of the Carpenters' Union at Zept's Hall on the night
of May 3d, from 8 until after 11 o'clock.

It is perfectly evident from the testimony of Seliger,
above quoted, that Lingg was not at the meeting at 54
West Lake street, and that he had no clear or intelligent
comprehension of the plan that was agreed upon at that
meeting, and particularly of the significance of the word
Ruhe if it should appear. He stated on the night of May
4th, so Seliger says, that the word *Ruhe* was a signal for
the armed men of the various sections to meet at 54 West
Lake street; but, according to Waller's testimony, no

such significance whatever attached to the use of that word.

The direct case against Louis Lingg consists of the following facts: (1) That he did manufacture bombs. (2) That he was specially active in preparing bombs on the 4th day of May, 1886, which bombs he assisted in carrying to Neff's saloon, 58 Clybourn avenue, a point more than two miles distant from the Haymarket, and where he arrived with Seliger about a quarter-past 8 o'clock. And (3) that he proposed to Seliger, if we accept Seliger's testimony, an attack upon the police out on Larrabee street, also two miles from the Haymarket.

As to Seliger's testimony, it must be borne in mind that it is the evidence of a man, who, upon his own showing, supposed himself to be swearing for his life. Such testimony should always be taken with great caution, and scrutinized with extreme care—particularly where, as in this case, the party admits that he had been led up to the point of the testimony given through repeated statements extorted by the police, while both himself and his wife were under arrest, and practically as the price of their liberty. Contradictions in the testimony of such a witness are matters for grave consideration. When, therefore, Mr. Seliger says that there was, on the afternoon of May 4th a remark made that the bombs were to be used that night, but practically in the same breath says: "Nothing was said about when they wanted the " bombs completed or ready, and nothing positive was " mentioned as to the time when the bombs were to be " used " (A., 46), such a contradiction is not without significance.

Again, it is rather singular that the only person who did anything which looked like acting upon the signal "Ruhe" should have been Lingg (namely, his proposal to attack the police on Larrabee street), who at the time *did not know that that signal was published*, but learned of it only after he had returned home late at night. (A., 47; I, 521.)

In the face of the proof that Lingg did not attend the Haymarket meeting, and was not in direct communication with anybody shown to have been at that meeting, in the absence of all evidence that any one of his bombs was taken to that meeting, we submit that it cannot be presumed, cannot legally be inferred, that he knew or understood that any one of the bombs manufactured by him was to be taken to the Haymarket meeting, or to be thrown by any person upon that occasion. The most we think that can fairly be concluded in reference to Lingg is, that he was completing the manufacture of a number of bombs which had been begun weeks before by him, and when a Haymarket meeting was not in the imagination of any mortal, in order to have them ready generally for use by the workingmen in the event of a general outbreak in the city, or a general conflict between the police and the strikers, and not with reference to their particular use upon the occasion of the Haymarket meeting.

We are brought, then, to the simple question whether a conviction in this case was justified as against Louis Lingg because he was a bomb-maker.

Upon this point an instruction was asked to be given to the jury, which was refused by the court. We desire to call attention, not only to that instruction, which we believe presented a correct principle of law, but to the circumstances attending the refusal of that instruction by Judge Gary. The instruction asked was as follows (1 A., 23; O, 32):

" It is not enough to warrant the conviction of the

" defendant Lingg that he may have manufactured the
" bomb, the explosion of which killed Mathias J. Degan.
" He must have aided, abetted or advised the exploding
" of the bomb, or of the doing of some illegal act, or the
" doing of a legal act in an unlawful manner, in the
" furtherance of which, and as incident thereto, the same
" was exploded and said Degan killed. If, as to the
" defendant Lingg, the jury should find beyond all rea-
" sonable doubt that he did in fact manufacture said
" bomb, but are not satisfied beyond all reasonable doubt
" that he aided, advised, counseled or abetted the throw-
" ing of said missile, or the doing of any unlawful act
" which resulted in the explosion of said bomb, your
" verdict should acquit him, as far as the establishment
" of his guilt is attempted by the manufacture of said
" missile or bomb."

The circumstances attending this instruction, and its
handling by Judge Gary, present some peculiar features.
(1 A., 23; O, 33.) The instruction, after being examined
by Judge Gary, was marked as " given." The judge proceeded to read it to the jury in connection with the other
instructions given in behalf of the defendants. The record
shows that he read it half way through. In other words,
he read it far enough to show to the jury that it was an
instruction applicable to the case of Louis Lingg, and
presenting broadly the doctrine that a man could not be
hung for a murder accomplished by a weapon manufactured by him simply because he manufactured the
weapon, without other evidence connecting him with its
use. Judge Gary then stopped, and, in the presence of
the jury, said, in effect, as disclosed by the record
(1 A., 23; O, 33), that an instruction often impressed one differently when read aloud, and thereupon, in the presence of the jury, marked the instruc-

tion " refused," and declined to read the balance of it.
That this conduct could not fail to prejudice the jury
against Louis Lingg, is manifest. The action of the
court itself was erroneous; its effect was just as prejudicial to Louis Lingg as if he had read the instruction
through, and then orally said: " Gentlemen of the jury,
that is not the law." Such a verbal statement would
have amounted to an instruction to the jury, not in writing, and, therefore, clearly illegal.

McEwen v. *Morcy*, 60 Ill., 32.

Rev. Stat. Ill., Chap. 110, Sec. 52.

That this instruction asked in behalf of Louis Lingg
should have been given, we think too clear to admit of
serious doubt. It even so commended itself to the judgment of the trial court as to secure in the first instance
his sanction. But not only did the court thus act in
reference to this particular instruction naming Louis
Lingg, but even a general instruction asked in his interest
was denied. The instruction was as follows, viz. (1 A.,
16; O, 15):

" The court further instructs the jury that the mere
" manufacture and disposition of deadly weapons does not
" of itself make the party so manufacturing or disposing
" thereof responsible for murder committed therewith by
" third parties. Before such manufacturer or distributor
" can be held liable for a murder committed by a third
" party, it must be made to appear by credible evidence,
" beyond all reasonable doubt, that such manufacturer or
" distributor countenanced, advised, aided, encouraged
" or abetted the particular act of such third party, which
" resulted in the homicide, and was thus himself in con-
" templation of law accessory to the particular act
" charged as a crime."

Does not this instruction announce a correct rule of

law? No equivalent for it is to be found in the instructions given. And certainly the situation of the case upon the evidence justified the asking of this instruction. If so, was not the refusal to give it clear error?

Whatever may be our criticism upon the matter of manufacturing dynamite bombs for any purpose, there is no law within this State which makes the mere manufacture of such missiles a crime punishable with death or otherwise. Louis Lingg could not have been convicted of murder because of all this matter detailed by Seliger and his wife and Lehmann, even if it were clear that the bomb thrown at the Haymarket had come from his hands, if it had been thrown by a third party acting upon his own responsibility and without Lingg's knowledge, consent, aid, assistance, advice or encouragement. For example, the manufacturers of revolvers, bowie knives, dirks, poisoned daggers, Gatling guns, air guns, have never been held responsible for the consequences of the use of these weapons by a third party acting *sua sponte*. These weapons are harmless in themselves, and cannot be involved in the commission of crime until some free moral agent intelligently applies them to some purpose of destruction. Nor is this rule affected by the fact, if conceded, that the manufacturer must have known that the natural use to which the implement manufactured would be put would be the taking of human life. We may deprecate such industry, but we cannot say that the mere pursuit of the industry makes the man engaged in it responsible for every use of the implement produced. By way of illustration, we may suppose that some third party, an enemy of Lingg's, had obtained one of the bombs of his manufacture and use for the purpose of deliberate murder, with the design of involving Lingg himself in ruin, and with it committed a crime to

which Lingg was a stranger; such result would not
follow. In order to justify a legal conviction of murder,
there must be satisfactory and conclusive proof of the
commission by the party accused, in his own person or
through another acting under his aid and advice, of the
crime alleged. It will not do to allow our horror over the
use of this terrible explosive to carry us away from the
moorings of the law. It will not do for us to allow the
realm of jurisprudence to be invaded by the mere dic-
tates of supposed policy. We must stand by fixed principles of general application. Only thus can the law be
administered as a science, and be made the protection of
the innocent and the terror only of the guilty.

We submit and insist that this record is barren of evidence justifying the conclusion by the jury that Louis
Lingg was a party to a conspiracy to throw a bomb on
the night of May 4, 1886, or to a common object in the
attempt to execute which that bomb was thrown. The
evidence is conclusive that Lingg did not throw the
bomb, did not stand by and assist the perpetration of
the crime. It follows as an irresistable conclusion from
Seliger's testimony, that whatever Lingg did, whatever
he may have attempted or proposed on the north side, he
had no knowledge that a bomb would be thrown at the
Haymarket meeting. The evidence fails to show, that
without being present, he had advised, encouraged, aided
or abetted the perpetration of the crime charged in the
indictment.

THE HAYMARKET MEETING.

It is perhaps fitting that at this juncture a little space
should be devoted to the consideration of the Haymarket
meeting itself, its special features, and the facts leading up

to, and resulting in, the tragedy of the night of May 4, 1886.

The Haymarket, so-called, is a widening of Randolph street between Desplaines and Halsted streets, extending a distance of two blocks. (People's Exhibit 1, Vol. of Ex.) The territory was sufficiently large for the holding of an immense meeting, and the evidence shows that when it was called a very large attendance was expected. This expectation was not realized. Only here and there small groups of men gathered on the Haymarket square, and the speakers were late in arriving. At the hour named, 7:30 P. M., no one was upon the ground to call the people together or to open the meeting. There is no contradiction of the testimony as to these points. It is proved alike by the witnesses for the State and for the defense, that no move was made toward the calling to order of the meeting itself until August Spies, looking around for a suitable rostrum from which to address the crowd, selected the truck wagon which he found standing close to the edge of the sidewalk in Desplaines street, and directly in front of the steps leading up to the door entering into the Crane Bros. manufacturing establishment. The wagon stood with the rear to the south, the tongue to the north; and the end of the wagon was some six or eight feet, or more, north of the north line of the Crane Bros.' alley. This is a short alley, as shown by the plat, which enters the block from Desplaines street toward the east upon the south line of Crane Bros.' building, and extends about half way through the block, then makes a junction with another short alley extending out from the point of junction southward to Randolph street. This alley is a perfect *cul-de-sac* as it there existed, and all egress from it could be stopped by a handful of men at the Randolph street exit.

Having selected this wagon Mr. Spies mounted it at
about half-past eight o'clock and inquired for Parsons.
Parsons not responding, Spies dismounted from the
wagon and went in search of him, being absent, as
estimated by the different witnesses, from five to ten
minutes, and returning again, mounted the wagon and
commenced to speak. He spoke about twenty minutes.
As soon as Parsons and Fielden arrived Spies brought
his remarks to a close and introduced Parsons. Parsons
did not commence to speak until about nine o'clock; he
spoke from three-quarters of an hour to an hour. At the
end of Parsons' speech Fielden was introduced. He
spoke about twenty minutes; and about twenty minutes
past 10 o'clock at night, his speech was interrupted by the
arrival of the police, the order to disperse, and the subsequent explosion of the bomb.

From its beginning to its close, the meeting was as
orderly as any ordinary outdoor meeting. Mr. English,
the Tribune reporter, says (A., 133; K, 284): "*It was
"a peaceable and quiet meeting* for an outdoor meeting.
"I didn't see any turbulence. I was there all the time."

Mayor Harrison tells us (A., 174; L, 27 *et seq.*), that
having had a conversation with Inspector John Bonfield,
and arranged for the presence of the police at the Desplaines street station, to be held in readiness against possible violence by the Haymarket meeting, he concluded to
attend the same in person, so as to personally order its
dispersion if, in his judgment, it assumed a dangerous tendency. It was his own determination to do this, against
the will of the police. He attended the meeting from its
beginning until near the close of Parson's address. Here
is his testimony (A., 175; L, 36 *et seq.*):

"I did, in fact, take no action at the meeting about dis-
"persing it. There were occasional replies from the

" audience, as ' Shoot him,' ' Hang him,' or the like, but I
" don't think, from the directions in which they came,
" here and there and around, that there were more than
" two or three hundred actual sympathizers with the
" speakers. Several times cries of ' Hang him ' would
" come from a boy in the outskirts, and the crowd would
" laugh. I felt that the majority of the crowd were idle
" spectators, and the replies nearly as much what might
" be called ' guying ' as absolute applause. Some of the
" replies were evidently bitter; they came from immedi-
" ately around the stand. The audience numbered from
" eight hundred to one thousand. The people in attend-
" ance, so far as I could see during the half hour before
" the speaking commenced, were apparently laborers or
" mechanics, and the majority of them not English-speak-
" ing people, mostly Germans. There was no sug-
" gestion made by either of the speakers look-
" ing toward calling for the immediate use of
" force or violence towards any person that night;
" if there had been, I should have dispersed them at once.
" After I came back from the station Parsons was still
" speaking, but evidently approaching a close. It was
" becoming cloudy, and looked like threatening rain, and
" I thought the thing was about over. *There was not*
" *one-fourth of the crowd that had been there during the*
" *evening*, listening to the speakers at that time. In the
" crowd I heard a great many Germans use expressions
" of their being dissatisfied with bringing them there for
" this speaking. When I went to the station, during Par-
" sons' speech, I stated to Capt. Bonfield that I thought
" the speeches were about over; *that nothing had occurred*
" *yet, or looked likely to occur, to require interference*, and
" that he had better issue orders to his reserves at the
" other stations to go home. Bonfield replied that he *had*

" *reached the same conclusion from reports brought to him,*
" but he thought it would be best to retain the men in the
" station until the meeting broke up, and then referred to
" a rumor that he had heard that night, which he thought
" would make it necessary for him to keep his men there,
" which I concurred in. During my attendance of the
" meeting I saw no weapons at all upon any person."

Upon cross-examination he says (A., 176) the rumor
referred to was related to him by Capt. Bonfield
immediately after his reaching the station. Bonfield
told him that he had just received information that
the Haymarket meeting, or a part of it, would go
over to the Milwaukee and St. Paul freight houses, then
filled with scabs, and blow it up. There was also an apprehension or fear on Mayor Harrison's part that this
meeting might be held merely to attract the 'attention of
the police to the Haymarket, while the real attack, if any,
should be made that night on McCormick's. Those
were the contingencies in regard to which he was listening to those speeches. In listening to the speeches, he
concluded it was not an organization to destroy property
that night, and went home.

This is the testimony of the chief executive officer of
the city, who was there upon the ground, charged with
the duty of preserving the peace and preventing violence.
We think it useless to quote from the testimony of a
score of other witnesses, in order to show that the meeting was peaceable and orderly during the time that Mayor
Harrison was present. We shall only attempt to answer
the question: Did the meeting change its character after
Mr. Harrison left it?

If the meeting commenced to disintegrate while Parsons was speaking, it had practically dissolved before Mr.
Fielden was interrupted by the arrival of the police.

Upon the proposal by Parsons of an adjournment of the meeting to Zepf's Hall, the meeting dwindled to about one-third or one-fourth of its original proportions. Mayor Harrison's statement that there were at no time more than eight hundred to one thousand men in attendance, is supported by substantially all the witnesses who testified in regard to the size of the meeting.

It is also admitted by substantially all the witnesses that not more than three to five hundred were left upon the ground, when the meeting came to a close, some standing immediately around the wagon, others upon the opposite sidewalks of the street. Fielden continued his address, approaching a close, and had in fact said the words, " In " conclusion," as he neared the end of his speech. Suddenly he was stopped by the arrival of a police force of about one hundred and eighty men, the head of the column being halted by the officer in command about the north line of the alley projected, and within six or eight feet of the wagon itself. There is no pretense that there was any difficulty experienced by the head of the column in reaching this position. There was no such crowd as to interfere with their free and rapid movement.

As to the character of this movement of the police, the testimony of the officers themselves shows that the order to fall in was given urgently; there was no halting of the head of the column until the complete column was formed; the head of the column moved without halting, at a rapid march, so that those who came later out of the station and formed the second and third companies of the column were compelled to proceed almost, if not quite, at a double quick, in order to get their position in the line, and that they did not in fact gain that position until the head of the column had reached the position of the halt. This appears from the

testimony of Lieut. Stanton (A., 16; I, 216); Ferguson
(A., 183; L, 133), and Gleason (A., 203; L, 362, 363).
No explanation is given by any of the officers in charge
of the force that night of this haste. Here was in process
of dissolution, a meeting from which no violence or danger was apprehended a few minutes before. Capt. Bonfield says that he was in receipt of constant information
from this meeting. We are, therefore, warranted in saying that when he ordered his men to fall in, he must have
known that the meeting was about to break up and the
people to go home: that he knew up to the time of the
latest advices received by him no proposal to do any
unlawful act had been advanced, and no turbulent or lawless character had been developed in the meeting itself.
Substantially all of the witnesses concur in saying that
the meeting was more enthusiastic and responsive while
Parsons spoke than when Fielden spoke, a position
vouched for by the fact that the audience was rapidly
scattering during the progress of Mr. Fielden's speech,
and explained by the fact that those present were wearied
of their long standing in the cold street.

This meeting, being reached by the police, Capt. Ward
gave at once the command: " In the name of the people
" of the State of Illinois, I command this meeting immedi-
" ately and peaceably to disperse," followed in the very
same breath by the words: " And I call upon you and
" you (turning to bystanders) to assist."

To assist in what? In dispersing a meeting that was
refusing to peaceably disperse upon lawful command? In
dispersing a riotous or unlawful assemblage and arresting
and securing the rioters? In suppressing a disorderly and
tumultuous gathering that was threatening the peace and
dignity of the city and of the State?

The law of the State of Illinois in reference to the

suppression of unlawful assemblages, as found in sections
253 and 254 of Div. 1, Chap. 38, R. S. Ill. Crim. Code,
clearly contemplates that when a meeting admittedly of
a riotous or tumultuous character, is ordered to disperse
by proper authority, a reasonable opportunity to comply
with such order shall be afforded before any demonstration of violence or force shall be made, so likely in itself
to precipitate the very evil to be guarded against, by
unnecessarily irritating the populace. Nothing of this
kind occurred at the Haymarket meeting. When the
order to disperse was given, no reasonable and proper
opportunity for compliance with that order was afforded
in the first instance, but there was an immediate call upon
the bystanders to assist in the forcible dispersion of a
meeting that was confessedly quiet, orderly, peaceable,
small in numbers, and upon the very eve of voluntary
dispersion.

Replying simply that the meeting was peaceable, Mr.
Fielden at once dismounted from the truck, and the
others that were on it in like manner proceeded to alight,
and were in the act of separating promptly and without
any delay whatever, as is conceded in all the testimony,
when the bomb was thrown.

Immediately following the explosion of the bomb, there
was a great amount of pistol shooting. It is claimed by
the police that somewhere from fifty to seventy-five, or
possibly one hundred shots were fired into them from
both sides of the street, before any shot was fired by the
police. We believe we are justified in saying that the
claim that the explosion of the bomb was followed by a
volley from the crowd, as though the one had been the
signal for the other, is a claim that grew up after the
Haymarket meeting, finding support from the assertions
of men who, like Mr. Hull, could remember what oc-

curred on that night several months afterwards much better than they could the next morning. Mr. Hull was a reporter for the Daily News, attended the meeting that night, standing at the head of the stairs on the northwest corner of Desplaines and Randolph. On cross-examination he says (A., 117, 118; K, 129, 135 *et seq.*):

"I wrote the account of the Haymarket meeting, de-"scribing the throwing of the bomb and what followed "immediately, which account was published in the Daily "News on the following morning. It was correct, ac-"cording to my impression at that time. My impression "has decidedly improved since. I was as well advised at "the time as I am now, but my recollection was not "clear at the time. *I have said nowhere in this report* "(report in the Daily News of May 5, 1886) *that the* "*crowd fired upon the police.* I did say that the police "required no orders before firing upon the crowd. I "wrote this about an hour after the occurrence. After "describing the explosion of the bomb I used this lan-"guage in my report: 'For an instant after the explo-"sion, the crowd seemed paralyzed, but with the revolver "shots cracking like a tattoo on a mighty drum, and the "bullets flying in the air, the mob plunged away in the "darkness with a yell of rage and fear.'"

That the crowd opened fire upon the police is explicitly denied by the following witnesses: Simondson (A., 179: L, 73); Zeller (A., 185; L, 157); Richter (A., 187; L, 181); Liebel (A., 189; L., 202, 203); Taylor (A., 192; L, 233); Stenner (A., 196; L, 283); Gutscher (A., 197; L, 301, 302); Raab (A., 198; L, 315, 316); Urban (A., 202; L, 349); Hiersemenzel (A., 207; L, 387); Messer (A., 208; L, 401); Lindinger (A., 216; L, 475); Koehler (A., 219; L, 514, 515); Heidekrueger (A., 222; L, 545, 546); Schmidt (A., 223; L, 552); Schwindt (A., 223;

L, 557); Holloway (A., 230; M, 64); Lehnert (A., 234; M, 91); Snyder (A., 237; M, 112); Waldo (A., 245; M, 170); Ingram (A., 287, 288; M, 451); Schultz (A., 278; M, 382), from whose testimony it also appears that the police pursued fleeing, inoffensive, defenseless citizens, clubbing and shooting them.

In this connection we beg to cite the following testimony of Dr. Taylor: " When I revisited the ground the " next morning I noticed bullet-marks on the wall of " Crane's building, which forms the *north side of Crane's* " *alley. I could not find one bullet-mark on the wall at* " *the south side of the alley.* I examined a telegraph pole " on the west side of Desplaines street, north of Crane's " alley. I noticed that *all the perforations were on the* " *south side of that telegraph pole.* I did not find one " pistol shot or fresh mark upon the north side. *The* " *pole is not there now:* about a week and a half ago I " observed for the first time that it was not there any " longer." This testimony was not attempted to be contradicted. Comment upon that seems to us unnecessary.

Even of the witnesses for the state, the following honestly admit that they cannot say that the crowd first fired upon the police:

Lieut. Stanton says (A., 16; I, 222) he *fired imme-diately upon the explosion of the bomb,* and he could not swear whether the police or the crowd fired first.

Reporter Freeman says (A., 106; K, 41, 42) he don't know where the firing began first, and that he *retreated into the alley because he saw no firing from there,* while the police claimed that the crowd fired from the sidewalk and the alley.

Officer Cosgrove (A., 121; K, 170) says he can't tell, whether the police fired first or the other side.

Reporter Heinemann (A., 126; K, 253) says he could

not say, whether the first shots came from the police or the crowd.

The police, after the explosion of the bomb, fired indiscriminately, and in wild confusion, shooting each other as well as pursuing the fleeing people in every direction and firing upon them.

Compare the testimony of Simondson: "The police "were not only shooting upon the crowd, but I noticed "several of them shoot just as they happened to throw "their arms" (A., 179; L, 74), with that of Dr. Fleming, that the bullet which he extracted from officer Krueger's knee was a police regulation bullet (A., 246, 247; M, 179 *et seq.*)

This is, perhaps, not the proper place for an arraignment of the police for their action in menacingly marching in such numbers and in the manner specified upon a peaceable meeting of citizens upon the eve of its adjournment. Neither shall we enter into a consideration of the unconstitutionality of this dispersion. We shall only ask: What excuse is there for this movement? What occasion was there for the police to thus interfere with this meeting?

While the foregoing evidence shows the peaceable and orderly character of the meeting until its dispersion, it also appears that none of the parties connected with the calling of that meeting had any criminal design in view in the calling thereof. It was believed by the parties who called the meeting that a great wrong had been done in the city of Chicago shortly prior thereto, and the call itself referred to this alleged grievance. Perhaps they were mistaken as to their view of the occurrence to which they referred, but certainly they had a right, and there was no crime involved in the exercise of that right, to call a meeting of citizens for the purpose of protesting against those supposed grievances; and this was all that was done in connection with the calling of the Haymarket meeting, and all that was designed. The impression that got abroad, that it was a part of the design of the meeting to make a disturbance, was expressly disclaimed by Mr. Spies when he took the speakers' stand, and the entire tendency of the addresses was the very reverse of inciting to any present riot or lawlessness.

The evidence utterly fails to show that any of these plaintiffs in error knew that a bomb was to be thrown by any one. It presents an instance of a meeting where some one, unknown to the public and to the plaintiffs in error, threw the bomb and did the killing; and the question is, whether the plaintiffs in error are to be convicted as accessories to a crime they did not know was to be committed, did not advise, aid or abet, and in which the really guilty party is as unknown to them as to the public.

OUR POSITIONS UPON THIS STATE OF THE CASE.

It is proper that at this point we should present to the court our views, and the authorities sustaining them, touching the case attempted to be made by the state upon the evidence thus far considered, and which in our view certainly includes all the testimony in this record which was properly before the jury for their consideration in the determination of the issues presented to them.

1. MERE PARTICIPATION IN AN UNLAWFUL ASSEMBLY DOES NOT MAKE RESPONSIBLE FOR THE INDEPENDENT CRIME OF A PARTICIPANT.

The only two plaintiffs in error who were shown by credible evidence to have been present at the meeting of May 4, 1886, at the time of the explosion of the bomb, are Fielden and Spies. Neither of them, however, had procured its being called. The evidence shows that it was a lawful assemblage. But even if there were grounds to question its legality, if, for the sake of argument, we should admit that the meeting were an unlawful meeting: though in that case all who attended it were equally touched with its unlawful character; yet mere presence at, participation in, or responsibility for, the calling of an *unlawful* assemblage, does not make such participants or attendants responsible for the independent, lawless or criminal conduct of persons attending that meeting, foreign to the general purposes and design thereof. Even if this meeting of May 4th should be deemed an unlawful meeting because of its purpose or of its character, yet the plaintiffs in error attendant at that meeting would not, for that reason, be responsible for a crime committed at the meeting by some person unknown to them and a stranger to their counsels, or acting without reference to their views, and not under their procurement. The law upon this subject is clearly and well stated in 1 Wharton Criminal Law, the latter part of sec. 220, where it is said:

" Where homicide is committed collaterally by one or " more of a body unlawfully associated, from causes hav- " ing no connection with the common object, the respon- " sibility for such homicide attaches exclusively to its " actual perpetrators. * * * It must also be remem- " bered that a rioter is not responsible on an indictment " for murder for a death incidentally caused by officers " engaged in suppressing a riot, nor in an affray are the " original parties responsible for a death caused by strang- " ers wantonly and adversely breaking in."

And the same author further says in the same work, section 397:

" It should be observed, however, that while the parties
" are responsible for consequent acts growing out of gen-
" eral design, they are not for independent acts growing
" out of the particular malice of individuals. Thus, if
" one of the party on his own hook turn aside to commit
" a felony foreign to the original design, his companions
" do not participate in his guilt. It must be remembered
" that to make out the *corpus delicti* in such cases, it is
" essential to show that the party charged struck either
" actually or constructively the fatal blow, and consented
" to the common design."

This rule is based upon natural right, and may be
stated perhaps in these words: that ONE MAN'S MALICE
OR MISCONDUCT SHALL NOT CREATE ANOTHER MAN'S
GUILT.

Speaking under this point, Mr. Wharton says (Criminal Law, § 160):

" We may expand this rule still further, and hold that
" the defendant, no matter how wrongful may have
" been his conduct, is not responsible for the acts of in-
" dependent parties performed on the objects of the crime
" without his concert." And many illustrations are given
by the learned author in the section referred to of this
doctrine, which show its reasonableness and propriety.

So Mr. Bishop, in the first volume of his work on
Criminal Law, seventh edition, in his chapter treating
upon " Combinations of persons in crime," speaks as follows (Sec. 633):

" A mere presence is not sufficient; nor is it alone
" sufficient in addition, that the person present, unknown
" to the other, mentally approves what is done. There
" must be something going a little further; as, for exam-
" ple, some word or act. The party to be charged 'must,'
" in the language of Cockburn, chief justice, 'incite or

" procure or encourage *the act*.' His will must in some
" degree contribute to what is done."

And further, the same author says in Sec. 634 of the
same work, as follows:

" From the proposition that mere presence at the com-
" mission of a crime does not render a person guilty, it
" results, that, if two or more are lawfully together, and
" one does a criminal thing without the concurrence of the
" others, they are not thereby involved in his guilt. * * *
" Even where persons are unlawfully together, and by
" concurrent understanding are in the actual perpetration
" of some crime, if one of them, of his sole volition and
" not in pursuance of the main purpose, does a criminal
" thing, in no way connected with what was mutually
" contemplated, he only is liable."

The learned author follows with many cases illustrating
the doctrine thus laid down, and, in summing up his observations on this subject, he says, in Sec. 641:

" The true view is doubtless as follows: One is re-
" sponsible for what of wrong flows directly from his
" corrupt intentions; but not, though intending wrong,
" for the product of another's independent act. * * *
" If the wrong done was a further and independent
" product of the mind of the doer, the other is not crimi-
" nal therein merely because when it was done he meant
" to be a partaker with the doer in a different wrong."

Among the cases cited by the authors above quoted in
support of the text as advanced by them, we single out
the following, by way of illustrating and enforcing the
rule:

In *Regina* v. *Skeet et al.*, 4 Foster & Fin., N. P. Cases,
931, the evidence showed that the defendants were joined
in the misdemeanor of poaching. Being attacked by the
gamekeeper of the premises upon which they were tres-

passing, a struggle ensued, in the course of which the gun of Skeet was discharged, killing the gamekeeper. The indictment was for murder. Charging the jury, POLLACK, C. B., said:

"As regards the other prisoners—there is no evidence "against them; and it is admitted that they cannot be "liable except upon the doctrine of constructive homi- "cide, which, as I have already laid down, does not ap- "ply where the only evidence is that the parties were "engaged in an unlawful purpose: not being *felonious*. It "only applies in cases where the common purpose is "felonious, as in cases of burglary: where *all the parties* "*are aware that deadly weapons are taken* with a view to "inflict death or commit felonious violence if resistance is "offered. That doctrine arose from the desire on the "part of the old lawyers to render all parties who were "jointly engaged in the commission of a felony responsi- "ble for deadly violence committed in the course of its "execution. But that doctrine has been much limited in "later times, and only applies in cases of felony, where "there is evidence of a felonious design to carry out the "unlawful purpose at all hazards, and whatever may be "the consequences. The possession of a gun would not "be any evidence of this, for a gun is used in poaching. "And poaching of itself is only an unlawful act and a "mere misdemeanor. Therefore, as there is no evidence "against the other prisoners of complicity in any such "design, or in the act of firing, they must all be acquitted "both of murder and of manslaughter."

In *Rex v. Hawkins*, 3 Car. & Payne, 392, it appears that a gang of poachers attacked the gamekeeper, beat him and left him senseless upon the ground, after which one of the number returned and robbed him. Under an indictment against defendants, and one Williams, who

did the robbing, but who was not in custody, the defendants were acquitted under the charge of PARK, Justice,.
who, in his instruction, used the following language:

"It appears to me that Williams is alone guilty of this
"robbery. It appears that there was no common intent to
"steal the keeper's property. They went out with the
"common intent to kill game, and perhaps to resist the
"keepers; but the whole intention of stealing the prop-
"erty is confined to Williams alone. They must be
"acquitted of the robbery."

In support of the doctrine of this case the learned anno-
tators append the following note: "To make all guilty,
"'the fact must appear to have been committed strictly in
"'prosecution of the purpose for which the party was
"'assembled; and, therefore, if divers persons be engaged
"'in an unlawful act, and one of them, with malice pre-
"'pense against one of his companions, kills him, the rest
"'are not concerned in the guilt of that act, because it
"'hath no connection with the crime in contemplation.'
"So, where two men were beating a third in the street,
"and a stranger made an observation of the cruelty of
"the act, and one of them stabbed him, this was not mur-
"der in both, though both were committing an unlawful
"act; because only one of them intended to do injury to
"the person killed. 1 Curw. Hawk., p. 101.

"In *Plummer's* case, a smuggler, in a scuffle with the
"revenue officers, shot one of his comrades (upon a
"grudge of his own); the question was, whether the
"whole gang was guilty of murder: and it was held, *that*
"*as it did not appear that the gun was discharged* in
"prosecution of *the purpose for which the party had assem-*
"*bled*, it was only murder *in him who did it.* Cited 1 Rus-
"sell, 652; *Hodgson* case, 1 Leach, 6 S. P. And if sev-
"eral are out for the purpose of committing a felony,

" and upon an alarm run different ways, and one of
" them maim a pursuer to avoid being taken, the others
" are not to be considered principals in such act. *Rex* v.
" *White*, Russell & Ry. C. C. R., 99."

So in *Rex* v. *Collison*, 4 Car. & Payne's, 565, the doctrine was laid down that in order to hold one guilty as an
accessory before the fact, it must be proved *that the criminal act was the result of a common purpose.* The facts in
that case were as follows: Two private watchmen, seeing
the prisoner and another person with two carts laden with
apples, went up and walked along with them, intending
as soon as they could procure assistance to secure them,
believing the apples to be stolen. One of the watchmen
walked beside one prisoner, and the other beside the other
person at some distance from the first. While walking
along, the prisoner's companion stepped back, and, with
a bludgeon which he carried, struck and wounded the
watchman with whom he had been walking. The law
in that case was laid down as follows:

" To make the prisoner a principal, the jury must be
" satisfied that, when he and his companion went out with
" a common illegal purpose of committing the felony of
" stealing apples, they also entertained the common guilty
" purpose of resisting to death, or with extreme violence,
" all who might endeavor to apprehend them; but if they
" had only the common purpose of stealing apples, and
" the violence of the prisoner's companion was merely the
" result of the situation in which he found himself, and
" proceeded from the impulse of the moment, without
" any previous concert, the prisoner will be entitled to an
" acquittal."

In *Regina* v. *Price*, 8 Cox's Criminal Cases, 96, the
facts briefly were: that the prisoners, six in number, who
were shipmates, for some unknown cause, chased a Ger-

man sailor belonging to another ship through the streets of Falmouth, brutally assaulting him, and as he took refuge from their attack against a railing, he was stabbed by one of them with a knife, of which wound he died in a few minutes. The evidence as to whose hands inflicted the wound was absolutely conflicting. Two of the witnesses who saw the transaction at the same spot and the same moment differed in their identification, one of them swearing positively that the stabber was one of the prisoners who had whiskers, and the other as positively swearing that the murderer was another of the prisoners who had no whiskers, and each swore that he had marked his man at the time by this very peculiarity. Byles, Justice, in charging the jury, laid down the law as follows:

"Six men were charged with the willful murder of a " German sailor by stabbing him. The deceased was a " peaceable unoffending person. The stab was given by " one individual of the six. Now, supposing they could " fix upon the hand that stabbed, the first question would " be what was his offense, and what was the offense of " the other five? The individual who stabbed was clearly " guilty of murder, whether he intended to kill or not. " If they could point out the man who gave that stab, and " they should be of opinion that they had selected the " right man, he was guilty of murder. The next ques- " tion would be, in what condition were the other five " men? The deceased sailor was leaning against some " iron railings when the stab was given, but before that " he had been assaulted in a barbarous and dastardly " manner by these six men; but did the other five men " contemplate the use of the knife, or was it the inde- " pendent act of the man who used it? First, then, they " were all guilty of murder if they participated in the " common design and intention to kill. If they should

" think the others did not intend and design to kill, yet
" these others would also be guilty of murder if the knife
" were used in pursuance of one common design to use
" it, because then the hand that used the knife was the
" hand of all of them. Supposing there was no common
" design to use the knife, if, being present at the moment
" of stabbing, they assented and manifested their assent
" *by assisting* in the offense, they were guilty of murder.
" First, then, *there must be a common design to kill;*
" secondly, *there must be a common design to use a mur-*
" *derous instrument;* thirdly, *there must be presence at*
" *the time and assent to and assistance in the use of the*
" *knife.* If, however, the jury should find neither of
" these three modes of putting the cases proved against
" the five, it would be their duty to find the stabber guilty
" and to acquit the others."

There was a verdict of not guilty.

In *Duffey's* case, 1 Lewin, C. C., 194, PARK, Justice,
laid down the law that " if three go out to commit a felony
" and one of them, unknown to the others, puts a pistol in
" his pocket and commits a felony of another kind, such as
" *murder*, the two who did not concur in this second felony
" will not be guilty of it, notwithstanding it happened while
" they were engaged with him in the felonious act for
" which they went out."

In *Regina* v. *Luck*, 3 Foster & Fin, N. P. Cases, 483,
it appears that more than nine men, of whom seven were
armed with guns, being out at night in pursuit of game,
were met as they passed through a field from one wood
to another by a party of gamekeepers without firearms,
but who at once assaulted them with sticks, and one of
them with a dangerous weapon, a flail, liable to inflict
deadly injury, with which he struck one of the parties,
upon which another one of them fired and killed him.

The grand jury were directed to throw out the bills for murder, and the whole party were indicted for manslaughter. The case was tried before BYLES, Justice, who charged the jury as follows:

" The questions are, who fired the fatal shot, and who " were parties to the act? for, whoever it was that fired the " fatal shot was clearly guilty of manslaughter. The use of " the flail, although it might reduce the offense from murder " to manslaughter, could not reduce it any lower. * * * So " all who were aiding and abetting in the act were equally " guilty of that crime. Now, as to Luck—the prisoner " chiefly charged with the offense—the chief evidence " against him was that of an accomplice, and it was per- " fectly true that the evidence of an accomplice required " corroboration, and that not merely as to the fringe and " margin of the case, but as to its substance, and above all as " to the persons accused: but here, although the accomplice " who had been admitted evidence stated that the man who " fired the shot was Luck, the other accomplice who had " made statements inculpating the others—Allchin—had " said that it was Burgess. So that it had depended merely " on the choice by the police of one or the other of those " prisoners as witnesses for the crown, whether the man " charged with firing the shot would be Luck or Bur- " gess;" [as in the case at bar, it depended wholly upon the choice by the representatives of the state as to their choice between Gilmer and Burnett, the testimony of both of whom they knew since weeks before the trial, whether the state would undertake to prove that the bomb in question was thrown by Schnaubelt or thrown by the unknown party described by Burnett.] "The question then was as to " the other and independent evidence against Luck; and " as to that, although there was ample and abundant evi- " dence that he was there [which there is not as to Schnau-

" belt in the case at bar], there was no positive evidence
" that he had fired the fatal shot. There was positive
" evidence that the gun was seen pointed at the game-
" keepers, and that was not reconcilable with the theory
" of an accident. There was evidence of belief that the
" man was Luck, but no positive evidence, and at night,
" in a scuffle like this, it was very difficult to get such evi-
" dence. The jury might vehemently suspect that Luck
" was the man that fired the gun, but in a case of this
" nature, on a charge on which very serious punishment
" must follow on conviction, and on which, indeed, his life
" had been in danger, they must be satisfied, beyond all
" reasonable doubt, that he did fire it in order to convict
" him on the present charge on that ground. But in the
" next place, even assuming that it could not be ascer-
" tained who fired the shot, all who were present and
" *were parties to the act* were certainly guilty; and it had
" been held and admitted that if all were in a row or line
" when the gun was pointed and fired, that would be
" strong evidence of a common purpose or design to shoot.
" It is, however, for your consideration that though there
" were seven guns, only one was fired, and it is not clear
" that it was fired when the men were in a line. And on
" the point, whether there was a common purpose to
" shoot, it is most material, for, if the men had all a design
" to shoot—and many of them had guns—why did they not
" all shoot? Or, at all events, why did not more than
" one shoot? This argument equally applies, whoever it
" was that fired the gun. But if Luck fired the shot, was
" it so fired by him in consequence of a severe personal
" encounter he had had with the keeper? If so, then it
" would not be fired in pursuance of any common design.
" *Now, if you cannot say who fired the shot, then you*
" *should not convict any of the prisoners unless satisfied*

"*that all of them were parties to the act.*" The jury found a verdict of not guilty as to all the prisoners.

A strong case supporting this doctrine which we contend for is *State* v. *Hildreth*, 9th Ired. Law, 440. also reported in 51st Am. Decisions, 369. In that case two brothers were present at the homicide, one doing the killing, and the other standing by, and not attempting in any way to interfere. The jury were instructed in effect on this state of facts, that the bystanding brother was guilty of murder if, after he entered the field where the homicide was committed and, joining his brother, he discovered that his brother intended to use the knife in time to prevent it, but did not act so as to effect a prevention. The court in commenting upon this instruction said:

" We think it inaccurate. For supposing the prisoner " to have no previous concert with his brother, and that " during the combat he first discovered that the other in-" tended to use the fatal weapon, we think he was not " guilty of murder, although he made the discovery in " time to prevent Robert from actually giving the stab. " If one who is present and sees that a felony is about " being committed does in no manner interfere, he does " not thereby participate in the felony committed. Every " person may upon such occasion prevent, if he can, the " perpetration of so high a crime; but he is not bound to " do so at the peril otherwise of partaking of the guilt. It " is necessary in order to convict that he should do or " say something, showing his consent to the violence " proposed *and* contributing to its execution."

In an able note to the case, as printed in the 51st Am. Decisions, the author says:

" A mere presence of a person at the place of the com-" mission of a crime is not of itself sufficient to justify the " conclusion that he assents to it. There must be some

" evidence of his participation in the offense to render him
" guilty either as accessory or as the aider and abettor.
" His presence is, of course, a circumstance which may
" be taken into consideration in determining whether or
" not he is guilty of aiding and abetting. 'In order
" to render a person an accomplice to the principal in the
" felony he must be aiding and abetting at the fact, or
" ready to offer assistance, if necessary; therefore if A
" happeneth to be present at a murder, for instance, and
" taketh no part in it, nor interfereth to prevent it nor
" punisheth the murderer, nor levyeth hue and crie after
" him, this strange behavior, though highly criminal, will
" not of itself render him either principal or accessory.
" Foster, 350.' " And a large number of cases are cited
by the author in support of the doctrine of the text.

So, in the case of *White* v. *The People*, 81 Ill., 333, this
court, in reversing a judgment for error in an instruction
in a case where two were present at the homicide, which
was committed by one of them, but there was no evidence
that the other aided, abetted or assisted in the killing,
recognize clearly the distinction for which we contend,
namely, that in order to hold the defendant guilty as accessory before the fact to the perpetration of a crime,
there must be more than his mere presence at the commission of the criminal act, or even his consent to the
perpetration of the crime; there must be, within the contemplation of our statute, an aiding, abetting or assisting
in its perpetration. The language of this court upon this
point is as follows (page 337):

" By the second instruction the jury are told that one
" who stands by when a crime is committed in his pres-
" ence by another, and *consents* to the perpetration of the
" crime, is a principal in the offense, and must be punished
" as such. The law is, that one who 'stands by and aids,

"abets or assists * * * the perpetration of the crime '
"is an accessory, and ' shall be considered as principal,
"etc. (R. S., 1874, page 393, sec. 274.)

"There is a plain distinction between '*consenting*' to a
"crime and ' aiding, abetting or assisting ' in its perpe-
"tration. Aiding, abetting or assisting are affirmative in
"their character. The consenting may be a mere nega-
"tive acquiescence, not in any way made known at the
"time to the principal malefactor. Such consenting,
"though involving moral turpitude, does not come up to
"the meaning of the words of the statute."

We do not understand that the law of the above cases
has ever been seriously questioned or qualified since its
enunciation, or that there is any substantial conflict as to
the rule above stated and considered. Whatever variance may be found in the text writers or in the authorities will, we think, be found to be simply the enunciation
of modified or different rules as applicable to different circumstances appearing in the cases respectively.

All the cases above quoted proceed upon the theory
that the accused was associated with the criminal actor in
an unlawful enterprise, but not a party by act or advice
in the crime. Our position, of course, is, that the Haymarket meeting was a lawful meeting under our constitutions, and that participation in that meeting and its
avowed purposes was lawful. At this meeting an unlawful
act was done, in which the plaintiffs in error did not participate, even those present. Of course, such presence
would not cast upon those who were there responsibility
for a crime thus committed. This position follows from
the cases above cited; and in its support we will cite but
one other authority.

The case of *U. S. v. Jones*, 3 Washington C. C. R.,
209, is a strong case in point. There the defendant, who

was the first lieutenant of an American privateer, the Revenge, was indicted for piracy committed on a Portuguese vessel, and for assaulting the Portguese captain and crew, and putting them in bodily fear, etc. The defendant was charged with boarding the vessel, and, by force and intimidation, taking from her many articles, not claiming the vessel as prize, but pretending that the Revenge was an English vessel, and that the articles would be paid for by an order on the English consul.

The evidence showed that a party, of whom the defendant was one, visited the Portuguese vessel for the ostensible purpose of searching her, and that while upon the vessel, there were various acts of lawlessness, including robbery or theft, committed, but the testimony was conflicting as to whether the defendant had any personal participation therein. After presenting to the jury the testimony for their consideration, WASHINGTON, Justice, closed a very careful and elaborate charge, as follows:

"Should you incline to acquit the prisoner of any active "participation in this robbery, he cannot be convicted "upon the ground of his being a member of the society "which committed the offense. * * * If the thing to be "accomplished be lawful, as the visitation of this vessel "was, and all but one of the party commit felony, though "in the presence of that one, but without his participation, "the crime of his companions is not imputable to him." There was a verdict of not guilty in the case.

We therefore maintain that neither the presence of Spies and Fielden at the Haymarket meeting at the time of the explosion of the bomb, nor the prior presence of Parsons, Fischer and Engel thereat, nor anything disclosed in this record, made them respectively liable criminally for the consequences of the bomb-throwing.

So much for the law, as we understand it, applicable

to those of the plaintiffs in error who were shown by the testimony to have been present at the Haymarket meeting when the bomb was thrown, but as to whom the proof utterly fails to show that they personally advised, aided, abetted, encouraged or procured the throwing of the missile. Their mere presence is no proof of their guilt, and does not attach to them any liability for the consequences of the act which resulted in the death of Mr. Degan; and the state, we insist, utterly failed to make out such a case on the evidence as entitled them to a verdict and judgment, even as against these plaintiffs in error.

II. IN ORDER TO HOLD THE ACCUSED AS ACCESSORIES ON THE GROUND OF CONSPIRACY, THE PRINCIPAL ACTOR MUST BE IDENTIFIED AS A CO-CONSPIRATOR.

Let us now turn to the law applicable, in our judgment, to the case made by the state against the plaintiffs in error connected with or involved in the so-called conspiracy meeting on Monday night, May 3d, and the Emma street meeting the day preceding.

Laying out of view, for a moment, our position upon the evidence, that the crime of the Haymarket was not at all within the scope or purview of the alleged conspiracy, or agreement, of Monday night, as demonstrated above (pp. 91–93), our position upon the law is, that there could be no legal conviction of the parties to that Monday night conspiracy (in this case plaintiffs in error, Fisher and Engel), without proof beyond all reasonable doubt that the bomb was in fact thrown by the hand of one of the conspirators, or by the procurement of some of them; and to this end, there must be *such an identification of the doer of the crime as brings him into casual relationship with the alleged conspirators.*

We cite, as sustaining this proposition, the text of Sec. 325 Wharton's Criminal Evidence, as follows: " The *corpus delicti*, the proof of which is essential to " sustain a conviction, consists of a criminal act; and to " sustain a conviction there must be proof of the defend- " ants' guilty agency in the production of such act." And from the note to the same section as follows: " The " latter feature, namely, criminal agency, is often lost sight " of, but is as essential as is the object itself, of crime. " Acts, in some shape, are essential to the *corpus delicti*, " so far as concerns the guilt of the party accused. A. " *may have designed the death* of the deceased, yet, if " the death has been caused *by another*, A., no matter " how morally guilty, is not amenable, *if he has done and* " *advised nothing in respect to the death*, to the penalties " of the law. Gellius, VII, 3."

In *Ogden* v. *The State*, 12 Wis., 553, the court say: " In order to establish the guilt of *Ogden*, it was first " incumbent on the prosecutor to prove the guilt of " *Wright* as alleged in the indictment. This done, he " must then prove that Ogden previously procured, hired, " advised or commanded Wright to commit the felony. " Both these facts must be established by competent evi- " dence. Now, however the confessions of Wright, as " to the first, might have been used against him, had he " been indicted and put on his trial, it is very evident that " as against Ogden they were wholly inadmissible. As " to him, they were mere hearsay, and open to all the " objections which exist to that kind of testimony. *For,* " *however clearly it may have appeared that Ogden coun-* " *seled and advised Wright to commit the offense, yet, if* " *Wright never did so in point of fact, and the barn was* " *set on fire by some one else, or by other means, then Ogden* " *was innocent of the crime of the commission of which he* " *stood charged.*"

In *Hatchet v. Commonwealth*, 75 Virginia, 925, the court say: " It is necessary to show that *the substantive offense,* " to which he is charged as having been accessory, has " been *committed by the principal felon.*"

There can be, however, no principal felon in contemplation of the law, except in the case of one who has committed a crime in concert with or at the instance and under the advice, or with the aid and assistance of those who, in the law, are called accessories. The very idea of principal felon involves the idea of relationship between himself and the accessories; involves the exclusion by legal evidence of the idea that the felony may have been committed *sua sponte*, and without any reference whatever to third parties, and uninfluenced by them. If, then, it be the law that it is necessary to show that the crime has been committed by "the principal felon," this means that is necessary to show, when seeking to hold one responsible as an accessory to a crime, that the hand which committed the offense was, in law, the hand of the accessory; that is, a hand controlled or moved by him.

So, in the case of *Jones v. The State,* 64 Georgia, 697, a judgment finding Jones guilty of murder as principal in the second degree, he having been indicted jointly with Jackson Sellers, as principal in the first degree, but tried separately, was set aside, on the ground that *it did not appear in the record that there was evidence showing the guilt of the principal in the first degree:* the court holding that the guilt of the principal in the first degree was necessary to be established as a condition precedent to the conviction of the principal in the second degree.

We contend that in the case at bar the state failed to show by credible evidence who threw the bomb (pp. 93–96). For this reason we argue that no casual relationship between his act and the Monday night conspiracy,

or any other conspiracy, has been established; and therefore, even if it were conceded that some of the plaintiffs in
error sanctioned and approved of a crime, such as was
committed at the Haymarket, before its execution, this
alone does not make them liable as accessories to that
crime.

III. IN ORDER TO HOLD THE ACCUSED AS ACCESSORIES
ON THE GROUND OF CONSPIRACY, THE CRIME CHARGED
MUST HAVE BEEN WITHIN THE PURVIEW OF SUCH CON-
SPIRACY AND COMMITTED IN FURTHERANCE THEREOF.

The parties to the alleged Monday night conspiracy
could not, by reason of their participation therein, properly
be adjudged guilty, in view of the fact that the crime of
the Haymarket was not within the contemplation of the
conspirators, nor within the general scope and purpose of
the alleged conspiracy.

In the case of the *State* v. *Lucas*, 55 Iowa, 321, the
doctrine is broadly and correctly laid down, that " an ac-
' cessory to one crime does not thereby become answer-
" able for another and different crime committed inten-
" tionally by his principals at the same time." The statement of the case is very brief and is as follows: " The de-
" fendant, Frank Lucas, was indicted jointly with Charles
" Wood and James White for a robbery from the person
" of R. G. Edwards, perpetrated by assaulting and wound-
" ing him with deadly weapons. The defendant was
" tried, convicted, sentenced and committed to the peni-
" tentiary for twelve years."

It appears from the opinion of the court that the prosecutor was assaulted by Wood and White, knocked down
and robbed on the night of August 24, 1879. That on

the same night a safe in the mill where the prosecutor was night watchman was blown open and robbed. Lucas testified that he had nothing to do with robbing Edwards, was not at the mill at all, that he rowed Wood and Harris in a skiff from LaCrosse to Lansing and landed near the mill about 9 o'clock on the night of the robbery; that Wood and Harris went up-town and left him to watch the boat; that afterwards they came down to the boat in a hurry and directed him to row over to Wisconsin; that on the way he saw them dividing some money; that when they reached the Wisconsin shore they sunk the boat, and that on the way to LaCrosse Wood told him all that had happened and gave him two revolvers to carry. The court thereupon instructed the jury:

" If you believe from all the evidence that the defend-
" ant did not leave the boat after the arrival at Lansing;
" yet, if you also believe that he had knowledge of the in-
" tent of his associates *to commit crime*, either of robbery
" of the man Edwards or of robbing the safe in Barclay
" & Hemmingway's mill, *or any other crime*, and rowed
" them ashore for such purpose, and waited in the boat
" for them during their absence in committing the crime,
" then you will find him guilty." Concerning this instruction as applicable to that case, the court say:

" The doctrine of this instruction is, that if the defend-
" ant knew of the intent of his associates, to rob the safe
" in Barclay & Hemmingway's mill, and rowed them ashore
" for that purpose, and awaited their return, he is guilty
" of the robbery of Edwards. This doctrine is not cor-
" rect. It is true, the accessory is liable for all that en-
" sues *upon the execution of the unlawful act contemplated:*
" as, if A. commanded B. to beat C., and he beat him so
" that he dies, A. is accessory to the murder. So if A.
" commanded B. to burn the house of C., and in doing so

" the house of D. is also burned, A. is accessory to the
" burning of D.'s house. So, in this case, if Lucas had
" knowledge of the intention to rob the safe, and aided
" and abetted his associates in the commission of that of-
" fense, and if, in furthering that purpose, a fatal assault
" had been made on Edwards, the defendant would have
" been accessory to the crime.

" But, *if the accessory order or advise one crime, and*
" *the principal intentionally commit another;* as, for in-
" stance, to burn a house, and instead of that he committed
" a larceny; or, to commit a crime against A., and instead
" of so doing, he intentionally commit the same crime
" against B., *the accessory will not be answerable.* It follows
" that the defendant cannot be convicted of a robbery of
" Edwards, from the mere fact that he abetted his associates
" in the robbery of Barclay & Hemmingway's safe."

In *Watts* v. *The State*, 5th W. Va., 532, the defendant
was charged as accessory to the crime of felony and burglary. There was proof tending to show that Watts
hired two parties to whip a man named Saunders; that
these men went to the house where Saunders was a
lodger, and pursuing Perry and his wife to Saunders'
room, knocked Perry down and ravished Mrs. Perry,
Saunders having made his escape. There was no evidence that Watts incited or advised, in any manner, the
commission of the rape upon Mrs. Perry, evidence of
which was permitted to go to the jury. It was held that
this was error. In passing upon the question the court
uses the following language:

" If the crime by the principal felon was committed un-
" der the influence of the flagitious advice of the other
' party, and the event, though possibly falling out beyond
" the original intent of the latter, was, nevertheless, in
" the ordinary course of things, a probable consequence of

" that felony, he is guilty of being accessory to the crime
" actually committed.   But if the principal, following the
" suggestions of his own heart, willfully and knowingly
" commit a felony of another kind, on a different subject,.
" he alone is guilty.   (3 Greenleaf's Evidence, Sec. 50.)
" And *if the principal totally and substantially departs*
"*from his instructions, as if, being solicited to burn a barn,*
" *he, moreover, commits a robbery while so doing*" [as in
the case at bar, *supposing* the bomb-thrower to be a.
party to the Monday night conspiracy, he threw a bomb·
when the police attacked the meeting, instead of notifying
his co-conspirators in the manner agreed upon] "*he stands*
" *single in the latter crime, and the other is not held respons-*
" *ible for it as accessory.* (3 Greenleaf's Evidence, Sec. 44.)
    " It was certainly improper to admit the testimony of
" Perry and his wife as to the rape, because that was a
" distinct substantive offense from that charged in the
" indictment (1 Wharton's Criminal Law, Sec. 647), and
" had no connection whatever with the felony charged,
" because it was a total and substantial departure from
" that instruction (3 Greenleaf's Evidence, Sec. 44), and
" the defendant could not be held responsible as accessory
" thereto. The admitting of such testimony, being evidence
" of a crime ever shocking to civilized society, was well
" calculated to draw away the minds of the jurors from·
" the points in issue, and to excite prejudice and mislead
" them, and thus prevent a fair and impartial verdict."
    So the rule is laid down in 4th Blackstone's Comment-
aries, page 23, as cited with approbation in *The State* v.
Absence, 4 Porter, 397, that in order to establish the guilt
of the principal in the second degree (accessory) " there
" must be a participation in the felonious design, or, at least,
" the offense must be within the compass of the original
" intention to constitute a principal in the second degree."

THE ILLEGITIMATE EVIDENCE.

We believe we have in the preceding pages considered substantially the entire testimony which tends directly to connect the plaintiffs in error with the event of the 4th of May, 1886, or with the matters occurring in immediate connection with that meeting, and have stated our position thereon. It becomes necessary for us now to consider a vast amount of testimony, which was introduced on behalf of the state over the objection of the plaintiffs in error, and the rulings of the court in connection with the introduction of that testimony—testimony much of which had certainly no direct relation with or reference to the throwing of the bomb on May 4, 1886, but which was allowed to be introduced upon the theory that the plaintiffs in error were parties in a general combination or conspiracy to overthrow by force the existing order of society, which combination had been entered into by them at some unknown antecedent date. There was confessedly no direct evidence that they had so conspired, but this conspiracy was attempted to be made out by the proof of a series of facts and circumstances extending through a long period of time.

The attitude of the court in reference to this matter was developed in connection with the examination of Gottfried Waller on the first day of the trial of the cause after the jury had been impaneled. After Mr. Waller had testified as to the alleged conspiracy meeting of Monday night, May 3, 1886, this question was asked: " Mr. Waller, did you ever have any bombs ? " To this question objection was interposed and fully argued. Our objection to the question, in brief, was that the question called for immaterial and irrelevant testimony. Gottfried

Waller was not indicted with the plaintiffs in error for the
murder of Degan, and whether he did or did not have
bombs, or what he personally did or did not do, could
have no proper bearing upon the determination of the
issue whether the plaintiffs in error caused the throwing
of the bomb on the night of May 4th; but particularly it
was objected that there was no limitation in the question;
it was not proposed to inquire of Mr. Waller whether he
had a bomb on the night of May 4th, but as to whether
he ever had a bomb, thus practically allowing an unre-
stricted investigation as to outside occurrences not connected with the plaintiffs in error, and through an
unlimited period of time. When the answer to that question came in, it served to illustrate the force of our objections; being, that the witness had a gas-pipe bomb in his
possession on Thanksgiving day, 1885, which he received
from plaintiff in error Fischer, and which he disposed of
subsequently to some unknown person, who thereafter
exploded it in a hollow tree. We desire to call attention
in detail to the ruling of the court upon our objection to
this class of testimony, and which he persisted in during
the entire trial.

Let it be remembered that at the time this ruling was
announced, the only conspiracy attempted to be established
by the state was the agreement entered into at the Monday night meeting, as described by the witness Waller, at
which of all the plaintiffs in error *only Fischer and Engel
were present*, and with which none of the other plaintiffs
in error had been connected. The court's ruling was as
follows (T, 89, *et seq.*):

" If the fact be that a large number of men concurred
" with each other in preparing to use force for the de-
" struction of human life, *upon occasions which were not
" yet foreseen*, but upon some principles which they sub-

" stantially agreed upon, as, for example, taking the words
" of this witness, if a large number of men *agreed together*
" *to kill the police*, if they were found in conflict with
" strikers—I believe is the phrase—*leaving it to the agents*
" *of violence to determine whether the time and occasion*
" *had come for the use of the violence*, then if the time and
" occasion do come when the violence is used, are not all
" parties who agreed beforehand in preparing the means
" of death, and agreed in the use of them upon the time
" and occasion, equally liable?

There had been no proof whatever in the record, and
there was no proof afterwards introduced, of an agreement between a large number of men to " kill the police,"
" leaving it to the agents of violence to determine whether
" the time and occasion had come for the use of the
" violence."

Such a statement of the witness Waller's testimony was
an absolute perversion of his evidence. The witness
Waller had testified that certain parties in that meeting
agreed among themselves that if the police should attack
the strikers, then the parties to the alleged agreement
would come to the rescue of the strikers, and join in the
conflict with the police. But the witness Waller further
had expressly sworn that nothing was to be left to the
agents of violence, that is to say, the individual perpetrator
of the violent act, as to determining whether the time and
occasion had come for the use of violence. On the contrary, he had sworn positively that a committee was appointed whose duty it should be to observe the movements
throughout the city generally, and in the event of an attack
by the police, to report in a certain manner to the parties
to the agreement, who were thereupon to meet at certain
meeting places in the outskirts of the city and then unitedly
proceed to the rescue of the attacked workingmen, with

the understanding that each *group* in its joint capacity
should act independently, according to the general plan.
(A., 5; I, 65).

Where in all of Waller's testimony can anything be
found warranting the suggestion that there was an agreement entered into " to kill the police," or whereby it was
left to the *individual members* of the conspiracy " to deter-
" mine whether the time and occasion had come " for the
use of violence?   The court then proceeded and said:

" Suppose the state are prepared to prove that there
" was a general combination and agreement that *weapons*
" *of death should be prepared to use against the police*, if
" they came in conflict with the workingmen or strikers'
" meetings—that is, if the police undertook to enforce the
" laws of the state, and prevent breaches of the peace and
" destruction of property, that then they would assault
" and kill the police, but the time and occasion at which
" the assault was to be were not foreseen, but were to be
" determined by the parties who were to use the force
" when in their judgment the time and occasion had
" come, and then when the police are found attempting
" to preserve the peace, some one or more of the persons
" who have been parties to this combination or agreement
" do kill, are not all who entered into the combination and
" agreement equally liable? "

There was no evidence up to the time of this suggestion that the state were prepared to prove a general combination and agreement " for the preparation for weapons
" of death to be used against the police if they came in
" conflict with the workingmen or strikers' meeting, in
" an effort by the police to enforce the laws of the state,
" prevent breaches of the peace and destruction of prop-
" erty"; there was no proof of a proposal in such an
event to assault and kill the police.   And again we say

there was no proof that it was proposed to leave to the
determination and judgment of the individual using violence the time and occasion therefor, and there was no
proof, either then or at the end of the trial, that " some
" one or more of the parties to the conspiracy did kill."
Could anything be more calculated to mislead the jury,
more calculated to put into their minds a false and unfounded hypothesis which would color their judgment
in the way of all the testimony that might be presented
to them than a suggestion of this character coming out of
the lips of the judge presiding?

His suggestions were, in our opinion, fully as erroneous as would have been instructions presenting the same
hypothesis. It is error for the court to suggest in the
presence of the jury, either by instructions or in the
course of rulings or remarks, an hypothesis which is not
supported by the testimony before the jury. The tendency of such action upon the part of the court is to lead
the jury away from the true issue and to set them to im-
agining things not suggested by the testimony, because it
is made apparent to them that such views are in the
mind of the presiding judge.

> *State* v. *Harkin*, 7 Nev., 382.
> *Hair* v. *Little*, 28 Ala., 236.
> *Andrews* v. *Ketcham*, 77 Ill., 377.

Then the court proceeded as follows:

" Unless the state is permitted to prove, step by step,
" piece by piece, what did occur, it never can be proved,
" although it may have existed. The only way in which
" it can be made to appear, if it did exist, is by introduc-
" ing, piece by piece, what did occur."

Yet no rule of law is better established than that, in
the effort to establish the guilt of a party on the ground

that he is a member of a conspiracy having an unlawful object in view, there must be at least a *prima
facie* case made of the alleged conspiracy, before the
individual acts and utterances of one or other of the
alleged conspirators can be given in evidence as against
his alleged co-conspirators. It is true that in some
jurisdictions it has been the custom of the court to
accept in lieu of the proof of establishing a *prima facie*
conspiracy the assurance of the representatives of the
state that such proof would be produced, the court holding that unless such proof should subsequently be produced the evidence should be excluded. But we do
not understand that to be the rule established by this
court. This court has laid down the rule, justified by all
experience, that the erroneous introduction of testimony
likely to prejudice a party to the litigation is not cured by
the subsequent exclusion of that testimony.

Howe v. Rosine, 87 Ill., 105.

This rule being established by this court, there can be
no doubt that in a capital case, where a conspiracy is alleged as the basis of liability, the principle should be
rigidly adhered to that the state must make out, by legal
evidence, at least a *prima facie* case of conspiracy before
such testimony as was proposed here to be called for from
Mr. Waller should have been admitted by the judge
as evidence against all of the plaintiffs in error. It
may be that the burden of proving a conspiracy is
increased by adherence to this rule; but the rule is too
well established to admit of its being set aside at convenience, and it is too important to the just protection of the
rights of the accused to be lightly disregarded. No subsequent ruling in this case, for instance, could have obliterated from the minds of the jury the prejudice instilled

by such observations of the court as we are here criticising, and by such testimony as, under this rule, the court permitted to come before the jury.

And for a third repetition of the same unwarranted hypothesis, the court stated as follows:

" If there was a general combination and agreement
" among a great number of individuals *to kill policemen*
" if they came in conflict with parties who they were the
" friends of—meetings of workingmen and strikers—if
" there was a combination and agreement to kill the police
" if they were attempting to preserve the peace—if there
" was such a combination and agreement among a great
" number of men, the object of which was something
" beyond mere local disturbance, it don't make any differ-
" ence whether that object was to create a new form of
" civil society or not—if there was this combination and
" agreement among a great number of people, prepara-
" tion for it to assault and kill the police upon some
" occasion which might occur in the future, and *whether*
" *the proper occasion had occurred, was left to the parties*
" *who used the violence at that time*, and then that violence
" was used, and resulted in the death of the police, every-
" body who is a party to that combination and agreement
" is guilty of the results."

Here the hypothesis complained of was changed from the form of a question to the enunciation of a rule, a rule, we venture to say, absolutely without support in any accredited authority, as we will show more fully hereafter. But not content with this third restatement of this proposition, the presiding judge proceeded to say:

" If the time and occasion *were left to the different con-*
" *spirators, or to the different parties to the agreement,*
" and then when the time did come, in the judgment of

" some one of those, and he did use the force and kill,
" then they are all liable."

We challenge the production of a syllable of testimony
to show that the plaintiffs in error, or any of them, were
parties to an agreement at any time under which it was
proposed to use force and kill, the time and occasion of
the use of such force and the doing of such homicide
being left to the "judgment of some one" of the alleged
conspirators.

The vice of this hypothesis, thus continually reiterated
in the hearing of the jury, was not at all relieved by the
fact that the court added:

" Whether that is the case here or not is for this
" jury to determine, after they shall have heard all of
" the evidence that there is bearing upon that question."

Such a question was not before the jury upon any evidence that had up to that time been submitted, or was
thereafter adduced during the whole trial. Such a question was not before the jury in any of the pleadings in
the case. The trial court brought forward that question
upon his own motion, and without any support in the
record, thus suggesting a false issue, to the manifest
prejudice of the plaintiffs in error.

Then to rivet and doubly rivet the errors above pointed
out, the court added:

" I have not a particle of doubt in my own mind
" that it is entirely competent for the state to show,
" if they can, *that these several defendants have advocated
" the use of deadly missiles against the police* upon occa-
" sions which they anticipated might arise in the future—
" that it is competent for them to show *that they intended
" that that use should be made, not by an agreement before-
" hand as to the specific occasion* when they should be
" used, *but* that they should be used *when in the judgment*

" *of the person using them the time had come*, they have
" a right to go on to prove what they can upon that sub-
" ject—all that these parties have said and done, and all
" preparations which they have made in contemplation
" of an attack upon the civil authorities."

The record will be searched in vain for evidence of
any such agreement, to which the plaintiffs in error were
parties. Certainly Mr. Waller had not detailed anything
looking in that direction. Finally, to crown the vice of
the entire ruling, the judge closed as follows:

" A general plan of that sort would be composed of a
" great multitude of people; there would be a great many
" incidents; there would be a great many times and occa-
" sions, if it lasted long enough, in which some portion of
" what they contemplated doing would be done. Now,
" any one of those instances or occasions, any small por-
" tion of the whole which they contemplated, when it be-
" came the subject of an investigation, would involve the
" showing of that whole combination and agreement from
" beginning to end, so as to show, in fact, that it was a
" small portion of that great whole, that it was in fact an
" incident of the great plan which they had."

We need not further criticise this most erroneous ruling
and address in the presence of the jury.

From the time of its announcement by Judge Gary
the representatives of the state almost entirely abandoned the effort to establish any direct relationship
between the Monday night meeting conspiracy and the
throwing of the bomb at the Haymarket meeting. Under
the suggestion of the presiding judge the scheme was
adopted of establishing, in the dramatic language of counsel, " a gigantic conspiracy against the law," a supposed
" general conspiracy," broad enough in its general purpose to include every conceivable crime, from murder and

treason to assaults and street brawls. The effort was abandoned to show that the plaintiffs in error advised, designed, arranged, aided, encouraged or abetted " the perpetration " of the crime," that is, the throwing of the bomb, or the commission of a felony at the time and place, in the attempt to execute which the crime charged was perpetrated. Not one instruction was asked by the state based upon such a theory. But the avowed theory of the prosecution was to establish the responsibility of the plaintiffs in error for this murder, by showing that they were engaged in a general plan to bring about, if necessary by the use of force, a reorganization of society, the overthrow of the existing social order; the claim being that the violence used at the Haymarket meeting was the result and in furtherance of that plan.

Plainly stated, the position of the state, sanctioned by the ruling of the court, was substantially this: That if the plaintiffs in error were desiring to bring about at some time in the future a change in the organization of society, and were expecting and preparing to use force in connection with the accomplishment of that design, and had called upon people to arm themselves and prepare for the approaching revolution, then they should be responsible as for murder for a death resulting from violence at a public meeting, without proof that that meeting was intended by them to result in violence, without proof that any violence at that meeting was contemplated, advised or prepared for by any of them, without proof that any of them ever knew the party who threw the bomb, and in the face of the proof that several of them were not present at the meeting, and had no knowledge even of its holding. As a corrollary to this theory, the representatives of the state contended that these plaintiffs in error were guilty of murder if they had given *general advice* to the public to use violence, leaving it for the jury *to guess* that some individual, acting under such advice, committed this particular crime.

Under this ruling many days of the trial were devoted to the introduction of testimony which, in our judgment, was totally foreign to the issue in this case.

It would unduly extend this argument for us to present this testimony at length. It may be classified with reference to its subject matter into certain divisions, however, concerning which we may express at reasonable length our criticisms upon its introduction.

I. NEWSPAPER LITERATURE.

A vast amount of literature was introduced into the case, found in the volume of exhibits, which in our judgment had no proper place in the trial of the cause, and which could not but have a tendency to jeopardize the rights of the plaintiffs in error.

There were introduced and read in evidence a large number of editorials, notices, communications and reprints (1) from the files of the Arbeiter Zeitung, running through a period of nearly two years prior to the Haymarket meeting; (2) from the Alarm, running through substantially the same period of time; and (3) from one number of the Anarchist.

(1.) As to the Arbeiter Zeitung, it appeared from the testimony (A. 40 *et seq.*), that it was a German daily paper, having a Sunday issue called Die Fackel and a weekly issue called Vorbote, published by the Socialistic Publishing Society, a corporation duly organized under the laws of the State of Illinois; that Spies, Schwab, Fischer and Neebe were among the stockholders of that corporation, and that Spies and Schwab were the editors of the above publications. They were employed as such by the corporation at the salary of $18 per week each. (A., 297, 308); Fischer was a compositor in the Arbeiter Zeitung office (A., 40). But there is no evidence that any of the other plaintiffs in error had anything to do with the Arbeiter Zeitung, or that any of the editorials, communications, quotations from other publications or notices were ever known to or approved by any of the plaintiffs in error other than Spies and Schwab.

(2.) As to the Alarm, it appears that it was a semi-monthly English paper, published by the Socialistic Publishing Society, at 107 5th avenue, that Parsons was its editor (A., 40), and that, on one occasion, when Parsons was absent from the city, Spies assumed the temporary editorial management thereof (A., 308); Fielden had two dollars' worth of stock in the Alarm; but aside from Parsons and Spies, there is no evidence showing that any other of the plaintiffs in error had any responsibility for or connection with the publication of any of the matters appearing in the Alarm.

(3.) As to the Anarchist, it appears (A., 83; J, 270) that its publication was undertaken because the parties interested therein were not satisfied with the attitude of other socialistic publications in the city of Chicago. So far as the record discloses, there was but one issue of this paper, and apparently Engel had some connection with it, a note in the paper directing that complaints should be addressed to G. Engel, and it appearing that in an address to the north side group he solicited support for its publication. (A., 83.) There is no evidence that he wrote any of the matters appearing in the Anarchist, and no evidence that any of the plaintiffs in error had any connection with or responsibility for the contents of the single issue of that paper.

Some of the articles in the Alarm and Arbeiter Zeitung contained information or directions as to the manufacture and use of explosives, sometimes apparently contributed originally for one or the other of the papers; and sometimes copied from, and credited to, other publications. The whole information upon this subject was such as could be obtained from any scientific publication treating upon explosives and from any of our current periodicals, where such matters are occasionally considered.

Besides this, the worst that can be said of the publications referred to is that they strongly advocated the rights of labor, claimed that the capitalistic classes robbed the workingmen of their due, urged the wage classes to prepare for the impending conflict, and advised them to arm themselves with guns, revolvers and dynamite. Particularly the issues of these papers within several months prior to the 4th of May contained much denunciation of the capitalists, and predictions that the eight-hour demand would not be complied with, but that the attempt by the workingmen to enforce it would result in violence, owing to the determined resistance of the capitalistic class, supported by the police, militia and Pinkertons, and much exhortation to the laboring men to prepare for this contest, in order that they might sustain themselves as against the attacks which it was predicted would be made upon them, and which it was said were being made upon them.

But all this matter was *general in its character*, and had no reference to or bearing upon the meeting on the 4th of May, except that in the afternoon issue of the Arbeiter Zeitung of that date the circular calling the meeting and one or two little paragraphs urging the workingmen to attend the same in large numbers was published; but even in that issue there was no exhortation to prepare for nor any suggestion of violence, or the contemplated use of force at that meeting. The meeting was treated as a meeting, not of socialists and anarchists, but as a mass-meeting of wage-workers for the purpose of agitation.

Our claim is that all this mass of literature which was admitted against *all* plaintiffs in error, over their objection and exception, was incompetent, and that by its inevitable tendency to inflame the prejudices, its introduction tended manifestly to the wrong and injury of the plaintiffs in error.

But particularly, we complain as to those portions of these publications in which there was purported to be given *reports of alleged meetings* held in different parts of the city, and of speeches made at the same by some of the plaintiffs in error and other parties. Our position was, and is, that the fact of such meetings or what occurred thereat could not be proved by any such published reports, no matter in what publication appearing. The fact is, that the only proof attempted to be introduced by the state as to a great number of meetings was proof of published reports of this kind.

Let us illustrate the injurious tendency of this irrelevant matter. In overruling the motion to instruct the jury to find a verdict of not guilty as to Oscar Neebe at the close of the state's evidence, the presiding judge, in assigning grounds for refusing said motion, amongst other things, stated that it appeared that Oscar Neebe had presided at socialistic meetings. The only support for that claim is in the reports of one or two meetings published in these papers, in which it was stated that Neebe presided. There was no attempt made to identify the Mr. Neebe alleged to have presided with Oscar Neebe, the plaintiff in error in this case; and there was no attempt

made to show by affirmative and competent evidence
that he was in fact present at or presided over such meeting; while neither in these published reports thus
erroneously admitted, nor in any evidence submitted by
the state, was there any attempt made to show that
Neebe ever said a word at any of these meetings, or took
any part therein, beyond the published report of his occu-
pancy of the chair.

Upon what legal ground can the introduction of this
class of matter be justified? Was there ever before a
case where it was attempted to involve men in the consequences of crime by the wholesale introduction of newspapers upon the suggestion and inference that they were
either connected in some way, as stockholders or otherwise, with the issuance of these papers, or that they were
supposed to be in sympathy with the contents and attitude thereof? We submit that there is no rule of law
yet established in our jurisprudence which can justify the
ruling of the court admitting this mass of testimony.

An inspection of the volume of exhibits will further
show that there was allowed to be introduced, over the
objection and exception of the plaintiffs in error, a large
number of *communications* published in the Arbeiter
Zeitung, the Alarm and the Anarchist. So far as the
Arbeiter Zeitung is concerned, it is in evidence that most
of these communications were published in a column
which bore at the head the note that the paper was not
responsible for the views of correspondents. In spite of
all this, here was a large amount of matter permitted to
be brought in, confessedly having no relation whatever to
the Haymarket meeting or the occurrences there, the
writers not even being identified in any manner by the
evidence in this record. Is this the law? Is such evidence competent upon such an issue?

Not content to stop, however, with this latitude, the state went still further, and, under the ruling of the court, introduced in evidence, as against all the plaintiffs in error, a translation of the platform of the International Workingpeople's Association, adopted in convention in Pittsburg in 1883, as published in the Arbeiter Zeitung; in other words, a translation of a translation.

Further than this, articles copied by the Alarm and the Arbeiter Zeitung from other publications, such as Truth, San Francisco, and Die Freiheit, published in New York, were read *in extenso;* notably one article on street warfare contributed by an officer of the United States army to Truth, and reprinted therefrom (People's Exhibit 48; 1 A., 172); and several articles upon explosives published in the Freiheit and reprinted therefrom.

Another illustration of the same matter was the republication of an article by the Russian nihilist, Bakunin, upon the revolutionist; an article which has passed into the current literature of the day and may be found by searching the files of almost any of the great daily papers published in the civilized world during the last decade. Even such a publication as this was permitted to be read in evidence as against all the defendants, because it was found published in one of these papers referred to.

In short, the state was allowed to ransack the files of these papers for a period of years, and to introduce for the consideration of the jury whatever they chose to select out of this mass of printed matter. What had all this matter to do with the issue before the jury? Let the tendency of it be what it may; let the matter be wise or unwise; let it be mistaken in its claim of grievances, foolish in its denunciation of supposed wrongs, unwise in its advocacy of proposed remedies—still what has all this matter to do legitimately with the issue before the jury?

II. JOHANN MOST'S BOOK.

There was introduced in evidence, as against all the plaintiffs in error, over their objection and exception, a translation of Johann Most's book on the Science of Revolutionary Warfare, and read to the jury *in extenso*. (People's Exhibit 15, Vol. of Ex.; 1 A., 142, *et seq*.) It is a treatise of over fifty pages of printed matter upon explosives, and all the details of modern revolutionary warfare.

Our objection to the introduction of this work was two-fold.

First, on account of its irrelevancy and immateriality; *secondly*, because no connection between this work and its publication to the plaintiffs in error was established by the evidence.

This book is openly published by the International News Company in the city of New York, as appears from the imprint. Its writer is shown by the evidence to be a resident of that city. Confessedly it was published long before the Haymarket meeting was dreamed of. There *can* be no claim that the writer of the book or the publishers thereof knew that a meeting would be held on the 4th day of May, 1886, or at any other time, at the Haymarket in Chicago, or at any other place, at which a bomb would be thrown, resulting in the death of Mathias J. Degan. Here was an entirely foreign matter brought into this case for no other purpose than to prejudice the jury.

But neither was it connected by any legal evidence in any manner with the plaintiffs in error. The work is printed in German. Two of the plaintiffs in error, Fielden and Parsons, cannot read German (A., 269; M, 320), and therefore never could have read this work, which confessedly was never translated into English until this was done by the prosecution in connection with the trial of this case. There is no evidence showing that this book was ever in the possession of any of the plaintiffs in error, nor any evidence showing that it was ever read by any of them.

The evidence by which the introduction of this book in this case was attempted to be justified, and which evidence itself, in our judgment, was incompetent and came in, in each instance, over the objection and exception of plaintiffs in error, was as follows:

Fricke testified that he had seen the book in the library of the International Workingpeople's Association, in the Arbeiter Zeitung building (A., 41; I, 474); that Hirschberger, the librarian, sold copies of that book at socialistic picnics and mass-meetings; at some of them Spies, Parsons, Fielden were present; sometimes Neebe, sometimes Schwab, and perhaps Fischer (A., 41; I, 475-6).

On cross-examination he admitted that none of the plaintiffs in error had anything to do with the selling of that book at those picnics, and he could not even tell that any of them saw the book there sold or exposed for sale. (A., 42, 43; I, 485, 486.)

Schrade says (A., 11; I, 159) he saw the book sold at workingmen's meetings, but does not say who sold or bought it, or that any of the plaintiffs in error were connected with it.

Seliger testifies that he saw the book at public meetings of the north side group, where one Huebner, the librarian, sold them. (A., 49; T, 532.)

There was also in evidence a little announcement appearing in the announcement column of several issues of the Arbeiter Zeitung, which read substantially as follows:

" Most's Revolutionary Warfare has arrived and can be
" had of the librarian at ten cents a copy."

That this evidence was inadmissible and incompetent,
as bearing not the remotest relation to the Haymarket
meeting, and for the reason that it was not shown that
any of the plaintiffs in error ever saw the book at that
library, or knew anything about its selling at any of those
places, is too clear for argument. Still, it was admitted
by the court, and used as the basis for the admission of
the contents of the book itself. But does incompetent
evidence become competent because there is a foundation
for it which is itself incompetent?

Again, Officer Bonfield says that Fischer admitted to
him having read about fulminating caps in Most's Science
of War (A., 28; I, 354); and Capt. Schaack states that
Lingg said to him he had learned to make bombs from
scientific books of warfare published by Most, of New
York (A., 159; K, 507); both of these alleged admissions
were made after the 4th of May, and could at best be
evidence against Lingg and Fischer respectively, but not
as against any of the other plaintiffs in error. Besides, in
neither case was it attempted to show that the book referred to was the same as that introduced in evidence.
Does that make the contents of the book admissible? Suppose Lingg had said he learned to make bombs from articles
in the Encyclopædia Britannica (and information on that
subject can be found there), what rational man would
claim that thereby the contents of the Encyclopædia
Britannica became admissible and competent evidence?

The introduction of the book and the reading of it before the jury could have no other tendency than to stimu-
late the prejudices of the jury, and possibly arouse their
fears or at least their apprehension. And we confidently
submit that it is too clear to require or justify further

argument, that the admission of this publication in evidence was unwarranted by any precedent, and contrary to every known rule of law governing the admissibility of evidence. Here was a voluminous, incendiary, outrageous publication, going into the detail of the manufacture of explosives and arms, and the manner of preparing them, filled with vile suggestions as to how to apply the results of modern science to the work of destruction of the capitalistic system, abounding in advice to persons who, as members of the so-called revolutionary forces, might propose to engage in the use of these weapons and explosives. But the fact remains that it had nothing whatever to do either in its contents or in the circumstances of its publication with the Haymarket meeting, or the offense there committed; nor even with any supposed revolutionary movement in the city of Chicago. It was altogether general in its terms, suggestions and advice. We think it is safe to say that the state could not have made out even their *theory* of the conspiracy to bring about a revolution and use force for the overthrow of civil society against these defendants, or any of them, but for the introduction of Herr Most's book, and presenting it to the jury and inflaming their minds by a recital of the bloody theories therein suggested. These theories were *inter alios acta*, for which the defendants were in no wise responsible.

III. VARIOUS OBJECTS.

Another specification of incompetent evidence to which the plaintiffs in error, in each instance, objected, was the introduction before the jury of various objects, particulars of which may be suggested as follows:

First. The state was allowed to introduce and exhibit before the jury a large amount of soiled clothing, accompanied by the explanation that it had been worn on the night of the Haymarket by divers officers other than Mr. Degan; and as the soiled and blood-stained garments were held up before the jury, various holes therein, supposed to have been made by fragments of the shell, were pointed out. (A., 158; K, 501–503.) What had this soiled and rent clothing to do with the question whether or not the plaintiffs in error were responsible for the death of Mathias J. Degan? It was not his clothing that was thus introduced; and it was not shown that the clothing belonged to officers who died; but as much or as little of this soiled wear as the representatives of the state chose to bring into court was permitted to be paraded before the horrified gaze of the jury. Was it for the purpose of enabling the jury intelligently to determine the issue before it, upon the proper determination of which rested the fate of eight fellow-beings, or was it a vulgar appeal to their passions, fears and prejudices, calculated, if not designed, to pervert the judgment and to turn justice awry?

Second. The state was permitted to introduce a large mass of fragments of boxes, kegs and other articles which had been fractured in experiments made by police officers after the 4th of May, and in some instances after the beginning of the present trial, with dynamite, claimed to have been found at the Arbeiter Zeitung office, and dynamite alleged to have been removed from bombs found in a trunk of Louis Lingg, and admitted in both cases to have been seized unlawfully and without warrant. Testimony in regard to these experiments was given by Schaack (A., 160, 161; K, 516 *et seq.*), and Buck (A., 60). Ostensibly the purpose of this was to show the power of that dynamite. In making our objection to the introduction of this material, the plaintiffs in error admitted in open court that the material experimented with was dynamite, and that dynamite was one of the most powerful of modern explosives. What occasion was there to go beyond this, and to bring in such material as broken barrel staves, indented iron, torn links, etc., etc.? It may be said that this is not a vital point, even if its impropriety be admitted; but we desire to call attention to it as an indication of what we think may be properly called the atmosphere of the trial.

Third. Near the close of the state's case (A., 163) evidence was admitted of the finding under a sidewalk of four tin cans filled with some combustible material, in the north-western part of the city, on the 2d of June, 1886, *more than four weeks after the Haymarket meeting.* Two views of one of these cans are shown in the photograph "People's Exhibit 131." The location where these cans were found was about *three miles from the Haymarket,* and *about a mile and a half away from Wicker Park.* (A., 163; K, 554.) Evidence was permitted to be introduced as to an experiment made with one of them by Officer Coughlin (A., 164), and when the cans were themselves allowed to be introduced before the jury it appeared that they were provided with an inner chamber of glass filled with gunpowder, and reached by a slow-burning fuse. There was no pretense that any of these articles had anything to do with the murder of Degan. He was not killed by anything of this sort. There was no effort made to connect any of the plaintiffs in error directly or remotely with these cans or with their construction. It was not attempted to be shown that any of them had ever manufactured such cans, or advised their manufacture or use, or had anything whatever to do with the construction or distribution thereof.

One objection to the introduction of these cans is based upon the twofold ground that they were not found until nearly a month after the Haymarket meeting, and therefore might have been constructed and placed where they were as a part of a deliberate effort to manufacture testimony for a conviction; and upon the further ground that there was no connection shown between them, their manufacture or disposition and the plaintiffs in error or any of them. The court in the first place ruled them incompetent. But upon the suggestion on behalf of the state that such cans were described in Herr Most's book as adapted for the purposes of making conflagrations in cities where such a course was resolved upon, the court allowed the cans to be introduced in connection with the reading before the jury of the description from Most's book. Thus Most's book, itself illegitimate evidence, was used as a bridge for introducing other illegitimate evidence, such as the tin cans. This, and the fact that the detective, Johnson, described some such instrument, and testified as to having seen it in a meeting of the American group (A., 94; J, 408), was taken as an excuse for the introduction into evidence of those tin cans, although there was no pretense that they could be traced to the possession of any of the plaintiffs in error, or that any one of them had any connection with or knowledge of them. No attempt was made to show that any alleged conspiracy entered into between the plaintiffs in error, or between them or other parties, contemplated the conflagration of the city, or the use of implements of this character for any purpose. If such evidence had been attempted to be adduced, it would have been incompetent, because the throwing of the Haymarket bomb could not have been within the purview of such a conspiracy. In our judgment the court, in overruling our objection, and allowing this evidence to go before the jury, permitted a base appeal to be made to the passions of the jurors, with a view to produce in their minds the impression that these defendants, as supposed disciples of Johann Most, were plotting for a universal conflagration of the city of Chicago.

It was upon and by the introduction of such testimony as this that the State sought to support the charge that these plaintiffs in error murdered Mathias J. Degan on the night of May 4, 1886, by throwing or causing to be thrown the dynamite bomb whose explosion resulted in the destruction of his life. Further comment seems to us unnecessary.

Fourth. The state was allowed to introduce in evidence a galvanized iron structure which was given to the police by Mr Engel, being taken by him from his cellar, where it had been stored for a considerable period of time.

The evidence introduced by the state in reference to this structure was that the galvanized iron which formed the body of it was rolled and cut about a year before the 1st of May, 1886, by a tinner (A., 148; K, 428), upon the order of Mr. Engel. Officer Quinn testified that Engel stated, when this instrument was found in his basement, that he thought it was made for the purpose of making bombs. (A., 147; K, 416.) But the state's evidence also showed affirmatively that *this structure had never been in fact used for any purpose, that there never had been any fire in it.* (A., 148; K, 427.) Yet the state was permitted to show by the testimony of Bonfield, who claimed to be an expert, that, and in what manner, it *could be used* for the melting of metals. (A., 148.) What had that to do with the issue which the jury were called upon to determine in this case? Was the introduction of this structure legitimate, proper? Was such testimony relevant and material? And even if, by a stretch of dis-

cretion, considered competent as against Engel, was it
competent as against the other plaintiffs in error?

Fifth. There were introduced various flags and mottoes containing inscriptions, such as " Every government is
" a conspiracy against the people," and the like, which
were claimed to have been found by the police in a small
room off the library in the Arbeiter Zeitung building
(A., 171, 172), and admittedly like all the other stuff
found there taken without legal warrant. This evidence
was admitted as against *all* the plaintiffs in error.

Sixth. The following was the evidence introduced by
the state in regard to dynamite found in the Arbeiter
Zeitung building on May 5, 1886, and admitted as to all
plaintiffs in error:

Detective Jones and Officer Flynn say (A., 62;
J, 92; A., 65; J, 120) that they were present when
a locksmith opened a desk in the corner of the office on
the second floor of the building, in which desk was found
a coil of fuse, two bars of dynamite, and a box containing
ten fulminating caps.

That these articles had been in the possession of
Mr. Spies for a long period appears from the testimony of Mr. Williamson, a witness for the state, formerly
a reporter of the Chicago Daily News, who says
that these very articles were exhibited to him on the
night of the dedication of the new board of trade in
April, 1885. (A., 55; J, 7, *et seq.*) Mr. Spies says in
regard thereto (A., 307; N, 68): " I have had in
" my desk, for two years, two giant-powder cartridges,
" a roll of fuse and some detonating caps. Originally
" I bought them to experiment with them, as I had read
" a good deal about dynamite and wanted to get ac-
" quainted with it, but I never had occasion to go out for
" that purpose, as I was too much occupied. The re-

" porters used to bother me a good deal, and then when
" they would come to the office for something sensational
" I would show them these giant cartridges. They are
" the same that were referred to here by certain witnesses
" as having been shown on the evening of the board of
" trade demonstration. One of them will yet show a
" little hole in which I put that evening one of those caps
" to explain to the reporter how terrible a thing it was."

Besides, there was introduced by the state evidence
tending to show that a package of dynamite was found
on May 5th in the closet off the editorial room on the
third floor of the Arbeiter Zeitung building. The witnesses who testify in regard to this find are Officer Duffy
(A., 63) and Officer Marks (A., 138), while Officer Mc-
Keough (A., 64) testifies to having seen the package
there, and Officer Haas (A., 81) says that he saw the
package put on a chair by Officer Marks. Mr. Spies
says that *he knows absolutely nothing about that package
of dynamite*, and that he never saw it before it was
produced in court during the trial. (A., 307, 168.) Mr.
Lindemeyer says that he calcimined the Arbeiter Zeitung
building from May 2d until May 5th; that he kept his
clothes and tools in the closet in the rear of the editorial
room of the Arbeiter Zeitung, on the third floor. On
May 4th, about noon-time, he made search for a missing
brush in that closet, got on a chair and examined the
shelves in that closet; that *he found no large package,
no bundle, no dynamite on the shelf;* that there was no
indication of greasiness there (A, 232; N. 74, *et seq.*).
The package of dynamite being produced in court, in
substantially the same shape as when claimed to have
been found in the Arbeiter Zeitung building, and exhibited
to Mr. Lindemeyer, he said that he saw no such package
on May 4th in that closet so searched by him (A., 277;
N, 376).

A very suspicious circumstance regarding the finding of this dynamite is the fact that while Officers Haas and Marks stated positively that this dynamite was found *on the third floor of that building*, Officer Duffy, who was the first of these witnesses examined, just as positively claimed to have found the same *on the second floor of the building*. It will be found from examination of the testimony of Officer Duffy, that he locates the room in which the stuff was found, *first*, as being on the first floor of the Arbeiter Zeitung office; *second*, as on the second floor of the building; *third*, as two floors below the typesetting room, and *fourth*, as being one floor below the third floor. *All these locations refer to the same floor, namely, the second floor of the Arbeiter Zeitung building.* Mr. Duffy could not be more positive or unequivocal as to his location of that room. After, however, the other officers had just as unequivocally and positively located the finding of the dynamite on the third floor of that building, Mr. Duffy was recalled (A., 85), and stated that, at the request of the state's attorney, he had made another examination of the Arbeiter Zeitung building, and found that *he had made a mistake in regard to the floor on which the dynamite was found;* that, in fact, the closet from which it was taken was two floors above the saloon.

That Mr. Spies had no desire of concealing any fact within his knowledge will appear from his whole testimony, which we claim is a model of fairness and candor. Nobody, except a few officers, all of whom, at the time of their testifying, and for years, were in the detective service of the police force, testifies to having ever seen that package of dynamite in the Arbeiter Zeitung building on May 5th, or at any time prior thereto. It is at least singular that the different officers claim to have found it on different floors of the building. Was it put there for the purpose of manufacturing evidence?

Seventh. There were introduced and paraded before
the jury, as against all the plaintiffs in error, the following
articles found upon Fischer at the time of his arrest: A
file ground sharp to an edge, a revolver, one fulminating
cap, and a belt and sheath, the brass buckle on the belt
bearing the letters " L. & W. V." (A., 39, 40.)

On the morning of the 5th of May, these articles were in
the drawer of a table in the composing room of the Arbeiter
Zeitung building. They belonged to Fischer, and Asch-
enbrenner, one of the compositors, told him to take them
away so as not to get anybody else into trouble. (A., 89,
90.) At that time the officers were engaged in the building, making searches and arrests. Fischer strapped the
revolver and belt upon his body under his clothing. On
going out of the building he was arrested. This testimony introduced by the state (A., 90) sufficiently explains how these articles came to be found upon Fischer's
person at the time of his arrest. There is no pretense that
he wore any of them on the night of the 4th of May,
1886, or that either of these weapons were in any manner instrumental in producing the death of Mathias J.
Degan, or anybody else; yet they were allowed to be introduced, not simply as against Fischer as being found
upon him when arrested, but also as against all the plaintiffs
in error.

Eighth. The state was allowed, over the objection
of the plaintiffs in error, to introduce evidence of a
number of dynamite bombs of different construction, alleged to have been found long after the Haymarket
meeting, the manufacture or possession of which was
not traced to any of the plaintiffs in error, without any attempt to establish any connection between such "finds"
and any of the plaintiffs in error. Under this head belongs the evidence of Officer McNamara (A., 166), who

claimed to have found thirty loaded and one " empty gas-pipe bombs " (the latter would probably be called a piece of gas-pipe by ordinary mortals) on May 23d, *about three weeks after the Haymarket meeting*, and about *three and a half miles distant from the Haymarket*. For all that appears in this record, these various so-called bombs may have been manufactured after the 4th of May, and placed where they were found, for the express purpose of manufacturing evidence against the defendants. We submit that the introduction of such testimony, in the absence of the establishment by legal evidence of any connection between these articles and the plaintiffs in error, was clearly erroneous and had a manifest tendency to prejudice the case of the plaintiffs in error. We again ask, what bearing had the finding of these bombs upon the legitimate and proper determination of the question whether the plaintiffs in error threw or advised or caused to be thrown the bomb which killed Degan?

IV. COMPELLING THE ACCUSED TO GIVE EVIDENCE AGAINST THEMSELVES.

We complain that the court erred in compelling the plaintiffs in error to give evidence against themselves. In this regard the court erred (1) in overruling our objections to various questions asked by the state upon cross-examination of the plaintiffs in error, when upon the stand as witnesses, and (2) in permitting the state to introduce in evidence, over the objections and exceptions of plaintiffs in error, a number of objects and articles unlawfully seized by the representatives of the state.

(1.) IMPROPER CROSS-EXAMINATION.

We understand that under the statute allowing defendants to testify in their own behalf, the defendant, when he takes the stand, is subject to the most rigid and full cross-examination. But we do not understand that he hereby subjects himself to having one of his constitutional safeguards broken down and being required to give evidence against himself, upon the pretense of cross-examination as to matter which is not covered by any inquiry upon examination in chief, but which, if germane to the issue, should have been introduced by the state in the presentation of its case.

Called upon the stand as a witness in his own behalf, Mr. Fielden was definitely interrogated, after a few general questions as to age, place of birth, etc., as to his occupation, his engagement on the day of the Haymarket tragedy, his actions and utterances in that connection and immediately thereafter. That was all. He stated that he was a teamster, and on the 4th day of May, 1886, he was busy hauling stone, according to his custom, until a late hour in the afternoon. Upon cross-examination, over the objection of the plaintiffs in error, the state was allowed to interrogate Mr. Fielden as to whether he had not made various labor speeches, or socialistic speeches, at various places and on divers occasions. That he had made such speeches had been proved by the state as a part of their original case. No effort had been made by Mr. Fielden, when upon the stand, to contradict the state's testimony in that particular. Not one question had been asked of Mr. Fielden regarding his connection with the labor movement, or speeches made by him in its interest. But to this objection it was answered by the

presiding judge that Mr. Fielden had been examined with
reference to showing that his occupation was that of a
teamster, the tendency of which was to show that he
was leading an industrious and quiet life, and that it was
competent for the state in cross-examination to show
whether that was his whole life or only a part of it.
(M, 333.)

Under this ruling, Mr. Fielden was required to answer
such questions in cross-examination as the following
(A., 271 et seq.):

" Did you ever meet with any other English-speaking
" group in this city or county?"

" How many times have you spoken on the lake front
" on Sunday afternoons?"

" Did you make a speech there on the night of the
" opening of the new board of trade?"

" Did you have anything to do with the management
" of the Alarm?"

" Did you read the Alarm?"

" Didn't you read this paper to keep track of the
" socialistic history as it was being made?"

We submit that this ruling of the court was a palpable
violation of the spirit and letter of the constitution and
was clearly erroneous. There was the same setting
aside, under the ruling of the court, of this constitutional
safeguard, that no accused person shall be compelled to
give evidence against himself, in the case of Spies, who
was compelled to answer questions like the following
(A., 310):

" Were you in the habit of making speeches at the
meetings of the American group?"

" Have you addressed meetings on the lake front?"

" Do you know Herr Most?"

" How long have you known him?" etc.

In this connection, the state was permitted to ask, and the plaintiff in error, Spies, compelled to answer, questions as to his correspondence with Most, as to his having received or answered a certain letter and a certain postal card alleged to have been written by Most and addressed to Spies, etc.

Nothing can be found in the testimony of Mr. Spies on his direct examination by which it could be claimed the above inquiries are covered. It was illegitimate cross-examination, it materially tended to prejudice Mr. Spies, and the court clearly erred in overruling our objections to this line of inquiry.

But not content with that, the state introduced in evidence translations of that letter itself, as well as the postal, in connection with the cross-examination of Mr. Spies, and our objections to their introduction were overruled by the court, and the letter and postal admitted as evidence against *all* the plaintiffs in error.

The evidence in reference to this letter and postal was substantially this: They were found in the desk of August Spies in the Arbeiter Zeitung building after his arrest and upon the search of that building. When Mr. Spies was upon the witness stand he was compelled, under the ruling of the court, to testify, and upon this point the State made him their witness, that he had *no recollection as to having received or read either the letter or postal*, the matter having entirely passed out of his mind; but he recognized the handwriting as that of Most, and stated that he had no doubt that he must have received the same in due course of mail, as they were addressed to him. But *he did not think he had ever answered it, and he stated positively that he never carried on any correspondence with Most*. He further stated that he knows positively that he *did not give the directions where to ship the material mentioned in the letter.* (A., 310, 311).

The introduction of this letter and postal was clearly illegal and erroneous on four different grounds:

(1.) This evidence was immaterial and irrelevant to the issue before the jury. The letter was dated 1884; it related to the troubles in the Hocking Valley, and inquired of Mr. Spies as to whether a party named in the letter, and represented as residing somewhere in the Hocking Valley, was a reliable and proper party with whom to communicate, and in that connection the suggestion was made in the letter that the writer had some " medicine " which he could send to the Hocking Valley if sure it would reach the proper parties. It was a letter from a stranger to these proceedings, not one charged as jointly liable with the plaintiffs in error for participating in their design; a letter of questionable import, which was not answered by its recipient. Can such a letter be competent evidence even against a party to whom it was addressed, let alone a number of other parties joined with him in the defense, who are not shown to have ever seen, heard of or in any way been connected with it? What was the purpose of the introduction of this letter into this case? Was it to prove that Mr. Most was desiring to help the miners in the Hocking Valley to commit deeds of violence by furnishing them with the necessary material for that purpose? There was no suggestion in the letter that Mr. Spies was a party to any such plan, or that any dynamite or " medicine " was to be forwarded by him or through him. The inquiry upon that branch was simply as to whether Mr. Spies knew the party named and his character. What had the Hocking Valley troubles in 1884, settled years before the Haymarket tragedy, to do with the throwing of the bomb upon the night of the 4th of May, 1886? Was the real purpose of the forcing of this letter into the record to plant in the minds of the jury by illegitimate evidence the suspicion of some combination, arrangement or understanding between Mr. Most and the plaintiffs in error, because of his letter and postal addressed to Mr. Spies? If this was the real purpose sought to be accomplished through the introduction of this evidence, then we respectfully submit that the purpose condemns the action of the court as strongly as does the law.

(2.) This evidence came in through illegitimate cross-examination. Nothing in regard to it, nothing by which these matters can be conceived to have been covered, was adverted to upon the direct examination of Mr. Spies. In other words, it was new matter elicited from the plaintiff in error. It was therefore a compelling a witness to give evidence against himself and a palpable violation of the constitutional safeguard mentioned. This court has held that illegitimate cross-examination of the defendant in a criminal case is ground for a reversal.

Gifford v. *People*, 87 Ill., 210, 214.

(3.) It is never competent to introduce in evidence against a party an unanswered letter addressed to him, even when found among his effects and in his possession, without evidence that the letter has been acted upon or invited by the party to whom it is addressed, and even where a tacit recognition is claimed, the whole correspondence which constitutes the recognition must be given. In support of this proposition, we cite:

Wharton's Criminal Evidence, 9th Edition, §§ 644 and 682.

The case of *Commonwealth* v. *Edgerly*, 10th Allen, 184, is directly in point. The defendant there was indicted for having counterfeit money in his possession, knowing it to be counterfeit. There was offered in evidence a letter received by the defendant from the post-office, immediately before his arrest, containing one or more of the counterfeit bills, but which letter was not read by him, nor answered by him, being seized upon the arrest of the defendant, immediately after its receipt. The Supreme court, in reversing the case, used the following language (p. 187):

" An unanswered letter is inadmissible, although the "statements contained in it are well known to the party " to whom it was sent; and this is held on the ground " that a letter written to a party by a third person, to " which no reply is made, does not show an acquiescence " in the facts stated in the letter. * * *

" It would be an immaterial error if the contents of the " letter were unimportant; but on looking at them it is "clear that they were of a nature to prejudice the minds " of the jury against the defendant."

The case was reversed solely on this ground.

(4.) This evidence was illegal on the ground that the letter and postal referred to were seized without warrant of law. But this leads us to the second subdivision of our complaints under this head:

II. Objects unlawfully seized.

Officer Jones says (A., 62; J, 91, *et seq.*) he was present on May 5th at the Arbeiter Zeitung office when a locksmith opened different drawers in different offices. The locksmith opened the desk in the corner of the office on the second floor of the building. In the drawer of the desk he found, among other things, a number of letters directed to Mr. Spies. (A., 63; J., 106.) He

had no search warrant in going through the building.
(J., 103, 4.)

Officer Flynn was with Officer Jones at the time he
searched the desk of Mr. Spies. He says (A., 65): "We
"found this box of letters (indicating); they were all
"found in Mr. Spies' drawer; *the desk was pried open.*
"I took the letters, put them into this box, carried them
"to the station and delivered them to Mr. Furthmann"
(assistant state's attorney).

This search and seizure being in palpable violation of
the provisions of the federal constitution, fourth amend-
ment, and of the constitution of the State of Illinois, we respectfully submit that the admission of any of this matter
in this record was improper, as being in effect a compelling of the plaintiffs in error to give testimony against
themselves contrary to the provision of the fifth amend-
ment of the federal constitution and to the provision of
article 2 of our constitution of 1870. In support of this
position we cite *Boyd* v. *The United States*, 116 U. S.,
616. The case is a very late one and very fully considered by the Supreme court, and the opinion very ably
presents the views of that tribunal.

This case arose upon the question of the constitutionality of the act of Congress providing that upon any complaint for violation of the revenue laws the parties accused
are required by the courts to produce their books, in-
voices and papers for inspection and for use in evidence
against them; and upon their failure to do so the aver-
ments of the complaint would be taken against them as
confessed. The Supreme court of the United States, after
citing and commenting at length upon various decisions,
amongst others the opinion of Lord Camden in *Entick* v.
Carrington, 19th Howell State Trials, 1,029, proceeds as
follows:

" The principles laid down in this opinion (of Lord Cam-
" den) affect the very essence of constitutional liberty and
" security. They reach further than the concrete form of
" the case then before the court with its adventitious cir-
" cumstances; they apply to all invasions on the part of
" the government and its employes of the sanctity of a
" man's home and the privacies of life. It is not the
" breaking in of his doors and the rummaging of his draw-
" ers that constitutes the essence of the offense, but it is
" the invasion of his indefeasible right of personal secu-
" rity, personal liberty and private property, where that
" right has never been forfeited by his conviction of some
" public offense;—it is the invasion of this sacred right
" which underlies and constitutes the essence of Lord
" Camden's judgment. Breaking into a house and open-
" ing boxes and drawers are circumstances of aggrava-
" tion; but any forcible and compulsory extortion of a
" man's own testimony, or of his private papers to be used
" as evidence to convict him of crime, or to forfeit his
" goods, are within the condemnation of that judgment.
" In this regard the fourth and fifth amendments run
" almost into each other. * * * Any compulsory
" discovery by extorting the party's oath, or compelling
" the production of his private books and papers, to
" convict him of crime, or to forfeit his property, is con-
" trary to the principles of a free government. It is ab-
" horrent to the instincts of an Englishman; it is abhor-
" rent to the instincts of an American. It may suit the
" purposes of despotic power, but it cannot abide the
" pure atmosphere of political liberty and personal
" freedom. * * * We are further of opinion that
" a compulsory production of the private books and
" papers of the owner of goods sought to be forfeited
" in such a suit is compelling him to be a witness

" against himself, within the meaning of the fifth amend-
" ment to the constitution, and is the equivalent of
" a search and seizure—and an unreasonable search
" and seizure—within the meaning of the fourth amend-
" ment. Though the proceeding in question is di-
" vested of many of the aggravating incidents of actual
" search and seizure, yet, as before said, it contains their
" substance and essence, and effects their substantial pur-
" pose. It may be that it is an obnoxious thing in its
" mildest and least repulsive form; but illegitimate and
" unconstitutional practices get their first footing in that
" way, namely, by silent approaches and slight deviations
" from legal means of procedure. This can only be ob-
" viated by adhering to the rule that constitutional pro-
" visions for the security of persons and property should
" be liberally construed. A close and literal construc-
" tion deprives them of half their efficacy, and leads to
" gradual depreciation of the right, as if it consisted more
" in sound than in substance. It is the duty of courts to
" be watchful for the constitutional rights of the citizen
" and against any stealthy encroachments thereon. Their
" motto should be *obsta principiis*."

A vast amount of other evidence was introduced which
comes directly within the principle laid down in the case
of *Boyd* v. *U. S.*, *supra*, as, for instance, all of the matter taken from the Arbeiter Zeitung building, including
manuscripts, type, flags and mottoes, the dynamite
cartridges, percussion caps and fuse taken from the desk
of Mr. Spies, the articles taken from Fischer's person at
the time of his arrest, etc., etc. That all these articles
were unlawfully obtained by the representatives of the state
appears from the testimony of Bonfield (A., 29, I, 368),
Slayton (A., 39, I, 460), Furthmann (A., 43) and others.

Perhaps the most striking illustration of the violation

of this constitutional safeguard was the introduction in evidence of a bunch of keys (A., 62; J., 94), which Officer Jones says he got from Detective Bonfield, and tried into the drawer where he found the dynamite, fuse and the letters referred to. (A., 62; J., 91, 92.) As to the manner in which these keys, which were permitted to be introduced in evidence, were obtained from Mr. Spies, Detective Bonfield testifies as follows (A., 29; I., 369): " I took Spies and Schwab into the front room of the " Central Station; we searched Spies, and took the per- " sonal effects from him; *I took Mr. Spies' keys out of his* " *pocket;* everything I found, little slips of paper, etc. *I* " *literally went through him. I had no warrant for any-* " *thing of that kind.*"

These searches and seizures were clearly within the prohibition of the federal and the state constitutions. The entries and seizures were clearly unauthorized and illegal; and this character is not taken off by the fact that they were made by those claiming to be in the act the representatives of law, the servants of the government. Nay, the lawlessness of this act is all the more reprehensible in view of the parties to this conduct.

Unless we are prepared to say that the law laid down by the Supreme court of the United States in the case of *Boyd* v. *U. S.* is all nonsense and sentimentality, then all of this matter which came in over the objection and ex- ception of all the plaintiffs in error was evidence extorted from them, and there was error in the rulings of the court in admitting the same.

The principle is the same as that by which it is neces- sary to show that the confession of a defendant was not obtained by holding out promises or threats to him, be- fore his confession is admissible in evidence against him.

Wharton's Crim. Ev., §§ 646, *et seq.*

V. SPEECHES AND PRIVATE UTTERANCES OF PLAINTIFFS IN ERROR.

Evidence was permitted to be offered as against *all* the plaintiffs in error of speeches and private utterances made by *certain* of them running through an interval of about two years prior to the Haymarket meeting, such speeches being made at various places of gathering, notably on Sunday afternoons on the lake shore, at the meetings of the American group of the International Workingpeople's Association at a hall at 54 West Lake street, and other halls, meetings of workingmen at West Twelfth Street Turner Hall, at Mueller's Hall, and at others; also speeches made at Market square on Thanksgiving day, 1885, and on the night of the dedication of the new board of trade building in the city of Chicago, April 30, 1885. At none of these meetings were there present more than two or three of the plaintiffs in error, and two of them, namely, Fischer and Neebe, are not shown to have spoken at any of these meetings, while a large number of them was held before Louis Lingg had come to the United States; still this evidence was in each case permitted to come in as against all of the plaintiffs in error, over their objection and exception and against the special objection and exception in each instance of the plaintiffs in error not present on the occasion of said respective speakings. And the evidence included not only speeches made by plaintiffs in error, but also speeches made by others at the same meetings, the meetings being in every instance public, in many cases outdoor meetings, and attended by large numbers of persons, not only those in sympathy with the views of the speakers, but also those opposed.

At no one of these meetings from the beginning to the end of the series will it be pretended there was any special reference to the Haymarket meeting, or to the initiation of revolution at that or any other particular date. The talk was general in its character.

To emphasize our objection to this class of testimony, and at the same time to show its unreliable character in many instances, we shall call attention to some of the occasions testified of.

(a.) THE MEETING ON THE NIGHT OF THE OPENING OF THE NEW BOARD OF TRADE.

Concerning the proceedings and utterances on the evening of the dedication of the board of trade of the city of Chicago, occurring in April, 1885, it appears that a meeting of wage-workers was held on the Market square, and from there organized a procession which marched down to the neighborhood of the chamber of commerce; being met by cordons of police on the different streets, and prevented from getting nearer to the building than a block upon either side, marched around the building, halting at one point, and sang the Marseillaise, and thence marched to 5th avenue in front of the Arbeiter Zeitung building, where the crowd was briefly addressed from the windows of the building by Parsons and Fielden, after which they dispersed.

Detective Sullivan's testimony (A., 80, 81), with which detective Trehorn (A., 77, *et seq.*) substantially agrees, is to the effect that at the Market square Parsons made a speech about the board

of trade, showing by figures how the poor man was
robbed; then he denounced the police as blood-hounds,
the militia as servants of the capitalists, robbing the laboring classes, and invited them all in a body to go to the
board of trade, force their way into it, and partake of the
twenty-dollar dishes at that supper. Fielden spoke after
Parsons, denouncing the police and militia as blood-
hounds, and urging the crowd to force themselves in to
the board of trade and partake of that twenty-dollar
supper; at the time of this speaking there was a company
of militia drilling upon the Market square, to which
Schwab called attention, and the witness and detective
Trehorn went over and requested them to leave, which
they did. Then they formed a procession, some carrying
red flags, marching around the board of trade and finally
stopping at 107 5th avenue. Parsons then spoke from
the window again, denouncing the policemen and militia
as blood-hounds, stating that they had stopped them from
going into the board of trade; that a good many of his
audience could not afford to pay twenty cents for a meal,
let alone twenty dollars; and that if they would follow
him he would raid different places, mentioning Marshall
Field's; then Fielden spoke from the window and wanted
the crowd to follow him; that arguments had failed, and
they would have to use the gun and dynamite. As to the
occurrences while the procession was in motion, and during
and after the speeches from the window at 5th avenue,
the witnesses named are substantially corroborated by M.
H. Williamson, a reporter. (A., 54, 55.) These witnesses
admit, however, that no movement was made or attempted
from 5th avenue, but the crowd quietly dispersed and
went home, Parsons and Fielden stepped quietly back
from the window into the rooms of the building, and remained there until after the audience had dispersed. Sulli-

van, Trehorn and Williamson then had a conversation
with Parsons in the room from which the addresses had
been made, while Fielden, Spies and Schwab were in the
room, in which they say they were shown a dynamite
cartridge, a coil of fuse, and some fulminating caps.
Parsons made some talk as to the possible use of dynamite in the future in the event of contests with the police,
and spoke of its power as an explosive, and said, in answer
to an inquiry by them, that they did not attack the board
of trade building that night because the blood-hounds
were in the way, and they were not prepared for action.

The testimony of Sullivan, Trehorn and Williamson
differs materially from that of another witness, detective
Johnson, called by the prosecution, who testifies with reference to the same occurrence. While the first three
witnesses testified simply from *recollection* as to alleged
proceedings and utterances occurring about fifteen months
before they were upon the stand as witnesses, Johnson, in
testifying, had before him, for the purpose of refreshing
his recollection, *detailed reports in writing*, which had
been made by him officially to the superintendent of Pinkerton's national detective agency, by which he was employed (A., 94); and it appeared from endorsements
thereon that these reports were at some time submitted
to other parties for examination, most of them being
endorsed by the name of Lyman J. Gage. (A., 103;
K, 2.)

Johnson's testimony, based upon his written reports,
and fortified by them directly, contradicts the testimony of the three witnesses above mentioned, as to
what was said in all the speeches on the occasion
in question, in the matter of any suggestion or proposal to use violence. Testifying from h's notes, he
says (A., 97; J, 402) that at this meeting on the night of

the 30th of April, 1885, Parsons and Fielden were present; that Parsons said they had assembled to determine in what way best to celebrate the dedication of the new board of trade building. Fielden said: "I want all the "workingmen in Chicago to arm themselves and sweep "the capitalists off the face of the earth." Parsons then said: "Every workingman in Chicago must save a little "of his wages each week until he can buy a Colt re- "volver and Winchester rifle, for the only way that "workingmen can get their rights is at the point of the "bayonet. We want you to form a procession now, and "we will march to the board of trade; we will halt there, "and while the band is playing, we will sing the Mar- "seillaise." Witness was himself in the procession.

On cross-examination (A., 103; J, 450, 457) he stated that he never at any of the meetings heard of an arrangement for blowing up the board of trade building or any other building in the city of Chicago, or for taking the life of any one, or for the sacking of any store in the city of Chicago. At the meeting on the night of the opening of the new board of trade, *no violence was proposed in any of the speeches:* witness heard of no proposal of violence of any kind. He heard Parsons when he first got up state the object of the meeting; heard Fielden speak and Parsons when he replied, and was there when the procession moved. Parsons said there were the board of trade men sitting down to this twenty-dollar supper, while the poor workingmen had to starve; but *witness did not hear* either Parsons or Fielden or anybody else say *that they would go down by force into the board of trade and eat of that twenty-dollar supper;* he says he was listening all the time.

The importance of this testimony of Johnson, in its contradiction of the testimony of Williamson, Sullivan and Trehorn, cannot be overestimated. Johnson was a Pinkerton detective, who, under the direction of that agency, joined the socialists in Chicago; became a member of the American group, and attended through nearly one year substantially all of their meetings, making written reports of what he heard and saw there (A., 94). He swears positively that he heard no proposal to invade the board of trade building by force, to take the supper there by force, to blow up that building, or any other building in the city of Chicago, to sack any building or place, and that he never heard such propositions in any of the meetings he attended, and of which he made detailed reports. If the testimony of this witness is reliable, and he is accredited by the state, and certainly had no inducement to favor the plaintiffs in error, and testified "by the book," then the testimony of the other witnesses as to this board of trade meeting must be taken with much allowance.

Now, what had all this testimony about the occurrences on the night of the dedication of the new board of trade building to do with the Haymarket meeting and the killing of Degan thereat?

(*b.*) The West 12th Street Turner Hall Meeting.

Take, as another illustration, the testimony of M. E. Dickson, formerly a Times reporter (A., 113), concerning a meeting at West 12th street Turner Hall. Witness says that this was a meeting publicly called for the discussion of the socialistic platform; that a circular had been issued, in which public men, clergymen, employers and others were invited to be present to discuss the question; that the hall was crowded; that during the meeting Parsons, Fielden and Spies spoke,

Parsons referring to the degradation of labor, claiming it was brought about by what was known as the rights of private property, and from statistics showing that the average man with a capital of five thousand dollars was enabled to make four thousand a year and thus get rich, while his employe, who made money for him, obtained but three hundred and forty dollars; that there were over two million heads of families in the United States who were in want, or bordering upon want, and it would be hard for the man who stood in the way of liberty and equality to all. Fielden said that the majority were starving because of over-production; that as a socialist he believed in the equal right of every man to live; that the present condition of the laboring man was due to the domination of capital, and they could expect no remedy from legislatures; that there were enough present in that hall to take Chicago from the grasp of the capitalists; that capital must divide with labor; and that the time was coming when a contest would arise; he was no alarmist, but the socialist should be prepared for the victory when it did come. Spies spoke in German, advising the workingmen to organize in order to obtain their rights, and that they might be prepared for the emergency. Then resolutions were adopted denouncing the capitalistic class and those who had refused to come and hear the truth spoken and discuss the question.

(c.) The American Group.

A large amount of evidence was permitted to be introduced in reference to the meetings of the American group, so called, particularly in connection with the testimony of Johnson, the Pinkerton detective.

It appears from the testimony that Parsons, Fielden
and Spies were members of the American Group of the
International Workingpeople's Association. The latter
is an association of working people throughout the civilized world, formed for the purpose of agitating for a
change in the existing social conditions. The meetings
of the American group were *always public and open to
everybody*. Those who joined the group were furnished
with a membership card, the dues were ten cents per
month; but if any person was unable, or for any reason
indisposed to pay the dues, he did not thereby lose his
membership or standing in the society. All this appears
from the testimony of Johnson himself. (A., 102.) It
also appears that the attendance of these meetings was
never larger than *twenty-five* people (A., 56; J, 24),
and that the proceedings were always reported in the
newspapers the next morning (A., 56; J, 16.)

The effect of the testimony referred to, which came
in under objection, was that at the various meetings of
this group there were speeches, statistical and otherwise,
and airing of the supposed grievances of the working people, urging to organize, and advice to prepare and arm
for resistance against the alleged oppressions which they
were suffering. But there is no pretense that the American
group, in any of its meetings, ever considered the holding
of the Haymarket meeting or the use of violence in connection with the same. It was therefore irrelevant and
incompetent, and, because prejudicial, its admission was
error. What place f. i. had in this record the testimony
of Johnson, that at the meeting of March 22, 1885, a
resolution of sympathy was introduced by a man named
Bishop, not one of the plaintiffs, for a girl alleged to have
been outraged by her master, a man of high social standing, and whose case had been refused consideration by

the magistrate to whom it was presented. Johnson says that, in connection with the offering of this resolution, Mr. Spies stated in effect that this was a fine opportunity for some young man to go and shoot the wrongdoer, and thus avenge the girl. (A., 96; I, 394-5.) He was, however, compelled to admit upon cross-examination that here, also, his memory ran beyond his report; for, with his report before him, he had to admit (A., 103; J, 440) that his *written official report* states that another man, named Keagan, made that remark, and that no such remark is there attributed to Spies. Was testimony of this kind admissible?

But we go a step beyond, to consider the unarmed "armed section" of the American group, of which Johnson testifies *in extenso.* (A., 98, 99.) He describes a meeting at which the suggestion was made that those members of the American group who desired to do so could join the armed section, and that thereupon a number of them, including himself, expressed their willingness to become members thereof. Fielden and Parsons also belonged to it. Several meetings were held at which the members present were put through certain marching maneuvers, *but they were never, in fact, armed; never practiced or drilled with arms.* Johnson also describes an alleged improved dynamite bomb which he claims was exhibited there by the drill-master at the first meeting. Certain it is that the armed section, so-called, was simply *an unarmed body of less than a score of men*—members of the American group—who held, all told, probably not more than half a dozen meetings, in which they drilled simply in marching maneuvers. There is no pretense that this "armed" section without arms called the Haymarket meeting, or plotted the throwing of the bomb or any other violence at the same. This testimony, as all of Johnson's, came in under objection. (A., 95; J, 391.)

(*d.*) Private Conversations of Mr. Spies.

(1.) Luther Moulton and George W. Shook testified that on the 22d of February, 1885, at Grand Rapids, in the State of Michigan, Spies stated, in a conversation with them, that he belonged to an organization whose purpose was the reorganization of society upon a more equitable basis, that the laboring man might have a better and a fairer division of the products of labor; that he expressed no confidence in the ballot as a means to accomplish this end, and stated that force and arms was the only way in which the result could be reached; that they were prepared for such a demonstration in Chicago, and in all the commercial centers of the country; that they had about three thousand men organized in Chicago; that they had superior means of warfare; that they would rapidly gain accessions to their ranks, if they were successful, from the laboring men, to whom they would hold out inducements. The demonstrations would be made when laboring men were idle in large numbers. He thought there might be bloodshed, for that happened frequently in the case of revolution, which might be crime if the revolution failed, but not otherwise. Moulton says that no details were given in regard to the means or mode of warfare, but thinks the term " explosives " was used in connection with arms, though he remembers nothing definite; that nothing was said about the police or militia, except in general terms that they were prepared to successfully resist and destroy such forces. (A., 20, 21.) This testimony came in over the objections and exceptions of the plaintiffs in error, and particularly of those other than Spies, and a motion to exclude it was likewise overruled. *Testimony of declaratory statements made in a private conversation*

*by Spies outside of this state, a year and a quarter before
the Haymarket evening, was here admitted not only as
evidence against Spies, but against all plaintiffs in error.*

(2.) Harry Wilkinson testified (A., 67 *et seq.*) that he
was a reporter for the Chicago Daily News, and in January, 1886, had several interviews with Spies, as a result
of which he wrote up an article published in the Chicago
Daily News of January 14th. He says that he was introduced to Spies for the purposes of that conversation,
which occurred at the Arbeiter Zeitung, by Joseph
Gruenhut. Later Mr. Gruenhut, Mr. Spies and Mr.
Wilkinson went to a restaurant together, where Mr.
Wilkinson set up the wine, and a conversation ensued,
illustrated by Mr. Spies by the use of tooth-picks laid
upon the table-cloth, in which Mr. Spies indicated a policy
of street warfare, much the same as that detailed by an
officer of the United States army as published in the San
Francisco Truth, and republished in the Alarm. (People's
Exhibit 48; 1A., 172.) Among other things Mr. Spies told
him that the socialists in Chicago had a body of very tall
and very strong men, *who could throw five-pound bombs
150 paces with their hands.* He says distinctly he tried to
find out from Spies when the social revolution was to be
inaugurated, but that Spies did not fix any date, either
precisely or approximately. He says, however, that at
another interview Spies said it would probably occur in
the first conflict with the police and militia; that if there
should be an universal strike for the eight-hour system
there would probably be a conflict brought about. He
further states that Spies showed him an empty shell of a
proposed dynamite bomb, which, by Spies' permission,
he carried away and gave to Mr. M. E. Stone, editor of
the Chicago Daily News, who retained the same, and
that shell was introduced in evidence in the case. He

195

further says that Spies spoke of there being a large number of men organized and ready for service in the event of a revolution, and that he got the idea, from what Spies said, that they had a number of thousand bombs ready for use. The witness had advised Mr. Spies, previous to his interviews, that he was assigned to this work by Mr. Stone, editor of the Daily News.

Mr. Joseph Gruenhut, also testified in behalf of the state, and examined as to the same conversation, says (A., 109; K, 59) that the conversation between Wilkinson and Spies was carried on *in an half joking manner*, lasting perhaps a quarter of an hour, while they were taking their supper; and he says distinctly on cross-examination (A., 109; K, 66) that in this conversation *no date was fixed when there was going to begin trouble in Chicago; that Spies' conversation was wholly upon general principles*, and that nothing was said as to any attack about May 1st.

Mr. Spies' version of these conversations with Mr. Wilkinson may be found in his testimony (A., 304–306); he says it was *a general discussion of the possibilities of street warfare under modern science* (A., 306), with no suggestion whatever of any time or place for the inauguration of the conflict with the constituted authorities.

(c.) THE EIGHT-HOUR AGITATION MEETING AT WEST 12TH STREET TURNER HALL.

James K. Magie (A., 23; I, 309 *et seq.*) and H. E. O. Heinemann (A., 30, 31; I, 380 *et seq.*) show that in October, 1885, at a meeting at West 12th street Turner Hall, the intended eight-hour movement was under discussion. Only Spies and Fielden, of the plaintiffs in error, were present. Resolutions were adopted which stated that the probabilities were that the property-owning class would resist any attempt of the laborers to enforce the eight-hour demand, by calling to aid the police and militia, and if the workingmen were determined on carrying their point they would have to arm themselves and be ready to enforce their demands by the same means that the property-owning class would use. The resolution concluded with the sentence: " Death to the " enemies of the human race—our despoilers." Mr. Heinemann expressly says (A., 31; I, 385): " I would " not be certain whether the resolutions stated the time " when this should culminate; the 1st of May was desig- " nated in so far as a commencement of the eight-hour " movement was fixed for that date."

There were about 500 people present, and after full discussion, pro and con, the resolutions were adopted by a very strong vote (A., 24; I., 319, 320.)

That the wage-workers throughout the United States fixed upon the 1st of May, 1886, for the inauguration of the eight-hour movement as early as two years before that date, is historic and furthermore appears from the record. But the above testimony in regard to the resolutions passed at the meeting at West 12th street Turner Hall, and that of Moulton and Wilkinson above considered, was used by the state as a basis for their claim, that the plaintiffs in error were engaged in a conspiracy to inaugurate the social revolution on May 1st.

This claim is too absurd to deserve serious refutation. Perhaps the best answer to it is the reply which Spies gave Wilkinson when he asked him if the anarchists and socialists were going to make a revolution: " Revolutions are " not made by individuals or conspirators, but are simply " the logic of events resting in the condition of things."

(*f.*) THE GENERAL TENDENCY OF THESE UTTERANCES.

There is a vast amount of other testimony concerning speeches and conversations attributed to the various accused, which was admitted in every instance as against all the plaintiffs in error, over their objection and exception, and particularly of those not present at the respective occasions. The worst that can be said of these utterances is that they were full of predictions of an impending conflict between laborers and capitalists, urging the laboring men to prepare for that conflict by arming themselves, advising them to buy guns and revolvers, and particularly commending to them as a weapon for such warfare the latest product of science in the development of explosives, namely, dynamite. But a careful inspection of all these speeches will show that none of them ever counseled an initiation of a conflict by the working people, nor fixed any date, nor designated any place for the bringing on of such contest—the position of the speakers being that the present societary relations were wrong; that the producing classes did not get the share they were entitled to; that the power held by the capitalists was founded upon force; that the capitatists would not, in all probability, yield peaceably to the just demands of the working classes, but in case the latter should insist upon their rights, would call out the militia and police force against them, and that they should be prepared to meet, when that conflict came, force with force, coupled with the suggestion, at times, that if they should thoroughly prepare themselves for the conflict, *they might achieve a bloodless victory*. None of the speeches ever referred directly or indirectly to the meeting of the night of May 4, 1886, or any other particular occasion, or counseled any act of violence, or suggested the use of explosives of any kind at that meeting.

Again, we ask, what has this testimony to do with the issue before the jury? What proper place had it in this record? That such testimony had a tendency to prejudice the jury against plaintiffs in error, or, more properly speaking, to intensify the prejudice with which they entered the jury box, we freely admit, and for this very reason claim that its introduction was material error.

VI. OTHER ILLEGITIMATE EVIDENCE.

Dr. Murphy (A., 152–157), Dr. Lee (A., 163, 164), and Dr. Baxter] (A., 162), were permitted to testify, at great length, to the details of the wounds *and their medical treatment* of a large number of police officers other than Degan, supposed to have been injured or killed by the explosion of the Haymarket bomb, or by pistol-balls. These horrifying details poured into the ears of the jury, through hours of the examination of these witnesses, were calculated to stir their prejudices to such an extent as perhaps to absolutely unsettle the judgment; but certainly no man can claim that this class of testimony had any proper place in the investigation of the issue, which was not the extent of the injuries resulting from the explosion of the bomb, but simply whether the plaintiffs in error were legally responsible for the explosion of that bomb, which confessedly resulted in the death of Mathias J. Degan.

Another illustration of the admission of improper testimony occurred in the examination of Fred. P. Rosback, for the State. Upon his examination the following took place (A., 84, 85; J, 282, 283), viz.:

" Q. What is your business?

" A. Machinist.

" Q. Where is your place of business?

" A. 224 East Washington street.

" Q. Do you know Rudolph Schnaubelt?

" A. Yes, sir.

" Q. Did he work for you?

" A. Yes, sir.

" Q. Do you remember the night of the throwing of
" the bomb?

" A. Yes.

*   *   *   *   *   *   *

" Q. Did you see him on Tuesday?

" A. Yes.

" Q. On Tuesday, when you saw him, did he have a
" beard on?

" A. Yes.

" Q. When did you next see him?

" A. I next saw him Wednesday morning.

" Q. At what hour?

" A. He came to work at 7 o'clock?

" Q. Did he have a beard on that day?
  (Objected to.)

" Mr. GRINNELL: It is for the purpose of identification.
  (Objection overruled; exception.)

" Q. Did he have a beard on on Wednesday?

" A. Yes.

" Q. Did you see him Thursday?

" A. Yes.

" Q. Did he have a beard on then?
  (Objected to; objection overruled, and exception.)

" A. Thursday morning he had his beard shaved off.

" Q. Did he have a mustache on?

" A. He had a mustache, but it was clipped off."

What was the purpose of this examination? Was it for
the purpose of identification, as suggested by the state's
attorney? How was that purpose aided by this examination? Is it not obvious that this evidence served not at
all for the purpose of identification, but that it did serve to
get before the jury the fact that Mr. Schnaubelt, shortly
after the bomb-throwing, shaved his beard and clipped
his mustache, thus suggesting disguise? And if this was
the sole tendency of this evidence, and the natural and obvious tendency thereof, are we not justified in charging
that such was the purpose of its offering, despite the contrary suggestion by the state's attorney, on the familiar
principle that every man is presumed to intend the natural consequences of his action? But whether this result
was intended or not, this evidence was clearly incompetent, upon the familiar principle that no evidence of the
acts of alleged conspirators *post* the crime, are competent
against their supposed co-conspirators. Schnaubelt was
not on trial. The alleged change in his appearance
specially inquired of, even to the point of asking a leading
question, occurred, if at all, as shown by the above tes-
mony, after the night of May 4. It was *grossly* improper
to allow this evidence, and the testimony could not but
have a strong tendency to prejudice the jury. It was evidence that might have been competent against Schnaubelt upon the issue raised by the testimony of Gilmer, had
Schnaubelt been on trial. Its introduction in his absence
cannot be excused.

It is said by Mr. Wharton (Crim. Ev., § 750,) that when
a suspected person attempt to escape or to evade
threatened prosecution, or resorts to flight or acts of disguise, this may be shown as tending to evidence consciousness of guilt; but in § 699 of the same work, he
says:

" When the common enterprise is at an end, whether
" by accomplishment or abandonment, no one of the con-
" spirators is permitted by any subsequent act or declara-
" tion of his own to affect the others. Even the most
" solemn admission made by him after the conspiracy is
" at an end is not evidence against accomplices. Nor can
" the flight of one conspirator after such time be put in
" evidence against the others."

In the case of *People* v. *Stanley*, 47 Cal., 112, the Supreme court of California used the following language:

" It is well settled that the flight of a person suspected
" of a crime is a circumstance to be weighed by the jury,
" as tending in some degree to prove a consciousness of
" guilt, and is entitled to more or less weight according
" to the circumstance of the particular case. Such evi-
" dence is received, ' not as a part of the *res gestæ*, of the
" criminal act itself, but as indicative of a guilty mind.'
" (Roscoe on Criminal Evidence, 18.) At most, it is but
" a circumstance tending to establish a consciousness of
" guilt in the person fleeing; and it would be extending
" the principle to a great length to hold that the flight of
" one person tends to establish the guilt of another person.
" We have been referred to no case which goes to that
" extent." In that case there was a reversal upon the
sole ground that evidence was admitted of the flight of
an alleged co-conspirator.

In support of the general proposition that " when the
" common purpose is at an end, whether by accomplish-
" ment or abandonment, no one of the conspirators is per-
" mitted by any subsequent act or declaration of his own
" to affect the others," we cite, without special comment:

Snowden v. *State*, 7 Baxter, 482.
People v. *Aleck*, 61 Cal., 137.
State v. *Soule*, 14 Nev., 453.

Commonwealth v. *Thompson*, 99 Mass., 444-

State v. *Westfall*, 49 Iowa, 328.

Strady v. *State*, 5 Caldwell, 300.

State v. *Fuller*, 39 Vermont, 74.

Hunter v. *Commonwealth*, 7 Grattan, 641.

Hudson v. *Commonwealth*, 2 Duval, 531 (Ky).

Rueber v. *State*, 25 Ohio State, 464.

People v. *Stevens*, 47 Mich., 411.

People v. *Arnold*, 46 Mich., 68.

Spencer v. *State*, 31 Tex., 64.

Abe v. *State*, 31 Texas, 416.

Commonwealth v. *Ingraham*, 7 Gray, 46.

Ormsbee v. *People*, 53 New York, 472.

Morris v. *State*, 50 Ohio, 439.

State v. *Arnold*, 48 Iowa, 566.

State v. *Rawler*, 65 N. C., 334.

Phillips v. *State*, 6 Tex. Appeal, 314.

We cannot, without unduly extending the limits of this argument, attempt to review in detail all of the testimony which was permitted to be introduced in the prosecution of this cause over the objection of plaintiffs in error, that in our view was illegitimate as being immaterial and irrelevant to the issue before the jury. The specifications of this class of testimony which we have above given were intended to bring into clear relief the general scope of the inquiry which was permitted to be entered upon by the court, and to show how far from the real issue the case was permitted to drift.

OUR POSITIONS UPON THE EVIDENCE ILLEGITI-
MATELY INTRODUCED.

The apparent purpose of the proofs thus specified was to establish a general conspiracy against the law; a plan to bring about a revolution in the order of society—a purpose to change the existing social condition, and to that end, if necessary, to resort to force.

There was no pretense that that testimony tended to show that the commission of the particular crime charged in the indictment was ever arranged for or advised. The claim was that such acts of violence were likely to fall out if an attempt should be made at any time to accomplish the purposes of this general conspiracy or agreement.

I. THERE IS NO RESPONSIBILITY FOR THE ACT OF AN ASSOCIATE IN PURPOSE, BUT NOT IN ACTION.

The evidence tends to show, that all of the plaintiffs in error favored the idea of a change in the order of society, and especially of the abolition of the wage system; and that some of the plaintiffs advocated the use of force, if this should become necessary, in order to bring about that change. The most which all that evidence tends to show, is that there was a community of purpose or desire among the plaintiffs in error in regard to these principles. But the state's own evidence shows that the different plaintiffs in error worked in different directions, under different plans, with different means. And it is a well established principle, that if a body of associates, entertaining a common purpose, start for the attainment of that result by different processes, acting independently of each other in their attempts to reach the common end, *the mere community of purpose or desire does not make the parties entertaining it responsible for the acts of their associates in desire, but not associates in action.* In other words, if a number of persons start out to accomplish a certain end, but afterwards divide their forces, one set adopting one plan to reach that end, without the knowledge or concurrence of the other set, such other set are not responsible for the independent plan or conspiracy of the supposed actors.

Our claim is that the liability of an accessory to the penalties of the law is conditioned upon legal proof that the accessory advised, abetted or encouraged *the perpetration of the particular crime charged,* or engaged in *some felony which,* in contemplation of the law, *involved the particular crime* as a probable result, at the time and under the circumstances of the perpetration of the offense.

The law is well settled that where different parties are engaged in a like conspiracy, but as to the particular act done are proceeding independently and without concert, only the parties to the act can be held responsible for it. In other words, parties cannot be held criminally liable because of sympathy with or participation in a general desire, but only because of aiding, abetting, assisting or encouraging " the perpetration of the crime."

The law upon this subject is well stated in 2 Starkey on Evidence, Part I, Philadelphia Ed. 1842, *324, as follows:

" Where it appeared that there was a conspiracy to " raise war in the North riding of Yorkshire, and that " there was at the same time a conspiracy in the West " riding, in which latter one it took place, and there was " no evidence to show that those in the one riding knew

" of the conspiracy in the other, it was held that the
" former could not be implicated in the acts of the latter,
" although they concurred at the same time to the same
" object."

We think it desirable, in order to show the full scope
of this ruling, to refer to the original text of Kellyng's
Crown Cases on the Law of High Treason, *24, where
the action of the justices upon this case is stated as follows:

" In the next place, we being informed that there was
" a conspiracy to raise a war in the North riding of
" Yorkshire, as well as the West riding, where some did
" actually appear in arms, yet it could not be proved that
" those in the North riding did agree to the rising that
" there was in the West riding, or that they knew any-
" thing about it, and so would not be within the first reso-
" lution," namely, would not be responsible for the acts of
the conspirators in the West riding. To apply the doctrine of this case to the case at bar, even if it should be
conceded that upon the part of all the plaintiffs in error
there was a general unity of design to bring about a revolution in the order of society; yet, if certain of the plaintiffs in error, of their own motion, and without any concert of action or consultation with the other plaintiffs in
error, proceeded to do an act of their own volition, and
upon their own responsibility, which was not at the time
within the contemplation or expectation of the other
plaintiffs in error, such other plaintiffs in error would not
be implicated in the consequences of such independent
act.

Another case which recognizes the same doctrine is that
of *State* v. *Trice*, 88 North Carolina, 627. In that case,
Cuff Trice was indicted, together with Charles Trice and
Mack Cross, for conspiracy to commit rape, and for the

preparation of certain powders to be used in that connection, and for conspiracy and agreement to give such powders to some person to the jurymen unknown. The
evidence tended to show that Cuff Trice did pretend to
be a manufacturer and vendor of powders calculated to
overcome the resistance of women, and that he gave some
of these powders to the co-defendants, telling them at the
same time that by using the powders they could overcome
any woman. There was a verdict and judgment against
the defendants, which was set aside by the court on the
ground, amongst others, that the evidence did not connect
the defendant Cuff Trice with the particular assault made
by Charles Trice upon Fidelia Upchurch or Effie Upchurch, both of whom it was charged Charles Trice attempted to rape. The position taken by the court was,
in effect, that the mere selling of the powder in question,
even when accompanied by a statement of its alleged
purpose, would not make the vendor a party to a crime
subsequently attempted to be committed by the vendee,
nor bring the vendor in as a conspirator with the vendee
in an assault made by the vendee upon some person or
persons unknown to the vendor, and without the vendor's
direct concurrence and advice. [This case, by the way,
fits exactly the facts, upon which alone Louis Lingg was
attempted to be made responsible for the Haymarket
tragedy. Unless it could be shown that he gave a bomb
of his manufacture to a person for the purpose of throwing it at the particular time and place—in other words,
unless he advised and aided "*the perpetration of* THE
crime," he should have been acquitted under the doctrine
laid down in this case.]

II. Evidence of Distinct Substantive Offenses is Inadmissible.

The proof offered and received, under the theory adopted and declared by the trial court, was proof tending to establish a conspiracy, not for the object of using violence at the Haymarket, but one unconnected with that crime. Conspiracy, under our law is a separate and independent crime. The effort made by the State was therefore in effect an effort to convict the plaintiffs in error of the crime charged under this indictment by offering proof that they were parties to a separate crime which did not specially relate to or contemplate the particular crime charged. As applicable to such an effort, we call attention to the statement of the rule, as given in Wharton's Criminal Evidence, §30, where it is said:

"A defendant ought not to be convicted of the offense "charged, simply because he has been guilty of another "offense. Hence, when offered simply for the purpose of "proving his commission of the offense on trial, evidence "of his participation, either in act or design, in commis- "sion or in preparation, in other independent crimes, can- "not be received."

This is laid down as the general rule.

In *Schaffner* v. *The Commonwealth*, 72 Penn. State, 60, the law is thus stated by Agnew, Justice, delivering the opinion of the court:

"It is a general rule that a distinct crime, unconnected "with that laid in the indictment, cannot be given in evi- "dence against a prisoner. It is not proper to raise a "presumption of guilt on the ground that, having com- "mitted one crime, the depravity it exhibits makes it "likely he would commit another. Logically, the com-

" mission of an independent offense is not proof in itself of
" the commission of another crime. Yet, it cannot be said to
" be without influence on the mind, for certainly, if one be
" shown to be guilty of another crime, equally heinous, it
" will prompt a more ready belief that he might have com-
" mitted the one with which he is charged; it therefore pre-
" disposes the mind of the juror to believe the prisoner
" guilty.   To make one criminal act evidence of another,
" the connection between them must have existed in the
" mind of the actor, linking them together for some purpose
" he intended to accomplish; or it must be necessary to
" identify the person of the actor by a connection which
" shows that he who committed the one must have done
" the other.   Without this obvious connection, it is not
" only unjust to the prisoner to compel him to acquit
" himself of two offenses instead of one, but it is detri-
" mental to justice to burthen a trial with multiplied issues
" that tend to confuse and mislead the jury."

This rule has been very strongly laid down by this
court.   It is said in *Kribs* v. *The People*, 82 Ill., 424, as
follows (p. 426):

" On the trial the court allowed the people, over the
" objection of the defendant (who was indicted for em-
" bezzlement), to prove that the defendant had collected or
" received money belonging to other parties, and on several
" occasions, which he had fraudulently converted to his
" own use.   This was error.   The evidence should have
" been confined to the charge for which the defendant was
" indicted.   On the trial of this indictment the law did not
" require him to come prepared to meet other charges,
" nor does it follow, because he may have been guilty of
" other like offenses, that he was guilty of the offense
" charged in the indictment."

" The evidence should have been confined strictly to

" the offense charged in the indictment. This was not,
" however, done, but improper testimony allowed to go
" to the jury, which could not fail to prejudice the rights
" of the defendant."

For the error above indicated alone the case was reversed.

To the same effect, we cite *Watts* v. *The State*, 5 W.
Va., 532.

So in *Devine* v. *The People*, 100 Ill., 290, it is said
(p. 293):

" In view of * * the consideration that the life of the
" accused was involved in the issue, it became highly im-
" portant to him, as well as essential to the due adminis-
" tration of justice in the prosecution of the case, that
" the state should be held to at least a substantial,
" if not a strict observance of the well-established rules
" governing the production of testimony, in its efforts to
" establish the charge against him. The trial should have
" been conducted with the utmost fairness, and no matter
" or thing should have been admitted in evidence, against
" the objections of the accused, which did not prove or
" tend to prove the issue, more especially if the evidence,
" when admitted, would have had an improper influence
" upon the minds of the jury, or place the accused at a
" disadvantage before them."

The same rule was applied in *Sutton* v. *Johnson*, 62
Ill., 209.

Under this head, we desire to quote further from 1
Phillips on Evidence, 765, 766 (p. 644, 5th Am. Ed.):

" In criminal cases, it is purely the duty of courts of
" justice to prevent evidence being given which would
" support a charge against prisoner of which he was not
" previously apprised under the pretext of it supporting
" some presumption of the offense which is the subject of

" the indictment. In treason, therefore, no evidence is to
" be admitted of any overt act that is not expressly laid
" in the indictment. This was the rule at common law.
" It is again prescribed and enforced by the statute of
" William III, which contains an express provision to that
" effect in consequence of some encroachments that had
" been made in several state prosecutions. The meaning
" of the rule is not that the whole detail of facts should
" be set forth, but that no overt act, amounting to a
" distinct, independent charge, though falling under the
" same head of treason, shall be given in evidence, unless
" it be expressly laid in the indictment; but still, not con-
" duced to the proof of any of the overt acts that are
" made, it may be admitted as evidence of such overt
" acts."

While Roscoe, in his work upon criminal evidence, 7th
Am. Ed., § 90, p. 90, thus states the rule:

" It may be laid down, as a general rule, that in criminal
" as in civil cases the evidence shall be confined to the
" point in issue. In criminal proceedings it has been
" observed that the necessity is stronger, if possible, than
" in civil cases of strictly enforcing this rule; for where a
" prisoner is charged with an offense, it is of the utmost
" importance to him that the facts laid before the jury
" shall consist exclusively of the transaction which forms
" the subject of the indictment and matters relating
" thereto, which alone he could be expected to come pre-
" pared to answer."

In *Kinchillow* v. *The State*, 5 Humph., 9, the court say
(p. 12):

" It is well settled that no proof of the admission of one
" distinct substantive offense shall be received upon a trial
" for the commission of another; *a fortiori*, shall not state-
" ments of an intention to commit it; the only tendency of

" such testimony necessarily is to prejudice the minds of
" of a jury, as it can by no possibility establish or eluci-
" date the crime charged."

The same court, in 3 Coldwell's Reports, 362, *Wiley* v.
The State, uses the following language (p. 372): "The
" general rule is that nothing shall be given in evidence
" which does not directly tend to the proof or disproof
" of the matter in issue; and evidence of a distinct sub-
" stantive offense cannot be admitted in support of an-
" other offense."

We think we may here pause for a moment to apply
the rule thus well expressed to the case at bar, and the
improper evidence adverted to. Here is a vast amount
of testimony of speeches, public utterances and publications tending to show the expression of *an intention or
purpose* on the part of some of the plaintiffs in error to
bring about a change in the order of society, and, if needs
be to the accomplishment of that end, to resort to force.
How can these statements of their intent to engage in this
enterprise, which may, for the sake of the argument, be
conceded to be criminal, if purposed to be accomplished
by the use of force, be competent upon an inquiry as to
whether or not these particular parties are responsible
for *the commission of a particular offense at the particular
time and place*, where all the evidence shows there was
no intent or design on the part of any of them to then or
there attempt to carry out their supposed general plan or
illegal design, but where the crime charged is committed by some unknown party, not shown to have been
acting under their advice, direction or encouragement in
the perpetration of the crime. Take, for an illustration,
the testimony of detective Johnson, above quoted, that at
a meeting of the American group, at which an outrage
committed by one Wright upon his servant, a young girl,

was under discussion, Spies said that this was a fine opportunity for one of our young men to shoot Wright; or the testimony of other detectives, that on the night of the board of trade demonstration Parsons said, the next time they would be prepared with dynamite, and many such alleged expressions of an intention to do unlawful acts in the future. Can we not say, adopting the language of the Supreme court of Tennessee just quoted, "the only tendency of such testimony necessarily is to "prejudice the minds of the jury, as it can by no possibil- "ity establish or elucidate the crime charged?"

III. A prima facie Conspiracy must be estab-lished before the Acts and Declarations of an alleged Co-conspirator can be Evidence against another.

In the case of the *State* v. *George*, 7 Ired., 321, where acts and declarations of a party other than the defendant were allowed to be introduced against him, upon the statement made by the prosecutor that he intended to in-troduce witnesses to prove a conspiracy between the pris-oner and such third person, a reversal was ordered upon this ground. Separate but concurring opinions were submitted by different members of the court. We quote, as, perhaps, one of the best expositions of the law upon this point, from the opinion of Ruffin, Chief Justice, com-mencing at page 328 of the report:

"I think there ought to be a *venire de novo* upon the "ground, simply, that the acts and declarations of the "woman, which were given in evidence, are not of such "a nature as can affect the prisoner. To make the acts "and declarations of one prisoner those of another, or to "allow them to operate against another, *it must appear*

" that there was a common interest or purpose between
" them; as applied to the case before us, *that there was*
" *a conspiracy to murder* the deceased formed between
his wife and the prisoner.

In further support of this proposition we cite Roscoe's
Criminal Evidence (7 Am. Ed., 1874, § 417, p. 416).
The learned author there speaks as follows: " Supposing
" that the existence of a conspiracy may in the first in-
" stance be proved, without showing the participation or
" knowledge of the defendants, *it is still a question whether*
" *the declarations of some of the persons engaged in the*
" *conspiracy may be given in evidence against others, in*
" *order to prove its existence;* and upon principle such
" evidence appears to be inadmissible."

Mr. Roscoe then further says (same Ed., p. 417, § 418)
as follows: " *After the existence of a conspiracy is estab-*
" *lished and the particular defendants have been proved to*
" *have been parties to it,* the acts of other conspirators
" may in all cases be given in evidence against them, if
" done in furtherance of the common object of the con-
" spiracy, as also may letters written and declarations
" made by other conspirators, if they are part of the *res*
" *gestæ* of the conspiracy and no mere admissions."

See further on this point, 1 Greenleaf, Evid., § 111.

That the erroneous introduction of evidence is not
cured by its subsequent exclusion was decided in *Howe*
v. *Rosine*, 87 Ill., 105.

IV. ACTS AND DECLARATIONS OF AN ALLEGED CO-
CONSPIRATOR, TO BE EVIDENCE AGAINST ANOTHER, MUST
BE IN THE PROSECUTION OF THE CRIMINAL CONSPIRACY.

In *People* v. *Stanley*, 47 Cal., 113, the court used the
following language (p. 118):

" The rule is well settled that the acts of an accomplice

" are not evidence against the accused, unless they con-
" stitute part of the *res gestæ*, and occur during the pend-
" ency of the criminal enterprise, and are in furtherance
" of its objects."

In *State* v. *George*, 7 Ired., 321, the court say:

" Before the acts and declarations of one of the conspira-
" tors can be received against another, it must be shown
" that they were acts done and declarations uttered in
" furtherance of the common design, or in execution of
" the conspiracy. They must be acts and declarations of
" the one that were authorized by the other, or such
" as became necessary in the prosecution of the joint
" business or criminal conspiracy."

In *Rex* v. *Hardy*, 25th State Trials, 1, the majority of
the judges held that a letter purported to be written from
one alleged conspirator to another was not admissible in
evidence save as against the party writing it, using the
following language: " A bare relation of facts by an
" alleged conspirator to a stranger was merely an admis-
" sion which might affect himself, but which could not
" affect a co-conspirator, since it was not an act done in
" the prosecution of that conspiracy." This rule is approved by Mr. Starkie in his valuable work on evidence,
2d ed., vol. 2, page 326.

Concerning the propriety of this rule there can be nc
question or doubt whatever. In the light of this rule, how
stands the action of the court in allowing the introduction
into the record of bombs, tin cans filled with explosive
material, and other materials of that sort, found long after
the Haymarket meeting? There is no evidence by whom
these instruments were manufactured, and it cannot be
presumed that they were manufactured by some parties
to a conspiracy in which the plaintiffs in error were implicated, and had been manufactured for use in carrying

out the purposes of that conspiracy. Besides, they were found *weeks after the 4th of May*, and for all that appears in the record, such manufacture may have been after the occurrences of the 4th of May. Can it be said, that this was evidence of " acts of accomplices," and can it be claimed that the manufacture and secretion of the articles occurred " during the pendency of a criminal en-" terprise, and in furtherance of its objects? "

How, in the light of this rule, stands the introduction of evidence *against all plaintiffs in error* of the testimony as to Mr. Spies' conduct and utterances at Grand Rapids, or as to his conversations with the reporter Wilkinson in January, 1886? A declaration made by Spies, more than a year before the Haymarket meeting, outside of this state, or a private conversation with a reporter at the dinner table, months before the 4th of May, and in either instance *merely narrative of what had or would be done*, certainly constitute no part of the *res gestae*, and were not in furtherance of the objects of the alleged criminal enterprise. Is not such talk as that to Wilkinson, who was at the time engaged in securing the material for an article in the News of Chicago, the very thing to frustrate any criminal design, if such an one had existed?

A further illustration of the disregard of the above rule, is the evidence of Rosback as to the change in Schnau-belt's appearance made by the shaving of his beard *two days after the Haymarket meeting*. Was this the act of an accomplice "during the pendency of the criminal en-terprise," was it part of the *res gestae*, was it in further-ance of the objects of the alleged criminal enterprise?

Or the admission of evidence, with which the record abounds, as to the utterances and writings of third par-ties, not attempted by the evidence to be connected in any manner with the alleged conspiracy? For example, the introduction in evidence of the platform of the International Workingpeople's Association; or of the translation of Herr Most's book? Under the law, as above declared, all this testimony was clearly incompetent, especially in the manner in which it was permitted to come in by the court, to wit, as against all the plaintiffs in error.

The errors of the court in the rulings in reference to the admissibility of the evidence were the more flagrant in this case, in our judgment, in view of the fact that upon an application formally made to the court, a separate trial asked for on behalf of four of the plaintiffs in error, in the first instance, namely, Spies, Schwab, Fielden and Neebe, and a like application on behalf of Parsons when he came into court and presented himself at the bar for trial, were denied. The motion for separate trial first interposed was supported by affidavits, and was substantially as set forth in pages 4 and 5 of Vol. 1 of the abstract. The grounds for the application for a separate trial were:

First. That the testimony against them would be materially different from that against the other defendants with whom they were jointly indicted.

Second. Testimony which might be competent against their co-defendants might be incompetent and prejudicial as to them.

Third. That they were advised that evidence of an alleged conspiracy would be introduced, with which said petitioners were not connected.

Fourth. That their defense would be imperiled by such testimony because of its length.

Fifth. That they were advised that illegitimate evidence would be submitted to the jury with regard to an alleged conspiracy, which might be competent as against their co-defendants.

Sixth. That they did not believe that they could have a fair and impartial trial jointly with their co-defendants.

The affidavit of Spies, Fielden, Schwab and Neebe showed upon information that upon the trial the prosecution intended to introduce evidence to show that some of the defendants participated in a meeting held May 2d, and in a meeting held May 3d, in which it was agreed that violence might or would be used thereafter, and that it would be claimed that Degan's death was caused by such conspiracy; that affiants had been furnished with a list of over a hundred witnesses, from which it was apprehended that the trial would be very protracted; that if the great mass of testimony was brought in, it would be impossible for the jury to intelligently keep the testimony, as applicable to them, separate from that which might be applicable to their co-defendants; and that by a separate trial alone could they be sure of securing an impartial trial. To this was appended the affidavit of counsel for the plaintiffs in error, that they believed the statements of the foregoing affidavit to be true.

This motion for a separate trial was overruled, to which the plaintiffs excepted. It seems to us that it cannot be necessary to argue at any great length that the plaintiffs in error who joined in this application were entitled to have the same granted, and that the denial to grant them was error.

It is true that the matter of a separate trial, while secured in many states by legislation as a right to a prisoner in pursuance of what is believed to be an enlightened and humane policy, is declared, in this state, to be a matter of discretion. But here, as always, the discretion means not an arbitrary choice by the judge, but the exercise of a sound, and, under the circumstances, fair judgment upon the application made, and the case as presented.

In the case of *White* v. *The People*, 81 Ill., 333, the court, in reversing the judgment, remanded the cause with directions to give the parties charged separate trials, using this language: "This is a case wherein it is eminently fit "that these plaintiffs in error should have separate trials."

The rule is laid down in Wharton's Criminal Proceedings and Practice, 8th Ed., Sec. 302, that where offenses are necessarily several, there can be no joinder, and among cases illustrating the text, he cites:

"If A and B are jointly indicted and tried for gaming, "and the evidence shows A and others played at one time "when B was not present, and that B and others played "at a time when A was not present, no conviction can be "had against them. If also the offense charged does not "fully arise through the joint act of all the defendants, "but from some personal or particular act or omission of "each defendant, the indictment must charge them sev- "erally and not jointly."

To the same effect we cite: *People* v. *Vermilyea*, 7 Cowan, *108.

Certainly much of the testimony in this record, which was introduced as against all of the plaintiffs in error, cannot be reasonably claimed to be relevant or competent as against certain of the plaintiffs in error. Take for instance the testimony introduced by the state in reference to the Emma street meeting, so-called, and the Monday night meeting conspiracy, so-called, at which Fischer and Engel are shown to have been present, but none of the other parties; and where a distinct line of policy or action was agreed upon to which none other of the plaintiffs in error are shown ever to have given their assent. Whether or not this testimony was relevant to the issue before the jury, and therefore admissible even as against Fischer and Engel, certainly it was not competent as against the other plaintiffs in error. It was testimony calculated to prejudice the jury, and under all the circumstances calculated to prejudice their cause seriously. It seems to us there can be no doubt whatever that the case was one where separate trials should have been ordered upon the application presented to the court, and that there was error in the action of the court in this respect.

THE COURT ERRED IN HIS RULING UPON THE MOTION, AT THE CLOSE OF THE STATE'S CASE, FOR AN INSTRUCTION TO THE JURY TO FIND OSCAR NEEBE AND OTHER OF THE PLAINTIFFS IN ERROR NOT GUILTY.

I. THE MOTION IN BEHALF OF OSCAR NEEBE.

At the time this motion was submitted, the only evidence in the record against Oscar Neebe tended to establish these and no other facts:

(1.) That Neebe was an acquaintance of certain other of the plaintiffs in error, and was met by the witness Gruenhut on different occasions at the office of the Arbeiter Zeitung, when there was under discussion the organization of certain unorganized trades for the eight-hour movement in the city of Chicago.

(2.) The testimony of Franz Hein (A., 71, 72), that on the night of May 3, 1886, Neebe came into his saloon between 9 and 10 o'clock, showed him a copy of the Revenge circular, and laid some upon the counter and some upon the table, asking the witness if he had heard about the McCormick riot. Witness responded that he had. Thereupon Neebe said, " It is a shame the police act that way, but may be the time comes that it goes the other way— that they get the chance, too." Neebe said: "That is just printed now," when he came in, and that he had got the circulars at Turner Hall, where he had attended a brewers' meeting. He stayed five or ten minutes, drank some beer, and left.

(3.)   Detective Marks (A., 138) testified that about 10 A. M., on the 5th of May, he visited the Arbeiter Zeitung building, met Neebe on the second floor, and asked who had charge of the office, to which Neebe replied, " I am in charge in the absence of Mr. Spies and Schwab" (who had then been arrested).   Upon Marks' suggestion that he would go upstairs and make a search of the floor, Neebe responded, " All right, you can go, but you will not find anything there but papers and writing materials." Marks went up, and says he found, in one of the closets, a package of loose dynamite; he put it on a chair, and asked Neebe what it was, to which Neebe replied that he didn't know, but guessed it was for cleaning type.

Detective Haas testified (A., 81) that when he went to the Arbeiter Zeitung office on May 5th, he found Neebe in charge of the office, and Mayor Harrison in conversation with him there; that the mayor asked who was in charge, to which Neebe replied, " I am in charge, or will take charge in the absence of Spies and Schwab." He swears that he then went up on the third floor, and was *present when Officer Marks placed the alleged package of dynamite just found on a chair in the center of the room, but does not pretend that Neebe was present, or made the remark* that he guessed the material found was for cleaning type, from which we feel justified in arguing that this alleged remark by Neebe was never in fact made.

(4.)   Officer John Stift (A., 170) says that he was at the house of Neebe, on the 7th of May, and there

found a thirty-eight caliber Colt's pistol, a sword, a breech-
loading gun, and a red flag. On cross-examination he
admitted that the gun may have been a sporting gun.

(5.) A number of other witnesses stated that they
knew Neebe (!).

(6.) It appeared from the testimony of Fricke (A., 41),
Henry E. O. Heineman (A., 126) and Seliger (A., 49)
that Neebe was at one time a member of the north side
group of the International Workingpeople's Association.

(7.) Fricke testifies (A., 41) that Neebe belongs to
the corporation publishing the Arbeiter Zeitung, and that
the witness had seen him at picnics and in the Arbeiter
Zeitung office.

Up to the time of the motion to have the jury instructed
to bring in a verdict of not guilty as to Neebe, the above
is, we believe, a fair presentation of all the testimony in
the record against him. There was no evidence showing
or tending to show that he attended the Haymarket meeting or knew of it or of the purpose of holding it, or was
a party to any agreement that violence of any kind should
be used on this or on any other occasion.

Upon these facts the motion was urged for this instruction in his behalf, and that he should not be put to his defense, or further jeopardized in the case. In reference to
the action of the court upon this motion we desire to call
particular attention to the record.

First of all, counsel for plaintiffs in error suggested
that they wished to make a motion which they desired to
argue to the court, and to that end requested that the jury
might be sent from the room pending the argument. The
court refused this application, and required that any motion should be made and argued in the presence of the
jury, to which ruling an exception was preserved. Thereupon the motion was made, and attention was called to

the want of evidence connecting Mr. Neebe in anywise with the crime committed at the Haymarket. The court undertook to argue this question with counsel, and in doing so made use of certain expressions and suggestions which in our opinion were highly improper, and tended to the manifest prejudice of Mr. Neebe, as well as of the other plaintiffs in error. (A., 172, 173; L, 1 to 25.) Amongst other things, the court said: " There is tes-" timony from which the state will be permitted to urge " upon the jury that he (Neebe) presided at meetings at " which some of the speeches were made *urging the kill-*" *ing of people.*" . We maintain that that statement of the court was utterly unsupported in the record. There was a statement in the report of a meeting published in one of the papers which the court permitted to be read, that Neebe presided at such a meeting, but it was not a meeting where speeches were made " urging the killing of " people," and such a report read from a paper was not evidence showing, nor even tending to show—not evidence from which the state would be " permitted to urge " upon the jury " that Neebe in fact presided at that meeting. Aside from this, even if there had been such evidence, would it be material to the issue?

The court, further proceeding, said: " Is there not evi-" dence in the case from which the state will be permitted " to urge upon the jury that he, without being an active " man in the Arbeiter Zeitung, yet was interested in it, " and it was published with his co-operation and consent, " and that, therefore, what was contained in it received " his assent? What inference can they urge upon this " jury from the testimony, that when the officers went " there after he was in charge, and asked who " was in charge, he replied that he supposed that " in the absence of Spies and Schwab he was in charge?

" Whether he had anything to do with the dissemina-
" tion of advice to commit murder is, I think, a debata-
" ble question which the jury ought to pass upon." Can
the making of such a remark as this, in the presence of
the jury, be excused or justified for one moment? It
practically assumes that the Arbeiter Zeitung was engaged in "the dissemination of advice to commit mur-
" der," and then expresses the opinion to the jury that it
was debatable upon the evidence, whether or not Mr.
Neebe had anything to do with the dissemination of such
advice.

Evidence of "advice to commit murder," or its dissemination, would, we respectfully submit, be wholly irrelevant, without evidence tending to show advice to commit
the murder charged in the indictment. In other words,
to put our case strongly, we submit that a man might
stand upon the street corners of a populous city and
cry "kill, kill, kill, murder, murder, murder," by the
hour, day and week, without making himself thereby
criminally responsible for some murder committed by
some unknown party not connected by the evidence with
him in any manner whatever. If the question of the dissemination of "advice to commit murder," in the general
terms stated by the court, was not a question legally relevant to the issue before the jury, then whether Neebe
had anything to do with the dissemination of such advice
was not "a debatable question which the jury ought to
" pass upon." The question, and the only question,
which the jury were to pass upon was whether Mr.
Neebe advised the commission of the murder charged in
the indictment, and not whether " he had anything to do
" with the dissemination of advice to commit murder."

Besides, is a man who has a property interest in a paper responsible for everything published therein? And

can anything be urged from the fact that Neebe took charge of the Arbeiter Zeitung office after the arrest of Schwab and Spies, except that he was interested in preserving the property of the corporation, to which he belonged, at a time when the police were unlawfully trespassing upon its premises?

Then the following took place (L, 21):

"The COURT: If it depended upon prior knowledge and "participation at the Haymarket meeting, the question "would be quite different; but if there is *general advice to* "*commit murder, the time and occasion not being foreseen,* "*the adviser is guilty when it* (*!*) *is committed.*"

The impropriety of this observation of the court in connection with this motion, in the presence of the jury, with the inevitable tendency that it would have to impress upon the minds of the jury the conviction that the court believed that Mr. Neebe had been a party to advise to commit the Haymarket murder, and was responsible therefor, cannot be overstated. As to the viciousness of the principle here announced by Judge Gary as the law we shall have occasion to speak further on in considering the instructions given by the court. For the present we beg to say, with all due respect, that the suggestions of the court in the course of the argument of this motion in Mr. Neebe's behalf, and in ruling upon it, constituted a specious and improper argument, calculated to influence the jury, and to prejudice their minds against Mr. Neebe by suggestions having no support in any legal evidence in the case, and that were utterly unwarranted by any accredited theory of law. We maintain that there was no evidence in the record at the close of the case attempted to be made by the state which called upon Mr. Neebe to enter upon his defense, or which justified his retention for one moment in the case at the hazard of his life. The motion should have been granted, and its refusal was palpable error.

The attitude thus assumed by the presiding judge as to Mr. Neebe was maintained to the end of the case. No further inculpatory evidence affecting Mr. Neebe being brought out in the presentation of the case of the plaintiffs in error, the following instructions were asked on his behalf, viz. (1 A., 18; O, 18):

" 22.   The fact, if such is the fact, that the defendant
" Neebe circulated or distributed or handled a few copies
" of the so-called Revenge circular, and while doing so
" said substantially: 'Six workmen have been killed at
" McCormick's last night by the police; perhaps the time
" will 'come when it may go the other way,' is not of
" itself sufficient to connect him with the killing of De-
" gan, nor is the fact that he had in his house a red flag,
" a gun, a revolver and a sword sufficient, even when
" taken together with the other statement contained in
" this instruction, to connect said Neebe with the act
" which resulted in the death of Degan, as charged in
" this indictment.

" 23.   There has not been introduced any evidence in
" this case to either show that the defendant Neebe, by
" any declaration, either spoken or written, has advised
" or encouraged the use of violence or the doing of any
" act in any way connected with the offense at the Hay-
" market, at which Degan was killed; nor is there any
" evidence that he was engaged at any time in any con-
" spiracy to do any unlawful act, or the doing of any act
" in an unlawful manner, in the furtherance of which said
" Degan was killed, and therefore the state has not es-
" tablished any case as against the defendant Neebe, and
" you are therefore instructed to render a verdict of not
" guilty as to him.

" 24. The jury are instructed to return a verdict of
" not guilty as to the defendant Neebe."

These instructions, we maintain, fairly brought to the
attention of the jury all the evidence, legitimate and
irrevelant, tending to inculpate Mr. Neebe, and charged
that such evidence was not sufficient to sustain a verdict.
Can there be any doubt as to this? If not, then the
charge asked, that the jury should acquit him, ought to
have been given, and the refusal to do so was clearly erroneous, resulting in the jeopardizing of his life unjustly,
and in a verdict and judgment unrighteously to take away
his liberty for fifteen years. We believe that no sufficient
excuse for this action of the court can be advanced.

II. THE MOTION IN BEHALF OF THE OTHER PLAINTIFFS IN ERROR, EXCEPT SPIES AND FISCHER.

After the motion in behalf of Mr. Neebe, above considered, had been argued and ruled upon, a motion was
made to the court to instruct the jury to find a verdict of
not guilty as to all the defendants except Spies and
Fischer, which motion was overruled, and an exception
saved. (A., 173; L, 25.)

When the state's case closed there had been an
attempt made to establish by proof three distinct offenses:

(1.) A general purpose or design, even to the extent
of using violence, for the bringing about of a change in
the order of society, in which all plaintiffs in error except·
Neebe participated.

(2.) A particular agreement entered into, on the
night of Monday, May 3d, to take particular action in
certain specified contingencies, to which only Fischer and
Engel were parties.

(3.) A combination between Spies, Schnaubelt and Fischer, on the night of May 4, 1886, in the throwing of the bomb which resulted in the death of Degan.

There was no evidence to show any inter-relation between these three distinct offenses; and no evidence to show that any of the plaintiffs in error other than Spies and Fischer were parties to the combination to throw the bomb, to perpetrate the crime charged in the indictment. We maintain that the state could have no right to experiment in this condition of the case—to rely upon the proof introduced tending directly to implicate Spies and Fischer, and at the same time rely upon proofs introduced attempting to involve Fischer and Engel on the ground of a distinct conspiracy, and all of the plaintiffs in error on the ground of the " general combination," which, too, was distinct and separate from, and unconnected by the evidence with, the combination of May 4th.

As to each of these issues the respective plaintiffs in error had a right to a trial disembarrassed of the consideration of the other special issues, with which they were not respectively connected by the evidence, and upon our motion above referred to it was the duty of the court to put the state to its election, and, upon election, to exclude all the evidence of the other distinct offenses.

In the case of *Baker* v. *The People*, 105 Ill., 452, there was an indictment charging Clarence Baker and Eliza Graves with the crime of attempting to procure and produce the miscarriage of Martha Van Antwerp, and there was a verdict and judgment of guilty. In that case there was the positive testimony of the prosecutrix, Van Antwerp, that she had had carnal intercourse with the defendant Baker; that he procured a bottle of medicine for the purpose of producing a miscarriage, and thereafter inserted a wire into her body with a hook upon the and. This evidence was admitted over the objection of the plaintiffs in error. There was further testimony to the effect that, these efforts at abortion having proved ineffective, the prosecutrix, under the advice of Baker, went with him to Eliza Graves, by whom the abortion was subsequently produced.

Upon this state of the case, upon a writ of error sued out by Baker, who was inculpated by all the evidence, this court held as follows, viz:

" It may be observed, in conclusion, at the close of the
" testimony, when it affirmatively appeared that Eliza
" Graves was in no manner connected with the transac-
" tion at the residence of the prosecutrix, in which she
" claims a wire was used by defendant Baker alone, *the
" people should have been put to their election*, whether
" they would proceed against Baker alone for using the
" wire, or against them both for what occurred at the
" house of defendant Graves. Assuming the evidence of
" the prosecutrix to be true, it established two offenses:
" One committed by Baker alone, and the other by him
" and Mrs. Graves jointly; and if the prosecution elected
" to proceed for the latter offense, *all evidence of the for-
" mer should have been excluded from the jury*, as it is
" well settled that *upon the trial of a party for one offense,
" growing out of a specific transaction, you cannot prove
" a similar substantive offense founded upon another and
" separate transaction*, but in such case the prosecution
" will be put to its election.   *   *   *   For the error in-
" dicated in the judgment of the court below, the judg-
" ment will be reversed and the cause remanded for fur-
" ther proceedings."

In *Womack* v. *The State*, 7 Coldwell's Reports, 508, the doctrine is laid down that where the indictment charges a single felony, but the proof shows two distinct felonies to have been committed, as, for example, the felonious killing of two men by one shot, the intent to kill one of the men being distinct and separate from the intent to kill the other, then the State will be required to confine its testimony to one of the felonies; or, if testimony as to the other felony necessarily comes in in connection with the testimony as to the one, then the court would instruct the jury to confine their verdict to the issue as to one felony, and *to disregard all testimony except that bearing upon the one felony considered.*

The effect of a granting of the motions interposed at the close of the state's case would have been to give to the different plaintiffs in error, apparently involved by the state's proof in these different alleged offenses, the benefit of a separate trial, to which, upon the evidence then in the record, they were most certainly entitled.

That our objection is well taken here is evidenced, first, by the fact that a motion for a separate trial in behalf of certain of the plaintiffs in error was aptly presented but overruled; and, second, from the further fact that the law awards to a defendant upon his motion for a new trial the benefit of every point of this character. (Wharton's Criminal Pleadings and Practice, Sec. 874.)

In *People* v. *Vermilyea*, 7 Cowan, *108, the rule in reference to cases of this character is thus stated by Mr. Justice WOODWARD (139), the rule in New York being the same as in our own State, that the granting of separate trials lies in the sound discretion of the court:

" I concur with the chief justice in his remark upon Mr. " Barker's motion, and particularly in the suggestion upon " the question of severance. We do not consider the case " before us for the purpose of deciding what the judge should " do in the exercise of that discretion which he undoubtedly " possesses. But I clearly hold, that were I presiding at the

" trial of a criminal charge against persons jointly indicted,
" but wholly disconnected in the acts through which they
" are sought to be convicted, on ascertaining that fact, I
" should deem it *my duty* to grant them separate trials."

In *State* v. *Roulstone*, 3 Sneed's Reports, 107, it was
held that two defendants cannot be jointly indicted for an
offense in its nature necessarily individual, as, for example, the uttering of obscene or libelous language, where
each offender must answer for his own act. In presenting
the rule, the court states (p. 109) that the duplicity in criminal proceedings, which is prohibited by the rule of law,
" consists in including two different and distinct crimes in
" the same count, or more than one person in a count where
" the acts charged were in fact several, or in their nature
" incapable of unity of agency." As applicable to the
case at bar, where is charged the single offense of murder,
and where the testimony in behalf of the state, if believed
to be true, proved the actual commission of the offense by
the separate and concurrent act of the plaintiffs in error,
Spies and Fischer, without showing any concert between
them and the other plaintiffs in error, or showing that their
act, then and there committed, was done under the aid,
advice, encouragement or counsel of the other plaintiffs in
error; in other words, where the testimony, if believed,
established the guilt of two of the plaintiffs in error, by
virtue of a several and independent act, disconnected from
the remaining plaintiffs in error, there should have been a
severance, which would have been accomplished by the
granting of the motion made; and it was error to require
the plaintiffs in error, other than Fischer and Spies, to
meet the effect in the minds of the jury of the particular
testimony as to their separate and independent acts.

B. ERRORS COMPLAINED OF.

We have thus far argued in support of our contention that, upon this record, the plaintiffs in error are not guilty. We have considered this case upon what we believe to be the legitimate evidence introduced, and have also reviewed measurably the illegitimate evidence, calling attention to the errors obtaining in connection with the introduction thereof. We have shown that even upon this illegitimate evidence the state failed to make a just claim to a conviction, under the law applicable to the case, we have further considered the erroneous action of the court in refusing to grant our motions interposed at the close of the evidence offered in behalf of the state, and have called special attention to the errors of the court in refusing the instructions having particular reference to the plaintiffs in error, Louis Lingg and Oscar Neebe.•

We come now to the consideration of the errors committed by the court on the trial other than those considered in connection with our review of the evidence. This field of review embraces, as its principal features, the errors committed by the court in the matter of the instructions, given and refused; the errors obtaining in connection with the empaneling of the jury; the improper remarks of the court; the improprieties of the closing argument of the state's attorney, and the errors obtaining after the verdict. To this branch of the case we most earnestly ask the court's patient attention; satisfied of our ability to demonstrate the truth of the proposition that under all of the above heads our clients have been aggrieved by material error appearing of record.

AA. ERRORS IN THE MATTER OF INSTRUCTIONS.

SUMMARY OF OUR COMPLAINTS.

First. In the instructions given in behalf of the people and in the refusal of certain of those by the defendants, the court proceeded upon the erroneous theory that parties not present at and aiding the perpetration of the crime, may be held as accessories on the ground of *prior* advice and aid, without the State being required to in any manner identify the criminal actor.

Second. The instructions given in behalf of the people with reference to finding the defendants guilty as accessories to an *unknown* principal, were further erroneous, in view of the fact that the evidence offered by the State tended to identify the bomb-thrower as *Rudolph Schnaubelt.* The people's instructions should have conformed to their evidence.

Third. The court based a number of instructions on hypotheses unwarranted by any evidence.

Fourth. The instructions given for the people were erroneous in assuming that there is *in law* such a thing as advice to commit *murder*, without designating the victim, time, place or occasion; in other words, that mere *general advice* to the public at large to commit deeds of violence, as contained in speeches or publications, without reference to the particular crime charged, and without specifying object, manner, time or place, works responsibility as for murder.

Fifth. In the most vital instruction given on behalf of the People, to which we shall call particular attention further on, there was the fatal error of an *omission of all reference to the evidence.*

Sixth. The instructions given for the people in regard to what constitutes reasonable doubt were erroneous.

Seventh. The instruction to the jury limiting their right to judge of the law was erroneous.

Eighth. The court refused to give an instruction allowing the jury to consider whether the bomb in question might not have been thrown by some unknown person under some sudden provocation, by reason of a supposed unlawful attack by the police upon a peaceable and lawful assemblage, without the knowledge, aid, counsel, procurement or encouragement of the plaintiffs in error, or any of them.

Ninth. After giving the instructions which were given on behalf of the people, and such instructions as were given on behalf of the defendants, the court, of its own motion, gave an instruction in which he undertook to summarize and condense all of the instructions in the case. But this instruction was fatally defective under the rule laid down by this court, in that it wholly failed to present all the law of the case fully and correctly.

Tenth. The instruction given by the court in reference to the form of the verdict, which was given as the last of the entire series, was fatally defective in that it left to the jury no alternative but to find the defendants, respectively, guilty of *murder*, in manner and form as charged in this indictment, or to acquit them.

Eleventh. The instructions given for the state are bad for duplicity in presenting different theories of a supposed conspiracy, and certain of those instructions are repugnant and inconsistent in themselves.

I. The Necessity of Identifying the Principal in
the case at Bar.

In order to illustrate our complaint in this regard, we
beg to call attention to instruction 4 given for the state,
which is as follows (1 A., 7; O, 3):

" The court further instructs the jury, as a matter of law,
that if they believe from the evidence in this case, beyond
a reasonable doubt, that the defendants, or any of them,
conspired and agreed together, or with others, to overthrow the law by force, or to unlawfully resist the officers
of the law, and if they further believe from the evidence,
beyond a reasonable doubt, that in pursuance of such conspiracy, and in furtherance of the common object, a bomb
was thrown *by a member of such conspiracy* at the time,
and that Mathias J. Degan was killed, then such of the
defendants that the jury believe from the evidence, beyond
a reasonable doubt, to have been parties to such conspiracy, are guilty of murder, *whether present at the killing or
not, and whether the identity of the person throwing the
bomb be established or not.*"

It will appear from this instruction, as in fact from all instructions given for the people, that the state entirely
abandoned the theory that *Rudolph Schnaubelt* threw
the bomb, and that the plaintiffs in error were accessories
before the fact to *his* crime. The instructions will be
searched in vain for even the slightest allusion to Gilmer's
testimony, *the only evidence in the case by which the identity of the bomb-thrower was sought to be established,*
but the theory adopted was that the bomb was thrown
by an *unknown, undescribed, unidentified, unindividuated
person.* So instruction 4 says: "whether the *identity* of
the person throwing the bomb *be established or not.*" In-

struction 5½ says: " All of such conspirators are guilty of " such murder, whether the person who perpetrated such " murder *can be identified or not*," etc. With the abandonment of the theory that Rudolph Schnaubelt threw the bomb, the theory that Adolph Fischer and August Spies stood by and aided him was given up; and nothing contained in any of the instructions in the slightest degree indicates that that part of the evidence was relied upon by the state. From this it follows that the instructions called upon the jury to find the plaintiffs in error guilty on the ground of having, without being present at the time and place of the bomb-throwing, theretofore advised, encouraged, aided or abetted *an unknown, unidentified person* in the perpetration of that crime.

There can be no conviction under our statute of a party as an accessory before the fact, without legal *proof* showing a *causal relationship* between such alleged accessory and the principal in the offense.

Where the evidence shows the accused present and aiding, abetting or assisting the perpetration of the crime, such causal relationship sufficiently appears without proving the hand that did the act. But where a party is sought to be held on the sole ground of alleged *prior* advice, assistance, abetting or encouragement, such causal relationship can, in the nature of things, only be established by identifying the criminal actor; not necessarily by name or minute description, but the fact that he is the same person who was, at another time and place, advised, encouraged, etc., by the accused, must be shown by legal proof; the principal must be individuated, otherwise the hypothesis of the criminal actor being some person wholly unconnected with the accused is not excluded. In such a case the jury would be allowed to *guess* that the criminal actor was a person advised and assisted beforehand by the accused, and to *presume* the guilt of the defendant.

To illustrate our position. If A, the defendant, is present, and aiding X (the unknown, undescribed, unidentified principal actor) in the throwing of a bomb into a squad of police, this is sufficient to establish his guilt as accessory. But suppose that A advises C, D and E to throw a bomb into the police at a future time, and afterwards, *without* his being present, aiding or assisting, *somebody* throws a bomb among the police: now, unless it be shown that the *somebody* was either C, D or E, how can it be said that A advised or aided *him?* In other words, if the *somebody* is an entirely unknown, undescribed, unidentified, unindividuated person, an essential element in the chain of evidence connecting the defendant with the bomb-throwing is lacking. X, the unknown criminal actor, may have been a person who acted independently of A, unadvised, unassisted by him. We do not claim that the bomb-thrower must be described by name or details of personality, but sufficient must appear to establish his identity as *one* of the parties *shown* to have been advised and aided, etc., by A.

In reply to this contention upon our part it will doubtless be urged that the jury were, under the instructions, required to find that the bomb-thrower was a member of the alleged conspiracy, as a condition of finding the guilt of the accused; membership in the supposed conspiracy being advanced as in law the equivalent of that aid advice, assistance, etc., laid in the indictment. But our reply is that this general feature of these instructions does not help out the case of the people, for the reason that *membership in the supposed conspiracy could not be proved without some evidence of identification.* It cannot be proved that an altogether unidentified, undescribed, unindividuated person is a member of a band of conspirators. It is not a case where the membership of the criminal actor in the supposed conspiracy can be proved simply by showing the commission of such a crime as contemplated by the supposed conspirators. And in this case to tell the jury that any identification of the criminal actor in the Haymarket tragedy was unnecessary, was to tell them that if they found a conspiracy and then a crime, such as planned by that conspiracy, they might *guess* that the character of the crime sufficiently proved that the criminal actor was one of the conspirators. To illustrate our position:

Suppose that, in the case at bar, the only count was one charging Schnaubelt as principal and the accused as accessories. Would it be enough to prove a conspiracy between the accused and the commission of the crime by Schnaubelt? Would the jury, in such a case, be permitted to find a verdict without any other evidence of Schnaubelt's participation in the conspiracy than his commission of the crime? Of course not! The proof of his participation in the conspiracy is just as necessary to be made out clearly by the evidence, in order to meet the claim of advice, etc., as any other part of the case. On the other hand, if the charge were limited alone to that of accessoryship to an unknown bomb-thrower, here, also, must be proof not only that the bomb was in fact thrown by one unknown, but *proof* that *the unknown was* a member of the conspiracy charged. But this cannot be done without *some* identification; and the mere commission of the crime no more proves membership in the alleged conspiracy, or, in other words, meets the legal requirement of such proof, in the case of an unknown actor, than in the case of one whose name is known. It was, therefore, clearly repugnant for the court to tell the jury

that the bomb must have been thrown by a conspirator
with plaintiffs in error, and in the same breath tell them
that the state need not by evidence identify the bomb-
thrower, in a case where the claim that had to be established under the instructions was that the bomb was in
fact thrown by an unknown person, under the advice, aid,
encouragement, etc., of the accused theretofore given.
The repugnancy in this line of instruction was clearly
vicious.

Thompson on Charging the Jury, pages
97, 98.

Wood v. *Steamboat*, 19 Mo., 529, 531.

The jurors are not lawyers or expert grammarians, who
can apply in their true sense the various clauses of such instructions as No. 4 above set forth. This instruction in the
first clause requires of the jury that they must find " from
" the evidence, beyond a reasonable doubt, that in pursu-
" ance of such conspiracy and in furtherance of the com-
" mon object, *a bomb was thrown by a member of such
" conspiracy at the time*," and then in the concluding
clause, when the mind of an ordinarily intelligent person would forget, or be unable to interpret, the preceding section, by reason of the long clause intervening,
the jury are instructed that the defendants are guilty of
murder, " whether the identity of the person throwing the
" bomb be established or not."

If the bomb-thrower is an unknown, unidentified, unindividuated person, how can he be proved beyond a reasonable doubt to be a member of the conspiracy?

How can a person be shown to be a member of a conspiracy beyond a reasonable doubt when the person cannot be identified by the jury? If he is to be shown to be
a member of a conspiracy beyond a reasonable doubt,
surely his identity must be established, if not by name,

then in some other way, such as by showing that he had but one arm or one leg, or by some description.

If, *c. g.*, there had been evidence that the plaintiffs in error on Monday, May 3d, had held a meeting and agreed upon a plan of violence at a gathering to be called for the next evening; if there had further been evidence that a one-armed man with black whiskers was a party to that combination, and that at the meeting on the next evening a one-armed man with black whiskers threw a bomb, then, although his name were unknown, and no further description of details of personality could be given, still here would be evidence from which a jury might fairly be allowed to conclude that the identity was established with reasonable certainty. But if the only fact proved were that *a bomb was thrown* from the midst of a crowd of a few hundred people, while no living being could tell which one of them did the dastardly deed, if not the slightest indication existed even as to what kind of a looking man he was, how in the name of common sense can it be claimed that he is proved to be, " beyond all reasonable doubt," a member of the conspiracy supposed in this illustration?

At the common law, no person could be convicted as accessory until after a *conviction* of the chief offender; and no evidence could be introduced to prove this, except the record of his conviction. The English statute of 7 Geo. IV qualified this doctrine, and our own statute was passed with the intention of qualifying it.

Our statute declares that an accessory shall be considered as principal, and punished accordingly. This only places the principal and accessory upon the same footing, as far as the punishment is concerned, but it does not abolish the common law distinction between the principal, who actually commits the deed, and the

accessory, who simply lends assistance. This distinction
is clearly upheld by our statute when it says that the
" accessory " may be indicted, etc., with or without the
" principal." It does not say that the two crimes become
one. As a test of this let us suppose A advises B to take
his pistol and kill C. A goes alone and does it. Suppose, then, that A be indicted for advising and assisting B
in the killing, and B be indicted for the act of killing, and
in describing the body of the offense, the pleader avers
that B killed C " with a certain pistol, which in his right
" hand he there had and held," would not both have
to be acquitted on the doctrine of variance? It is
of the very essence of the conception of accessoryship
that somebody, *as principal*, should have committed the
criminal deed. Without a principal there can be no accessory, and therefore a person charged as accessory cannot be legally convicted, unless he is shown beyond a reasonable doubt to have assisted, etc., " THE " principal.

Wharton says in his Crim. Law, Vol. 1, Sec. 237:
" By statutes, however, now almost universally adopted,
" the offense of an accessory is made substantive and in-
" dependent, and consequently the accessory may be tried
" independently of the principal, *though in such case the
" guilt of the principal must be alleged and proved.*"

In *State* v. *Ricker*, 29 Me., 84, the court, in delivering
its opinion and interpreting a statute which, in legal effect,
is similar to our own, says:

" By the modification of the common law, in these pro-
" visions, *more effectual modes for the prosecution and pun-
" ishment of accessories* before the fact to felonies was in-
" tended. The change has the tendency to prevent the de-
" lays attending the trial and escape of accessories arising
" from the failure to bring the principals to trial. The his-
" tory of legislation upon this subject conclusively shows

" that such was the purpose. These provisions in the re-
" vised statutes are the same as those of the statute of 1831,
" Chap. 504, Sec. 1. The statute of Massachusetts of 1830,
" Chap. 49, Sec. 1, and the revised statutes of that com-
" monwealth of 1836 are identical with those of this state;
" and all are in the same terms as those in the statute of
" England, 7 Geo. IV, Chap. 64, Sec. 9, which section
" commences with the words, 'and for the more effectual
" prosecution of accessories before the fact to felony, be it
" enacted,' etc. * * * It is insisted in behalf of the
" prosecution, that by the last mode it was intended that
" such accessory could be indicted as a principal in all re-
" spects, in the manner and form that he would be in-
" dicted if he did the act, which at common law would
" constitute him as principal. It is obvious that, upon
" such a construction, the distinction of principal and ac-
" cessory before the fact may be entirely disregarded.
" Was this the design of the legislature? We cannot
" believe that it was.

    " In the former part of the section, the crimes of the
" principal and the accessory are presented as being dis-
" tinct. Nothing indicates an intention that they should
" not remain so."

The court, after reasoning the case, and giving a history of the question, etc., concludes as follows: " The
" guilt of the latter (the principal) will be alleged in the
" same manner as if he alone had been concerned, fol-
" lowed by the averment of the acts done by the procurer
" which constitute him accessory before the fact. *The
" guilt of the principal is a necessary fact to be shown on
" the trial, in order to obtain a conviction of the accessory,*
" but the record of a conviction is not required; other
" competent proof is sufficient."

From these cases it would seem that the object and

scope of the statute of 7 Geo. IV, which is the first, followed by other statutes of similar import, in Maine, Massachusetts, and other states, and in the State of Illinois, is to facilitate the punishment of accessories, and not destroy the distinction which had existed between principals and accessories. A person who was principal, without these statutes, would still be principal; an accessory would still be an accessory.

Now, what does it mean, when the Supreme court of Maine say that "the guilt of the principal is a necessary "fact to be shown on the trial, in order to obtain a con- "viction of the accessory"? It surely does not mean that the fact of a crime having been committed must be established. It would not be necessary to speak about principal and accessory in order to express this idea. The idea is, that there is no principal without an accessory, no accessory without a principal, and that no man can be held as an accessory, unless he be shown to have aided and advised HIS principal. The guilt of the " principal," as *the principal to an accessory*, must be shown, in order to convict the "accessory," as *the accessory to* THE *principal*.

In *Baxter* v. *People*, 2 Gil., 578, in passing upon the provisions of our statute, in reference to accessories before the fact, the following language is used by this court:

" Under our statute, an accessory may be indicted and " punished as principal, and *in such case it would be neces-* "*sary for the prosecution to make out* THE GUILT OF THE " PRINCIPAL, *before the jury could find the defendant guilty* " *of the murder by being an accessory to it.*"

The purpose of our statute to make the accessory before or at the fact the principal, is obviously based upon the theory " that what we advise or procure another to " do, in the eye of the law, we do ourselves," as has been declared by this court. But upon this theory, it cannot be doubted that to charge the principal for the act of his alleged agent, the agency, or as before stated, the causal relationship, must be made out by legal evidence. No liability as principal can in such case arise, without clear evidence of crime by a recognized or identified agent. Otherwise, for aught that appears, the criminal actor may be acting independently of any advice, or under the advice and instruction of *another* person.

By way of illustrating our position: Suppose A and B, being political agitators, and desiring to bring about a revolution in the conditions of society, plan and agree that B, at a certain time and place, for example, some public meeting, shall throw a bomb for the purpose of destroying the life of a number of the police. Suppose, further, that C and D, criminals, and thus having a natural antagonism to the police force, having learned of the proposed meeting, enter into a distinct agreement of their own that D shall attend said meeting and throw a bomb at the police with a view to committing theft and robbery in the confusion expected to ensue. Before A could be properly convicted of the results of the bomb thrown at the time and place arranged for, it would be necessary to show that the bomb was thrown by B, and to exclude the hypothesis of its being thrown by C or D, parties to the other and independent conspiracy. This serves to illustrate our point, that it is not sufficient to show a conspiracy, if such were shown, broad enough in its general scope to include the particular crime; and to supplement that proof by evidence of the commission of the crime. The proof must go further and show legally, and to the exclusion of every reasonable hypothesis, that the crime was committed by a party to or agent of *the conspiracy* attempted to be established; that, in other words, the perpetrator of the crime must be identified as an agent of the alleged accessories, before they can be held responsible for the act. But how can it be claimed that that was shown in the case at bar beyond a reasonable doubt, if the identity of the bomb-thrower is as unknown as that of the man in the moon?

Commenting upon such statutes as ours, making accessories indictable and punishable as principals, Mr. Bishop in his Criminal Law, Sec. 71 lays down the rule that statutes like these " do not supersede the necessity of "*proving the guilt of the principal.*"

Wharton, in his work on Crim. Ev., 9th Ed., § 325 and note, speaks as follows, viz.:

" The *corpus delicti*, the proof of which is essential to " sustain a conviction, consists of a criminal act; and to " sustain a conviction there must be *proof of the defend-* "*ant's guilty agency* in the production of such act."

" The latter feature, namely, criminal agency, is often " lost sight of, but is as assential as is the object itself " of crime. *Acts*, in some shape, are essential to the " *corpus delicti*, so far as concerns the guilt of the party " accused. A may have designed the death of the de- " ceased, yet if that death has been caused by another, " A, no matter how morally guilty, is not amenable to the " penalties of the law, if he has done and advised nothing " in respect to *the* death. Gellius, vii, 3."

The same rule is recognized and applied in *State* v. *Crank*, 13 S. C. Law Reports, 86.

Such also is the rule distinctly recognized in 2 Bishop's Criminal Procedure, sections 12 and 13, where the learned author speaks as follows: " Seeing that the ac- " cessory cannot be guilty unless his supposed principal " is guilty also, the former, whether indicted with the " latter or separately, can be convicted *only on evidence* " *showing*, together with his own participation in the

" crime, *the guilt of* his *principal.* * * * But by
" force of statutes in most or all of the states, the acces-
" sory may be tried even in advance of his principal. And
" whether the trial is in advance or the two are tried to-
" gether, there being already no conviction of the princi-
" pal, *there must be parol evidence produced against the*
" *accessory of the principal's guilt.*"

So in *Holmes* v. *Commonwealth*, 25 Penn. St., 221, it was
ruled that where an accessory was indicted the guilt of
the principal must be averred, and the evidence must
establish his guilt before the accessory can be convicted.

Starkie on Evidence, volume 2, part 2, edition 1842,
page 1,381, states the law as follows: " A. and others were
" indicted for feloniously demolishing the house of B. It
" was proved that A. and a mob of persons assembled at
" H. A. addressed the mob in violent language, and led
" them in a direction towards a police office, about a
" mile from H, some of the mob from time to time leav-
" ing and others joining. At the police office the mob
" broke the windows, and then went and attacked the
" house of B., and set it on fire, A. not being present at
" the attack on the house nor at the fire. It was held
" that on this state of facts A. ought not to be convicted
" of the demolition, as it did not sufficiently appear what
" the original design of the mob at H. was, *nor whether*
" *any of the mob who were at H.* were *the persons who*
" *demolished B.'s house.*"

R. v. *Howell*, 9 C. and P., 437.

To the same effect see

Roscoe's Criminal Ev., 86 and 87.

In *Fairlee* v. *The People*, 11 Ill., 5, this court, speaking by Mr. Justice Caton, held bad for uncertainty an indictment under which Fairlee had been tried and sentenced to punishment on the charge of murder. The

indictment set out that Fairlee, of his malice aforethought, with the intent to murder the deceased by the smallpox, inoculated certain third parties with the virus of such smallpox, whereby they became infected with the diseases as he had intended; and the grand jury further presented that the smallpox with which these third parties were infected, was a fatal and infectious disease, by means whereof the deceased became infected with the disease whereof he died, etc. The judgment in the case was reversed, and the prisoner ordered to be discharged on the ground that for aught that appeared to the contrary the deceased might have contracted the disease from some source other than through the procurement and instrumentality of the accused.

As applicable to the case at bar, [because the same certainty of proof is required in criminal proceedings that is required in the averment of the offense in the indictment], for aught that appears in the testimony in this case to the contrary Mathias J. Degan may have been killed by a bomb thrown by some third party wholly and utterly unknown to, and in the act altogether uninfluenced by the plaintiffs in error or any of them. And as the instructions tell the jury that the identity of the bomb-thrower need not be established, they were at liberty to exclude the hypothesis that he may have been a person unconnected with the plaintiffs in error.

The case of *Ritzman* v. *The People*, 110 Ill., 362, is not an authority militating in the least against the position we contend for.

There the evidence showed that Ritzman and others, being trespassers upon the premises of the deceased, were requested or orderd by him to leave such premises, whereupon the parties set upon the deceased and in the struggle the homicide resulted. It was admitted that the death resulted from a blow given *either by the accused or by some one of the party with whom the accused in that case was actually participating* in the unlawful act. It was urged there that no conviction could be sustained because the evidence did not show *which one of the co-trespassers* did the killing; and with reference to that contention the following language was used by this court:

"And yet we are told there can be no conviction in this "case because the evidence does not show beyond a "reasonable doubt the very hand that hurled the fatal "missile, which sent him into eternity without a moment's "warning. So far as the accused is concerned, under the "proofs in this case, we think it wholly immaterial whether "the missile in question was thrown by the hand of the "accused or of some one of his co-trespassers. That the "defendant *was present*,—and to say the least of it *en-* "*couraging the perpetration* of the offense,—cannot be "denied; * * * and if the defendant was so present "encouraging the perpetration of the offense, it is hardly "necessary to say that, by the express provisions of our "statute, he is made a principal, and equally guilty with "the one who personally gave the fatal blow."

In this case, surely, the causul relationship between the hand that did the act and the defendant was established. He was *present and encouraged* the perpetration of the crime, was identified with the criminal actor in the very act itself. This case does not apply to the facts assumed in the erroneous instructions complained of, namely, that the bomb-thrower is *unidentified*, and that the plaintiffs in error were *not present and encouraging*.

In the *Ritzman* case there was an absolute identification, or, if you please, positive proof, that the one who did strike the fatal blow was a co-actor in the trespass with the party accused, or the accused himself; and if

the accused did not in fact strike the fatal blow he was
yet actively co-operating with the man who did so inflict
the mortal injury. For the proof in the *Ritzman* case
showed that Ritzman joined in the assault, and participated actively in the combat. Alike in the case of *Brennan* v. *The People*, 15 Ill., 511, and in the *Ritzman* case,
as we understand, the defendants being present and participating in the felony, they were principals therein.
With the doctrine of this case we have absolutely no
contention whatever. But it does not apply to the case
at bar.

II. THE INSTRUCTIONS WERE AT VARIANCE WITH THE PROOF INTRODUCED BY THE STATE.

As to the general theory of the instructions given in
behalf of the people, there was an entire departure from
the case attempted to be made by the state's testimony.

The indictment which involved the plaintiffs in error,
together with William Seliger and Rudolph Schnaubelt,
as co-defendants, charged the act of throwing the bomb
upon each of the plaintiffs in error, in concert with others,
and then in another series of counts charged that the
criminal act was committed by Rudolph Schnaubelt, acting under the advice and with the aid and encouragement
or by the procurement of the plaintiffs in error. In support of the charge contained in this indictment, the state
introduced positive and direct evidence that the Haymarket bomb was thrown in fact by Rudolph Schnaubelt.

As to the plaintiffs in error, the testimony presented by
the state left the case as *advice and encouragement by them
to Rudolph Schnaubelt.*

This was the case that the plaintiffs in error were
called upon to meet when the state rested in the presenta-

tion of its evidence to the jury. This was the charge with which they were confronted, this the evidence they were to rebut.

There can be no question whatever that under the indictment it would have been incompetent for the state to have proved or attempted to prove, for example, that the bomb was thrown by John Smith or Thomas Jones, unless they had shown that such bomb thrower was to the grand jury unknown, and that his identity had been *subsequently* established. The rule of law is conclusively established, that if the name of the pridcipal criminal is known to the grand jury it must be stated in the indictment, that the defendants may know the charge which they have to confront; and that if it appears in the course of the trial that the name of the principal criminal was in fact known to the grand jury, and the indictment charged the principal as unknown, such indictment will be quashed.

In this case the indictment charged that Rudolph Schnaubelt threw the bomb, and there was direct and positive testimony introduced by the state that said Schnaubelt was in fact the bomb thrower. Such evidence, if believed, excluded absolutely the hypothesis that anyone other than Schnaubelt threw the bomb. There was absolutely no evidence introduced by the state that the bomb was thrown by an unknown, unidentified man. Not one count in the indictment, except the two charging Rudolph Schnaubelt with having thrown the bomb and the plaintiffs in error with being accessories thereto, were supported, or even attempted to be supported, by the state in its evidence. Our claim is that in this state of the case the state was bound to ask of the jury a conviction upon *that* theory, and upon none other. It had chosen to present to the jury testimony which, if credible, established *one particular charge* of the indictment, and to rest upon that testimony, and the plaintiffs in error were called upon to meet only *the case made out by the state*, and not one of which they were not apprised in any manner by the state's evidence.

Nor is this rule, we insist, affected in the least by the fact that in certain other counts the plaintiffs in error were charged as accessories to an unknown bomb-thrower. The state did not attempt to sustain that charge; and not having introduced evidence in support of that charge, was not entitled to ask a conviction upon that theory. *The instructions must follow the proofs. The state could have no right to ask instructions of the court that were altogether without support from the evidence in their case, altogether out of harmony with their own testimony.* The case may be likened to a civil action in assumpsit, with a special count upon a promissory note and the common counts. Suppose, in such a case, the plaintiff introduced the promissory note described in the declaration, and rested there. Suppose that the defendant then introduced evidence tending to show that that note was a forgery, and upon that testimony the case was submitted to the jury; would not the plaintiff in the action be required to recover, if at all, upon the theory of the genuineness of the note, and for the note alone? Could an instruction be given on his behalf upon the theory of some general indebtedness under his common counts? Would not his instructions have to conform with his proofs, and go upon the hypothesis supported by his testimony?

And if this is true in a civil action, can a different rule be sustained in reference to criminal matters, and especially in capital cases? Here was a special count charging that Schnaubelt threw the bomb, the plaintiffs in error being accessories to that act, and *only* this special count attempted to be supported by the testimony offered in behalf of the state.

But so completely, overwhelmingly and absolutely was this case met by the defendants—so conclusively was the falsehood of the state's testimony demonstrated, that the state in its instructions abandoned its own case. *Not a single instruction on behalf of the State presented to the jury the hypothesis of accessoryship to the throwing of the bomb by Schnaubelt.* Dropping their special count, the state attempted to recover under their common counts. We maintain that the instructions of the court in behalf of the state, inasmuch as they departed from the case which the state had attempted to make, and upon which the state rested, were altogether erroneous.

In support of the position above suggested we cite briefly the following authorities:

" An indictment will be bad against an accessory, " stating the principal to be unknown to the grand jury " contrary to the truth, and the judge will direct an ac- " quittal."

> Wharton's Criminal Pl. & Pr., 8th ed.,
> Section 112; citing in support of the text,
> 3 Campbell, 264, 265; 2 East's P. C., 781.

The same author says in section 104 of the same work: " A known party cannot be indicted as unknown."

> Citing Wharton's Cr. Ev., 8th ed., §97;
> *Geiger v. Steele*, 5 Iowa, 484.

That evidence cannot be admitted to prove accessory-ship to a felony *committed by a person other than the one named in the indictment*, where the indictment is special and purports to give the name of the principal felon, is also well settled by authority.

> See 2 East's Crown Law, 651, 781.

In *Simmons v. State*, 4th Georgia, 465, it was expressly held that where an indictment charged the defendant with an offense, or with being an accessory to a felony, committed by a party specially named, it was necessary to prove that the felony was committed *by that individual*

So it was held in *Moore* v. *State*, 65 Indiana, 213, that the proof must follow the indictment, and that if the indictment charged accessoryship to an offense committed "with '*persons*' whose names are unknown to the grand "jury," such indictment was not sustained by proof of commission of the offense "with *a person* whose name "to the grand jury was unknown." It was said by the Supreme court of Indiana, in that case, that *the description in the indictment must be literally proved*, in order that the record may be a sufficient bar to a subsequent prosecution for the same offense. The question there arose upon the instructions under the indictment, which instructions held that it was sufficient to sustain the indictment to show by the proofs the commission of the alleged offense with *some person* whose name was unknown. For this error in the instruction the conviction was set aside.

See also Wharton's Criminal Evidence, 9th edition, section 97, where it is said: "When a third person is de- "scribed as 'a person to the grand jurors unknown,' and "it turn out he was known to the grand jurors, the "variance is fatal. * * * *A 'person unknown' must* "*be individuated as a specific person, though his name* "*may not be ascertainable.*"

In *Regina* v. *Stroud*, 2 Moody, C. C., *270, there was an indictment against the prisoner for the murder of her infant child. In the first count of the indictment the child was described as Harriett Stroud. In the second count it was described as a female infant of tender age, whose name is to the jurors unknown. It appeared by the evidence that the prisoner, being a single woman, gave birth to a female child; that the child was called Harriett. The child was baptized by the name of Harriett only, not Harriett Stroud, and there was no evidence showing it had ever been called by any other name except Harriett. The prisoner drowned the child. The jury found the prisoner guilty. The judge passed sentence of death upon her.

A doubt was afterwards suggested, whether the conviction was right. It would seem, on the authority of *Rex* v. *Waters*, 1 Moody, 457, that she could not be convicted on the first count, and as the child was certainly known by the name of Harriett, it might be doubted whether the second count would warrant conviction for the murder of a child whose name is to the jurors unknown, and whether there ought not to have been a count for the murder of a child named Harriett. The execution of the sentence had been respited in order that the opinion of the judges might be obtained on the point. This case was considered at a meeting of the judges in Michaelmas term in 1842, and they held the conviction wrong. The proper description would have been Harriett, the base-born child of the prisoner, and the want of description is only excused when the name cannot be known.

Though this case applies to the name of the victim of the crime, still it shows the principle that the proof must strictly conform to the indictment. As applied to the case at bar, all counts in the indictment other than those charging accessoryship to *Rudolph Schnaubelt* as principal, could not form the basis of conviction, because at variance with the proof, and therefore could not be made the basis of the theory of the instructions.

In *Rex* v. *Russell and Ryan*, p. 489, it was decided, if the name of a prisoner is unknown, and he refuses to disclose it, an indictment against him as a person whose name is to the jury unknown, but who is the prisoner brought before the jurors by the keeper of the prison, would be good, but it would not be sufficient to base an indictment against him as a person to the jurors unknown, without something to ascertain who the grand jury meant to designate.

See also *Blodgett* v. *State*, 3d Indiana, 403.

In Russell's Law of Crimes, volume 2, page 297, it is said: "*Rex* v. *Robinson*, the averment in the indictment "always is 'to the jurors aforesaid, *i. e.*, grand jury un-": known;' and in *Rex* v. *Cory*, Gloucester S. PR. 1832, "upon it being stated in argument that it had been held "that if it were alleged that property was stolen by *a* "*person unknown*, and it was proved at the trial that the "person was *known*, the prisoner must be acquitted."

LITTLEDALE, judge, says: "That case has been decided, "and it is subject to some doubt. The question is, "whether the person is known to the grand jury. It "will be difficult to prove that he was so known; and "unless he was known to the grand jury I should have "doubt about that case. If the case should occur where "the witnesses who went before the grand jury were "wholly ignorant of the parties said to be unknown, and it "turned out by other evidence, *e. g.*, by a witness called "for the prisoner, that the party was known, it would "deserve consideration whether the prisoner would "thereby be entitled to be acquitted."

In *Rex* v. *Walker*, 3 Campbell's Reports, page 264, there was an indictment against the prisoner as accessory before the fact to a larceny. The indictment charged that a certain person, to the jurors unknown, feloniously stole, took and carried away six bushels of wheat.

The grand jury had found a bill upon the evidence of

Charles Ives, who had acknowledged that he had stolen the wheat. It was now proposed to call him as a witness to establish the guilt of the prisoner; but the fact being opened by the prosecution, the judge interposed and directed an acquittal. He said he considered the indictment wrong in stating that the wheat had been stolen by *a person unknown*, and asked how the person who was the principal felon could be alleged to be unknown to the jurors, *when they had him before them and his name was written on the back of the bill.*

See fully Russell on Crimes, *ubi supra.*

III. INSTRUCTIONS BASED UPON HYPOTHESES UNWARRANTED BY THE EVIDENCE.

Instruction 5, given on behalf of the people (1 A., 7; O, 3) presents to the jury substantially the hypothesis that the jury might find the plaintiffs in error guilty of murder, " although the jury may further " believe from " the evidence that the time and place for the bringing " about of such revolution, or the destruction of such " authorities, had not been definitely agreed upon by the " conspirators, *but was left to them and the exigencies of* " *time, or to the judgment of any of the co-conspirators.*" Our objection to this part of the instruction is that there was no evidence in the record to support this hypothesis. We have heretofore (pp. 146–149) presented to the court our views upon this point quite fully, and it may suffice here to repeat that there is absolutely no evidence in this record to show that under any agreement, understanding or conspiracy to which, it is claimed on the part of the state, the plaintiffs in error, or any of them, were parties, was there any provision, agreement or understanding that the time and place for

the "bringing about of revolution or the destruction of
"the authorities was left to the exigencies of time *or to*
"*the judgment of any of the co-conspirators.*" As before
suggested by us, there are perhaps in Bakunin's article
and in Most's book, and possibly in some other of the
literature introduced, suggestions by some of the writers
to the effect that revolutionists ought themselves to proceed with their own enterprises without involving therein
any more of their fellow revolutionists than seems absolutely necessary. But this is as far as possible from
evidence supporting a theory that there was a general
agreement by plaintiffs in error that the revolution was to
be brought on at the caprice, or upon the judgment, of
any individual member of the conspiracy, as to when the
time or the exigency had arisen for striking the deter-
minative blow. In this particular this instruction is absolutely vicious, and was calculated in the highest degree
to work prejudice to the plaintiffs in error.

IV. Mere general advice does not constitute accessoryship.

We come now to a consideration of the most important, in our view perhaps the most vicious, of all the
instructions asked and given in behalf of the people, to
wit: instruction $5\frac{1}{2}$ (1 A., 8: O, 4), which is as follows:

"If these defendants, or any two or more of them, con-
"spired together with or not with any other person or
"persons to excite the people or classes of the people of
"this city to sedition, tumult and riot, to use deadly
"weapons against and take the lives of other persons, as
"a means to carry their designs and purposes into effect,
"and in pursuance of such conspiracy, and in furtherance
"of its objects, any of the persons so conspiring publicly

" by print or speech advised or encouraged the commis-
" sion of murder without designating time, place or occa-
" sion at which it should be done, and in pursuance of,
" and induced by such advice or encouragement, murder
" was committed, then all of such conspirators are guilty
" of such murder, whether the person who perpetrated such
" murder can be identified or not. If such murder was com-
" mitted in pursuance of such advice or encouragement, and
" was induced thereby, it does not matter what change if
" any, in the order or condition of society, or what, if any,
" advantage to themselves or others, the conspirators pro-
" posed as the result of their conspiracy, nor does it matter
" whether such advice and encouragement had been fre-
" quent and long-continued or not, except in determining
" whether the perpetrator was or was not acting in pur-
" suance of such advice or encouragement, and was or
" was not induced thereby to commit the murder. If
" there was such conspiracy as in this instruction is recited,
" such advice or encouragement was given, and murder
" committed in pursuance of and induced thereby, then all
" such conspirators are guilty of murder. Nor does it
" matter, if there was such a conspiracy, how impractica-
" ble or impossible of success its end and aims were, nor
" how foolish or ill-arranged were the plans for its execu-
" tion, except as bearing upon the question whether there
" was or was not such conspiracy."

*The only act on the part of any of the plaintiffs in error
required to be found under this instruction by the jury is
the mere matter of conspiring together or with others to
excite the people or classes of the people to riot, tumult and
sedition, and to the use of deadly weapons against, and
taking the lives of other persons.*

Here is supposed a conspiracy, not to commit murder,
not to do any act of violence out of which murder might

result, but *a conspiracy to excite, a conspiracy to solicit crime.* To excite the people to deeds of violence is the only and final object of the conspiracy supposed in this instruction. The law is, that each member of an unlawful conspiracy is responsible for all the acts done by one of the conspirators in furtherance of the common design, or, as applied to the conspiracy supposed in instruction 5½, the act of soliciting crime by print or speech by one of the parties to that combination. If the mere fact of soliciting crime by print or speech were an indictable offense [and it may, perhaps, constitute a common law libel or a misdemeanor], then all of the conspirators would be guilty as accessories to *that* offense. But the instruction does not stop there. It goes on to say that if murder was committed in pursuance of and " *induced* " by such solicitation of crime, then all conspirators are guilty of murder.

" If murder was committed," by whom? The instruction is silent about that. This alone would make it vicious for uncertainty. But apart from that, the the ory of this instruction is that if *anybody*, "induced " by such advice, commits murder, then the parties to the " *conspiracy to excite*," are accessories to such murder. In other words, they are responsible as accessories to the act of one *who is not a member of their conspiracy*, accessories to an act which goes *beyond the common design*, which common design, under the theory of this instruction, is " excitement of the people to crime," and not the commission of any act of violence.

" If murder was committed," against whom, where, when? The instruction will be searched in vain from the first to the last word, for any reference to the charge in the indictment. The name of Degan is not mentioned, the instruction does not speak about a murder committed in Cook county, on the 4th of May, nor is the jury required to find that murder was committed by means of a bomb. But it says: "If murder was committed, then all "of such conspirators are guilty of such murder."

This instruction was bad by reason of its stating an abstract principle of law, erroneous in itself, and not based upon any evidence legitimately before the jury. That it was calculated to mislead is apparent.

Coughlin v. *The People*, 18 Ill., 266.

But, beyond this, instruction 5½ says that if "*any of* "*the persons* so conspiring publicly, by print or speech, "advised or encouraged the commission of murder, with- "out designating time, place or occasion at which it "should be done, and in pursuance of and induced by such "advice or encouragement murder was committed, then "all of such conspirators are guilty of such murder."

It will be observed that under this instruction it was not necessary for the jury to find that *any of the plaintiffs in error* advised or encouraged the commission of murder in order to hold them guilty; but if any other man, not one of the plaintiffs in error, but who was a *party to the conspiracy to excite* to crime, made public speeches advising or encouraging the commission of murder, and murder was committed, induced by such advice, then all of the conspirators, including the plaintiffs in error, are to be found guilty.

But the instruction now under consideration is, in our judgment, subject to still further special criticism. It is therein said: "If any of the persons so conspiring pub- "licly, by print or speech advised or encouraged the com- "mission of murder, without designating time, place or "occasion at which it should be done, and in pursuance of. "and *induced* by such advice or encouragement murder "was committed, then all of such conspirators are guilty," etc.

This assumes that there is, *in law*, such a thing as advice to *murder* in the abstract. As we said in another connection, a man might cry out in the public streets: " Kill, kill, murder, murder," by the day and by the hour, and would not advise murder in contemplation of law. Unless he designates the victim, the means, the manner, time or place, he has not done sufficient by his outcries alone to become amenable to the law as an accessory before the fact to the crime of murder.

Again, from the structure of this part of the instruction it is evident that the jury were left free to judge as to the nature of supposed public advice, without any instruction as to what would constitute advice to commit murder. Our point is that the advice should, in order to constitute accessoryship, be advice to the commission of *such act or acts* as would in law constitute murder, and that the express elimination in this part of the charge of any consideration by the jury of time, place or occasion, as designated for the proposed offense in the supposed advice, renders the charge vicious for uncertainty.

But this vice of the instruction was intensified by the suggestion of *inducement* under such advice. The statute does not make a man liable for a crime *induced* by what he may have said, but only for a crime advised directly by him.

For example. I may advise men to kill a particular class of people, as Chinese, or Pinkerton detectives, or Mormons. As a result of such advice, or its oft repetition, I may *induce* in the minds of my hearers a light regard for life, a disposition to homicide generally, so that *induced* by such advice a murder may be committed totally different from any advised. Will it be contended that in such a case I would be responsible for the murder thus induced and committed?

Again, this instruction is vicious because it does not require the jury to find that the advice to commit murder was *directed and addressed to the man who committed it.* This is absurd. Suppose A., a physician, in his consultation room advises a woman to commit abortion and tells her the means by which to accomplish it. Suppose further that in the ante-room, severed by a closed door from the consultation room, there is waiting, accidentally, another woman, sent on an errand to the doctor. She is pregnant. She is unmarried. She overhears the advice given by the physician to the woman inside. It prompts to her the suggestion that there would be a chance to conceal her shame. " Pursuant to the advice " given by the doctor to the other lady and " induced " by it, she goes off and commits the crime of abortion without ever seeing or talking to the doctor. Is the doctor an accessory before the fact to *her* crime? The suggestion is preposterous.

Considering the various vices of instruction $5\frac{1}{2}$, above criticized, it will appear that it admits of such a consequence as the following:

If, as supposed by this instruction the plaintiffs in error were parties to a conspiracy to excite the people to tumult, to the use of deadly weapons for the taking of human life, etc., and if in supposed furtherance of this conspiracy *some unknown member* of this band of conspirators (not one of the parties accused) published an article in *general terms* encouraging and advising assassination, without designating time, place or occasion, or naming any victim or class of victims, and if " in pursuance " of this general advice " and " induced " thereby some *unknown* person had murdered a policeman in London, in the course of a private altercation, all of the parties to the original conspiracy would be guilty of the London murder.

For observe, the instruction makes no limitation as to *where* the supposed murder might be committed; nor at what time, near or remote; nor on what occasion, a public meeting or a private brawl; nor who should be the victim, or even class of victims. Here would be liability for a crime never dreamed of by the original conspiracy, nor within its scope; for it is not said in the instruction that the *murder* done mnst be in pursuance of and induced by the *original conspiracy;* but only in pursuance of and induced by the public general speech or writing of *some one* of the supposed conspirators, which speech or writing is made in furtherance of a conspiracy " to excite the people " or classes of the people of this city to sedition, tumult " and riot, to' use deadly weapons against and take the " lives of other persons, as a means to carry their designs " and purposes into effect."

Isn't this a trifle remote? Isn't it importing into criminal law the exploded doctrine of " consequential " liability? Is it not an instruction in utter disregard of the maxim, " *Causa proxima non remota spectamur* "? Is it not the undue development of what may be termed a doctrine of constructive crime?

In this instruction 5½ again, the false proposition is repeated, that it is unnecessary to identify in any manner the bomb-thrower, if the jury imagine or conclude that it was thrown in pursuance of such advice or encouragement, and was induced thereby. How is it possible legally to conclude that an unknown party, absolutely unidentified, and with no evidence connecting him with the accused, ever heard their speeches, read their writings, or was in any relationship to them subjecting him to the slightest influence by them—how is it possible, legally to conclude that the act of such a man was done in pursuance of such advice or encouragement, and was induced thereby? Or, to put it in the language of Mr. Wharton in his Crim. Law, Vol. 1 §179: " What human judge can determine that there is such a " necessary connection between one man's advice and an- " other man's action as to make the former the cause of " the latter?" No legal relationship under this instruction is required to be established by the evidence, but the jury were left absolutely free to *guess* or conclude upon any basis satisfactory to them " *as men* " (*vid:* Instruction 13), that the unknown bomb-thrower at the Haymarket was influenced in his act, was incited to his crime, was en- couraged in his evil deed, by the plaintiffs in error.

When once the theory that Rudolph Schnaubelt threw the bomb was abandoned, there was no evidence which warranted the hypothesis assumed in the instruction that the unidentified bomb-thrower was in fact an associate in, their purposes and an instrument of their designs, or even, a disciple of one of the band of conspirators supposed in instruction 5½.

We beg to cite here again from Starkie on Evidence, volume 2, part 2, edition 1842, page 1381, who states the law as follows: "A. and others were indicted for feloni- " ously demolishing the house of B. It was proved that " A. and a mob of persons assembled at H. A. addressed " the mob in violent language, and led them in a direction " towards a police office, about a mile from H., some of " the mob from time to time leaving and others joining. " At the police office the mob broke the windows, and " then went and attacked the house of B., and set it on " fire, A. not being present at the attack on the house nor " at the fire. It was held that on this state of facts A. " ought not to be convicted of the demolition, as it did not " sufficiently appear what the original design of the mob " at H. was, *nor whether any of the mob who were at H,* " were *the persons who demolished B.'s house.*"

R. v. *Howell,* 9 C. and P., 437.

Wharton in his Criminal Law, 9th edition, volume 1, section 226, note entitled " Modes of Instigation," says: " *Counseling, to come up to the definition, must be special.* " Mere general counsel, for instance, that all property " should be regarded as held in common, will not consti- " tute the party offering it accessory before the fact to a " larceny; free-love publications will not constitute their " authors technical parties to sexual offenses which these " publications may have stimulated. Several youthful " highway robbers have said that they were led into " crime by reading Jack Shepard; but the author of " Jack Shepard was not an accessory before the fact to " the robberies to which he thus added impulse."

In volume 1, section 179, of the same work, the learned author says: " It would be hard, also, we must agree, if we " maintain such general responsibility, to defend, in pros- " ecutions for soliciting crime the publishers of Byron's " ' Don Juan,' of Rousseau's ' Emile ' or Goethe's ' Elective " Affinities.' Lord Chesterfield, in his letters to his son, " directly advised the latter to form illicit connection with " married women. Lord Chesterfield, on the reasoning " here contended, would be indictable for solicitation to " adultery. *What human judge can determine that there " is such a necessary connection between one man's advice " and another man's action as to make the former the cause " of the latter?* "

To further illustrate the doctrine of the text above quoted, we desire to cite some matters so familiar as to be historic.

Prior to the year 1860 slavery was an institution in the United States recognized by the constitution and pro- tected by the laws. Upon the one side arose a body of earnest and devoted men, constituting a very small minority of the people of the north, who denounced the

provision of the constitution and these laws passed thereunder in unmeasured terms—advocating the abolition of
property in slaves, and demanding, if needs be, the dissolution and reorganization of the union itself. These men
openly and constantly advocated the forcible, immediate
and unconditional abolition of slavery without compensa-
tion for the slave property thus proposed to be confiscated
or abolished. On the other side of the line arose practically a majority of the influential people of that section,
who, standing for the institution of slavery, and recogniz-
ing the tendency of these efforts of the abolitionist, demanded the dissolution of the Union as a means of but-
tressing about and perpetuating beyond question or interference this institution.

As a result of the agitation of the first-named body of
men, at last John Brown organized his raid in Virginia, resulting in the taking of human life, denounced by the law
as murder. He and his immediate associates, being arrested, were tried, found guilty, sentenced, and paid the
penalty of their alleged crimes with their lives. But,
meanwhile, back of John Brown, advocating precisely
what he attempted, namely, the abolition of slavery by
force and arms, was the abolition press of the north, the
abolition speakers, preachers and people. It would have
been easy to prove on the part of all these a general conspiracy to overthrow the law in reference to chattel
slavery, and to have shown upon their part such advice,
such sentiments, such predictions of violence, bloodshed,
disorder, as would have embraced the John Brown expedition.

In the light of history, what would be now said of a
proposal to indict Horace Greeley, Wendell Phillips, Ger-
rit Smith, William Lloyd Garrison, and the host of im-
mortals whose names were then a reproach and a by-

word, but are now honored in all lands, under the charge of murder, and to attempt to secure to them the scaffold as the end of their career, because of the act of John Brown?

On the other side, the result of the secession agitation for the preservation and perpetuity of slavery, an agitation participated in by almost every prominent speaker in the south, and by almost every leading newspaper; an agitation which boldly challenged and unhesitatingly predicted war; an agitation which made provision for the struggle, and that was ready in advance for the trial of arms; this agitation went forward for years, and at last resulted in the great struggle of 1861 to 1865, which involved our entire land and caused the sacrifice of hundreds of thousands of lives. In the light of history, what would now be said of a proposal to indict the participants of this movement for murder and to bring them to the scaffold, because of their advocacy of secession, because of their " gigantic conspiracy against the law?"

Let us take another illustration: At the close of the war, in many parts of the south, after the enfranchisement of the colored race, in large portions of the territory there was as to numbers a dominance of the colored people. The whites of these localities, in many instances, set themselves deliberately and resolutely to control by any and all means this colored majority, and to keep the control of their governmental affairs in their own hands. The result was what was familiarly called the " shot-gun policy." A large proportion of the press of the south joined in the continual expression of the sentiment that the white race should dominate— peaceably if possible, but forcibly if necessary. This position was advocated openly and undisguisedly in the editorial columns and communications of these papers, by speakers upon the rostrum and stump, and the resolution became in effect an agreement substantially to deprive the black race in these particular territories of the free exercise of their legal rights; a conspiracy to control the goverment for the time being as against what was believed to be an ignorant, incapable and misguided majority. The result was many massacres occurring in many parts of the country by organized bodies of men—the K. K. K. and other organizations—massacres as deliberate, inexcusable and cold-blooded as any perhaps which have ever disgraced the annals of civilized society, but which were excused or apologized for in large measure by the local press on the plea of necessity. Was it ever pretended that these newspaper editors and stockholders could be made liable upon indictments for murder for the lawless conduct of these night-riders? Who ever thought of attempting to hold as guilty of murder parties not shown by legal proof to have specially advised or participated in the particular crime referred to? What would have been thought of a deliberate suggestion to arrest in the locality of these atrocities the political leaders among the whites, including the newspaper editors, compositors and stockholders, and attempting to hold them for the murders committed in these massacres and assassinations, without any attempt to show that they participated in the crime or advised *the* perpetration of *the* offense?

Again, substantially the entire press of the Pacific slope for many years past has joined in the hue and cry—" the Chinese must go." Against this people, columns of editorials and communications were constantly appearing, denouncing them in the most violent terms, declaring them unworthy to live, and taking the position that any means were justifiable to get rid of them, even to the point of their physical extermination. They were in this country by legal right, by virtue of treaties and pro, visions deliberately entered into by this government, and solemnly sanctioned. This agitation to secure their exclusion and expulsion from our shores amounted in effect to a general conspiracy to produce the result desired. As a consequence of this opposition, thus stimulated and excited to the highest pitch, numerous massacres occurred from time to time in various portions of the far west, where armed bodies of men deliberately set upon the Chinese, in their own quarters and in their own homes, murdering them mercilessly and brutally. It is only within a very short time that the last of these massacres occurred in Wyoming. Many more lives were sacrificed in these massacres, on many different occasions, than were sacrificed at the Haymarket. But no suggestion was ever made that the newspaper editors and writers were criminally liable for these massacres, and should be executed on account of them. Still less did the claim ever find sane advocacy that men connected with these newspapers as stockholders, or in some other manner, should be indicted for the murder of these Chinese.

Let it not be said that these illustrations are far-fetched. The action of the people in reference to these cases serves to illustrate the consensus of enlightened humanity with reference to matters of this nature. It has been a part of the policy of our country, and of our laws, under the constitutional guaranty of free speech, to permit the utmost latitude in the matter of agitation for supposed reform. And let it be remembered that, as in the case of the abolition agitation, the claim of reform always in the first instance finds its advocacy only in the lips of the minority, while the majority deny that the proposed change is reformatory, usually contending that it is altogether pernicious. We repeat that the common sense of the community at large has applied this general rule to matters of this nature; that no matter what general advice looking to a general line of conduct may have been given by one party, or a set of parties; and no matter to what extent that general advice may have entered into the education, and into the formation of the opinions and views, of the particular individual subsequently committing, perhaps under the direct influence of this general advice, a particular crime; yet, if the individual committing the crime acts in the commission thereof upon his own volition and responsibility, he alone must bear the penalty of the crime; while the adviser can be held only when there is shown, passing entirely beyond the realm of general agitation, general advocacy of measures, general advice of processes, *special advice to the doer of the deed involving the commission of the particular crime, whereby the adviser becomes personally involved in the turpitude of the particular act*, as having been done at his suggestion at the time and under the circumstances of its commission.

We respectfully submit that the doctrine of instruction $5\frac{1}{2}$ and the other instructions for the people presenting the same view, substantially amount to the introduction, for the first time, into criminal jurisprudence, of the principle that a supposed or possible moral responsibility involves the penalty of legal offense.

V. Instruction $5\frac{1}{2}$ contained no reference to the evidence.

Aside from the general views of the doctrine of instruction $5\frac{1}{2}$ above considered, it is further subject to a special criticism, namely, that it contained no reference to the evidence as the basis of the contemplated or permitted action or finding of the jury. There is not from the opening to the close of this import-

ant and vital instruction, a single reference to the evidence. The jury are not told in it that *if they find
from the evidence* so and so, then they can conclude thus
and so, but they are left free to draw upon all sources of
information, and full rein is given to their prejudices,
preconceptions and even fancies. We do not need to
elaborate this criticism. A simple reading of the instruction shows its utter viciousness in the light of the well-
recognized principle of law, that the jury must, in their
findings, be limited to the evidence in the case.

As to the law on this point, we will only quote what
our Supreme court stated in *Ewing* v. *Runkle*, 20 Ill.,
448: " A jury should be permitted to believe nothing
" except that belief be occasioned by the evidence, and
" *their minds should always be directed to that, and that
" alone,* as the ground of their belief."

This doctrine, flowing from the provisions of our
statute (Chapter 110, Sec. 52, Hurd's R. S., 1885), has
been upheld by a long line of decisions in this court, collected in the recent case of *Chambers* v. *The People*, 105
Ill., 409, which again emphasizes that rule.

The error indicated is the more significant, as this
was the longest single instruction given in behalf of
the people, came early in the series, and was the
instruction which perhaps most thoroughly and completely presented the theory of the prosecution, and summarized the repeated rulings of the court upon the questions of evidence in the progress of the trial. It was,
therefore, pre-eminently the most important instruction
given in behalf of the people, and the one which, in view
of the arguments which had transpired, must have been
most influential with the jury, and must have most deeply
impressed itself upon their minds.

This instruction permits the jury to *surmise, without

reference to the evidence in the case, that the alleged murder was committed under the influence and encouragement of general advice from *some member* of a supposed conspiracy, given in public speeches and writings; it permits the jury to *guess, without reference to the evidence*, that the murder was committed by a disciple of one of those conspirators.

Nor will it do to say that this defect of this instruction is supplied in other instructions, for example, in the instruction given by the court upon its own motion, later, where an attempt was made to limit the investigation and determination of the jury to the evidence presented. In criminal practice, and particularly in capital cases, it is essential that each instruction (certainly every vital instruction, such as this) shall be complete and correct in itself, and its defects cannot be helped out if they exist by reference to other instructions. It is stated by Mr. Wharton (Cr. Pl. & Pr., 8th Ed., § 793), that "material error in " one instruction calculated to mislead is not cured by a " subsequent contradictory instruction."

Accordingly, in *Murray* v. *Commonwealth*, 79 Penn. State, 311, there was a reversal, because of an error in one part of the charge, although that error was apparently corrected in the general charge. So in *Clem* v. *State*, 31 Indiana, it was held that an erroneous charge given in behalf of the people was not cured by giving a contradictory and correct charge upon the same point at the request of the defendant.

So in *Howard* v. *The State*, 50 Indiana, the same rule is announced and followed, as also in *People* v. *Valencia*, 43 Cal., 543.

VI. Erroneous Instructions as to Reasonable Doubt.

Instruction 12, given on behalf of the people, was as follows (1 A., 10; O, 7):

" The court instructs the jury, as a matter of law, that " in considering the case the jury are not to go beyond " the evidence to hunt up doubts, nor must they entertain " such doubts as are merely chimerical or conjectural. A " doubt, to justify an acquittal, must be reasonable, and " it must arise from a candid and impartial investigation " of all the evidence in the case, and unless it is such that " were the same kind of doubt interposed in the graver " transactions of life, it would cause a reasonable and " prudent man to hesitate and pause, it is insufficient to " authorize a verdict of not guilty. If, after considering " all the evidence, you can say you have an abiding con-" viction of the truth of the charge, you are satisfied be-" yond a reasonable doubt."

In *Brown v. State*, 5 North-Eastern Reporter, 903, de-cided March 30, 1886, the Supreme court of Indiana said:

" In the third instruction the court undertook to " define what constituted a reasonable doubt. The jury " were told, in substance, that it was not their duty to go " beyond the evidence in search of doubts based on " merely groundless conjectures; that, in order to justify " an acquittal, the doubt should be reasonable, and arise " of an impartial consideration of the evidence in the case, " and that it must be such a doubt as would cause a pru-" dent and considerate man to hesitate before acting in " the gravest and most important affairs of life; that if, " upon a careful and impartial consideration of all the

" evidence, the jury had an abiding conviction of the de-
" fendant's guilt, then they were satisfied beyond a
" reasonable doubt. We cannot commend this instruction.
" It is not an accurate statement of the law upon the sub-
" ject of reasonable doubt. To the extent that the in-
" struction was liable to be understood as saying to the
" jury that, in order to justify an acquittal, the doubt of
" the defendant's guilt must arise out of the evidence, and
" be such as to cause a prudent man to hesitate before,
" acting in matters of the gravest concern, it was clearly
" wrong. It is not the law that in order to justify an
" acquittal the doubt must arise out of the evidence given,
" and be such as to cause a prudent man to hesitate. The
" doubt may arise from a want of evidence.

" In order to justify a conviction the evidence must be
" such as to produce in the minds of prudent men such
" certainty that they would act upon the conviction pro-
" duced without hesitation in their own most important
" affairs. *Jerrell* v. *State*, 58 Ind., 293; *Stout* v. *State*,
" 90 Ind., 1."

See also note to the above case, 5 N. E. R., 905.

To the same effect is,

> 1 Greenleaf Ev., 14th Ed., Sec. 13A and
> note A.
>
> Wharton Cr. Ev., 9th Ed., Sec. 718.

Instruction 13, given for the state, is also clearly obnoxious to the rule of law established by the above authorities. It is as follows (1 A., 10, 11; O, 7):

" The court further instructs the jury, as a matter of
" law, that the doubt which the juror is allowed to re-
" tain on his own mind, and under the influence of which
" he should frame a verdict of not guilty, must always be
" a reasonable one. A doubt produced by undue sensi-
" bility in the mind of any juror, in view of the conse-

" quences of his verdict, is not a reasonable doubt, and a
" juror is not allowed to create sources or materials of
" doubt by resorting to trivial and fanciful suppositions
" and remote conjectures as to possible states of fact
" differing from that established by the evidence. You
" are not at liberty to disbelieve as jurors, if from the evi-
" dence you believe as men; your oath imposes upon you
" no obligation to doubt where no doubt would exist if no
" oath had been administered."

We further specially object to this instruction, that it
permits the jury to find a verdict against the plaintiffs in
error upon any conviction in reference to the issue with
which they entered the jury box. In the closing clause,
" your oath imposes upon you no obligation to doubt where
"no doubt would exist if no oath had been administered,"
they are, in effect, told: If you entered this jury box convinced of the guilt of the defendants, you are not obliged
to lay that persuasion aside, but may resolve all possible
doubts by that prior conviction. No other interpretation
can possibly be given to this instruction, particularly in
the light of the rulings of the court as to the competency
of jurors, to which we shall have occasion to call attention later. Again and again during the impaneling of the
jury, the plaintiffs in error were denied the privilege of
asking a proposed juror whether, if a doubt arose in his
own mind upon the evidence, the conviction or opinion
entertained at the time of the examination would control
the verdict or determine the action of the juror. At times
such questions were allowed to be asked, but at other
times the answering of them was disallowed. Here was,
in effect, in this instruction, a charge that under their
oaths as jurors there was no obligation upon them to entertain any doubts which did not exist in their own minds
when they took their seats in the jury box.

The further statement of this instruction, "You are not "at liberty to disbelieve as jurors, if, from the evidence, "you believe as men," is, we maintain, an utterly perni-cious and illegal proposition. We are aware that one authority can be found to support this instruction. But we confidently submit that that authority is not law. Many a man as a man, from evidence produced before him, may be morally certain that a particular hypothesis is true, who yet, if a fair and reasonable man, will say without hesitation that the hypothesis, though fully be-lieved, is not supported by the evidence adduced beyond reasonable doubt. The old saw,

> " A man convinced against his will
> Is of the same opinion still,"

is merely a familiar expression of the truism, that many men believe not only without, but against, evidence. It is not true, therefore, that evidence which produces mere mental persuasion of the truth of a certain hypothesis, would legally support a verdict based upon such persuasion. It is not true that the jury " are not at liberty to disbelieve " as jurors, if, from the evidence, they believe as men "; but, on the contrary, they may, as honest jurors, be com-pelled to doubt, even where they are morally certain as to the issue presented. It seems to us that the closing part of this instruction is absolutely vicious.

The true test on a question of this kind is, What, as reasonable, prudent, fair-minded men, they *are justified in believing the legal evidence produced establishes*, and not what they may choose or be able to persuade themselves to believe " as men " from the evidence. Beliefs, even in their relations to evidence, are largely controlled in the every-day affairs of life by the prejudices or passions or predispositions of men; and it would be giving a most dangerous latitude to say that whatever they choose to

believe as men, from the evidence, they may act upon as
jurors. How much worse when, in the language of this
instruction, they are told in effect that they are not at
liberty to disbelieve as jurors anything which from the
evidence they believe as men, no matter by what influence or considerations that belief is induced or controlled.

VII.   The Jury are the Judges of the law in
CRIMINAL CASES.

By instruction 13½ the court told the jury as follows:
(1 A., 11; O, 7, 8).

" The court instructs the jury that they are the judges
" of the law as well as the facts in this case, and if they
" can say, upon their oaths, that they know the law bet-
" ter than the court itself, they have the right to do so;
" but before assuming so solemn a responsibility, they
" should be assured that they are not acting from caprice
" or prejudice, that they are not controlled by their will
" or their wishes, but from a deep and confident convic-
" tion that the court is wrong and that they are right.
" Before saying this, upon their oaths, it is their duty to
" reflect whether from their study and experience they
" are better qualified to judge of the law than the court.
" If, under all the circumstances, they are prepared to
" say that the court is wrong in its exposition of the law,
" the statute has given them that right."

This instruction is, as we understand the authorities,
wholly without warrant in the law. It is, in effect, an
attempt to destroy the statutory provision making the
jury judges of the law, and to constrain the jury into an
unquestioned acceptance of the law as delivered by the
presiding judge. This is not the intent of the statute.

The history of litigation is too full of the findings by the courts of review of grave errors as to the view of the law adopted by the trial court, and presented in the instructions, to make it permissible in a case of this kind for the judge to lecture the jury upon the solemnity of the responsibility which they would assume if they undertook to reach a conclusion based upon their views of the law as properly applicable to the case. The statute of our state, which makes the jury the judges of the law, ﹐ did not confine this provision to such jurors who have made the science of the law the study of their life, did not intend to limit the power conferred thereby to men " who from their study and experience are better quali-" fied to judge of the law than the court." The legislature could not possibly have in view a jury of that kind, because every day experience teaches that juries are seldom composed of lawyers; in fact lawyers are exempt from jury service.

In support of the correctness of instruction 13½ will probably be cited the case of *Schnier* v. *The People*, 23 Ill., 17. The language there used is the same as that embodied in this instruction, but it is apparent, from reading the opinion, that it was a general reasoning, and was not meant to sanction an instruction to the jury of that kind.

In the case of *Clem* v. *State*, 31 Indiana, 480, the propriety of such an instruction as this came directly under review. There the instruction, after stating that the jury might determine the law for themselves, proceeded to advise them that they should " be well satisfied in their own " minds of the incorrectness of the law as given by the " court before assuming the responsibility of determining " for themselves." It was held by the Supreme court of Indiana that upon careful analysis this instruction was in direct conflict with the provision of the constitution of that state that "in all criminal cases the jury shall have the " right to determine the law."

In commenting upon this matter the Supreme court of Indiana used the following language:

" If the judge adorns his high place by his learning and " impartiality, his jurors will be apt to rely upon his in- " structions, because they will deem them correct. They " may reasonably rely on them as a trustworthy source of " information concerning the law, as they would upon a " truthful witness concerning the facts, not because any " rule of law requires that they must, but because their " own common sense suggests the credit due to the legal " opinion of such a judge. But, on the other hand, a " magistrate destitute of character for either knowledge " of the law or uprightness in his administration, and who " so deports himself through the trial as to destroy con- " fidence in his fairness, will not be so apt to command " the confidence of his jury. He would not be worthy of " it. Distrust would, in such a case, result from the ex- " ercise of a sound judgment. The constitutional pro- " vision means that in criminal cases the jury shall be free " to exercise this judgment. It does not proceed upon " the presumption that all judges know the law, and will " impartially declare it, but, on the contrary, its necessity " was suggested by circumstances which proved that this " was not true. Judges had, in England, stained the " ermine by using their position to secure the conviction of " citizens in defiance of law, to serve the purposes of party. " It might be done again, and here. We were entering " upon the experiment of an elective judiciary under " which judges might be chosen for partisan services, and " might be too ready to serve the interest that had given " them position. Criminal prosecutions had ever been a

" favorite resort of those in power in times of high ex-
" citement. It would be some security against possible
" abuses to put the ultimate function of judgment of the
" law as well as the facts in the hands of the jury drawn
" from the body of the county; and hence it was done.
" It is enough that it is so written. * * * The courts
" have no authority to modify it, for that would be to de-
" feat, in a measure at least, the end which it was de-
" signed to secure."

VIII. Proper Instructions for the Defendants Refused.

We believe the proper rule of law, as applicable to the facts in the case at bar, is as presented in several of the instructions asked in behalf of the plaintiffs in error and which were refused by the court. We refer particularly under this head to instructions 3, 8, 9, 11 and 18, which are as follows (1 A., 12 *et seq.*):

" 3. The court instructs the jury that, in order to con-
" vict these defendants, they must not only find that they
" entered into an illegal conspiracy, and that the Hay-
" market meeting was an unlawful assembly in aid of said
" conspiracy, but in addition thereto that the bomb by
" which officer Degan lost his life was cast by a member
" of said conspiracy in aid of the common design, or by
" a person outside of said conspiracy, aided and ad-
" vised by all or some one of these defendants; but in any
" event, should you find such a conspiracy from the evi-
" dence to have been in existence, any one or more of
" these defendants not found beyond a reasonable doubt
" to have been a member thereof, and who is or are not
" proved beyond a reasonable doubt to have been present
" at the Haymarket meeting, or who, if present, did not

" knowingly counsel, aid or abet the throwing of the
" bomb by which officer Degan lost his life, such defend-
" ant or defendants you are bound to acquit.

" 8. If the jury believe from the evidence that the de-
" fendants or any one of them entered into a conspiracy
" to bring about a change of government for the ameliora-
" tion of the condition of the working classes by peace-
" able means, if possible, but if necessary to resort to
" force for that purpose, and that in addition thereto in
" pursuance of that object the Haymarket meeting was
" assembled by such conspirator or conspirators to discuss
" the best means to right the grievances of the working
" classes, without any intention of doing any unlawful act
" on that occasion, and while so assembled the bomb by
" which officer Degan lost his life was thrown by a person
" outside of said conspiracy, and without the knowledge
" and approval of the defendant or defendants, so found
" to have entered into said conspiracy, then and in
" that case the court instructs the jury that they are
" bound to acquit the defendants.

" 9. The court instructs the jury that it is not enough
" to find that the defendants unlawfully conspired to over-
" throw the present form of government, and that the
" Haymarket meeting was an unlawful assembly called
" by these defendants in furtherance of that conspiracy,
" but you must find, in addition thereto, that the bomb by
" which officer Degan lost his life was thrown by a mem-
" ber of said conspiracy, in aid of the common design; or
" if you should find that it was thrown by a person not
" proved beyond a reasonable doubt to have been a mem-
" ber of said conspiracy, then you must find that these de-
" fendants knowingly aided and abetted or advised such
" bomb-thrower to do the act, otherwise you are bound
" to acquit them.

" 11. The court further instructs the jury, that unless
" you find from the evidence, beyond all reasonable doubt,
" that there was a conspiracy existing to which the de-
" fendants or some of them were parties, and that the act
" resulting in the death of Mathias J. Degan was done by
" somebody who was a party to said conspiracy, and in
" pursuance of the common design of said conspiracy, you
" must find the defendants not guilty, unless the evidence
" convinces you, beyond all reasonable doubt, that the de-
" fendants or any of them personally committed the act
" resulting in the death of Mathias J. Degan, as charged
" in the indictment, or that the defendants or any of them
" stood by and aided, abetted or assisted, or not being
" present, had advised, aided, encouraged or abetted the
" perpetration of the crime charged in the indictment, and
" then you should find guilty only those defendants as to
" whom the evidence satisfies you, beyond all reasonable
" doubt, that they thus committed or aided in the commis-
" sion of the crime charged in the indictment.

" 18. Although certain of the defendants may have
" advised the use of force in opposition to the legally con-
" stituted authorities, or the overthrow of the laws of the
" land, yet unless the jury can find, beyond all reasonable
" doubt, that they specifically threw the bomb which
" killed Degan, or aided, advised, counseled, assisted or
" encouraged said act, or the doing of some illegal act or
" the accomplishment of some act by illegal means in the
" furtherance of which said bomb was thrown, you should
" return said defendants not guilty."

We respectfully submit that these instructions above
quoted correctly announce the law as applicable to the
case at bar, and insist that they should have been given
as asked, and that the refusal so to do was manifest error.
No other instructions given in the case presented this
theory.

Two other instructions, particularly, were asked by the plaintiffs in error and refused, which we insist should have been given. No. 1 (1 A., 12; O, 10) is as follows:

"No person can be legally convicted under the laws of Illinois on account of any opinion or principles entertained by him. It cannot be material in this case that defendants, or some of them, are or may be socialists, communists or anarchists, and no prejudice ought to be borne against them on account thereof by the jury, although the jury may believe their doctrines are false and pernicious."

What objection is there, what well-founded objection, to this instruction? And certainly, in view of the character of the jury examinations, and particularly in view of the appeals by the state's attorney in his closing argument to the passions and prejudices of the jury against the defendants, as supposed socialists, anarchists or communists, it was most fit and proper that an instruction of this character should be given, to, at least, measurably protect plaintiffs in error from the improper influence of these appeals. As to these features of the address of the state's attorney, we shall have occasion to comment later, but at present content ourselves with the mere reference as serving to illustrate the propriety of the instruction asked, and the error of its refusal.

Instruction 13 asked in behalf of the plaintiffs in error (1 A., 15; Vol. O, 15), was as follows:

"The court further instructs the jury, that under the constitution of this state, it is the right of the people to assemble in a peaceable manner to consult for what they believe to be the common good, and that so long as such meeting is peaceably conducted, orderly, and not tending to riot or a breach of the peace, no official or authority has or can have any legal right to attempt the dispersal thereof in a forcible manner. Such attempt, if made, would be unwarranted and illegal, and might legally be resisted with such necessary and reasonable degree of force as to prevent the consummation of such dispersal.

" If the jury believe from the evidence in this cause that the meeting of May 4, 1886, was called for a legal purpose, and at the time it was ordered to disperse by the police was being conducted in an orderly and peaceable manner, and was about peaceably to disperse; and that the defendants, or those participating in said meeting, had, in connection therewith, no illegal or felonious purpose or design, then the order for the dispersal thereof was unauthorized, illegal, and in violation of the rights of said assembly and of the people who were there gathered.

" And if the jury further believe from the evidence that the meeting was a quiet and orderly meeting, lawfully convened, and that the order for its dispersal was unauthorized and illegal under the provisions of the constitution of this state referred to, and that upon such order being given, some person in said gathering, without the knowledge, aid, counsel, procurement, encouragement or abetting of the defendants, or any of them, then or theretofore given, and solely because of his own passion, fear, hatred, malice or ill-will, or in pursuance of his view of the right of self-defense, threw a bomb among the police, wherefrom resulted the murder or homicide charged in the indictment, then the defendants would not be liable for the results of such bomb, and your verdict should be not guilty."

We respectfully submit and insist that this instruction is absolutely correct in its enunciation of the law, was applicable to the issue before the jury and the evidence which had been adduced upon that issue, and should have been given. We insist that no valid excuse can be urged for the refusal to give this instruction as asked. If, in point of fact, the jury should have been led, under this instruction, if given, to believe from the evidence that the bomb at the Haymarket was thrown by some one in that gathering, without the knowledge, aid, counsel, procurement, encouragement or abetting of the defendants, or any of them, then or theretofore given, and solely because of his own passion, fear, hatred, malice or ill-will, or in pursuance of his view of the right of self-defense, then the defendants would not have been liable for the results of such bomb, and the jury should, in that event, have found a verdict of not guilty; and should have been instructed so to do. The court erred, we submit, in refusing to give this instruction. It called particular attention of the jury to the evidence bearing upon the character of the meeting which was then and there being held, and to the evidence bearing upon the action of the police in attempting the dispersal of that meeting, and stated correctly the law under the constitution, as to the right to peaceable assemblage and discussion of alleged grievances. These were matters that, in the light of the evidence in this record, the plaintiffs in error had a right to have considered by the jury. All these matters were matters which might furnish to the jury some suggestion explanatory of the conduct of the unknown bomb-thrower, and tending to show that his action might have resulted from his own disposition and the special circumstances of the hour, and not at all from the advice, or by the aid or procurement of the plaintiffs in error. The law was correctly stated in this instruction; it presented correctly an hypothesis consistent with the theory of the innocence of the defendants, and explaining the alleged offense; and it should unquestionably have been given as asked. We submit that the refusal to give it was error.

An affidavit of John Philip Deluse, of Indianapolis, was filed in support of the motion for a new trial (1 A., 28; O, 81), in which he states that in the beginning of May, 1886, a man entered his saloon in Indianapolis, and while there inquired as to how the labor movement stood in that city. Being told that everything was quiet there, he stated that he came from New York, and believed he would go to Chicago, and then, pointing to his satchel, which he held in his hand, and which seemed to be heavy, he stated: " You will hear of some trouble there very soon. I have got something here that will work. You will hear of it." As he was passing out of the door he stopped, held up his satchel, and said again: " You will hear of it soon." Deluse says that the incident made no special impression upon his mind at the moment, but that when a day or two afterwards the news of the explosion of the bomb came, he immediately put the two things together and reached the conclusion that this stranger was the bomb-thrower.

Now, it be may be said that this story is improbable. Yet it is not impossible—it is not even unreasonable, and it *may* be the fact—that the bomb at the Haymarket was thrown by some one who was an entire stranger to these plaintiffs in error, only two of whom were present at the time of the explosion of the bomb, and that it was thrown by some one not at all influenced by their advice or prompted by their suggestions. Nay, it may have been thrown by some one who was an enemy of theirs, and not at all in their counsel. These suggestions serve to show the humanity and wisdom of the rule for which we contend, that the state must be required by its proof to connect the alleged accessories with the principal felon by legal proof,

before they can ask the conviction of the alleged accessories, and serves to illustrate the propriety of instruction
13, erroneously refused.

IX. THE INSTRUCTION GIVEN BY JUDGE GARY
SUA MOTU.

After having given the instructions in behalf of the
people, followed by those given on behalf of the defendants, the presiding judge of his own motion gave an instruction, which by its terms, could not but operate to
supersede all other instructions given in the case. The
instruction referred to was in the following language
(A., 23, 24; O, 35): " The statute requires that instruc-
" tions by the court to the jury shall be in writing, and
" only relate to the law of the case. The practice under
" the statute is that the counsel prepare, on each side, a
" set of instructions, and present them to the court, and if
" approved to be read by the court as the law of the case.
" It may happen, by reason of the great number pre-
" sented, and the hurry and confusion of passing on them
" in the midst of the trial, with a large audience to keep
" in order, that there may be some apparent inconsistency
" in them, but if they are carefully scrutinized such incon-
" sistencies will probably disappear. In any event, how-
" ever, the gist and pith of all is, that if advice and en-
" couragement to murder was given; if murder was done
" in pursuance of and materially induced by such ad-
" vice and encouragement, then those who gave such
" advice and encouragement are guilty of the murder.
" Unless the evidence, either direct or circumstantial, or
" both, proves the guilt of one or more of the defend-
" ants upon this principle so fully that there is no reason-
" able doubt of it, your duty to them requires you to

" acquit them; if it does so prove, then your duty to the
" state requires you to convict whoever is so proved
" guilty. The case of each defendant should be consid-
" ered with the same care and scrutiny as if he alone
" were on trial. If a conspiracy, having violence and
" murder as its object, is fully proved, then the acts
" and declarations of each conspirator in furtherance
" of the conspiracy are the acts and declarations of each
" one of the conspirators. But the declarations of any
" conspirator, before or after the 4th of May, which are
" merely narrative as to what had been or would be done,
" and not made to aid in carrying into effect the object of
" the conspiracy, are only evidence against the one who
" made them. What are the facts and what is the truth
" the jury must determine from the evidence, and from
" that alone. If there are any unguarded expressions in
" any of the instructions, which seem to assume the exist-
" ence of any facts, or to be any intimation as to what is
" proved, all such expressions must be disregarded, and
" the evidence only looked to to determine the facts."

Whatever may be said as to the effort of the court
here, in connection with a brief summary of the State's
formal instructions, to epitomize and again present to the
jury the theory suggested by the court for the trial of the
cause, in connection with his ruling upon our objection
interposed during Waller's examination, it will hardly be
pretended that in the above instruction the court made
any attempt to present, or summarize, the instructions
given in behalf of the defendants. For example, there was
no suggestion in this instruction, of the rule that the jury
were bound to reconcile the facts, if reasonably possible,
with any hypothesis of innocence advanced. Neither does it
present the substance of the instruction for the defendants,
commencing near the bottom of 1 A., 21. Neither

did it present the law in reference to what constitutes a reasonable doubt. We cite these points simply as illustrations. The instruction in fact merely attempting to summarize the instructions given for the state, it was exactly equivalent to saying: The instructions given for the defendants may seem to conflict with those given for the state, but the conflict is only apparent, and in fact the whole law is as given for the state, namely: and then repeating the substance of the state's instructions.

But beyond this, the instruction, we submit, was absolutely erroneous in the principal proposition laid down. It will not be denied, we think, that a man might advise one murder, or the perpetration of a homicide under certain circumstances; that a person listening thereto might be encouraged by such advice and materially induced thereby to go out and commit a totally different murder, or a totally different homicide. For example, it might be that the defendants advised resistance to an armed attack by the police to the extent of homicide. A party listening to such advice might go out, and, inflamed and encouraged thereby, kill a policeman who was at the time in the peace of the state. It will not be pretended that under such circumstances the mere giving of advice to murder generally, or to do one particular murder, would make the party responsible for a specific murder other than that covered by the advice, however much the murderer might be influenced thereby. Yet that is the scope of this instruction, wherein the court says: " If advice and " encouragement to murder [upon whom? where? when? " by what means?] was given, if murder was done " in pursuance of and materially induced by such advice " and encouragement, then those who gave such advice " and encouragement are guilty of the murder." The impropriety of the giving of this instruction, and par-

ticularly the giving of it at the close of the defendant's
instructions, whereby any impression that the defendant's
instructions might have made upon the minds of any of the
jury was likely to be obliterated, is obvious in the light alike
of reason and authority. This court, in *McEwen* v. *Morey*,
60 Ill., 32, used, with reference to a final instruction given
on the court's own motion, and attempting to epitomize
the entire law of the case, the following language:

" The counsel for appellant insists that the court erred
" in orally qualifying or superseding the instructions
" already given by the remark prefacing the giving of
" said instruction [which remark was as follows: ' I take
" upon myself to concentrate all there is in these instructions
" into this one, as embodying all the law necessary for
" the case.'] The bill of exceptions does not state that
" the remark was orally made, though it is fairly infer-
" able that it was. If oral, it was in violation of the
" the spirit of the statute, because it would have the direct
" effect, though directed to counsel in the hearing of
" the jury, to induce the jury to disregard all the other
" instructions, and regard only that given by the court of
" his own motion, ' as embodying all the law necessary
" for the case.' If in writing, and directed to the jury,
" it would operate as a supersedure of all the other in-
" structions; and the one given of the court's own motion
" did not embody all the law necessary for the case, be-
" cause it withdrew from the jury all consideration of the
" question respecting the issuing and acceptance of the
" receipt given in evidence. The evidence upon that
" point was properly before the jury, and the defendant
" had the clear right to have it passed upon by the jury
" under the instructions which the court had given as ap-
" plicable to it."

X. The Instruction as to the Form of the Verdict.
(1 A., 24; O, 37.)

"If all of the defendants are found guilty the form of "the verdict will be:

"We, the jury, find the defendants guilty of murder in manner and form as charged in the indictment, and fix "the penalty.

"If all are found not guilty the form of the verdict "will be:

"We, the jury, find the defendants not guilty.

"If part of the defendants are found guilty and part "not guilty, the form of the verdict will be:

"We, the jury, find the defendant or defendants (nam-"ing him or them) not guilty; we find the defendant or "defendants (naming him or them) guilty of murder in "manner and form as charged in the indictment, and fix "the penalty," which was duly excepted to.

As to this instruction, our objection is that it was fatally defective in that it left to the jury absolutely no alternative as to each and every one of the plaintiffs in error between a verdict of not guilty and a verdict of guilty of murder in manner and form as charged in the indictment.

Now, it will not be denied but that the jury were entitled, if in their judgment the evidence so warranted, to find that the offense committed was not murder, but was a lower grade of homicide. In fact, after the jury went from the bar, the court, upon the instance of the plaintiffs in error, permitted the preparation of an instruction embodying this principle of law, and thereafter sent for the jury, and upon their return into court, gave this instruction (1 A., 25; O, 38, 39); but the giving of this instruction at the time and under the circumstances it was given, without giving to them an instruction with reference to the form of the verdict, should they find any of the defendants guilty of manslaughter, certainly did not serve to cure the error in the instruction as to the form of the verdict above set forth. Let us take by way of illustrating our position, the case of Mr. Neebe. In our view there was no evidence whatever to justify his being held to answer to this indictment upon the evidence adduced by the state, but in the presence of the jury, the court had refused our motion for an instruction in Mr. Neebe's favor, and had argued the circumstantial evidence supposed to tend in some measure to criminate him, and thereupon refused to allow his discharge. Having done all this in the presence of the jury, he finally follows it up by an instruction which in effect said to them: "Gentlemen of the jury, you must either "acquit Mr. Neebe, or you must find him guilty of mur- "der in manner and form as charged in the indictment."

We cite Mr. Neebe's case simply for the purpose of illustrating the vice of the instruction, and not because it is more vicious in his case than in the case of any other of the plaintiffs in error. When the court undertakes upon its own motion to give an instruction as to the form of the verdict in a capital case, the instruction must be correct in every particular, such that in the nature of things it could not have wrought prejudice to the defendants.

XI. Theory of the Instructions as a Whole.

A brief consideration of the instructions given on behalf of the state as a whole is proper at this juncture. Do they, when read together, without reference to the special criticisms above urged, present a fair, just and full view of the law applicable to the case, so as to clearly and intelligently direct the jury in their investigation and determination of the issue submitted to them—such a summary of the law as it was the duty of the court to present, to avoid possible injustice to the accused? Do they secure certainly to the accused the benefit of every reasonable doubt, whether arising from a consideration of the evidence offered or the absence of evidence? They should be, as far as possible, simple, lucid, consistent homogeneous. They should not be contradictory nor unnecessarily involved. They should be free from duplicity, should fit the evidence, and should be fair to the accused.

In the instructions under consideration, in fact three different conspiracies, as to the object named, were presented. In instruction 4 the court presented the hypothesis of a conspiracy " to overthrow *the law* by force, *or* " to unlawfully resist the officers of the law." In instruction 5 the hypothesis was of "a conspiracy to over- "throw the existing order of society, and to bring about " social revolution by force, *or* to destroy the legal " authorities by force ": while instruction 5½ is based on the hypothesis of a conspiracy "*to excite the people* or "classes of the people of this city to sedition, tumult and " riot, to use deadly weapons against and take the lives of " other persons," etc.

Under which hypothesis did the jury find? The first of instruction 4? That is only a conspiracy " to over- " throw *the law* by force "—for the unlawful resistance of the officers of the law suggested is put *disjunctively*. Can murder be predicated upon a conspiracy "*to overthrow* "THE LAW?" Can *the law* be murdered, so as to affix the death penalty to the offender? Could Fielden's advice to stab, throttle, resist and impede *the law* be made the basis of responsibility for a murder by an unknown man? Did these instructions as a whole *fairly* present a homogeneous, consistent and uncontradictory hypothesis upon which to rest a verdict of guilt? But particularly, can such instructions as these be sustained when, under each of the hypotheses presented, conviction is allowed for the act of a wholly unidentified principal, upon the mere arbitrary finding by the jury, without support from competent evidence, that the criminal actor was a party with the plaintiffs in error in some one of these supposed conspiracies?

Was it *fair* to the accused to present to the jury these different hypotheses of conspiracy and to *require* a general verdict of guilty or not guilty of " murder in manner and "form as charged in the indictment," in view of the evidence which had been allowed to go to the jury? Should not the jury have been required to make their verdict special in view of that evidence? For that evidence tended to establish three different conspiracies, to some of which the state's evidence affirmatively showed that the accused were not *all* parties, *i. e.*, (1) the general conspiracy " to overthrow the law;" (2) the Monday night conspiracy, with which only Engel, Fischer, and possibly Lingg were connected; and (3) the special conspiracy to throw the Haymarket bomb, " *to perpetrate the crime,*" with which the state's evidence connected *only* Spies, Fischer, and possibly Schwab. With such diversity of proof, and under the distinct hypotheses of the different instructions, what did the jury in fact find?

Under a fair charge, requiring the jury to designate what they found from the evidence, they might have disclosed that in their judgment the evidence, under the doctrines announced by the court, showed Spies and Schwab to have been connected with conspiracies (1) and (3);

Fischer to have been connected with conspiracies (2) and (3); Engel and Lingg with conspiracies (1) and (2); Parsons and Fielden with conspiracy (1) alone; and Neebe with none of these conspiracies; and only such finding could be possibly justified on the state's own evidence. But upon such finding no judgment of guilty could legally have been entered in this cause.

In *O'Connell* v. *R.*, 11 C. & F., 155, it was held that upon a count in an indictment against eight defendants, charging one conspiracy to effect certain objects, a finding that three of the defendants were guilty generally; that five of them were guilty of conspiring to effect some, and not guilty as to the residue of these objects, is bad in law and repugnant; inasmuch as the finding that the three were guilty was a finding that they were guilty of conspiring with the other five to effect all the objects of the conspiracy, whereas, by the same finding it appears that the other five were guilty of conspiring to effect only some of the objects.

Was it fair to the accused to give the instruction as to the form of verdict, when under the instructions the court allowed the conclusion of guilt to be *guessed* out by the jury under such diverse and repugnant hypotheses, and upon such distinct proofs relating to different ones of the accused?

The Rule Recognized by this Court.

It will doubtless be urged, strenuously, that the doctrine presented in the instructions for the people has received the sanction of this court in the cases of *Brennan* v. *The People*, 15 Ill., 511, and *Lamb* v. *The People*, 96 Ill., 73; and it is proper that in this connection we should examine those cases. It is well settled, that only as the language of an opinion is applied to the facts of the case

before the court, can the true rule established by the
decision be accurately deduced. General expressions,
not directly pertinent to the case considered, cannot be
relied on as announcing a rule of general application.

Let us say here that with the rule of law as declared
in the cases now under review, we have no occasion to
differ. That rule, *as interpreted by the facts in those cases
respectively*, is no other than this: that if two or more
persons conspire to do *an unlawful act*, all of those shown
to be parties to the conspiracy are responsible for (1) the
execution of *the act planned, by any one of the conspirators;*
or (2), for the doing of *any act by any one of such conspirators which naturally or necessarily results in course of an
"attempt to execute the common design;"* on the doctrine
that such naturally or necessarily resultant act is at law
presumed to be within the intention of the conspirators.
There is not in the doctrine of these cases anything that
militates in the slightest degree against our contentions—
that if the act is an independent crime, attributable to the
unconstrained volition of the criminal actor; or if it be in
fact unadvised by, and foreign to the accomplishment of
the general design, of the alleged conspirators; or if the
legal proofs fail to establish beyond reasonable doubt, in
a case where the accused are not present aiding the act,
the identity of the criminal actor as a member or instrument of the alleged conspiracy, no conviction can be
legally had; because in every such case the evidence fails
to sustain the averment that the accused had " advised,
" assisted, abetted or encouraged THE *perpetration of*
" THE *crime.*"

As we read the case, our position was distinctly recognized in *Brennan* v. *People*, 15 Ill., 511, where, in defining
what was enough to establish the guilt of an accessory,
this language is used:

" It is sufficient that *they combined with those committing* "*the deed* to do an unlawful act. * * * If several "persons conspire to do an unlawful act, and death hap-"pen in the prosecution of the common object, all are "alike guilty of the homicide. The act of ONE OF "THEM *done in furtherance of the original design*, is "in consideration of law the act of all; and he who "advises or encourages another to do *an illegal act* is "responsible for all the natural or probable consequences "that may arise from this participation."

Here is distinctly recognized the rule that an accessory can be held guilty only in case it is made to appear that the criminal act was done by one acting in conjunction with, and under the advice and encouragement of, the accused; which would involve an identification of the doer of the criminal deed, as connected with and representing in the act the parties accused. The facts in that case may be briefly stated for the purpose of illustrating this rule. *Certain parties, of whom the defendant was one, started out together to make an illegal assault, in pursuance of which conspiracy and in execution of which purpose the party who was the object of the assault was killed by one of the parties to the conspiracy.* The evidence showed all this; and therefore established indisputably a case of direct relationship between the accused and the criminal actor in the *very act* of the commission of the crime. We understand that at the common law where parties combine deliberately in an assault, and murder results, all are guilty as principals. In the Brennan case the defense attempted to be interposed was that there was no *preconcert to kill;* and the real point ruled in the case was, that it was not necessary to prove *such* preconcert; *it was sufficient to show it was a conspiracy or agreement to do an unlawful act, and that* THE KILLING *was a natural consequence of* THE ACT *agreed to be done, and happened in the carrying out of the illegal purpose.*

The case of *Lamb* v. *The People*, 96 Ill., 73, was disposed of upon a totally different principle, involving the
application of the first branch of our position *supra*, the
sole point ruled in this case being, that to warrant a conviction the evidence must show that the crime charged
was naturally incidental to the conspiracy proved,
and not a result of the independent volition of the
criminal actor. It appears that in the Lamb case
there was proved against the accused a conspiracy to
commit a distinct felony, viz: a particular burglary. This
executed, the stolen goods were placed in the custody of
one of the conspirators other than Lamb for safe disposition. As these goods were being unloaded at a pawn-
shop, a police officer who came up was killed by the party
in charge of the goods; but this distinct felony was committed in the absence, and without the knowledge, participation or advice of Lamb. As applicable to this case
disclosed by the proofs, this court, while stating broadly
the doctrine of the liability of co-conspirators for acts
done *in the carrying out of the original design*, yet hold
that *there is no liability for a separate and independent
crime committed by one of the conspirators outside of the
original agreement*. The whole language of the case
must be read as applicable to an agreement between
parties to commit a *certain* offense, and their liability for
crimes naturally incident to the principal specific agreement committed *by a party to the original conspiracy* in
the prosecution thereof.

Surely, no support is afforded by these cases, fairly
considered, for the novel doctrines under which the conviction of plaintiffs in error was *induced;* that (to apply
these doctrines to the case at bar) if a conspiracy to overthrow the law, *or* change the order of society, *or* take the
lives of the officers of the law, OR unlawfully resist the

lawful authorities, OR " to excite the people to sedition, tu-
" mult and riot, to take the lives of people," in pursuance
of which some conspirator " advises murder " without
designating time, place or occasion for its commission;
and if some of these conspirators call and attend a meeting
for the sole purpose of denouncing an alleged grievance,
and at such meeting *somebody* does murder, *all* the conspirators are liable, without any evidence establishing in
any manner the identity of the murderer as a member of
the alleged conspiracy, or as advised at any time by any
of the alleged conspirators, the proofs of the state affirmatively showing that *the murder done, the act performed*, THE
crime perpetrated, was not contemplated, designed, advised, aided, abetted or encouraged by any of the accused.
Or to put the proposition in another form, without any
evidence whatever to show that the man who threw the
bomb at the Haymarket meeting had been advised, assisted, encouraged or abetted by the plaintiffs in error or
any of them to throw that bomb at that meeting. The
absence of this proof connecting the bomb-thrower as a
cognizable individual with the accused left a gap in the
case of the state which the law required to be bridged.
It was simply leaped by the whole crowd, the court in the
lead. It serves to illustrate how irresistible is the sweep-
ing current of an excited public opinion, and how under
it, as in a panic in an audience at the cry of fire, the cool-
est seem to lose their heads.

Such were the ruling and instructions under which the
plaintiffs in error were required in this cause to meet the
issue involving their lives. Let us now consider under
what rulings they were required to select the tribunal,
which was to pass upon the question of their guilt or innocence, and the character of the jury selected under
these rulings, to whom the issue upon which they were
arraigned was submitted.

BB. ERRORS IN CONNECTION WITH THE EMPANELING OF THE JURY.

I. THE LAW RELATING TO THE QUALIFICATIONS OF JURORS.

a. CONSTITUTIONAL PROVISIONS.

The constitution of the United States, 6th article of the amendments, provides as follows:

" In all criminal prosecutions the accused shall enjoy " the right to a speedy and public trial by *an impartial* "*jury* of the state and district wherein the crime shall " have been committed."

The constitution of this state of 1818, article 8, section 9, in the last clause, provides:

" In prosecutions by indictment or information the ac- " cused hath a right to a speedy public trial by *an im-* "*partial jury* of the vicinage."

The constitution of 1848, article 13, section 9, provides:

" That in all criminal prosecutions the accused hath a "right to be heard by himself and counsel,   *   *   * " and in prosecutions by indictment or information, a " speedy public trial by *an impartial jury* of the county " and district wherein the offense shall have been com- " mitted."

The constitution of this state, 1870, article 2, section 9, provides:

" In all criminal prosecutions the accused shall have the "right to appear and defend in person and by counsel, "   *   *   * and a speedy public trial by *an impartial* "*jury* of the county or district in which the offense is al- " leged to have been committed."

Therefore we have, all alike in their requirements, the constitution of the United States, the constitutions of Illinois of 1818, of 1848 and the new constitution of 1870.

No statute attempting to prescribe the qualifications of jurors with reference to their opinions was ever passed in the State of Illinois until after the adoption of the constitution of 1870, but the matter of such qualifications was left entirely to the decision of the courts, pursuant to the rules established by the common law and the law of this country, under the United States constitution and those of the various states of the Union.

b. CONSTRUCTION OF THE MEANING OF THE CONSTITUTION OF THE UNITED STATES AS TO WHAT CONSTITUTES AN IMPARTIAL JURY.

The trial of Aaron Burr, for treason, held at Richmond, in the Circuit court of the United States, in the summer of 1807, presents the ablest discussion and the clearest construction, by the highest authority, of the meaning of the constitution of the United States as to what constitutes an impartial jury. The circumstances which led to the trial of Aaron Burr were somewhat similar in their notoriety to the case at bar. Burr had organized an expedition for conquest south-west of the United States, and perhaps embracing New Orleans within them; the newspapers of the time were full of the details of this expedition, and every man of intelligence had read the papers on that subject, and most of them had formed an opinion of greater or less fixedness and weight. On Monday, August 10, 1807, the jurors were summoned into court, and an examination of them had, by the able attorneys engaged in that cause. Some of these jurymen were rejected for cause, and others were held over for argument and the decision of the court. After a very able argument by Mr. Martin, Mr. Botts, Mr. McCrea, Mr. Wirt, Mr. Hay, Mr. Wyckam and Mr. Randolph, the chief justice, MARSHALL, decided the question as follows:

" The great value of a trial by jury certainly consists
" in its fairness and impartiality. Those who most prize
" the institution prize it because it furnishes a tribunal
" which may be expected to be uninfluenced by any bias
" of the mind. I have always conceived, and still con-
" ceive, an impartial jury, as required by the common law,
" and as secured by the constitution, must be composed of
" men who will fairly hear the testimony which may be
" offered to them, and bring in their verdict according to
" that testimony and according to the law arising on it.
" This is not to be expected, certainly the law does not
" expect it, where the jurors, before they hear the testi-
" mony, have deliberately formed and delivered an opinion
" that the person whom they are to try is guilty or inno-
" cent of the charge alleged against him. The jury
" should enter upon the trial with minds open to those
" impressions which the testimony and law of the case
" ought to make, not with those preconceived opinions
" which will resist those impressions. All the provisions
" of the law are calculated to obtain this end.

" Why is it that the most distant relative of a party
" cannot serve upon his jury? Certainly the single cir-
" cumstance of relationship, taken in itself, unconnected
" with its consequences, would furnish no objection. The
" real reason of the rule is, that the law suspects the rela-
" tive of partiality; suspects his mind to be under a bias
" which will prevent his fairly hearing and fairly deciding
" on the testimony which may be offered to him. The
" end to be obtained is an impartial jury; to secure this

" end, a man is prohibited from serving on it whose
" connection with a party is such as to induce sus-
" picion of partiality. The relationship may be remote;
" the person may never have seen the party; he may de-
" clare that he feels no prejudice in the case, and yet the
" law cautiously incapacitates him from serving on the jury,
" because it suspects prejudice; because in general a per-
" son in a similar situation would feel prejudice. It would
" be strange if the law were chargeable with the inconsist-
" ency of carefully protecting the end from being defeated
" by particular means, and leaving it to be defeated by other
" means. It would be strange if the law would be so
" solicitous to secure a fair trial as to exclude a distant, un-
" known relative from the jury, and yet be totally regard-
" less of those in whose minds feelings existed much more
" unfavorable to an impartial decision of the case. It is
" admitted that where there are strong personal preju-
" dices, the person entertaining them is incapacitated as a
" juror, but it is denied that fixed opinions respecting guilt
" constitutes a similar incapacity. Why do personal preju-
" dices constitute a just cause of challenge? Solely because
" the individual who is under their influence is presumed
" to have a bias on his mind, which will prevent an impar-
" tial decision of the case according to the testimony.
" He may declare that, notwithstanding these prejudices,
" he is determined to listen to the evidence and be gov-
" erned by it; but the law will not trust him. Is there
" less reason to suspect him who has prejudged the case,
" and has deliberately formed and delivered an opin-
" ion upon it? Such a person may believe that he
" will be regulated by the testimony, but the law sus-
" pects him, and certainly not without reason. He will
" listen with more favor to that testimony which confirms
" than to that which would change his opinion. It is not

" to be expected he will weigh evidence or argument
" as fairly as a man whose judgment is not made up in the
" case. It is for this reason that a juror who has once ren-
" dered a verdict in a case, or who has been sworn in a
" jury which has been divided, cannot again be sworn on
" the same case. He is not suspected of personal preju-
" dices, but he has formed and delivered an opinion, and is,
" therefore, deemed unfit to be a juror in the case. * * *

" In reflecting upon this subject, which I have done
" since the adjournment of yesterday, my mind has been
" forcibly impressed in contemplating the question pre-
" cisely in its reverse. If, instead of a panel composed
" of gentlemen who had almost unanimously formed, and
" publicly delivered, an opinion that the prisoner was
" guilty, the marshal had returned one composed of per-
" sons who had openly and publicly maintained his inno-
" cence, and who insist that, notwithstanding all the tes-
" timony in the possession of the public, they had no
" doubt that his designs were perfectly innocent; who
" had been engaged in repeated, open and animated
" altercation to prove him innocent, and that his objects
" were entirely opposite of those with which he was
" charged; would such men be considered impartial
" jurors? I cannot believe they would be thought so; I
" am confident I should not think so. I cannot declare a
" juror to be impartial who has advanced opinions against
" the prisoner which would be cause of challenge if ad
" vanced in his favor."

There is another question passed upon by this court,
which is material in the case at bar, and that is: suppose
in the Burr trial a juryman, from reading the newspaper or
hearing rumors, had formed and expressed an opinion,
that Burr entertained treasonable designs and was making
treasonable preparations, and arming a force for a treason-

able expedition, but whether or not he had committed the overt act of treason the juryman had not formed and expressed an opinion. The court in passing upon this question decided, in substance, that mere impressions founded on rumor will not disqualify the juror, but the formation of an opinion which goes far toward the decision of the whole case does disqualify him. The court uses the following language:

" It would seem to the court that to say that any man " who had formed an opinion on any fact conducive to " the final decision of the case would therefore be con- " sidered as disqualified from serving on the jury would " exclude intelligent and observing men whose minds " were really in a situation to decide upon the whole case " according to the testimony, and would perhaps be ap- " plying the letter of the rule requiring an impartial jury " with a strictness which is not necessary for the preser- " vation of the rule itself. But if the *opinion formed* " be on a point so essential as to go far towards " a decision of the whole case, and to have a real " influence on the verdict to be rendered, the dis- " tinction between a person who has formed such an " opinion and one who has in his mind decided the whole " case appears too slight to furnish the court with solid " ground for distinguishing between them. *The ques- " tion must always depend on the strength and nature of " the opinion which has been formed.* * * * The " cases put by way of illustration appeared to the court " to be strongly applicable to that under consideration. " They are those of burglary, of homicide, of passing " counterfeit money knowing it to be counterfeit; cases " in which the intention and the fact combine to consti- " tute the crime.

" If, in case of homicide, where the fact of killing was

" admitted or was doubtful, a juror should have made up
" and delivered the opinion that, though uninformed
" relative to the fact of killing, he was confident as to
" malice; he was confident that the prisoner had deliber-
" ately formed the intention of murdering the deceased,
" and was prosecuting that intention up to the time of
" his death; or if on a charge of passing bank notes
" knowing them to be counterfeit, the juror had declared
" that, though uncertain as to the fact of passing the
" notes, he was confident that the prisoner knew them to
" be counterfeit, few would think such a person suffi-
" ciently impartial to try the case according to testimony.
" The court considers these cases as strikingly analo-
" gous."

c. Interpretation by the Supreme Court of Illinois of the Provisions of our Constitutions
Touching the Qualification of Jurors.

Prior to the adoption of the constitution of 1870, and,
therefore, prior to the passage of any enactment by the
legislature touching the qualifications of jurors, with ref-
ference to their opinions, the Supreme court of this state
had frequently given a construction to the provisions of
the constitutions of 1818 and 1848, touching the qualifications of jurors.

Among others may be noted *Neeley* v. *The People*
(June term, 1852), 13 Ill., 685, where Treat, Chief Justice, says:

" It was held in *Smith* v. *Eames*, 3 Scam., 76, that, if a
" juror has *made a decided opinion* respecting the merits
" of the controversy, either from a personal knowledge
" of the facts, from the statements of the witnesses,
" from the relations of the parties, or from rumor, he is

" disqualified from trying the case, if challenged for
" cause. The rule was adhered to in the case of *Gard-*
" *ner* v. *The People,* 3 Scam., 83; *Vennum* v. *Harwood,*
" 1 Gilman, 659, and *Baxter* v. *The People,* 3 Gil., 368,
" and must now be considered as the settled doctrine of
" this court.

" Applying this test to the present case, the jurors were
" clearly incompetent, and the court properly allowed the
" challenge for cause. Each of the jurors *had formed a*
" *definite opinion* as to the guilt or innocence of the pris-
" oner, *based upon information as to the facts of the case,*
" *which he believed to be true.* His *opinion* was of a
" *positive* and not a hypothetical character. He would
" have entered the jury-box with a *fixed opinion* as to the
" question to be determined, which would have controlled
" his action as a juror, unless the testimony disclosed a
" state of facts materially different from what he already
" believed them to be."

The next case to which we call attention is that of
Gray v. *The People,* 26 Ill., 344 (April term, 1861),
which is a decision under the constitution of 1848.
BREESE, Justice, in delivering the opinion, used the following language:

" It is objected that the challenge for cause of a juror,
" William H. Anderson, should have been allowed. A
" critical examination has satisfied us this is a good point.
" This juror, in his examination, stated that he had read
" about the case in the papers, that he did not know the
" defendants, that he believed the reports that there was
" a house-breaking; if these defendants are the persons
" named in the newspapers, *has an opinion* as to their
" guilt or innocence. In the papers one of the per-
" sons named may have been Silas Gray; and if it should
" turn out that Silas Gray was one of the defendants,

" should have an opinion as to their guilt or innocence;
" does not know that Silas Gray is one of the defendants,
" and has no opinion of the guilt or innocence of the de-
" fendants.   This juror, with others objected to, de-
" clared he had not formed or expressed an opinion of the
" guilt or innocence of the defendants; that he had no
" bias or prejudice upon his mind, and could give the
" defendants a fair trial, according to the law and the evi-
" dence.

" This possibly might be so, but he declared in his ex-
" amination that he believed the statements of the news-
" papers that there had been a housebreaking, and if the
" prisoners were the persons named in the newspapers, he
" had an opinion of their guilt or innocence. He has
" *formed an opinion*, if it should turn out that one of the
" defendants was Silas Gray.

" These opinions are not hypothetical if the newspaper
" statements were true, but he says he believed those
" statements.

" This court said, in the case of *Smith* v. *Eames* (3
" Scam., 80): ' If the *opinion of the juror* is positive,
" though founded on rumor, and not hypothetical, he is
" disqualified.'   And this has been adhered to in criminal
" cases.   (*Gardner* v. *The People, id.*, 88.)

" The prisoner ought not to be forced to encounter a
" pre-existing opinion, deliberately formed on statements
" believed to be true, and which he would be required to
" remove.   Had the witness said he neither believed
" nor disbelieved the statement, he would have been com-
" petent."

In *Collins* v. *The People* (September term, 1868), 48
Ill., 146, delivering the opinion of the court, WALKER,
Justice, says:

" It is insisted that the court below erred in refusing to

" allow the challenges of plaintiffs in error to a number of
" jurors, comprising a part of the panel that tried him.
" These jurors stated that they had heard of the circum-
" stances of the difficulty; that they believed the state-
" ments, and upon these statements had *fixed opinions* as
" to the merits of the case, such as would require evidence
" to remove or change, but that the opinion could be
" changed by sufficient evidence; but that they had no
" prejudice against the accused, and they believed they
" could render a fair and impartial verdict according to
" the evidence.

" These are substantially the statements of some five of
" the jurors who tried the case, and were the ground of
" challenge by plaintiffs in error, but which were disal-
" lowed by the court trying the case in the court below,
" and that ruling is assigned as one of the errors in the
" record brought to this court.

" It has been repeatedly held by this court, that if a
" juror *has a decided opinion* respecting the merits of the
" controversy, either from a personal knowledge of the
" facts, from the statements of witnesses, from the rela-
" tion of the parties, or from rumor, he is disqualified from
" trying the case, if challenged for cause (citing, among
" cases, *Gray* v. *The People*, 26 Ill., 344). These cases
" must govern this case. A prisoner should never be
" required to encounter *a pre-existing opinion deliberately*
" *formed* which the juror believes is true, and which the
" prisoner would be obliged to overcome. When tried by
" such jurors, he cannot be said to have had a fair trial,
" unless he choose to permit him to act in his case. He
" has a right to be tried by men who are wholly impartial,
" without prepossession or prejudice against him or his
" cause. Tested by these rules, these jurors were incom-
" petent when objected to by the accused, and the court

" below erred in not allowing the challenges to these
" jurors."

We next cite *Chicago & Alton Railway Company* v.
Adler, 56 Ill., 344 (September term, 1870), which is the
first case after the adoption of the new constitution.

In that case the court, Mr. Justice WALKER delivering
the opinion, says:

" It is first urged that the court erred in refusing to
" allow the challenges of jurors made by appellants.
" Four of the jurors who tried the case were asked
" on their *voir dire*, if the evidence were evenly bal-
" anced, which way they would be inclined to find, and
" each answered that he would, in such case, lean against
" the defendants, and one of them stated that he would
" do so because the company was able to stand it, and he
" thought a private individual should 'have a little mite
" the advantage.'

" It is a fundamental principle that every litigant has
" a right to be tried by an *impartial and disinterested*
" *tribunal*. Bias or prejudice has always been regarded as
" rendering a juryman incompetent. And when a juror
" avows that one litigant should have any other ad-
" vantage than law and evidence give him, he declares his
" incompetency to decide the case. He thereby proclaims
" that he is so far partial as to be unable to do justice
" between litigants, or that he is so far uninformed, and
" his sense of right is so blunt, that he cannot perceive
" justice, or, perceiving it, is unwilling to be governed
" by it.

" The rule is so plain and manifest that the party claim-
" ing to recover must prove his cause of action, it is a
" matter of surprise that an adult can be found who would
" not know that such is the common sense as well as the
" common honesty of the rule. No ordinary business

" man would be willing that a claim pressed against
" him should be allowed, and he be compelled to pay it,
" when the evidence for and against the claim was evenly
" balanced. And how such men can bring themselves to
" apply a different rule, as jurors, to the right of others,
" is incompatible with the principles of justice. *Nor does
" the fact that jurors who avow, under oath, that they
" would incline to favor recovery by the plaintiff on evi-
" dence evenly balanced declare that they are impartial,
" in the slightest degree, tend to prove their impartiality.*
" Their statement only tends to prove that they are so
" far lost to a sense of justice that they regard what all
" right-thinking men know to be wrong as just and
" impartial.

" To try a cause by such a jury is to authorize men
" who state that they will lean, in their finding, against one
" of the parties, unjustly to determine the right of others,
" and it would be no difficult task to predict, even before
" the evidence was heard, the verdict that would be re-
" turned."

We further cite *Winnesheik Insurance Company* v.
Schueller, 60 Ill., 465 (September term, 1871). Mr. Justice
THORNTON, delivering the opinion of the court, says:

" It was error to overrule the challenge of the juror,
" Samuel Askey. He said that he had *some prejudice* in
" his mind against insurance companies generally; that
" his prejudice was founded on the fact that he could not
" comprehend their proceedings, that the prejudice would
" not affect his verdict.

" A man may have a prejudice against crime; against
" a mean action; against dishonesty, and still be a com-
" petent juror. This is proper, and such prejudice will
" never force a jury to prejudge an innocent and honest
" man.

" As to this juror, the feeling he entertained against
" insurance companies was of a bigoted and reprehensible
" character. It was not founded upon any knowledge or
" information of conduct which should condemn them,
" but merely upon the fact of his inability to understand
" the proceedings of these corporations.

" They must then disclose all their operations—open to
" him all their business transactions—in order to remove
" his suspicions. His prejudice, based upon the reason
" assigned, must have been deep seated, and would neces-
" sarily have affected his verdict.

" A juror should *stand indifferent* between the parties.
" *No bias* should influence his judgment and swerve him
" from strict impartiality. It would have required as
" much evidence to remove his unfounded prejudice as
" to convince him of the justice of the defense.

" The juror said that he had no more prejudice against
" this than any other company, but that he had a preju-
" dice against all insurance companies. How is it possi-
" ble that his mind would not be biased, and his determin-
" ation, to some extent, influenced? It is not necessary
" that his unfavorable impressions should be so strong
" that they cannot be shaken by evidence. It is sufficient
" if proof be necessary to restore his impartiality. A
" party should never be compelled to produce proof to
" change *a preconceived opinion or prejudice* which may
" control the action of the juror."

d. THE STATUTE OF 1874 AND ITS CONSTRUCTION BY
OUR SUPREME COURT.

Section 14, of chapter 78 of the Revised Statutes, and
passed March 12, 1874, is, in substance, as follows:

" It shall be a sufficient cause of challenge of a petit

"juror that he lacks any one of the qualifications men-
"tioned in section two of this act." Then there follows
several other qualifications not material to be considered
in this case. The second proviso is as follows:

"*And provided, further*, that in the trial of any crimi-
"nal cause, the fact that a person called as a juror has
"formed an opinion or impression, based upon rumor or
"upon newspaper statements (about the truth of which
"he has expressed no opinion), shall not disqualify him
"to serve as a juror in such case, if he shall, upon oath,
"state that he believes he can fairly and impartially ren-
"der a verdict therein, in accordance with the law and
"the evidence, and the court shall be satisfied of the
"truth of such statement."

We now come to the cases under the statute heretofore set forth, and which have arisen since it was passed,
and in which this statute has received a construction;
and the essence of these cases is that this statute declares to be competent a juryman who has
a slight opinion, or an opinion based upon rumor or
newspaper statements, and where he will swear and the
court is satisfied that such opinions will not affect him in
the rendition of a fair and impartial verdict. This was
always the law, and cases which have been cited, in
which courts have held that such jurymen were competent, declare the law in accordance with this construction
of this statute. The qualifications of a juror are fixed by
the constitution. The constitution is paramount to the
statute, therefore this statute *must be construed* in conformity with the constitution, otherwise it is wholly void.

Recurring again to the case of Aaron Burr: The
Burr trial was one of great notoriety like the present.
Chief Justice MARSHALL, in commenting on this case
(Vol. 1, p. 416), says:

" Were it possible to obtain a jury without any pre-
" possessions whatever respecting the guilt or innocence
" of the accused, it would be extremely desirable to ob-
" tain such a jury; but this is perhaps impossible and there-
" fore will not be required.

" The opinion which has been avowed by the court is,
" that light impressions which may be fairly supposed to
" yield to the testimony that may be offered; which may
" leave the mind open to a fair consideration of that
" testimony, constitute no sufficient objection to a juror;
" but that those *strong and deep impressions, which will*
" *close the mind* against the testimony that may be offered
" in opposition to them; *which will combat that testimony*
" *and resist its force*, do constitute a sufficient objection
" to it."

We believe that the intention of the legislature in passing this statute was simply to secure the law as Judge
Marshall has declared it in the quotation above given.

Let us see what the Supreme court of Illinois have
decided:

The case of *Plummer* v. *The People*, 74 Ill., 361 (September term, 1874), is the first case in which the act of
March 12, 1874, came under consideration.

In that case Mr. Justice Scholfield, delivering the opinion
of the court, says:

" The juror Broubaker, we do not think was competent.
" He is unable to state that he could sit as an impartial
" juror in the case. He was, among others, asked
" this question: 'You think that you have heard reports
" which *you believe* to be true, in respect to the defend-
" ants, which would have a tendency, in some degree, to
" bias your mind in this respect?' and he answers: 'it
" may have.'

" Where the juror has been exposed to influences the

" probable effect of which is to create a prejudice in his
" mind against the defendant, which it would require evi-
" dence to overcome, to render him competent it should
" clearly appear that he can, when in the jury-box, en-
" tirely disregard those influences, and try the case with-
" out, in any degree being affected by them." Judgment
reversed.

The next case to which we would call your Honors'
attention is that of *Robinson* v. *Randall*, 82 Ill., 521.
We quote from the opinion of the court delivered by Mr.
Justice CRAIG as follows:

" As to the other juror (Mercer), we do not regard him
" competent. He said he had great prejudice against the
" traffic (the liquor traffic); could not give the testimony
" of a person engaged in the business the same weight he
" could a man engaged in other business. Under the law,
" the defendants were competent witnesses, and a juror
" who was so prejudiced that he could not give their evi-
" dence that weight which it was entitled to receive could
" not be regarded as a person standing indifferent between
" the parties, free from all bias which might swerve his
" judgment from all impartiality. But conceding that the
" court erred in not sustaining the challenge of the juror,
" it was an error that did appellants no harm. The
" jurors were challenged peremptorily and excused, and
" appellants did not exhaust their challenges in the selec-
" tion of the entire jury before which the cause was tried,
" therefore appellants were not injured by the ruling of
" the court; and, as was held in *Winnesheik Insurance*
" *Company* v. *Shreller*, 60 Ill., 465, we cannot reverse
" for an error that worked no injury.

" If appellants, in consequence of the ruling of the
" court, had exhausted their peremptory challenges. and
" had been compelled to accept a juror whom they might

"have otherwise rejected, the rule might be otherwise,
"but this record does not disclose such a state of facts."

Construing this statute also in the case of *Wilson* v.
The People, 94 Ill., 299, the opinion of the court, delivered
by Mr. Justice SCHOLFIELD, bears upon the point under
consideration, and is as follows:

" While empaneling the jury, William Gray was called
" as a juror in the case, and, being first duly sworn, testi-
" fied in response to questions touching his qualifications
" as a juror: ' I have read newspaper accounts of the
" commission of the crime with which the defendant is
" charged, and have also conversed with several persons in
" regard to it since coming to Carthage and during my at-
" tendance upon this term of court; do not know whether
" they are witnesses in the case or not; do not know who
" the witnesses in the case are. From accounts I have
" read and from conversations I have had, *I have formed*
" *an opinion* in the case; would have an opinion in the
" case now, if the facts should turn out as I have heard
" them, and I think it would take some evidence to re-
" move that opinion; would be governed by the evidence
" in the case, and can give the defendant a fair and im-
" partial trial, according to the law and the evidence.'

" The defendant, by his counsel, thereupon challenged
" said Gray for cause, but the court refused to allow the
" challenge, and held that he was a competent juror to try
" the case. To this the defendant excepted, and then
" challenged Gray peremptorily. * * * We think
" all objection to Gray's competency is clearly removed
" by the statute, if indeed he would have been incom-
" petent otherwise. It provides in two of the clauses of
" section 14, chapter 78, of the revised statutes of 1874,
" page 633, as follows:

" Provided, further, that it shall not be a cause of chal-

"lenge that a juror has read in the newspapers an account "of the commission of the crime with which the prisoner "is charged, if such juror shall state, on oath, that he "believes that he can render an impartial verdict accord- "ing to the law and the evidence; and provided, fur- "ther, that in the trial of any criminal cause, the fact "that a person called as a juror has formed an opinion "or impression, based upon rumor or upon newspaper "statements (about the truth of which he has expressed "no opinion), shall not disqualify him to serve as a juror "in such case, if he shall, upon oath, state that he be- "lieves he can fairly and impartially render a verdict "therein in accordance with the law and the evidence, "and the court shall be satisfied of the truth of such "statement.

"The opinion formed seems not to have been decided, "but one of a light and transient character which, at no "time, would have disqualified the juror from serving. It "was said in *Smith* v. *Eames*, 3 Scam., 81: 'If the "opinion be merely of a light and transient character such "as is usually formed by persons in every community, "upon hearing a current report, and which may be "changed by the relation of the next person met with, "and which does not show a conviction of the mind and "a fixed conclusion thereon, or if it be hypothetical, the "challenge ought not to be allowed.' * * * * "But even if the juror had been incompetent, still under "the ruling in *Robinson* v. *Randall*, 82 Ill., 522, holding "that he was competent was an error that did no harm "and could not therefore be held to be ground for reversal. "The defendant exhausted but two of his peremptory "challenges, and hence, when he accepted the jurors by "whom he was tried, he was entitled to eighteen peremp- "tory challenges, and it must, therefore, be presumed

"the jurors by whom he was tried were entirely unob-
"jectionable to him."

The foregoing Illinois cases, we believe, present the decisions of our Supreme court upon the right of a defendant to an impartial jury, and the construction of the
statute passed since our last constitution. From these decisions it appears:

1. That the constitutionality of this law has never
been challenged. It was intended to cover cases where
the juror would have been held competent at common
law, without such statute, and where, under the decisions,
in this country, made under our various constitutions, he
should also have been held competent. The substance of
these decisions our legislature put into a statute. It seems
also, from these decisions, that the deliberate *formation of
an opinion* by the juror, and having that opinion at the
time of his examination, of itself disqualifies such juror,
and the having a bias against a class of people existing in the community, or a class under the law competent as witnesses, so that the same consideration and
heed would not be given them in reference to their testimony as to other persons, of itself also disqualifies such
juryman. But having an opinion or impression not deliberately formed, but based upon rumor or newspaper
accounts, does not disqualify him, provided he will swear
that notwithstanding such opinion or impression he believes he can try the defendant fairly, and the court is
satisfied that the juror's judgment on this point is correct.

2. That when the juror has once by his statements
become disqualified, he cannot, after that, by swearing that
he can disregard his opinion or prejudice, become a competent juror.

(*c.*) DECISIONS IN OTHER STATES IN CONSTRUCTION
OF SIMILAR STATUTES.

In Michigan is a statute similar to our own, except that after the word " formed " are " or expressed." In the 38th Michigan, in the case of *Stevens* v. *The People*, 742, Judge COOLEY uses the following language: " The con-
" stitution of this state provides that in every criminal
" prosecution the accused shall have the right to a speedy
" public trial by an *impartial jury*. Of course no legisla-
" tion can take this right away. In *Holt* v. *The People*,
" 13 Mich., '224, decided long before the act of 1873
" was passed, it was decided by this court that the law
" did not require that a juror should be *entirely unim-*
" *pressed* with any views as to the guilt or innocence of
" the person on trial, but only that he should *not have an*
" *opinion of such a fixed and definite character* as to
" leave a bias on his mind which would preclude his giv-
" ing due weight to the presumption of innocence. In
" that decision we followed what we believed to be the
" settled law of the country, citing in support of it, among
" others, the opinion of Chief Justice Marshall in Burr's
" case.   *   *   *   The question on this record is,
" whether that jury can be an impartial one whose mem-
" bers are already so impressed with the guilt of the ac-
" cused that evidence would be required to overcome such
" impression. It seems to us that this question needs only
" to be stated; it calls for no discussion. This woman,
" instead of entering upon her trial supported by a pre-
" sumption of innocence, was, in the minds of the jury,
" when they were empaneled, condemned already; and
" by their own statements, under oath, it is manifest that
" this condemnation would stand against her until re-

" moved by evidence. Under such circumstances, it is
" idle to inquire of jurors whether or not they can return
" just and impartial verdicts; the more clear and positive
" were their previous impressions of guilt, the more cer-
" tain may they be that they can act impartially in con-
" demning the guilty party. They go into the jury box
" in a state of mind that is well calculated to give a color
" of guilt to all the evidence; and if the accused escapes
" conviction, it will not be because the evidence has estab-
" lished guilt beyond a reasonable doubt, but because an
" accused party, condemned in advance, and called upon
" to exculpate himself before a prejudiced tribunal, has
" succeeded in doing so."

As to the importance of the action of Judge Gary in substantially importing into the statute of 1874 the words, " *and expressed*," or, in other words, disregarding wholly the fact that our act of 1874 does not attempt to provide for the relief from disqualification of a juror who has formed *and expressed* an opinion, etc., we call attention to the case of *State* v. *Clarke*, 42 Vermont, 629. PIERPONT, Chief Justice, delivering the opinion of the court, says:

" The first exception taken upon the trial was to the
" decision of the court allowing one Manly to sit as a
" juror in the trial of respondent, against his objection. It
" appears that, upon being inquired of, the juror said that
" he had expressed an opinion as to the guilt of the re-
" spondent, on reading a newspaper account of the exam-
" ination of the respondent before the magistrate, some
" month or six weeks before; but that he has no opinion,
" and has formed none, and can try the case impartially
" on the evidence.

" This question was before this court in the case of
" *Boardman et al.* v. *Wood et al.*, 3 Vermont, 270. That
" was a civil action, and the question arose upon the an-

" swer of a juror that he had formed an opinion, but did
" not know that he had expressed it. The court decided
" that to have formed an opinion did not disqualify a juror,
" but to render him incompetent, he must have expressed
" that opinion.

" Judge Williams, in delivering the opinion of the court,
" carefully reviews the authorities bearing upon the ques-
" tion, and shows very clearly and satisfactorily that the
" rule, both in England and in this country, is that a juror
" who has *formed and expressed* an opinion is disqualified,
" and that one who has formed an opinion without express-
" ing it is not. So far as my experience and observation ex-
" tend, this rule has been recognized and practiced upon,
" both by the courts and the bar, ever since, in this
" state; and the practice, I think, has been the same,
" both in civil and criminal cases. There certainly can be
" no good reason for relaxing the rule against the respond-
" ent in a criminal prosecution. In this case the juror says
" he expressed an opinion. That necessarily involves the
" forming of one, as he could not otherwise express it.
" Having formed and expressed an opinion, he is thereby
" disqualified, unless what he further says shall have the
" effect to take the case out of the rule. It is not quite
" clear what the juror meant when he said that, at the
" time of the trial, he had no opinion, and had formed none,
" after having just stated that a few weeks before he had
" expressed one. Probably these expressions should be
" taken in connection with the following one: that he could
" try the case impartially, and that what he meant was,
" that he had no opinion, and had formed none, that would
" prevent his trying the case impartially, and undoubtedly
" he thought so. Men are very apt to think they can try
" cases fairly, even though they have a strong feeling in
" favor of one side or the other; but whether a man who

" has expressed an opinion on the subject to be considered
" can try the question fairly or not, does not depend upon
" his own opinion of his impartiality. The rule of law is
" that he cannot, or, at least, that the parties shall not be
" required to take the risk."

In the State of Texas, with the same constitutional provision as to the right of the accused to be tried by *an impartial jury*, there is a provision in their code that a juror shall be disqualified when, from hearsay or otherwise, there has been established in his mind such a conclusion as to the guilt or innocence of the defendant as will influence him in finding the verdict. It is provided further that, to determine whether there is such a conclusion in the juror's mind, the juror shall first be asked whether, in his opinion, the conclusion will influence his verdict. If he answers affirmatively, he shall be discharged; if he answers negatively, he shall be examined by the court, and if the court is satisfied that he will be influenced by the opinion, he shall still be discharged. In the case of *Black* v. *The State*, 42 Texas, 377, a juror, having answered the questions put to him satisfactorily, was accepted by the court, after due examination, and the challenge for cause was disallowed, which was assigned for error. The examination of the juror was to this effect: " That he had read the report of the evidence in "the case of *The State* v. *A. J. Walker;* that he had "*formed an opinion* thereon as to the guilt or innocence of " the accused; that it would require other and different " evidence to change that opinion; that the opinion so " formed would not influence his verdict in the slightest " degree, and that he would go into the jury-box and give " the accused a fair and impartial trial, according to the " law and the evidence appearing on this trial." In sustaining the error and reversing the cause, on the ground that the challenge to this juror was improperly overruled, the court say:

"In this case the juror had read the report of the evidence in the Walker case—Walker and the defendant being charged with the commission of the same offense, in the same indictment. The report referred to may be presumed to be the detail of the evidence at a former trial as given in the newspapers of the city, which is usually published in cases exciting any general interest. He must have placed reliance in the report of the evidence which he read, in order to have enabled him to have formed a conclusion at all, and the fact that, as he says himself, it would require other and different evidence to change that opinion shows, or at least renders it probable, that it was with some considerable attention to, and a consideration of the facts reported, that he had formed his conclusion. Under such circumstances, we are of opinion that the court below, in judging of the qualification of the juror, should not have been satisfied that he was an impartial juror.

"The juror took his seat in the jury-box with a conclusion formed, when the defendant had not been heard, and without the benefit of the instruction of the court as to the law applicable to the case. If his conclusion was in favor of the prisoner's guilt, it was as a weight put in the scales of justice before the trial commenced. Whatever of obstinacy of character and pride of opinion he possessed had to be overcome by other evidence. There are, perhaps, but few men who do not lean in favor of preconceived opinion, founded on what they deem to be an authentic source. They look favorably upon whatever will support it, and examine with increased caution whatever will oppose it. The love of consistency in the formation of their judgments re-

" quires this of them. No authority has been found for
" holding that this juror was qualified, and an abundance
" that is in opposition to it. See Graham & Waterman
" New Trials, p. 377, and American authorities cited,
" 378, 379."

As particularly applicable to the examination of the
jurors in the case at bar, we now cite the case of *Wright*
v. *Commonwealth*, 32 Grattan, 941. In that case one of
the proposed jurors objected to stated " that he had
" read newspaper accounts of the offense with which
" prisoner was chaiged, and had heard rumors of the
" same; that upon what he had heard and read he had
" made up and expressed an opinion in the case; that the
" opinion so made up and expressed was still upon his
" mind; that he did not think he could do the prisoner
" justice; but in answer to a question from the judge,
" should the evidence before the jury be different from
" that he had read, he said his opinion would be changed;
" *that he could come to the trial with an unbiased and an*
" *unprejudiced mind, and give the accused a fair and*
" *impartial trial.*" Upon this examination the challenge
for cause was overruled, and the juror was accepted and
sworn. In reversing the case for this error the Supreme
court used the following language (page 943):

" If the juror has made up and expressed a *decided*
" opinion as to the guilt or innocence of the accused, he is
" incompetent; and it does not matter whether the opin-
" ion be founded on conversations with the witnesses or
" upon mere hearsay or rumor. It is sufficient that the
" opinion is decided, and has been expressed. * * *
" He must be able to give him a fair and impartial trial.
" Upon this point nothing should be left to inference or
" doubt. All the tests supplied by the courts, all the in-
" quiries made into the state of the juror's mind, are

" merely to ascertain whether he comes to the trial free
" from partiality and prejudice.

" If there be a reasonable doubt whether the juror pos-
" sesses these qualifications, that doubt is sufficient to in-
" sure his exclusion. For, as has been well said, it is not
" only important that justice should be impartially admin-
" istered, but that it should also flow through channels
" as free from suspicion as possible.

" Now, in the case before us, the juror had heard of the
" homicide, and he had read the newspaper accounts of the
" occurrence, and upon these he had made up and expressed
" an opinion, which he then entertained; and such was
" the state of his mind, ' he did not think he could do the
" prisoner justice.' It is true he subsequently stated, in
" answer to a question propounded by the court, *that he
" could come to the trial with an unbiased and unprejudiced
" mind, and give to the accused a fair and impartial trial.*
" But how was the court to decide which of these state-
" ments was true and which was false? How was it to
" say that the second statement more correctly and truly
" represented the juror's feelings than the first? His first
" avowal showed alone he was not a fit person to sit
" upon the trial of the accused ; his ready disavowal of
" all prejudice under the interrogation of the court fur-
" nished no satisfactory evidence of his impartiality or
" competency. A man who could assert in one breath
" that he had prejudged the accused and could not do
" him justice, and in the next assert that his mind was
" free from all prejudice, is not to be trusted with the
" grave and responsible duty of passing upon the guilt or
" innocence of a fellow-being. Such a man may per-
" suade himself that he is impartial, but the law does not
" so regard him. Unconsciously to himself, it may be,
" his prejudices will follow him into the jury box and in-

" fluence and control his judgment there. We are, there-
" fore, of opinion that this juror is incompetent, and the
" County court erred in permitting him to be sworn as
" such."

In *Curry* v. *The State*, 4 Neb., 545 (January term,
1876), the question arose as to the constitutionality of a
statute substantially like our act of March 12, 1874, in
view of a constitutional provision similar to our own.
The court unhesitatingly declares that if the statute con-
flicted in any particular with the constitution it was of
course inoperative, but proceeded to give the statute such
a construction as we contend should have been given to
our statute in the present case. The following is the
language of the court (pp. 549, 550):

" The juror Corby was of opinion that 'he might
" lean a little the other way,' that is, against the return of
" an impartial verdict. But it is altogether immaterial
" whether he leaned little or much; to render him com-
" petent he must not lean at all, neither for or against one
" party or the other. *No inquiry can be entered upon as
" to the extent of a juror's bias or prejudice;* if he be not
" certain of their non-existence he ought not to be per-
" mitted to sit upon the jury in any case."

*   *   *   *   *   *   *

" If, however, the opinion of a juror, based upon news-
" paper statements or common rumor, be not merely hypo-
" thetical but decided and so fixed as to require testimony
" to overcome it, should he be retained if challenged for
" that reason? We think not. Surely such a juror
" cannot be said to stand impartially between the parties,
" and to hold him to be competent would in our opinion
" violate not only the constitutional guaranty of a free and
" impartial jury, but also the spirit, if not the letter, of the
" section of the statute above quoted."

To the same effect is the decision of the same court in *Farmer* v. *The People*, 4 Neb., 68.

We have not regarded it necessary in the contention which we make before this court to attack the constitutionality of the act of March 12, 1874, because we have supposed that the act was susceptible of such a construction as might relieve it from such objection. But our contention is that the construction given to it by Judge Gary makes the statute obnoxious to, and a limitation upon, the constitutional provision under consideration; and that such construction must, therefore, be held to be erroneous.

Upon the proposition that the clause of the constitution of 1870 is to be construed in the light of the prior decisions of this court, proceeding under a like clause in our earlier constitutions; and that if this statute is necessarily to receive such construction as will materially infringe upon the right of the accused to an *impartial jury* as thus secured, it would be unconstitutional, we beg to cite the case of *Eason* v. *The State*, 6 Baxter (Tenn.), 466, (April term, 1873). From that case it appears (page 468) that the constitution of Tennessee adopted in 1870 contains a provision guaranteeing defendants in criminal cases a trial by an impartial jury; and that, in an act of the legislature thereafter passed, there was the following provision:

" That hereafter no citizen, in any criminal prosecution
" in this state, shall be adjudged incompetent to act as a
" juror by reason of having *formed or expressed* an opin-
" ion touching the guilt or innocence of the accused upon
" information derived exclusively from any published ac-
" count of the facts of the offense with which the defend-
" ant stands charged, unless the writer of said statement
" in said article professed to have been a witness to the
" same at the time of their occurrence, which must affirm-

" atively appear: and provided that said juror will state,
" upon the law and the testimony, on trial, he believes he
" can give the accused a fair and impartial verdict."

It will be observed that the provisions of this statute,
while differing in some particulars from our own, and
going beyond ours in the provision as to the *expression* of
the opinion formed, are otherwise of the same general
purport as our own, and were designed to accomplish the
same end to which Judge Gary used our statute of March
12, 1874. The constitutionality of this Tennessee act
was challenged in the case cited, and the court, in its
opinion, used the following language (470):

" The guarantee of a trial by an ' impartial jury ' has
" been secured to the accused in exactly the same lan-
" guage in the constitutions of 1796, 1834 and 1870. They
" were introduced into ' the Bill of Rights ' of 1796, and
" we are to presume that they were adopted with a full
" understanding of their legal import, as ascertained and
" settled by judicial interpretations in England. But if
" there was any doubt as to this proposition, if we shall
" find that there has been an unbroken chain of judicial
" construction, from 1796 down to 1834, when the same
" words were again adopted in the constitution of that
" year; and also from 1834 down to 1870, when the
" same words were adopted for the third time in the con-
" stitution of that year; and if we find, throughout this
" succession of decisions, the same construction has been
" uniformly placed upon the words, we are forced to the
" conclusion that that construction is to be regarded as
" the true legal, judicial and constitutional meaning of an
" ' impartial jury.' "

The court then proceeded to cite the earlier decisions
of that state, including *Rice* v. *State*, 1 Yer., 432; *Mc-
Gollan* v. *The State*, 9 Yer., 192; *Baine* v. *State*, 3 Hum-

phrey, 275; *Brackfield* v. *State*, 1 Sneed, 215, and *North-field* v. *State*, 4 Sneed, 340, and then said:

" When the constitution of 1870 was adopted, the same
" language, which had thus been judicially interpreted,
" was again re-adopted, and, we have the right to pre-
" sume, with full knowledge of its uniform interpretation
" in the constitution of 1796 and 1834. This being so,
" this interpretation of the language becomes incorpo-
" rated with the constitution of 1870 as part of the
" fundamental law of the state. The decisions which
" have fixed the true meaning of the words ' impartial
" jury' also established the position, that a juror who is
" incompetent from having formed or expressed an opinion
" as to the guilt or innocence of the accused cannot ren-
" der himself ' impartial' by expressing his belief, on his
" examination, that he can render a fair and impartial
" verdict according to law and proof, notwithstanding the
" opinion then in his mind. * * *
" When the constitution guarantees to the accused an
" ' impartial jury,' it necessarily means that he is entitled
" to a jury which can enter upon the examination of his
" case, conceding to him the full benefit of that pre-
" sumption of innocence which the law gives to every
" prisoner as a matter of right. This presumption en-
" titles him to an acquittal until it has been overturned
" by plenary proof. In the formation of a jury under the
" statute in question, the prisoner may have forced on
" him as his tryers twelve men who will enter the box
" with a conviction on their minds that he is guilty, and
" he must stand convicted, in their judgment, until he
" has, by full proof, overcome their conviction of his
" guilt, and established his innocence, This would be a
" virtual reversal of the fundamental principle that the
" law presumes the accused to be innocent until proof

" shows him to be guilty. It is little else than a mockery
" to try the competency of a juror by asking if he has
" formed and expressed his opinion of the guilt or inno-
" cence of the accused, and when he answers that he has
" upon having heard or read the facts, then to take him
" as an impartial juror, upon his belief that he can divest
" himself of his convictions and render a fair and impar-
" tial verdict. A prisoner whose life or liberty is sub-
" mitted to a jury composed of such men cannot be
" said to have a fair trial by an impartial jury. We hold
" that an impartial juror is one who enters the box in-
" different between the parties, indifferent in feeling and
" in opinion. Either partiality or prejudice in the usual
" acceptance of those words, or an opinion based on the
" supposed facts of the case, already existing in his mind,
" renders it impossible for him to be indifferent and there-
" fore to be impartial. If he is partial or prejudiced, he
" will enter upon the trial predisposed to follow his par-
" tiality or prejudice in weighing testimony. If he enters
" the box with an opinion already made up, he will be
" in danger of so viewing and weighing the testimony as
" to sustain and confirm his existing impressions. One
" of the jurors who was put to the prisoner in this case
" as competent stated that the impressions made on his
" mind by reading details of the facts as they were given
" in the newspaper were such that the proof to remove
" them must be full. When could a jury composed of
" men such as the juror referred to, be said to be indif-
" ferent? Certainly never until their convictions of guilt
" had been removed by full proof of innocence. Is it not
" an abuse of language to call such a jury an impartial
" one? To be an impartial jury, they should enter the
" box indifferent at the time of entering it between the
" state and the accused. The courts have gone to the

" verge of the law in holding that a juror who has formed
" and expressed an opinion on mere rumor may be an
" impartial juror. We recognize such to be the settled
" law, but we are not disposed to go further in that di-
" rection. It has been urged with much earnestness and
" force that the act of the legislature in question ought to
" be sustained upon considerations of public policy. Con-
" siderations of this character can have no place in con-
" sidering questions involving the constitutionality of
" laws, except in cases where there is doubt as to the
" power of the legislature to enact the laws.

*   *   *   *   *   *

" But it is our duty, and the highest and most responsible
" imposed upon us, to guard the constitution against in-
" fractions. When we are called upon to determine con-
" stitutional questions, if we are in no doubt, our path of
" duty is plain and straightforward."

(f.)   As to the Propriety of Questions in Refer- ence to Peremptory Challenges.

The law is settled so directly in the case of *C. & A. R. R. Co.* v. *Mary A. Buttolf*, 66 Ill., 347, that we cite that case as especially bearing on this subject. That case was tried before one Joseph E. Gary, judge, at Chicago— the same judge who tried the present case. The point saved in that case was exactly like the points saved with reference to such questions in the case at bar, and is stated as follows, in the language of the court:

" Upon impaneling the jury, several of the jurors were
" asked by defendant's counsel this question: If, upon
" hearing the testimony, they should find it evenly bal-
" anced, which way they would be inclined to decide the
" case? The plaintiff's counsel objected to the question,

" and the court sustained the objection, and defendant
" excepted.

" On one ground, if no other, the question was proper
" as determining the exercise of the defendant's right
" to a peremptory challenge."   *   *   *

The court reversed the judgment on this point alone.
It says: " On the first point (that is the point we have
" suggested) the judgment must be reversed."

The precise point in question was also settled in the
case of *Lavin* v. *The People*, 69 Ill., 303. The question
now considered is the only question presented in that
case to the Supreme court to pass upon. The opinion
of Justice CRAIG states the case and uses the following
language:

" In selecting a jury to try the cause in the Criminal
" court, the defendant propounded to each juror called,
" the following questions: *First*. Are you a member of
" a temperance society? *Second*. Are you connected
" with any society or league organized for the purpose of
" prosecuting a certain class of people, under what is
" called the new temperance law of the state; or have
" you ever contributed any funds for such a purpose?"

    (Objection by the state's attorney; objection sus-
    tained, and exception by the defendant.)

The court continues: " It is the policy of our laws to
" afford each and every person who may have a cause
" for trial in our courts a fair and impartial trial. This
" can only be done by having the mind of each juror who
" sits to pass judgment upon the life, liberty or rights
" of a suitor entirely free from bias or prejudice. In
" order to determine whether the person who may be
" called as a juror possesses the necessary qualifications,
" whether he has prejudged the case, whether his mind is
" free from prejudice or bias, the suitor has the right to

" ask him questions, the answer to which may tend to
" show he may be challenged for cause, or disclose a
" state of facts from which the suitor may see proper to
" reject such juror peremptorily."

The court cites and quotes, in strengthening itself in
this position, from *The Commonwealth* v. *Egan*, 4 Gray,
18; *People* v. *Rogers*, 5 Cal., 347, in each of which cases
the precise question is decided.

For the error indicated, and for that error alone, the
Supreme court reversed the judgment in that case.

In the case at bar two motives operated upon the mind
of the person asking the questions which Judge Gary
refused to permit to be answered. One was to elicit
answers furnishing ground of challenge for cause. The
other was to call out facts with a view to satisfy his own
mind whether the juror should be challenged peremptorily.
At the time of asking these questions defendants still had
the right to challenge peremptorily; and we maintain that
there is no limit to the range of inquiry in reference to
the exercise of the right of peremptory challenge, except
impertinence or questions involving improprieties of life.

II. JUDGE GARY'S RULINGS ON THE QUALIFICA-TION OF JURORS, AND OUR CONTENTIONS.

The complaints that we have to make with Judge Gary's
rulings on that point are, in substance, as follows:

His Positions are:

1. Judge Gary, in this trial, adopted the statute alone
as the basis of the right of trial by jury. He absolutely
ignored the constitutional right of trial by an *impartial
jury*, and construed the statute broadly against the de-

fendants in reference to its meaning, as though it were the only provision in existence in reference to the right named, and the only source of the right of trial by jury.

2. The court held that jurors were competent who had *formed and expressed* an opinion of the guilt or innocence of the accused, based upon newspaper articles and rumors, and held such opinions at the time of their examination and which it would require evidence to remove, provided they would swear they could " fairly and impartially " render a verdict therein."

The court carried his ruling to the extent of holding that even where the proposed juror stated that he had formed and expressed an opinion in reference to the guilt or innocence of the defendants, based upon what he had read, heard and believed to be true, and admitted that he had talked with parties who were present at the Hay-market, witnessing the occurrences there, and who detailed the same to the juror, and whose statements were believed by the juror to be true; still this did not disqualify the proposed juror; while continually, by the questions asked by the court, the position was in fact assumed that a prejudice against the defendants, if it were based only upon what he had heard and read in connection with the Haymarket trouble, did not disqualify the proposed juror, if he would state that he believed he could fairly and impartially try the case and render his verdict.

3. The court held that a juryman, who had *formed and expressed* an opinion of the guilt or innocence of the accused, based upon rumors or newspaper articles, and had also, in the past, expressed an opinion of the truth or falsity of such rumors or articles, was thereby disqualified as a juror; but the present statement by the juror, at the time of his examination on his *voir dire*, that he believed

then what he had heard and read to be true, and that he had *formed and expressed* an opinion of the guilt or innocence of the defendants, based on what he had so heard, read and believed, did not disqualify him.

In other words, Judge Gary held that if a proposed juryman, who had formed and expressed an opinion as to the guilt or innocence of the accused, based upon newspaper accounts and rumors, had also expressed an opinion about the truth of such newspaper accounts and rumors previous to his examination as a juror, that, in itself, disqualified him. But if he, for the first time during his examination, stated that he then believed such accounts and rumors to be true, and still had such an opinion of the guilt or innocence of the accused, that, in itself, did not disqualify him.

In his construction of the statute (Chap. 78, Sec. 14), Judge Gary introduces the words "and expressed" after the word "formed," and made it read, "formed "and expressed"; and introduces, after the words in parentheses, "about the truth of which he has expressed an opinion," the words "previous to his examination," and not applying to a present fixed belief.

4. The fact that the proposed juror swore that the opinion or prejudice which he had *at the time of the examination* was fixed and positive, and that the juror had *expressed such opinion*, and would require evidence, and even a good deal of evidence, for its removal, the court held, did not disqualify the juror, provided he would swear that he believed he could render a fair and impartial verdict in the case.

Judge Gary finally refused to allow the proposed jurors to be asked whether their opinion concerning the guilt or innocence of the defendants or their prejudice against them was such as would require evidence for its removal, even for the purposes of determining as to exercising a peremptory challenge.

5. Where proposed jurors admitted a prejudice or bias against socialists, anarchists or communists, as a class, the judge refused to allow the defendants to ask questions as to whether that prejudice was such as materially to affect the credence they would accord to the evidence of the defendants, or as probably to affect them in determining the question of the guilt or innocence of said defendants, if it should appear or be conceded that said defendants, or some of them, were socialists, anarchists or communists; and refused to allow challenges for cause on account of any such confessed prejudice or bias against such classes; and refused to allow this question to be asked, even as to determining upon a peremptory challenge.

OUR POSITIONS ARE AS FOLLOWS:

1. That, when the people adopted the constitution of 1870, they adopted section 9 of article 2 thereof, with reference to the construction it had theretofore received from our Supreme court, as a provision of the constitutions of 1818 and 1848 as to what constituted an impartial jury. That the statute of 1874, in the particular under consideration, is to be construed with reference and subject to this provision of this constitution of 1870, and the interpretation theretofore given by the Supreme court. If the statute necessarily requires such a construction as impairs the right to an *impartial jury*, as heretofore held by this court under the constitutions of Illinois of 1818, 1848 and 1870, all of which are alike, and have received the same construction, it must then be held unconstitutional and void. And, least of all, is the court permitted to interpolate words into the statute of 1870 not found

there, the effect of which, when thus incorporated, would necessarily be to enlarge its scope or extend its operation, and deny the right of the defendant to a fair and impartial jury, guaranteed by the constitution.

The statute in question only goes the length in terms of holding as follows: (a) That the formation of an opinion or impression, based upon newspaper report or rumor, shall not disqualify, provided, etc. Nothing is said in the statute tending to remove the disqualification incident to the *deliberate formation of an opinion*, or to the *formation and expression* of such an opinion. (b.) As to the clause in the statute, introduced parenthetically, "con-"cerning the truth of which he has expressed no opinion," if construed as relating to an expression of an opinion or impression as to the truth of the report or rumor, read or heard, it is not subject to any limitation as to time, but must be taken as it reads. If the juror, upon his *voir dire*, states unequivocally that he did believe and does believe the truth of the accounts and rumors heard and read by him, and which formed the basis of the opinion as to the guilt or innocence of the defendants, formed and expressed by him, and he is thereafter challenged upon that ground, then the juror, at the time of the challenge, *has*, in the past tense, expressed an opinion concerning the truth of the account or rumor; and there is no warrant for the position that the expression of the opinion must have preceded the examination in order to disqualify him. In other words, the legislature cannot be presumed to have intended the absurdity that the casual expression of an opinion, as to the truth, for example, of a newspaper report, communicated upon the street to an acquaintance or friend, *should* be effective to disqualify a man from service as a juror, when the deliberate expression of the same opinion, under the sanction of an oath, at the time of his examination, should *not* be a ground for his rejection.

This distinction is not technical, but substantial. The reason is this: If the opinion is based on reports which, on his voir dire or on any other occasion, the proposed juror says he believes to be true, this statement furnishes a demonstration that the opinion, inasmuch as it is founded on accredited report, is such as will require evidence for its removal. Such an opinion is not hypothetical, but positive. The talesman is not in the position of one saying, "If this "report be true, then my opinion is," etc.; but he says deliberately: " I believe what I have heard and read "to be true, and because I believe the truth of this "report, I have a positive opinion on the question of "the guilt of the accused." Clearly, this opinion would disqualify, and it was manifest error for the court to import into the interpretation of the statute a provision which, contrary to the manifest intention of the legislature, would make the statute palpably obnoxious to the constitutional objection above considered.

2. We maintain that it was a proper subject of inquiry as to the extent to which the prejudice of the proposed juror against certain classes of citizens, to wit: socialists, communists and anarchists, would affect the credence by the proposed juror of the testimony of the defendants, in the event of its being shown by proofs, or admitted, that the defendants belong to such classes; and also, that it was proper to inquire whether the verdict of the juror would, in the juror's opinion, be influenced by the fact supposed. Certainly such inquiry and examination were proper, if for no other reason than for the purpose of informing defendants, so that they could intelligently determine whether

or not they should exercise, in the case of the proposed juror, their right of *peremptory* challenge, even if the answers to the proposed inquiries did not furnish ground to sustain a challenge *for cause.*

3. If, *having formed a decided opinion* or *having expressed it*, or as to having a *bias or prejudice*, the juror answers that he has formed, or formed *and expressed* such an opinion, that he cannot try the case fairly, he stands disqualified by the law; notwithstanding that, by a *teasing and coaching* process, he may be finally got to say he thinks he can try the case fairly. *A fortiori*, if he says six times that he cannot try the case fairly, and once that he can, he is the more clearly disqualified.

We have stated the rulings of Judge Gary as to the competency of jurors and our positions as to the law on these points. We now beg leave to refer your Honors to the examinations of jurors in this case, for the purpose of illustrating and proving what we have asserted. We give the substance of the examination, and in some cases the words.

III. EXAMINATIONS OF JURORS AS ILLUSTRATING JUDGE GARY'S RULINGS.

MELON T. CAREY, on the first day (Vol. A., 117 to 121), discloses that he had read an account of the case, had talked of it, *believed what he had heard and read to be true*, and had formed *and expressed* an opinion as to the guilt or innocence of defendants. This juryman also expressed the belief that he could try the case fairly. He was asked the question whether that was *such an opinion as would require evidence to remove.*

The court decided that was an incompetent question,

because it called for the opinion of the juror as to the future effect of evidence upon his mind. The defendants excepted. This juror was subsequently challenged for cause, but upon another ground.

FRANK JACOBSON (1 A., 43; Vol. A., 312 to 321) said he had not, previous to this examination, expressed an opinion about the truth of the newspaper accounts or rumors on which he based the opinion of the guilt or innocence of the defendants, but admitted on his *voir dire* that *he now believed the newspaper accounts and rumors on which he formed and expressed* his opinion as to the guilt or innocence of the defendants, and that he still entertained that opinion. He also said he believed he could try the case fairly. This panelman was challenged for cause, the court overruled this challenge, taking the position in his ruling that if a juryman had, before his examination, read an account of the circumstances, and *then* expressed an opinion that he believed the accounts which he read to be true, and upon those accounts had formed and expressed an opinion as to the guilt or innocence of the defendants, he was subject to challenge for cause; but if he had not, previous to his examination, expressed an opinion that he believed that account, but, for the first time, on his *voir dire*, stated that he does believe the account, and upon that belief had *formed and expressed* and still entertained that opinion of the guilt or innocence of the accused, that did not constitute a ground for challenge.

JOHN JOHNSON (1 A., 53; Vol. B, 155 to 159) upon his examination, stated that he had heard and read the reports concerning the Haymarket affair, and had discussed the matter from time to time, and had formed *and expressed* an opinion as to the guilt or innocence of the defendants, which he still entertained, and

that he believed in substance what he had read and heard.
He stated further that the opinion was such as *might possibly be removed by evidence* contrary to what he had
read. He also said he believed he could try the case
fairly. When asked as to whether his opinion was such
as would require evidence for its removal, and whether it
would require strong evidence, the court refused to allow
the questions to be answered, and overruled the challenge
for cause, to which defendants excepted, and the juror was
then challenged peremptorily.

CLARENCE H. HILL (1 A., 53; Vol. B, 187 to 196)
stated that he had read accounts of the Haymarket meeting, had conversations in reference to it, and, upon the information derived from all sources, had formed an opinion as to the guilt or innocence of the defendants, which
he still entertained, and which was *based upon his belief in
the truth of what he had read,* and that he was prejudiced
against socialists, anarchists, etc. He was finally asked:
" Q. You have no opinions, biases or prejudices which
" *it would require testimony to overcome? A. Yes, sir;*
" *I have.*" This juror was challenged for cause, the
challenge was overruled, to which defendants excepted,
and he was thereupon challenged peremptorily by defendants.

W. N. UPHAM was examined the first day. He
stated that he had read the newspaper accounts of the
Haymarket affair, and had conversations with various persons upon the subject; that from all sources of information
he had formed an opinion upon the question of the guilt or
innocence of some of the defendants, which he believed he
had expressed to others; that he *believed to be true the
statements which he had heard and read,* and that he *expressed a belief that what he had heard was true.* Subsequently he modified these statements through the following

question and answer by and to the court: " Q. The question " is whether you have ever formed or expressed an opin- " ion as to the guilt or innocence of any one of these eight " men of the murder of Officer Degan? A. I can't say " what I have expressed in words, but *my opinion was that* " *some of them are guilty.*" He also said he believed he could render a fair verdict on the evidence. The COURT: " That is not any ground of challenge under the law."

He stated further that he still had the same opinion as to the guilt of some of the defendants, and then the ques- tion was asked as to whether testimony would be required to remove that opinion before he would be unbiased and free to act upon the evidence. The question was objected to, quite fully argued, and the objection was then sustained by the court. This juror was challenged for cause, the challenge was overruled, the defendants excepted, and then challenged peremptorily. (1 A., 36; Vol. A., pp. 61 to 70.)

E. F. SHEDD, examined on Wednesday, June 23d, stated that he had read of the Haymarket affair in the papers, and at the time formed an opinion as to the guilt or innocence of the defendants, which opinion he still entertained, no circumstances having occurred to change it. That such opinion was formed from the belief by him of the truth of the statements which he had heard and read, and that he *had expressed* the opinion to others. He said also, " I " would have my opinion, my own opinion, until it was set " aside by the whole testimony," and that *it would require* *evidence to remove the opinion which he had.* (1 A., 45; A., 390.) He was thereupon challenged for cause, and a long argument ensued (Vol. A., pp. 391 to 399), at the end of which the court overruled the challenge, and the defendants excepted.

The same person was thereupon further interrogated,

and stated that he had a *prejudice* against communists, anarchists and socialists as a class, which was of such a character that it would *prevent his listening to the testimony and rendering an impartial verdict* if it were conceded or proved that the defendants belonged to such class. He stated further: "*I think the mere fact of their* " *being communists would influence my opinion as a juror.* " Q. And therefore you would not find the same verdict " upon the same evidence as you would if they were not " so—you would require additional evidence? A. Yes, " sir"; and that he "*would find the defendants guilty upon* " *less evidence than if they were law-abiding citizens.*" But he also said that he thought he could try the cause fairly. The challenge for cause was renewed upon this examination (Vol. A., 400), was overruled, the defendants excepted, and thereafter challenged said Shedd peremptorily.

A. F. BRADLEY (1 A., 42; Vol. A., 198 to 206) stated that he had heard and read accounts of the Haymarket meeting, that he had a strong prejudice against anarchists, socialists and communists, so strong that he could not tell whether it would affect his verdict if selected as a juror in this case or not. He was then asked whether he would receive the testimony of anarchists, communists or socialists as freely and readily as that of other witnesses, which question was objected to, and the objection sustained, to which defendants excepted. Thereupon the following question and answer occurred: "Q. You " feel that you could lay the prejudice all to one side and " be governed exclusively by the testimony as it was in- " troduced, and the law governing the case as given you " by the court? A. No, I don't know about that, as I " told you before. I don't know whether I could or not. " I don't know whether I can answer that, because I

" don't know." But the juror also stated that he thought he could render a fair and impartial verdict. The juror was thereupon challenged for cause, the challenge over-ruled, and the defendants excepted, and Mr. Bradley was subsequently challenged peremptorily by the defendants.

WILLIAM NEIL (1 A., 57; Vol. C, 50 to 57) stated that he had heard and read about the Haymarket difficulty and *believed enough of what he had so heard and read to form an opinion* as to the guilt or innocence of some of the defendants, which he still entertained, but thought *strong evidence to the contrary would change that opinion;* that he *had expressed* said opinion and said, " it would take " pretty strong evidence to change my opinion." And again he said, " it would take strong evidence to remove " the impression that I now have." That he believed his opinion, based upon what he had heard and read, would accompany him through the trial, and *would influence* him in determining and getting at a result. But he also stated that he believed he could give a fair verdict on whatever evidence he should hear. Thereupon the juror was challenged for cause on all his answers, and particularly on the ground that he had expressed the opinion which he still entertained, which challenge was overruled; the defendants excepted, and thereupon the juror was challenged peremptorily.

JAMES S. OAKLEY (1 A., 59; Vol. C, 91 to 102), stated that he had heard and read of the Haymarket difficulty, and *believed enough of what he had so read and heard to form an opinion* as to the guilt or innocence of some of the defendants, which opinion he *had expressed* and still entertained. He was asked if that opinion was so strong and firmly fixed that it would take strong evidence to the contrary to remove it. The question was refused by the court, and the defendants excepted. He also stated that he believed he could determine the question of the guilt or innocence of the defendants upon the evidence alone; but he still further stated as follows:

" Q. Still you think that the opinion you now have and " what you have read and heard would influence you in " arriving at a verdict? A. I do. Q. *You do think it would influence you?* A. *I do.*" He was further asked as to his prejudice against socialists, anarchists, etc., and admitted that he had such prejudice, and was then asked· " Q. If it should be proven or conceded on the " trial of this case that the defendants, or some of them, " are anarchists or communists, would this opinion of yours " in regard to these classes, that you have now expressed, " influence you in arriving at a just and impartial verdict?" The question was refused by the court and the defendants excepted. Mr. Oakley, again stating that he had expressed his opinion as to the guilt or innocence of the defendants, or some of them, was challenged for cause on all his answers, and particularly on the ground of the expression of his opinion. The challenge was overruled, defendants excepted, and challenged peremptorily.

H. F. CHANDLER (1 A., Vol. C, 149 to 157) stated that he had read and heard of the Haymarket matter, and from what he had so read and heard, had *formed an opinion* as to the guilt or innocence of one or more of the defendants, which he still entertained, and which he *had expressed.* That he *believed in the truth of the statements he had read and heard,* and had never questioned it. He was asked and answered as follows: " Q. Is that a decided " opinion as to the guilt or innocence? A. It is a de- " *cided opinion;* yes, sir. Q. Your mind is pretty well " made up now as to their guilt or innocence? A. Yes, " sir. Well, it will take evidence to satisfy me on that " point. I don't know. I have simply heard one side of

" the case. I have just read the newspaper matter. I
" have formed an opinion as far as that goes. Q. Would
" it be hard to change your opinion? A. It might be
" hard; I can't say. I don't know whether it would be
" hard or not."

He also stated that he had a strong prejudice against
socialists, anarchists and communists, and was then asked
if that prejudice would influence his verdict; which
question was refused by the court, and the defendants
excepted. He further stated that he thought he *had
expressed* his opinion as to the guilt or innocence of the
defendants quite frequently, and was thereupon challenged for cause.

The court thereupon proceeded to interrogate Mr.
Chandler (Vol. C, 210 to 213). He stated that he
had an opinion as to whether the defendants did the act
which caused the death of Degan, but that that opinion
was based wholly upon what he had heard and read
and not from any conversation with any person who
was present at the time of the transaction. Thereupon
the court announced the following ruling (pages 212 to
213): " It don't seem to me that it makes any difference
" in the competency of a juror whether he has simply
" formed an opinion, *or expressed* an opinion which he
" has formed. I don't see how it makes a particle of
" difference in his state of mind. *Every man* is in favor
" of justice and fair dealings as between other people
" where his own interests are not affected; and as I have
" said before, I think it must be—I think it is in the nature
" of any man, when he wants to find out the truth of any
" transaction, that he will, when the original sources are
" presented to him, follow them, and not any hearsay that
" he has ever heard."

The challenge for cause was thereupon overruled, to

which defendants excepted, and then challenged Mr.
Chandler peremptorily.

A. L. KETCHUM stated that he had read and heard
about the Haymarket difficulty sufficiently to form an
opinion as to the guilt or innocence of some of the defendants, which opinion he *had expressed* and still entertained. Asked the question, "Is it a *strong opinion?*" he
answered, "*Yes, it is.*" He stated, however, that he could
render a fair and impartial verdict, and be governed alone
by the testimony in the case. But he admitted that he
still had an opinion, which was firm. Asked if it would
require testimony to overcome the opinion, the court refused the question, to which the defendants excepted
(1 A., 61; Vol. C, 131 to 136).

Further examined (Vol. C, 179 to 180), Mr.
Ketchum stated that he had formed a *decided opinion* as
to the guilt or innocence of the defendants, which he still
entertained and *had theretofore expressed*. He was challenged for cause on all his answers, the challenge was
overruled, and the defendants excepted, and thereupon
challenged peremptorily.

D. F. SWAN (1 A., 63; Vol. C, 195 to 203) stated that
he had read and heard about the Haymarket trouble; had
formed an opinion as to the guilt or innocence of the defendants, or some of them, which he still entertained, and
had frequently expressed. That the opinion was *firmly
fixed in his mind* at the time of his examination. He
stated, however, that he believed he could be governed
by the evidence and the law; that he had discussed the
case with his neighbors and friends, and was prejudiced
in a general way against labor organizers. The court refused to allow him to be questioned as to whether his admitted prejudice against socialists, anarchists, etc., would
influence his verdict, to which defendants excepted.

Thereupon the defendants challenged Mr. Swan for cause, when the court interrogated him as follows (page 203): " Q. *Have you any feelings against either one* " *of them (the defendants), other than such as grows out* " *of what you have heard about their connection with the* " *Haymarket?* A. No, sir. Q. That is the only feel- " ing you have? A. Yes, sir. Q. And that feeling is " based upon the assumption—you have taken it for " granted that what you have read and heard about them " was true, substantially? A. Yes, sir. Q. Now, do " you believe you can sit here as a juror and listen to the " evidence on both sides that may be presented here on " their trial, and from that evidence only make up your " mind fairly and impartially as to what the real truth is " about their connection with the matter? A. I guess I " could. Q. Without any reference to what you have " heard about it heretofore, or what you have read about " it, or what you feel about it? A. Yes, sir."

Thereupon the challenge for cause was overruled, to which defendants excepted, and thereupon challenged peremptorily.

EDWARD KNAUER (1 A., 60; Vol. C, 103 to 109) stated he had formed a *pretty strong opinion* as to the guilt or innocence of the defendants; *had expressed* that opinion, and still entertained it. Thought he could deter- mine the guilt or innocence of defendants upon the proof presented in court, but stated also that *it would take pretty good evidence to change his present opinion.*

In answer to questions by the court, Mr. Knauer stated he had no ill feeling against any of the defendants person- ally, that he would go by the evidence, but *his opinion would influence him some.* He said: "I believe I could " take the evidence, although some of it I have my opin- " ion of." Q. You believe that you could take the evi-

" dence alone, and not be influenced by any opinion you
" have had hitherto, or that you have now? Do you be-
" lieve you can or cannot? A. Well, I guess I could."

Further interrogated by counsel for the defense, Mr.
Knauer said that in making up his mind as to what the
facts are in the case, after all the evidence should be in,
he *would to some extent call upon the facts now in his mind
and be influenced some thereby*, but he believed that he
could arrive at a fair and impartial verdict. He admitted
a strong prejudice against anarchists, socialists and communists. He was asked whether he believed that that
prejudice would influence him in a trial in which the defendants were conceded to be anarchists. Question refused by the court and defendants excepted. Mr. Knauer
was challenged for cause, the challenge was overruled, to
which defendants excepted, and challenged peremptorily.

F. I. WILSON (1 A., 65; Vol. C, 284 to
289) stated he had formed *and expressed* an opinion as to the guilt or innocence of some of the
defendants, based upon what he had read and
heard about the Haymarket trouble. That he believed *such opinion would influence him in rendering his
verdict.* In answer to the court's question, he stated that
he had no acquaintance with any of the defendants.
" Are you conscious in your own mind of *any wish or de-
" sire* that there should be evidence produced on this
" trial which shall prove some of these men, or any of
" them, to be guilty? A. Well, I think, possibly, I
" have. I think I have." The only feeling he had
against them was based upon having taken it for granted
that what he read about them was in the main, or part of
it at least, true. He believed that, sitting as a juror, the
effect of the evidence, either for or against the defendants,
would be *increased or diminished* by what he had heard or

read about the case. Thereupon said Wilson was challenged for cause; challenge overruled, and defendants excepted. Further on he modified his answers, upon further questions by the court, by saying: " Well, I feel " that I hope that the guilty one will be discovered or " punished; not necessarily these men. * * * Q. " Are you conscious of any other wish or desire about " the business than that the actual truth may be dis- " covered? A. I don't think I am." Thereupon the court overruled the challenge for cause; defendants excepted, and challenged said Wilson peremptorily.

JOHN CONNOLLY (1 A., 67; Vol. C, 338 to 344) said he had heard and read about the Haymarket meeting; formed and *frequently expressed a pretty strong opinion* as to the guilt or innocence of the defendants; thought he was open to conversion, and *might change his opinion if evidence contrary to the same would be presented.* Thought he could determine the case upon proof presented in court " if I tried pretty hard "; thought he *would be influenced* by his opinion in determining the question whether the proof presented was sufficient in fact to prove the guilt of the defendants beyond all reasonable doubt. Whereupon Mr. Connolly was challenged for cause.

In answer to questions of the court, he said he could fairly and impartially try the case upon the evidence presented in court; " at least I would try hard to." Didn't know any of the defendants; had no feeling about them one way or the other, except what grows out of what he had read or heard about them.

Whereupon said challenge for cause was overruled; defendants excepted, and said Connolly was peremptorily challenged by defendants.

GEORGE N. PORTER (1 A., 77; Vol. D, 191 to 204) stated he had formed *and expressed* an opinion as to the guilt or innocence of defendants, which opinion he thought *would bias his judgment.* He would try to go by the evidence, but *what he had read would have a great deal to do with his verdict.* His mind was certainly biased now, and *it would take a great deal of evidence to change it.* Whereupon said Porter was challenged for cause.

On examination by the state, in answer to the question whether he believed he could determine alone from the proof the guilt or innocence of the defendants, without consulting his opinion, or without being influenced by it, he said, " I hardly know how to answer that question. " I should certainly try to." Being asked the same question over again, he said: " Well, I rather think I could."

In answer to the court's question, Mr. Porter said: " I " think what I have heard and read before I came into " court *would have some influence with me.*" He was afraid that what he had read and heard before and the opinion he entertained *would have some effect* upon the kind of verdict which he should render. But finally he said he believed he could fairly and impartially try the case and render a verdict according to the law and the evidence; he certainly would try to. Challenge for cause was overruled by the court, and defendants excepted.

Upon further inquiry, by defendants' counsel, Mr. Porter admitted that he had a prejudice against communists, socialists and anarchists, and said he should certainly try to go by the evidence, but he thought in this case it would be awful hard work for him to do it. He should try very hard to do it, and he believed he could. He was asked whether he ever expressed his opinion that he believed the narration. He said: " Well, I don't know " that I ever said it in that many words, but I meant that, " of course, certainly. * * * Q. You don't know, " then, that you ever did say that you believed what you

" had read, or that you believed what you heard? A.
" Why, we have talked about it there a great many times,
" and *I have always expressed my opinion. I believe what
" I have read in the papers—believe that the parties are
" guilty.* Q. Now, then, you say that you did, in the
" discussion of it, in substance, say that you believed what
" you had read in the papers? A. Yes, sir; I have.
" Q. And it was from what you had read in the papers
" that you formed an opinion. A. Yes, sir."

Whereupon counsel for defendants renewed their challenge for cause to Mr. Porter.

Further interrogated by the court, whether he had
expressed an opinion as to the truthfulness of the account
itself which he had read or heard, he said: " Well, that is
" a pretty hard question to answer; I don't know. I
" have expressed myself as believing it. I don't know.
" Q. Well, believing— A. Believing what I read in
" the papers. Q. Believing the opinion that you had
" about the case and the defendants, or believing the
" story as it was printed? A. Why, believing, of course,
" the opinion of the defendants, and the story, believing
" it all, believing it just as I read it in the papers." * * *
" Q. Did you ever express any opinion as to whether
" the newspapers had got bodily or the substance of the
" story right or not? A. Oh, I don't know that I ever
" did; no, sir."

This is an instance of what we call *teasing the juryman*
up to the proper point, or " *coaching* " him, by the court.

The challenge for cause was overruled by the court, defendants excepted, and challenged Mr. Porter peremptorily.

H. N. SMITH (A., 81; Vol. D, 311 to 315) said he
had formed *quite a decided opinion* as to the guilt or innocence of the defendants; had read the newspapers at the

time, had had frequent conversations in regard to the matter; *had expressed* his opinion and still entertained it. He said he was *afraid he would listen a little more intently to testimony which concurred with his opinion than to testimony on the other side.* "Q. That is, you would be willing " to have your opinion strengthened, and would hate very " much to have it dissolved? A. I would. Q. Under " these circumstances, do you think you could render a " fair and impartial verdict? A. I don't think I could. " Q. You think you would be prejudiced? A. *I think* " *I would be prejudiced, because my feeling is very bitter.* " * * * Q. The question is whether or not your " prejudice would in any way influence you in coming to " an opinion, arriving at a verdict? A. I think it would. " Q. You think it would take less testimony as a jury- " man to come to the conclusion which you now have "than to come to the opposite conclusion? A. Yes, " sir. Q. That is your best judgment now? A. Yes, " sir." Whereupon said Smith was challenged for cause by the defendants.

On examination by the state, this talesman said he thought he could determine the guilt or innocence of the defendants upon the proof presented in court regardless of what he had read or heard, or of his opinion. Upon questions by the court he said he didn't know any of the defendants; he had a personal feeling; some of the officers were personal friends of his, but he had no feeling towards any of the defendants upon any ground other than what he had heard or read. He *had talked with persons who were at the Haymarket at the time of the explosion,* but the name of no man was mentioned.

The challenge for cause was overruled, the defendants excepted and challenged said Smith peremptorily.

ISAAC W. PINKHAM (A., 82; Vol. D, 339 to 344)

said he had formed *and expressed* an opinion as to the guilt or innocence of the defendants, which he still entertained. That opinion would not influence him *if the evidence showed that he was in error.* He believed he could, notwithstanding that opinion, listen to the testimony and the charge of the court and render an impartial verdict. He thought he could change his opinion if he saw any necessity for it. *The evidence would have to show that he was in error.* "I suppose that my present opinion would "*naturally prejudice* me slightly. I do not think that " would prejudice me so that the evidence would not be " weighed. * * *

"I believe I could weigh the evidence. I can't say " any more than that. I can't tell until the time comes. " Q. You don't know whether you could lay your opin- "ion aside or not? A. If the evidence should show I " was in error, I would. Q. The evidence would have "to show you were in error before you would change " your mind? A. Yes, sir. Q. *In other words, it* "*would take testimony to overcome your present opinion?* " A. *Yes, sir.*" Challenged for cause by defendants.

Upon examination by the state, this talesman said he could determine the guilt or innocence of the defendants upon the proof presented in court alone, and under the instructions of the court.

The challenge for cause was overruled, defendants excepted, and challenged Mr. Pinkham peremptorily.

Leonard Gould (A., 97; Vol. E, 477 to 490) said he had read about the Haymarket meeting, had discussed it, and had formed a rather decided opinion on the question of the guilt or innocence of the defendants, and still entertained that opinion. He thought he could be persuaded, thought he could listen to the evidence, whatever evidence was offered. Had a pretty decided prejudice against socialism, did not believe he could be governed by the evidence alone, irrespective of all prejudices and opinions, and all conclusions he then had.

Challenged for cause by defendants.

On examination by the state, he said: "I think I could "weigh the evidence impartially, but then to put that "thing just as it should be put, when you come to sepa-"rate a man's idea and his prejudice, but take the two "together, I really don't know that I could do the case "justice. * * * If I was to sit on the case, I should "just give my undivided attention to the evidence, and "calculate to be governed by that." He thought he could do that.

Further interrogated by counsel for defendants, he said he had some bias and some prejudice in the matter. He should do just the very best he could. As to whether he could act upon the proof produced and the charge of the court uninfluenced, unbiased and unswerved by any prejudice, opinion or conclusion that he then had, Mr. Gould said: "That is a question that it is almost impossible for a "man to answer." "Q. Do you believe that *you can* "*return a verdict*, under the evidence and proofs and "the charge of the court, and that alone, uninfluenced "by any opinion, prejudice or feeling that you now "have? A. I will leave out the last part of that question "entirely."

The court ruled that the question was improper, on the ground of ambiguity, because not stating whether it meant that the *juror* would be uninfluenced, or the *verdict* uninfluenced. To which ruling defendants excepted. We respectfully submit that this question, when printed, does not seem to be as ambiguous as one seeing from the other side might imagine.

Mr. Gould further said he believed what he had read

and heard, and his opinion was formed from that, and he supposed it was true.

" Q. I want to ask you whether you believe you can " listen to the testimony and other proofs that may be here " introduced in court, and the charge of the judge, and " render an absolutely impartial verdict in this case, not- " withstanding your present opinion, bias, or any preju- " dices that you may have? A. Well that is the same " question over again. Q. Do you say that you can't " answer it? A. Well, I answered it as far as I could " answer it. * * * Q. You say you don't know " that you can answer that either yes or no? A. No, I " don't know that I can."

Challenge for cause renewed.

In answer to the question by the court whether he believed that he could fairly and impartially render a verdict in accordance with the law and the evidence, he said: " Well, in a general way, I think I could listen to the law " and the evidence and form my verdict from that. * * " Q. Now, do you believe that you can, that you have " sufficiently reflected upon it so as to examine your own " state of mind, then say yes or no? A. It is a difficult " question for me to answer. Q. Well, make up your " mind as to whether you believe you can fairly and im- " partially render a verdict in accordance with the law and " the evidence. Most men in business possibly have not " gone through metaphysical investigations of this sort, so " as to be prepared to answer off-hand, without some " reflection? A. Judge, I don't believe that I can answer " the question. Q. Can't you answer whether you *believe* " you know? A. I should try. If I had to do it I " should do the best I could. Q. The question is, " whether you *believe* you can or not. I suppose Mr. " Gould, that you know the law is that no man is to be

" convicted of any offense with which he is charged un-
" less the evidence proves that he is guilty beyond a rea-
" sonable doubt?   A. That is true.   Q. The evidence
" heard in this case in court?   A. Yes.   Q. Do you
" *believe* that you can render a verdict in accordance with
" that law?   A. Well, I don't know that I could.   Q.
" Do you believe that you can; *if you don't know of any*
" *reason why you cannot*, do you believe you can?
" A. I could not answer that question.   *   *   *
" Q. Have you a belief, one way or the other, as to
" whether you can or cannot?   A. If I were to sit on
" the case, I should get just as near to it as possible, but
" when it comes to laying aside all bias and all preju-
" dice, and making it up in that way, it is a pretty fine
" point to them.   Q. Not, whether you are going to
" do it, but what do you *believe* you can—that is the
" only thing.   You are not required to state what is
" going to happen next week, or the week after, but
" what do you *believe* about yourself, whether you can
" or cannot?   A. I am just about where I was when I
" started."

The same question was asked again. Mr. Gould replied: " Well, I believe I have got just as far as I can in
" reply to that question."   *   *   *   " Q. This question,
" naked and simple of itself, is, do you *believe* that you
" can fairly and impartially render a verdict in the case
" in accordance with the law and the evidence?   A. I
" believe I could."

Question by counsel for defendants: " Do you believe
" that you can do that uninfluenced by any impression,
" prejudice or opinion which you now have?   A. You
" bring in that point that I object to, and I do not feel
" quite competent to answer."

Challenged for cause on all answers. Challenge overruled. Defendants excepted, and challenged Mr. Gould peremptorily.

The examination of this juror shows particularly what ran through all the examinations. After the juror had stated that he had formed and expressed an opinion, or that he could not try the case fairly and impartially without being influenced by bias or prejudice, six or eight times, he was taken in hand by the prosecution and by the court, and coached and coaxed up to a point where he would answer once that he thought he could. He was then decided by the court to be a competent juror.

We respectfully submit this examination as an instance of "*coaching*," and we most respectfully suggest that *we believe* the court itself was not representing the Goddess of Justice, and was not blind, and was not holding the scales level, when he was doing this.

Another examination which admirably illustrates the same process of questioning by the representatives of the state and the court, and the line of ruling adopted by Judge Gary, was that of JAMES II. WALKER (1 A., 104; Vol. F, 35 to 42). Mr. Walker said that he had formed an opinion on the question of the guilt or innocence of the defendants of the murder of Mr. Degan, which opinion he still entertained, and had expressed to others. Asked as to whether this opinion would influence his verdict, he replied: " Well, I am willing to " admit that *my opinion would handicap my judgment*, " possibly. I feel that I could be governed by the testi-" mony."

Further on he was asked:

" Then your belief now is that you could listen to the " testimony and any other proof that might be introduced, " and the charge of the court, and decide upon that " alone, uninfluenced, unprejudiced and unbiased by the

" opinion that you now have? A. *No, I don't say that.*
" Q. That is what I asked you? A. I said *I would be*
" *handicapped.*" He also stated that he was *prejudiced*
against socialists, anarchists and communists.

And then the following question was asked him
(p. 39; Vol. F.):

" Q. Now, considering all prejudice and all opinions
" that you now have, is there anything which, if the testi-
" mony was equally balanced, would require you to
" decide one way or the other, in accordance with your
" opinion or your prejudice? A. *If the testimony was*
" *equally balanced, I should hold my present opinion, sir.*
" Q. That is, you would throw your opinion upon the
" scale, which would give it a greater weight, your pres-
" ent opinion would turn the balance of the scale in favor
" of your present opinion? That is, assuming that your
" present opinion is that you believe the defendants
" guilty—or some of them—now suppose, if the testimo-
" mony were equally balanced, your present opinion would
" warrant you in convicting them, you believe, assuming
" your present opinion is that they are guilty? A. *I*
" *presume it would.* Q. Well, you *believe* it would—
" that is your present belief, is it? A *Yes.*"

Thereupon counsel for defense challenged Mr. Walker
for cause.

Upon examination of Mr. Grinnell, Mr. Walker answered the so-called statutory questions satisfactorily, and
thereupon the court interrogated him as follows:

" The COURT: Mr. Walker, I suppose you know that
" the law is that no man is to be convicted of any crime
" unless the evidence upon his trial, unless that evidence
" proves that he is guilty beyond a reasonable doubt?
" A. Yes, sir. Q. Now, this confusion about opinions
" and verdicts I want to clear up if I can. I suppose

" that you know that no man is to be tried upon prior
" impression or prior opinion of the jurors that are called
" into the case? A. Yes, sir. Q. But only upon the
" evidence. That you are familiar with, of course. Now,
" do you believe that you can fairly and impartially ren-
" der a verdict without any regard to rumor and what
" you may have in your mind in the way of suspicion and
" impression, etc., but do you *believe* that you can fairly
" and impartially render a verdict in accordance with the
" law and evidence in the case? A. I shall try to do it,
" sir." The COURT, interrupting: " But do you *believe* that
" you can sit here and fairly and impartially make up
" your mind from the evidence whether that evidence
" proves that they are guilty beyond a reasonable doubt or
" not? A. I think I could, but I should feel that I was
" a little handicapped in my judgment, sir." The COURT:
" *Well, that is a sufficient qualification for a juror in the*
" *case. Of course, the more a man feels that he is handi-*
" *capped, the more he will be guarded against it.*"

Thereupon counsel for defendants excepted to the remark of the court, stating that the court's position did
not correspond with observation or judgment, and objected to such remark being made as shown by the record in the presence of a large number of talesmen who
were in attendance, awaiting examination.

The court overruled the challenge for cause, to which
the defendants excepted, and thereupon peremptorily challenged Mr. Walker.

We beg leave to state that not only is the remark given
above contrary to experience, but to all the authorities.
According to the remark of the court, the stronger the
opinion of the juror against the defendant, and the more
bias and prejudice he has, the better juryman he will
make, because, having this hostile opinion and this bias

and prejudice, he will be conscious of it, and will isolate it from himself, and that will leave his mind to act on the evidence alone. The common experience is that a previously formed opinion or prejudice is like the sand-drift that permeates and mixes with everything, or, like green spectacles, that colors everything within the vision. The authorities all agree the defendant is not bound to take such a juryman, or, as Chief Justice Marshall says in the Burr case, "*the law will not trust him.*" Judge Gary seems to think the provision of the constitution is all wrong. This provision should have been that the defendant should be entitled to a juryman "*handicapped*" by previous opinions and prejudices, and the more he is *handicapped* the better the juryman will be.

W. D. ALLEN (1 A., 61; Vol. C, 125–130) stated that he had heard and read about the Haymarket difficulty, and from what he had so read and heard had formed an opinion as to the guilt of some or all the defendants, which opinion he still had, and which he had frequently expressed to others. Then came these questions and answers:

"Q. I will ask you whether what you have formed "from what you read and heard is a slight impression, or "an opinion, or perhaps a conviction? A. It is a de- "cided conviction. Q. You have made up your mind "as to whether these men are guilty or innocent? A. "Yes. Q. It would be difficult to change that convic- "tion, or impossible, perhaps? A. Yes. Q. It would "be impossible to change your conviction? A. It would "be hard to change my conviction." (Page 126.)

Thereupon Mr. Allen was challenged for cause. Whereupon Mr. Grinnell asked him if he could determine the guilt or innocence of the defendants, regardless of his opinion, and he stated he could; and thereupon the court proceeded to interrogate him, asking whether he had any personal acquaintance with any of the defendants, or had ever seen them before, which he replied to in the negative. Then the following occurred:

"Q. Have you any feeling with regard to them ex-
"cept such as grows out of what you have read or heard
"in connection with the matter which was referred to as
"the Haymarket difficulty? A. No, sir. Q. If you
"should be impaneled here as a juror, do you believe that
"you would endeavor to get at the real truth by the evi-
"dence without regard to any former opinion that you
"have had, or any opinion that you have now, or any-
"thing that you have read or heard? A. I should, yes.
"Q. And in trying the case, you believe that you could
"fairly and impartially try it only upon the evidence here
"in court, with the instructions of the court? A. I do.
"Q. I suppose you are familiar with the rule of law,
"that if there is no evidence which entirely satisfies the
"jury beyond a reasonable doubt of the guilt of the person
"charged with the offense, he must be acquited—you
"are familiar with that? A. Yes. Q. Do you believe
"that you will fairly and impartially apply that rule in
"this case, and unless the evidence which is here heard is
"of that character, that you can acquit these defendants?
"A. Yes." The COURT: "It don't make much differ-
"ence what a man calls his own state of mind—whether
"he calls it an impression, an opinion or a conviction.
"The thing is the same—any bias or prejudice or state
"of mind which will prevent him from trying the case
"upon the evidence."

Thereupon continued discussion between counsel and court as to the attitude of Mr. Allen as disclosed by his answers, at the end of which the court overruled the challenge for cause, to which defendants excepted, and thereupon challenged Mr. Allen peremptorily.

Perhaps the attitude of Judge Gary with reference to
the scope to be allowed defendants in their examination of
proposed jurors cannot be better illustrated than by calling attention to his action in reference to one particular
question which was formulated carefully and was asked
of a great number of the proposed jurors, but which
Judge Gary in every instance refused to allow the proposed jurors to answer, although the representatives of the
state formally withdrew all objection to the question in
open court. The question asked appears in 1 A., 39,
as follows:

" Suppose it should appear in evidence that the meet-
" ing held at the Haymarket square was a meeting called
" by socialists or anarchists, and was attended by them
" and others; suppose that it should further appear that
" the bomb which is alleged to have produced the death
" of Mr. Degan was thrown by some one in sympathy
" with the socialists or anarchists; now, I will ask you,
" provided it was not established beyond all reasonable
" doubt that these defendants actually threw the bomb,
" or that they aided, participated in or advised the com-
" mission of that wrong, would the fact that they were
" socialists or communists have any influence upon your
" mind in determining their innocence?" Mr. Grinnell,
the state's attorney, then said: " I *will not object* to that
" question." But the question was refused by the court,
not only in that instance, but in every other case where
it was propounded, to which defendants excepted in every
instance.

This course of action upon the part of Judge Gary
appears at page 148, Vol. A.; 1 A., 40.

Mr. CROWLEY was under examination, and stated that
he would not give the same effect to the testimony of an
anarchist upon the stand, or a communist, that he would

to any other unimpeached testimony. He was challenged for cause, the challenge was overruled, to which defendants excepted, and then asked the following question, by defendants' counsel:

"Q. I will ask you whether your prejudice against "communists and anarchists is such, that if they should "testify as witnesses you would not give to their evidence "the weight which it was entitled to, had they not been "anarchists or communists?" Mr. Grinnell stated: "We "don't make any objection." But the court held the question to be improper, and refused to allow it to be answered.

Thereupon the defendants' counsel asked the following:

"You have answered that you are prejudiced against "socialists, communists and anarchists. Now, upon the "trial of this cause, if it should be established by compe- "tent evidence that a meeting of socialists and anarch- "ists, communists and others, was held at the Haymarket "square, in this city, on May 4th, and that a bomb was "maliciously thrown by some one in sympathy with such "meeting, and in sympathy with the principles advocated "by socialists, communists and anarchists, and that by "reason thereof Mathias J. Degan was killed; but if the "evidence introduced upon the trial fails to show beyond a "reasonable doubt that such bomb was thrown by these "defendants, or any one of them, and that they, nor any "one of them, neither assisted, aided, abetted, advised or "counseled the throwing of the bomb, would your preju- "dice against socialists, communists and anarchists pre- "vent you from rendering an impartial verdict and ac- "quitting the defendants, or are you now so prejudiced "against the classes to which I have referred that you "cannot act impartialy and fairly as a juror in this case "under the facts assumed in the question?"

This question was refused by the court, to which the defendants excepted, and then asked:

"Q. I will ask you whether, if the defendants should "testify as witnesses in their own behalf in this trial, "and it should appear that they were communists, social-"ists or anarchists, that you would give credence to their "testimony?"

The question was objected to, and the objection sustained, and defendants excepted, and then asked:

"Q. Would you consider their testimony, under these "circumstances, the same as the testimony of any other "witness?"

Which question was objected to, and objection sustained, and defendants excepted, and then asked:

"If the testimony was equally divided upon the trial of "this case, would you find against the defendants or in "favor of the defendants, because of their being commun-"ists, socialists or anarchists?"

Which question the court, on its own motion, refused, to which defendants excepted.

Mr. Crowley was thereupon peremptorily challenged by defendants.

JAMES H. COLE was one of the jurors who tried the case. He was asked the same questions as Mr. Crowley. The rulings of the court were the same as in the case of Crowley, and the exceptions the same, the court refusing to allow any of said questions to be answered. In addition to this, it may be mentioned that Mr. Cole admitted that he had a prejudice against socialists, communists and anarchists. (1 A., 41; Vol. A., 172 to 181.)

In Mr. SHEDD's examination, heretofore referred to (1 A., 46; Vol. A., 396 to 398), defendants' counsel examining, the following occurred:

"Q. Have you any prejudice against the class known

" as socialists, communists or anarchists? A. I have;
" yes.

"Q. A decided prejudice against them? A. It is.

"Q. I will ask you whether that prejudice would
" prevent your rendering an impartial verdict in this case,
" provided it was conceded or proved that the defendants
" belonged to this class? A. It would; yes, sir."

The juror was thereupon challenged for cause. Challenge overruled, and exception.

The following discussion then occurred:

" The COURT: I know, or the court judicially knows,
" what are the objects of socialists, communists or an-
" archists.

" Mr. FOSTER: Beg your pardon, it presumes that the
" juror knows.

" The COURT: You must presume that I know, be-
" cause it has been decided that for a man to say that he
" was prejudiced against horse-thieves is no ground to
" impute to him any misconduct as a juror. Now, you
" must assume that I know either that anarchists, social-
" ists and communists are a worthy, a praiseworthy class
" of people, having worthy objects, or else I can't say
" that a prejudice against them is wrong. I don't know."

Later on, in the examination of the same proposed juror, this talesman stated, as we have before called attention to, that the mere fact of the defendants being communists would influence his opinion as a juror, and that he would find a verdict of "guilty" upon less evidence than if they were law-abiding citizens.

Thereupon the court asked this question:

" Well, that prejudice of yours, then, is based upon your
" understanding that they are not law-abiding citizens, is
" it? A. That is what it is."

T. H. DOWD (1 A., 50; Vol. B, 99-104), having

stated that he was prejudiced against socialists, anarchists and communists, was asked if such prejudice was so strong that it would influence his verdict if selected as a juror. The court on his own motion refused to allow the question to be answered. To which defendants excepted. Then he was asked if his prejudice was such that it would influence his verdict should it be established or conceded during the trial that the defendants were socialists, communists or anarchists; which question the court refused to allow to be answered, and the defendants excepted. And then he was asked whether, if it should appear that the defendants were socialists, anarchists or communists, it would require less evidence to convict or more evidence to acquit than if such fact should not appear. Which question the court also refused to allow to be answered. To which defendants excepted.

H. F. Chandler (1 A., 62, Vol. C; 149 *et seq.*): Stated that he had heard and read of the Haymarket trouble, had formed an opinion as to the guilt or innocence of the defendants, which he still entertained and had expressed before coming into court. That he believed what he heard and read, but had not expressed an opinion as to the truth of the accounts received. *That his opinion was decided and his mind pretty well made up.* He stated: "*It will take evidence to satisfy me,*" *and that it might be hard to change his opinion;* but he stated further that he believed he could determine the question of the guilt or innocence of the defendants solely upon the evidence in court; admitted he had a strong prejudice against anarchists and communists. He was asked: "Q. "If it were proved or conceded on this trial that all the "defendants or some of them are socialists, anarchists or "communists, do you think your prejudice would in any

" way influence your verdict?" Which question the court refused, and defendants excepted.

He stated that he was pointed out to the deputy sheriff by his employer to be subpœnaed as a juror, and that he had quite frequently expressed his opinion as to the guilt or innocence of the defendants.

Challenged for cause, he was examined by the court, to whom he stated that he did not know the defendants, *but thought he had some feeling against them, not only based upon what he had read about the Haymarket trouble, but on matters which he had heard before that.* That his opinion was based alone on what he had heard and read, and he believed he could try the case fairly upon the evidence. That he had now an opinion upon the question as to whether the defendants did the act which resulted in the death of Degan.

Thereupon the court suggested, in effect: " It don't " seem to me it makes any difference in the competency " of a juror, whether he has simply formed an opinion, " or expressed an opinion which he has formed. I don't " see how it makes a particle of difference in his state of " mind. Every man is in favor of justice and fair deal- " ing as between other people, where his own interests " are not affected; and, as I have said before, I think it " is in the nature of any man when he wants to find out " the truth of any transaction that he will, when the " original sources are presented to him, follow them and " not any hearsay that he has ever heard."

Thereupon the challenge for cause was overruled to which defendants excepted, and challenged peremptorily.

H. L. ANDERSON (1 A., 69; Vol. C, 517) stated that he had heard and read about the Haymarket affair, and formed an opinion as to the guilt or innocence of some of the defendants; that he had frequently talked the matter over with other people, and expressed his opinion as to the guilt or innocence of the defendants, which opinion he still retained, and which was based not only upon what he had read but what he heard; that he was sure he could lay aside his prejudice and grant a fair trial upon the evidence. *That he was well acquainted with some of the police force who were present at the Haymarket, and they had given him their views of the matter since that meeting, and told him what occurred there in connection with the effort to disperse the crowd.* That some of them were injured by the explosion of the bomb, and that he knew well one of the parties killed by the bomb. *That he had formed an unqualified opinion as to the guilt or innocence of the defendants which he regarded as deep-seated, a firm conviction that* THESE DEFENDANTS, OR SOME OR THEM, WERE GUILTY. *That as a result of the conversation that he had with the policemen present at the meeting, he reached his opinion as to the guilt or innocence of some of the defendants.*

He was thereupon challenged for cause by the defendants; challenge was overruled; defendants excepted and challenged peremptorily.

T. E. KEEFE (1 A., 724; Vol. D, 42–61) stated that he had heard of the Haymarket affair, and from what he heard and read had formed an opinion as to the guilt or innocence of the defendants of the murder of Degan, which opinion he still had, and which was a firm opinion; thought such opinion would not influence his verdict; knew Officer Degan for several months before he was killed, and knowing him, what he had heard and read caused him to form a very strong opinion upon the question of the guilt or innocence of these defendants or some of them, which he had expressed to others; that he believed what he had heard and read, and expressed his

opinion on that belief; *had stated to others that he believed
what he had heard and read, and did, in fact, believe the
accounts as published and repeatedly so stated,* and at the
same time told others his opinion.

Challenged for cause, he stated to Mr. Grinnell that
he got the opinion from what he read, which he expressed
to others, but that he did not say to anybody that he believed what he read—did believe it, but did not say so;
and that the opinion he had was as to who was respon-
si ble.

Thereupon to the court he stated that he had never had
any discussion as to the truth of the reports he had
heard, but had expressed his opinion to others as to the
transaction and as to the parties.

Examined again by defendants' counsel, he stated that
he had expressed his opinion, which was based upon what
he had heard and read, which he believed, more on what
he had heard than what he had read, and he had repeated
what he had heard to others —*that he had stated to others
that he believed what he had heard,* but did not state that
he believed what he had read—stated to others that he
believed what he had heard and gave them his opinion—
*that there is no mistake about this; that he said to others
that he believed what he had heard.*

The challenge for cause was here renewed, when to the
court he stated that he had heard the Haymarket trasac-
tion talked of, but never told anybody that he believed the
newspapers had got the story straight, nor that he believed that he himself had got it straight from any one
who talked with him.

Thereupon to defendants' counsel he further stated that
his opinion was formed from what he had heard largely,
and that in communicating that opinion to others *he stated
that he believed what he had heard—that there was no mis-*

take about this; that he told them his opinion, which was based upon what he had heard and read.

Thereupon the challenge for cause was again renewed, when to Mr. Grinnell he stated that in discussing the matter with others he had repeated what he had heard and had expressed his opinion, but did not state that he believed every word or any particular word that had been told; and to the court he stated that he had never said anything as to whether he thought those that he talked with got the story straight.

Finally to defendant's counsel he again stated that he had heard the story from several parties whose names he could not give, and had discussed the matter with a good many; that he believed what he had heard, though he did not say so; and thereupon *he stated further that in talking with others he told them that he did believe what he had heard,* but did not repeat the substance fully—*that he was sure that he did tell them that he believed what he had heard,* and this in conversation with different people.

Challenge for cause was thereupon overruled, to which the defendant excepted, and challenged peremptorily.

The examination of M. D. Flavin (1 A., 84; Vol. D, 411 to 418) brings out another point in the ruling of the trial court as to the qualification of jurors not heretofore suggested, namely, that even *relationship of the proposed juror to one of the parties killed by the Haymarket bomb, coupled with admitted prejudice,* would not, in the judgment of the court, disqualify. It needs no citation of authority to show the absolute error of this ruling. The examination was in substance as follows:

He stated that he had heard and read about the Haymarket affair and formed an opinion as to the guilt or innocence of the defendants of the murder of Degan, which opinion still stood pretty strong, which he still entertained and had expressed to others. *That one of the officers killed, Officer Flavin, was a relative, although his relationship was distant, and for this reason his feeling was perhaps different from what it would have been, and occasioned a very strong opinion as to the guilt or innocence of the defendants, or some of them. That he stated in discussing this matter with others that he believed what he had heard and read, not so much what he had read as what he had heard.* That he believed he expressed the opinion that what he had heard was a true narrative. He was thereupon challenged for cause.

To Mr. Grinnell he stated that he read the accounts of the Haymarket, but did not believe he had ever told anybody that he believed the story that he had heard and read was a true story; did not express any opinion as to the truth of the details; but stating he believed he could give a fair and impartial verdict, challenge for cause was overruled, to which defendants excepted and challenged peremptorily.

RUSH HARRISON (1 A., 106-7; Vol. F, 56-65) stated that he had been working for Edson Keith & Co., in their silk department, for eleven years. Had read and heard of the Haymarket meeting, and formed an opinion touching the guilt or innocence of the accused, or some of them, of the murder, which he had expressed to others, and there had been nothing to change it. The examination given in the abstract then proceeds as follows:

" *It would have considerable weight with me*, if selected
" as a juror. *It is pretty deeply rooted, the opinion is, and
" it would take a large preponderance of evidence to remove
" it.* Think I could listen to the testimony and render a
" verdict upon that alone, uninfluenced by my present
" opinion. Am prejudiced against socialists, communists
" and anarchists. I still think it would take a preponder-

" ance of evidence to remove my present opinion. I should
" naturally take the law from the court and the evidence
" from the witnesses. *I should give the defendants the*
" *benefit of a reasonable doubt, if the evidence were equally*
" *balanced, but to some extent I should be governed by my*
" *present opinion.* My opinion is based more upon what
" I have read than what I have heard. ' *It would require*
" *the preponderance of evidence to remove the opinion I now*
" *possess. I feel like every other good citizen does feel, a*
" *feeling that* THESE MEN ARE GUILTY; we don't know
" which. We have formed this opinion by general re-
" ports and the newspapers. *Now, with that feeling, it*
" *would take some very positive evidence to make me think*
" *these men were not guilty if I should acquit them;* that
" is what I mean.' I should act entirely upon the testi-
" mony. I would do so as near as the main evidence
" would permit me to do. Probably I should take the
" testimony alone. ' Q. *But you say it would take posi-*
" *tive evidence of their innocence before you could consent*
" *to return them not guilty?* A. *Yes. I should want*
" *some strong evidence.* Q. *Well, if that strong evidence*
" *of their innocence was not introduced, then you would*
" *want to convict them, of course?* A. *Certainly.'*
" Don't know whether, if the testimony was evenly bal-
" lanced, my opinion would turn the scale, but I think it
" would. I think if the testimony was evenly balanced
" my present opinion would convict them."

(Challenged for cause by defendants.)

To Mr. Grinnell: "If I did not believe, beyond a rea-
" sonable doubt, these defendants, or some of them, were
" guilty, I would be willing to acquit them upon the proof
" presented in court. I would give the defendants the
" benefit of the doubt.

"*If the testimony was equally balanced, I think my present*

" *opinion would convict the defendants. I said so, and I* " *still think so."*

To the COURT: " I understand that a defendant must " be proved guilty by the evidence beyond a reasonable " doubt or he is entitled to be acquitted. I should give " the benefit of the doubt to the prisoners, unless they " were proved to be guilty by the evidence."

The challenge for cause by the defendants to Mr. Harrison was thereupon overruled, to which the defendants excepted, and challenged peremptorily.

We submit that if Mr. Harrison, as shown by this examination, was a fair and impartial juror within the contemplation of our constitution and laws, then there is no such thing as a prejudiced juror. Here was a man who stated positively that he shared in the general belief that the defendants, or some of them, were guilty: that this opinion of his was deep-rooted, and that " it would take " a *large preponderance* of the evidence to remove "; " that it would take some pretty positive evidence to make " me think these men were not guilty, if *I* should acquit " them." That if the testimony was evenly balanced the opinion he entertained at the time would convict the defendants. Even to the state's representative, upon cross-examination, he repeated that, if the testimony was equally balanced, his present opinion would, in his judgment, convict the defendants. While to the court, upon further interrogation, stating that he recognized that it would be his duty to acquit, unless the evidence convicted beyond a reasonable doubt, he would only say that he would give the benefit of such doubt to the prisoners, " unless they were proved to be guilty by the evidence." Not, observe, by a clear preponderance of the evidence, but by such amount of evidence as he might deem necessary to satisfy the opinion that he then held.

We repeat that this juror was an incompetent juror, and if Judge Gary's ruling upon his examination was correct, then we have studied the constitution and the law to little purpose.

LeRoy Hannah (1 A., 118; Vol. G, 165-171) stated that he had heard and read of the Haymarket meeting; that he had a prejudice against socialists, communists and anarchists; *that if he were a juror in this case his verdict might be prejudiced by his present bias and opinion, and that he* BELIEVED THAT HE COULD NOT *act upon the proof presented in court alone, uninfluenced thereby.*

He was thereupon challenged for cause by the defendants.

To the state's attorney he said that he would try to determine the question of the guilt or innocence of the defendants, if taken as a juror, without reference to what he had heard or read, and believed he could do so. To the court he stated that he had no personal acquaintance with the defendants, and the only opinion he had was from what he had read and heard. That *he had talked with a policeman who was present at the Haymarket*, but that the names of the defendants were not mentioned, and that if selected as a juror he thought he could be governed by the evidence alone. The challenge for cause was thereupon overruled, and he was further examined by defendant's counsel.

He stated that he had talked with a policeman who was present at the Haymarket, and who described the occurrence there, the throwing of the bomb, etc., but did not mention the names of the particular persons present; that he had heard the names of Spies, Parsons and Fielden, and whatever opinion he had upon the matter had reference to parties bearing those names; and the prejudice which he had was against parties

*bearing these names, and the principles they advocated.
That it was so strong that it would probably influence
him in considering the testimony. That he was prejudiced against the principles which they advocated
and against them, and that he felt that this prejudice
might influence his verdict:* and he said, " I don't know
" but we deceive ourselves sometimes, when we say we
" can do so and so. My prejudice might bias my ver-
" dict."

The challenge for cause, being thereupon renewed, was
fully argued, overruled, and exception; and the defendants
thereupon challenged peremptorily.

We think we may be justified here in citing one or two
illustrations, for the purpose of showing, by the questions
asked and the expressions made use of by Judge Gary,
the extent to which he went in this matter of the qualification for jury service, despite the matters upon which we
relied as evidencing disqualification; and also further
showing the attitude taken by the court in the course of
these jury examinations.

In the course of the examination of J. R. Adams (1 A.,
75; Vol. D, 84–89), after he had been challenged for
cause, this occurred:

The COURT: " Q. Do you believe that after you
" have heard all the evidence that can be presented, or
" that shall be presented on either side—examination and
" cross-examination—that your conclusions then as to
" what is the truth will be at all affected by what people
" have said or written about it before you heard any tes-
" timony? Do you believe that your conclusions as to
" what that evidence proved or failed to prove will be at
" all affected by what anybody had ever said or written
" about that matter before? A. I believe it would.

" The COURT: It is incomprehensible to me."

The challenge was, of course, allowed on this answer, but the remark was excepted to by defendants' counsel, the remark being made in the presence of other jurors.

In connection with the examination of B. L. Ames (1 A., 95; Vol. E, 400–408), after he had been challenged for cause on his answers made to defendants' counsel, the court took him in hand and proceeded to examine him. This appears: *He stated to the court that he did not believe, everything considered, that he could sit as a juror, listen to the evidence, and from that alone make up his mind as to the guilt or innocence of the defendants:* that he did not know the defendants, but had frequently been with the police, and didn't think he would listen to the evidence presented, and make up his mind from that alone as to whether it proved the defendants guilty beyond a reasonable doubt. Thereupon the following examination occurred:

"The COURT: Q. Why not? What is to prevent "your listening to the evidence and acting only upon that? "Why can't you listen to the evidence and make up your "mind on that?"

(Exception by defendants to said question.)

"A. I can, I suppose, make up my mind, but I may "be prejudiced just the same. Q. Can you make up "your mind whether the evidence proves beyond a rea- "sonable doubt whether they are guilty or does not "prove it? A. Yes, I could come to a conclusion. Q. "Can't you do that impartially? The question in this "case for a juror is, not what he may think will be the "effect upon his mind as to his private impressions, "suspicions or notions, but what effect the state of his mind "will have on his verdict. Will your verdict be influenced "by anything other than the evidence in the case and the in- "struction of the court? A. I am afraid it would, for

" certain reasons. Q. You don't believe that you could " fairly and impartially try the case and render a verdict " on the law and evidence? A. I don't think I could."

This challenge also was allowed; but the questions of the court, and the manner of their putting to the proposed juror, illustrate the attitude of the court upon these questions, and the manner in which proposed jurors were led or urged to give answers that would, in the view of the presiding judge, establish their competency.

Still another illustration we select from the many abounding in the record, as afforded in connection with the examination of H. D. Bogardus (1 A., 102–104). For convenience we shall present this examination precisely as it stands in the abstract, as follows, to wit:

H. D. BOGARDUS (1 A.), flour and fruit merchant, examined, stated: Have heard and read of the Haymarket meeting; and from what I have read and heard, have formed an opinion as to the guilt or innocence of the defendants of the crime now charged, which opinion I have expressed to others, and still entertain; it certainly would influence my verdict if selected as a juror; I could not act independent of the opinion; it would "require very " strong proof to overcome my opinion. I would be in- " fluenced by it, of course," and I would not render my verdict upon the testimony alone, fairly and impartially.

(Challenged for cause.)

To Mr. GRINNELL: I have talked with some policemen about the Haymarket affair, but whether they were there or not, I do not know. I have heard no testimony upon the matter. I would be influenced as a juror by my prejudices and opinions against the defendants; " it would " require very strong proof to overcome it." I don't believe I could give them a fair trial upon the proof, for it would require very strong proof to overcome my preju-

dices; " I hardly think that you could bring proof enough
" to change my opinion." If accepted on the jury, I
would try to do my duty according to the evidence, and
might do so; think I could do my duty, " but it would re-
" quire pretty strong evidence to overcome my prejudice."
Would not convict without some evidence. If taken as
a juror in this case, I think I could " determine the guilt
" or innocence of the defendants upon the proof produced
" alone, * * * but being prejudiced, it would take
" very strong evidence to overcome my prejudice."

To the Court: I know the law as to defendants not
being convicted except upon evidence on the trial, and I
think I might fairly and impartially determine whether the
evidence proved that they are guilty beyond a reasonable
doubt, " but it would require pretty strong proof." I can
fairly and impartially render a verdict in this case in accordance with the law and the evidence, I think.

(Challenge for cause overruled, and exception.)

To Defendants' Counsel: " I say it would require
" pretty strong testimony to overcome my opinion at
" the present time." Still I think I could act independent
of my opinion. I would start with an opinion, however, and " I think that the preponderance of proof
" would have to be against my opinion strong." I think
the defendants are responsible for what occurred at the
Haymarket meeting. The preponderance of evidence
would have to be in favor of the defendants' innocence
with me.

(Challenge for cause renewed.)

" The COURT: The question is, what will the verdict
" be? The statute says that if a man says that he be-
" lieves that he can fairly and impartially render a verdict
" in accordance with the law and evidence, that then the
" formation of opinions from rumor or newspaper state-

" ment is not a ground of challenge; of course, leaving it
" to the judgment of the tryer, whether that belief of his
" is well founded or not.   But I have expressed my opin-
" ion upon that part of the case here, so that it is not
" necessary to repeat it.   Every fairly intelligent and
" honest man, when he comes to investigate the question
" originally for himself upon authentic sources of infor-
" mation, will, in fact, make his opinion from the authen-
" tic sources instead of the hearsays that he had before."

(Exception to the ruling of the court.)

Upon further examination of this talesman, he finally
stated to the court directly that he would find the .de-
fendants guilty unless the evidence was very strong and
clear, and that, if evenly balanced, his prejudice would
condemn them (page 26); and thereupon the juror was
finally discharged from the panel and the challenge for
cause allowed.

We could go on through the eight volumes of the
record containing the jury examination, and cite hundreds
of illustrations of these rulings, but we do not feel that we
would be justified in so far trespassing upon your Honors'
time and patience.   We have selected the cases above
specially referred to simply as examples running all
through the case, which illustrate the positions assumed
by Judge Gary, and which seem to us to demonstrate the
absolutely fatal error which pervaded his rulings, and
which vitiated the construction which he attempted to
give to the statute of March 12, 1874: a construction
which, as above shown, disregarded the omission from
the statute of any suggestion indicating a design to remove the disqualification from a juror who *had expressed*
his opinion, and had committed himself to its advocacy,
disregarding wholly the long line of judical decisions, to
which there had never been any notable exception, prior

to the adoption of our constitution of 1870. That while the formation of an opinion or impression based upon newspaper statements or rumor, and which was slight in its character, does not necessarily disqualify a juror otherwise apparently candid, fair and impartial, yet the confession of a fixed or decided opinion, or a decided conviction, no matter upon what sources of information based, was always held to disqualify. The fixed belief in the truth of the information is material, as bearing upon the character of the opinion as to defendant's guilt or innocence, and showing that the opinion is not hypothetical, but deliberate, based on what is deemed credible information, and therefore a disqualifying bias, prejudice or opinion.

It was under such rulings, announced at the outset of the trial, as appears from the examinations transcribed in volume I of the abstract, that the defendants were compelled to select the jurors. Under such rulings the defendants proceeded to secure a jury as best they could. It was our duty, in view of the responsibilities devolving upon us in the defense of eight lives, to select the least objectionable, out of those presented for examination, whom we could obtain under the rulings fixed by the court, and to which we were compelled to submit.

IV. THE TWELVE WHO TRIED THE CASE.

As a matter of fact the record discloses concerning the twelve jurors *who tried the case*, the following:

Juror COLE. We have already referred to this juryman's examination above, in connection with which was disclosed his prejudice against socialists, anarchists and communists as a class, and the refusal of the court to allow us to interrogate him as to whether that prejudice would influence his verdict, or the weight he would give to the testimony of the defendants if they should be sworn, and to their witnesses, in his determination of the cause.

Mr. JAMES H. BRAYTON, one of the twelve, said that he had formed an opinion as to the nature and character of the crime perpetrated at the Haymarket, and, based upon his reading, as to the guilt or innocence of the defendants of that crime. He also stated that he had as a result of his investigations a prejudice against socialists, anarchists and communists (1 A., 108; Vol. F, 134, 135, 139); but he also stated that he believed that he could render a fair and impartial verdict, and was accepted notwithstanding his bias or prejudice.

JOHN B. GREINER, one of the twelve, said that he had heard and read of the Haymarket meeting, and from his reading had formed an opinion as to the guilt of the defendants, or some of them. The following further occurred in his examination (1 A., 121; Vol. G, 356):

" The distinction is this, whether or not your opinion " is that an offense was committed at the Haymarket " merely, or whether it is that the defendants are con- " nected with the offense that was so committed? A. " Well, it is evident that the defendants are connected " with it from their being here, as far as that is con- " cerned.

" Q. You regard that as being evidence? A. Well, " —well, I don't know exactly; I would expect of course " that it connected them, or they would not be here.

" Q. Well, that would infer that somebody thought so, " anyhow, or else the whole thing would be a very foolish " proceeding. So then the opinion that you have has " reference to the guilt or innocence of some of these men,

" or all of them? Now, is that opinion one, Mr. Greiner, " which would influence your verdict if you should be " selected as a juror to try the case, do you believe? A. " I certainly think it would affect it to some extent. I " don't see how it could be otherwise."

Mr. Greiner, however, stated that he believed he could render fairly and impartially a verdict upon the law and the evidence in the case, and was accepted.

CHAS. A. LUDWIG, one of the twelve, admitted a prejudice against socialists, communists and anarchists, but inasmuch as his answers to other questions were comparatively unobjectionable he was accepted. (1 A., 83; Vol. D, 352, 362, 392.)

ALANSON H. REED, one of the twelve, stated that he had an opinion concerning the commission of the offense at the Haymarket, and from newspaper reports had an opinion concerning the guilt or innocence of the defendants, or some of them, and that he had a prejudice derived from his reading against socialists and communists. Further on he stated that the opinion which he formed, touching the guilt or innocence of the defendants, was both from what he read in the paper and what he heard, but principally from the newspaper reports. His answers upon other questions, however, in the main, were satisfactory, and he was accepted. (Vol. G, 253 *et seq.*)

C. B. TODD, one of the jurors, stated that he had heard and read about the Haymarket affair, and from all sources of information, he had an opinion upon the question of the guilt or innocence of the defendants of the crime of murder, which opinion he had expressed to others in the course of discussions upon the matter. (1 A., 55; Vol. B, 279–300.)

Aside from these matters, however, his answers were substantially unobjectionable, and he was accepted.

G. W. Adams, one of the twelve jurors, upon his direct examination by Mr. Grinnell, admitted that he had read and heard about the Haymarket affair, and had formed an opinion as to the character of the crime there committed, but denied that he had formed any opinion as to whether or not the defendants were guilty. (1 A., 124; Vol. II, 33.) But upon cross-examination by defendants, he admitted that he had formed an opinion that some of the defendants were interested in that crime, which opinion he still entertained. (Vol. II, 39, 40.) He stated, however, that he did not think the opinion was a strong one, and that he believed that he could fairly and impartially render a verdict in the case, and lay aside all prejudice, bias and opinion in reaching his verdict. He was thereupon accepted.

Andrew Hamilton (1 A., 79; Vol. D, 259 *et seq.*) stated, in substance, that he had said that somebody ought to be made an example of in connection with this affair, and that if it should be proved that the defendants were the men whose names he saw in the papers, connected with the affair, then he thought they should be made examples of. Otherwise his answers were satisfactory, and he was sworn.

H. T. Sanford, who was the last juror examined (1 A., 139: Vol. H, 293 *et seq.*), stated that he had an opinion from what he had read and heard as to the guilt or innocence of the eight defendants of the throwing of the bomb. He also said that he had a decided prejudice against socialists, communists and anarchists. He was thereupon challenged for cause by the defendants, despite his statement that he believed that he could fairly and impartially render a verdict in the case. He was thereupon interrogated by the state, when the following occurred:

" Q. Have you ever said to any one whether or not
" you believed the statement of facts in the newspapers
" to be true? A. I had never expressed it exactly in
" that way, but still I have no reason to think they were
" false.

" Q. The question is not what your opinion of that
" was. The question simply is—it is a question made
" necessary by our statute, perhaps? A. Well, I don't
" recall whether I have or not."

Thereupon the challenge for cause was overruled,
and defendants excepted.

Prior to the examination of this juror, as the record
discloses, the defendants had exhausted all their peremptory challenges, and, their challenge for cause being overruled, they stopped and refused to accept Mr. Sanford as
a juror. (Vol. II, 301.)

Subsequently Mr. Sanford was accepted by the state,
and was sworn as a juror.

The nine jurors last above named, together with Mr.
Frank Osborne, Mr. Samuel G. Randall and Theodore
Denker, constituted the panel by which the defendants
were tried.

As to Mr. Adams and Mr. Denker, we would like to
offer a few remarks in particular.

Upon the motion for a new trial there was filed by the
defendants, in support of their motion, the affidavit of
Michael Cull, who stated that shortly after the Haymarket
affair he had a conversation with said Adams, at which a
number of other persons were present, in reference thereto,
in which said Cull stated: " That the police had no right
" to interfere with the meeting; that if they, the police,
" had let the meeting alone they would have gone home
" in a little while," to which said Adams replied that the
police ought to have shot them all down; that they, mean-

ing the defendants, had no rights in this country, and that
" if I was on the jury I would hang all the damned bug-
" gars." That Adams evinced a good deal of bitter
feeling against the defendants. It is true that an affidavit
of Mr. Adams was filed in behalf of the state, which denied the statements of Cull's affidavit. But the fact stands
with reference to Mr. Adams that after first stating, on
his *voir dire*, that he had formed no opinion as to the
guilt or innocence of the defendants touching the Haymarket affair, he subsequently, on cross-examination, admitted that he had formed such an opinion, thus directly
contradicting himself; while Cull's affidavit, if believed,
shows the expression of a strong feeling, and a strong
adverse opinion upon his part.

The case of THEODORE DENKER, one of the twelve
who tried the case, presents special features, to which we
wish to call attention. He was examined on the fourth
day of the proceedings (Vol. B, 125 *et seq*). He admitted that he had heard of the Haymarket affair, and
that he had expressed an opinion as to the guilt or innocence of the defendants of the murder charged, which he
still entertained. That he believed what he had read
and heard upon the subject, and that he thought that the
opinion was such as would prevent him from rendering
an impartial verdict. He was thereupon challenged for
cause.

Mr. Grinnell then asked him if he believed he could
determine the guilt or innocence of the defendants upon
the proof presented in court, without reference to his
prejudice or opinion, and regardless of what he had
heard, and he stated that he believed he could. Thereupon the court asked this question:

" Do you believe that you can fairly and impartially
" try the case, and render an impartial verdict, upon the

" evidence as it may be presented here, and the instruc-
" tions of the court?"

To which he replied: "Yes; I think I could." Thereupon the court overruled the challenge for cause, and defendants excepted. Thereupon he was re-examined by
defendants, and again admitted that he had formed an
opinion as to the guilt or innocence of the defendants,
which he had expressed frequently and without hesitation. He persisted, however, in stating that he believed
that he could lay aside his prejudice or opinion and try
the case fairly, and was finally accepted.

In support of the motion for a new trial, the defendants
introduced the affidavits of Thomas J. Morgan and of
Thomas S. Morgan, who both testified unequivocally that
on the morning of the 6th of May, Denker stated to
them, and in their hearing, referring to Spies, Fielden,
Schwab and Fischer particularly, who had been arrested
on the 5th of May for alleged complicity with the Haymarket affair, and referring particularly to Spies: " He
" and the whole damned crowd ought to be hung."
This remark of Denker's was made with much feeling
and emphasis (Vol. O, 56.) It is true that the affidavit of Mr. Denker himself to contradict these statements
of Thomas J. and Thomas S. Morgan was permitted to
be read (Vol. O, 100), in which he denied that he
made the remark sworn to by the Morgans, although he
again admitted that he had an opinion, and had expressed
that opinion.

That the court erred in overruling our motion for a
new trial, even if that motion had been based alone on the
ground of the showing that the juror DENKER was not
an impartial and competent juror, admits, we respectfully
submit, of no doubt, in the light of well-considered
authority. Let it be remembered that the juror ad-

mitted, upon his *voir dire*, that he was prejudiced, had an opinion, which he had expressed frequently to others, and did not think that he could fairly try the case. Challenged for cause on these answers, he was coached into a retraction thereof, and into the statement that he believed he could fairly and impartially try the case; and thereupon the challenge was overruled, etc. Upon the motion for a new trial two affidavits were produced showing that Denker had, several days after the 4th of May, stated, referring to Spies and other of the defendants then under arrest, that " he and the whole " damned crowd ought to be hung." These affidavits are altogether unimpeached, and the only effort to meet them is the unsupported affidavit of Denker. The new trial should have been granted on this ground, if for no other reason.

Closely parallel to the case made against Mr. Denker on these affidavits was the case against the juror Finley, on account of whose prejudice alone there was a reversal in *Vennum* v. *Harwood*, 1 Gil., 659, a case that arose under the constitution of 1818. In support of a motion for a new trial in that case, one Wilson swore to statements made by Finley before being taken as a juror, to the effect that the plaintiff ought to recover heavy damages; and one Crawford swore that he heard Finley, after the trial, say to Wilson that he, Finley, had told him how the case would go, etc. Finley's affidavit was read, in which he swore that while he had talked with Wilson and Crawford since the trial, he had never, as he believed, made any such declarations as they stated; and that prior to the trial he had never in fact formed or expressed any opinion about the case, and that he had acted impartially as a juror: a much stronger affidavit than Denker's, as will be observed. Yet our Supreme court unhesitatingly reversed the judgment on this sole ground, citing and approving the language used in *Smith* v. *Eames*, 3 Scam., 76, and *Gardner* v. *The People,* id., 83.

In *Brakefield* v. *The State*, 1 Sneed, 215, the Supreme court of Tennessee used the following language:

" It is said that William Perry, one of the jurors, had " prejudged the case, and was therefore incompetent. To " support this fact, two affidavits were produced on the " motion for a new trial; first, Oscar states that as he came " to court with Perry, the morning he was taken on the " jury, he asked him if he was not afraid to go to town. " Perry replied: 'No; I have formed my opinion as to the " last case therein; as to Brakefield, I believe he ought " to be hung'; and Edwards states that he was in com-" pany with Perry on his way to the court, who inquired " of him if he was not a witness in this case. Affiant " replied that he was a witness for the state. Perry then " said, alluding to the prisoner, ' Damn him, he ought to " be hung.' The prisoner states in his affidavit that he " had no knowledge of these facts when Perry was taken " on the jury.

" It is well settled that loose impressions and conversa-" tions of a juror, founded upon rumor, will not, if disclosed " by him or others to the court, have the effect to set him " aside as incompetent.

" But was Perry's remark a mere loose impression " founded upon rumor? We think not. His statement is " in the strongest terms of opinion, conviction and preju-" dice; he pronounced the prisoner as guilty, and guilty of " the highest grade of murder. He stands clearly convicted " of having prejudged the case. His examination upon his " *voir dire* before the court does not appear. His counter-" affidavit is produced to explain the matter, but *it is a set-" tled rule that the affidavit of an offending juror cannot be*

"*relied upon to exculpate himself and prejudice the*
"*prisoner.*" *Hynes* v. *The State*, 8 Humph., 602; *Luster*
v. *The State*, 11 Humph., 170.

"We are to presume that his statement before the
"court made him apparently competent as a juror; after
"the trial he is accused upon the evidence of the wit-
"nesses as having prejudged the case.   The juror stands
"criminated before the court, and in such case his own
"affidavit cannot be credited or relied on when it involves
"the rights of the accused.   Other affidavits of jurors
"were made to the effect that Perry, the juror, was favor-
"able to the prisoner on the trial.   This fact we regard
"as not competent to the issue, which is, was the juror
"competent?   Not what his conduct was after he was
"taken on the jury.   If he was put to the prisoner as a
"competent juror, when he was in fact incompetent, the
"rights of the prisoner were violated, and it is a legal
"presumption that he was injured.   *   *   *   A verdict
"thus tainted cannot be permitted to stand.   The pris-
"oner was entitled to an impartial jury."

While it may be that under our practice the affidavit of
Denker in contradiction of the affidavits of T. J and T.
S. Morgan may be entitled to be read and considered,
yet, as said by the Supreme Court of Tennessee, "the
"affidavit of an offending juror cannot be relied on to ex-
"culpate himself.   *   *   *   The juror stands crimi-
"nated before the court, and in such case *his own affidavit*
"*cannot be credited or relied on, when it involves the rights*
"*of the accused.*"   With reference to his affidavit, we
beg to submit the following further criticism.   There is
no statement in Denker's affidavit that he never used to
any person the language attributed to him, to wit: "He
and the whole damned crowd ought to be hung"; the
denial is specific, namely, that he never made that state-

ment to the particular affiants; while he admits, in substance, that he did have an opinion adverse to the prisoners, an opinion as to their guilt, which he had freely
expressed. Was he a competent and proper juror to be
put to these prisoners? And is a "verdict thus tainted,"
one that should be sustained in the due administration of
justice?

As bearing upon the contradictory answers given by
Mr. Denker, and as showing that he ought to have been
excluded from the panel by the court upon our challenge
for cause, we cite again the case of *Wright* v. *Commonwealth*, 32 Grattan, 941. There, as in the case at bar,
the juror first stated "he had made up and expressed an
" opinion in the case; that the opinion so made up and
"expressed was still upon his mind; that he did not think
"he could do the prisoner justice"; but in answer to the
questions of the court whether, should the evidence be
different from what he had heard, his opinion would be
changed, he stated that it would, and that he could come
to the trial with an unbiased and unprejudiced mind, and
give the accused a fair trial, and thereupon the trial court
overruled the challenge. The case is exactly parallel
in these regards with the action of Judge Gary as to juror
Denker. The Supreme court of Virginia held that this
action was error, for which the case was reversed, and
laid down the law, *in favorem vitæ*, as follows:

"* * * If the juror has made up and expressed a
"*decided* opinion as to the guilt or innocence of the
"accused, he is incompetent; and it does not matter
"whether the opinion be founded on conversations with a
"witness or on mere hearsay or rumor; it is sufficient that
"the opinion is decided, and has been expressed. When,
"however, the opinion is founded on common rumor, the
"presumption is that it is merely hypothetical, and it

" will be so considered in the absence of proof to the con-
" trary. But whether the opinion be hypothetical or de-
" cided, whether founded on rumor or on evidence heard
" at the trial, the juror *must be free from prejudice against*
" *the accused.* He must be able to give him a fair and an
" impartial trial. Upon this point nothing should be left.
" to inference or doubt. All the tests applied by the
" court, all the inquiries made into the state of the juror's
" mind, are merely to ascertain whether he comes to the
" trial free from partiality and prejudice. If there be a
" reasonable doubt whether the juror possesses these
" qualities, the doubt is sufficient to insure his exclusion.
" For, as has been well said, it is not only important that
" justice should be impartially administered, but that it
" should flow through channels as free from suspicion *as*
" *possible.*"

V. THE CONDUCT OF THE SPECIAL BAILIFF.

We deem it proper also to call attention to the fact that
we were subjected to most outrageous misconduct on the
part of a special baliff, who had in charge the summoning of the talesmen.

In support of our motion for a new trial we filed an
application for leave to examine as a witness in open
court Otis Favor, and to use his examination upon the
motion. We filed, beside the formal affidavit of defendants, the affidavit of E. A. Stevens, who stated that Favor was an intimate acquaintance of the special bailiff,
Ryce, and that affiant had learned from Favor that while
said Ryce was serving the venires in the present case he
stated to said Favor, and to others in Favor's presence,
in substance, this: " I am managing this case and I know

" what I am about. Those fellows will hang, as certain
" as death. I am summoning as jurors such men as they
" will be compelled to challenge peremptorily, and when
" they have exhausted their peremptory challenges, they
" will have to take such a jury as is satisfactory to the
" state." (I A., 25; Vol. O, 51.)

Judge Gary refused to order the examination of Mr.
Favor upon this application, to which the defendants excepted. Nevertheless, we are convinced that the bailiff
did make these declarations, and did act upon the line of
policy therein indicated. We submit that the court erred
in not allowing the examination of Mr. Favor, and that
it was an abuse of judicial power to refuse such examination, it appearing from the affidavits filed that Favor
refused to make an affidavit in the case to be used in support of the motion for a new trial, but expressed a readiness to appear and testify, if required.

The refusal of Judge Gary to order Mr. Favor's examination, as appears from the record, was based prima-
rily on a denial by him of his *power* to so do. We submit
that the court was wrong in this position. This is not
and cannot be the law. Had we been permitted to show,
and had we established by proofs in support of our motion for a new trial, this villainy practiced against the rights
and lives of the defendants, there can be no question that
we would, on this ground alone, have been entitled to a
new trial.

But the power of the court to order the examination
admits of no doubt. The case was still in court awaiting
final disposition—and the court was possessed of plenary
power to require the appearance and testimony of witnesses so far as requisite to the due administration of
justice. The power of the court to require witnesses to
appear and testify, even after judgment, is distinctly

recognized in such cases as when one is examined as to
his testimony on a trial, in order to settle a point for a bill
of exceptions. *People* v. *Jameson*, 40 Ill., 93. And the
granting of such a motion as was here made is recognized
as proper practice in those jurisdictions (as in England
and Pennsylvania), where, upon a motion for new trial, a
rule to show cause is entered. Under such a rule deposi-
tions may be taken on notice, or under a special rule witnesses may be examined in open court. (Troubat &
Holz's Pr., §§1,459 and 1,472, pages 852 and 853.)
Under our practice a motion is filed, supported by affidavits. But justice forbids that one should be denied an
opportunity to support his motion because of the refusal
of a party to give an affidavit, to compel which there is
no statutory provision; and in such case requires an order
that he should be examined. To refuse such order on
the application and showing made in this case was so
flagrantly unjust as to be palpably erroneous.

VI. MISCONDUCT OF JURY.

There is one point, as to the conduct of the jury upon
this trial, which, alike upon reason and authority, we deem
it proper to present to this court upon consideration of
this record. It appears from one of the affidavits filed in
support of the motion for a new trial (1 A., 29; O, 84),
and it is not in any manner contradicted, that after the
jury were sworn to try the issues, before any testimony
was offered, the presiding judge proposed to counsel that
the jury should be furnished from day to day with a
short-hand writer's transcript of the testimony taken upon
the previous day. This proposition defendants, by their
counsel, declined to accede to.

It appears, however, that from day to day, during the progress of the trial, various of the jurors took notes, short-hand or otherwise, of portions of the testimony as it was being offered, which they carried with them from the jury box from day to day. We believe this conduct was erroneous, and that it should not have been allowed. The objections to it are obvious. Instead of the jurors preserving, as far as possible, a clear mind, listening, as far as possible, with impartial attention to *all* of the testimony, and giving equal consideration to it all, their attention, those of them who were engaged in taking notes, would from time to time be drawn off from what was currently passing, by their own exercise in taking down the notes of the testimony; while, still further, in a subsequent consideration of the testimony, that which they had thus noted was likely to be given undue weight and prominence in their deliberations. Such conduct upon the part of a jury has been expressly held to be error for which a reversal should be ordered.

> Thompson and Merriam on Jury, Sec. 390.
> *Cheek* v. *State*, 35 Indiana, 492.
> *Palmer* v. *State*, 29 Arkansas, 249.

If this be the law, then here also was ground on which a new trial should have been granted, and the refusal to grant a new trial under the circumstances was error for which there should be a reversal.

VII. AS TO THE NUMBER OF PEREMPTORY CHALLENGES ALLOWED THE STATE.

The next point to which we desire to call attention, arising in connection with the selection of the jury, is this: When the state had, by its representative, peremptorily challenged twenty proposed jurors, it happened that there was tendered to the state as a juror acceptable to the defendants, August Berg, who was thereupon peremptorily challenged by the state. Whereupon the defendants interposed respectively the following objection (1 A., 83; Vol. D, 367):

"August Spies, the accused, objects to any further "peremptory challenge by the attorney prosecuting on "behalf of the people, because the said attorney has "already been admitted to, and has exercised against this "accused, twenty peremptory challenges, being the full "number of peremptory challenges allowed to this "accused under the statute; and in the exercise of such "challenges has excluded from the jury divers jurors "who were acceptable to, and accepted by, this accused."

The same objection was interposed in behalf of each of the accused at that juncture. The objection being overruled, the peremptory challenge was allowed; and thereafter in the progress of the trial more than thirty additional peremptory challenges were exercised by the attorney prosecuting on behalf of the people, and making the total number of peremptory challenges exercised by said attorney between fifty and sixty. In each and every instance of such peremptory challenge by the state, after the first twenty, the same objection was interposed in behalf of each of the several defendants, and in each and every instance each and every of the defendants excepted to the ruling of the court allowing such additional peremptory challenges.

The disposition of this objection involved a discussion as to the proper construction of the provision of our statute with reference to peremptory challenges.

The argument on that point appears somewhat fully in Vol. D, pp. 368 to 391.

The positions taken in support of the objection may be summarized as follows: That while the statute provides that "*every person* arraigned for any crime punishable " with death or imprisonment in the penitentiary for life " shall be admitted to a peremptory challenge of twenty " jurors," etc., "the attorney prosecuting on behalf of " the people shall be admitted to a peremptory challenge " of the same number of jurors that *the accused* is en-" titled to." In contemplation of law, the defendants in a criminal action, no matter how many of them there may be, constitute but one party, and the trial is a trial, in each instance, between the people on one side and *one defendant or accused* upon the other, whose rights are to be guarded. That the state cannot multiply its challenges by increasing the number of parties defendant, any more than it can abridge the right of each person defending to his separate number of challenges by joining such person with others. That any other construction of the statute would enable the attorney prosecuting on behalf of the people to multiply his challenges indefinitely, by joining as defendants persons against whom he might know that he had no evidence. In the case at bar, under the construction contended for by the state's attorney, the state might have exercised 160 peremptory challenges, and then, before offering a particle of proof, might have dismissed as to every defendant except one, and proceeded against him. That in such case the state would have exercised 160 challenges peremptorily as against the defendant tried, to the manifest perversion of the provision of the statute. That if the state elects to try the defendants jointly, and, as in the case at bar, opposes a separate trial, the state must take that position, subject to the possible disadvantage of the defendants jointly exercising more peremptory challenges than the state is in

such case entitled to. The language of the statute in
reference to the peremptory challenges by the attorney
prosecuting in behalf of the people, is explained by referring to the fact that in the previous parts of the section
the number of peremptory challenges allowed to every
person arraigned is stated with reference to different
crimes; and then comes the general provision that the attorney for the people " shall be admitted to a peremptory
" challenge of the same number of jurors that the accused
" is entitled to " ; the language of the statute being in
the singular, and not to be enlarged. In support of our
construction of this statute, and of our objection to the exercise of these additional peremptory challenges, we beg
to call the attention of the court, without citing at length,
to the following authorities:

The question considered arises upon a construction of
section 432 of the Criminal Code, Hurd's Rev. Stat.
1885.

Schaefer v. *The State*, 3 Wis., 730.
Wiggins v. *The State*, 1 Lea (Tenn.), 738.
Mayhon v. *The State*, 10 Ohio, 232.
State v. *Earle*, 24 La. Ann., 38.
State v. *Gay*, 25 La. Ann., 472.
Savage v. *The State*, 18 Fla., 925.
Wylie v. *The State*, 4 Blackf. (Ind.), 458.
State v. *Reed*, 47 N. H., 466.

VIII. THE MANNER OF EMPANELING THE JURY.

Sec. 21 of Starr and Curtis' Annotated Statutes, Vol.
2, Chap. 78, provides:

" Upon the empaneling of any jury in any civil cause
" now pending, or to be hereafter commenced in any court

" in this state, it shall be the duty of the court, upon
" request of either party to the suit, or upon its
" own motion, to order its (the) full number of twelve
" jurors into the jury box, before either party shall
" be required to examine any of said jurors touching
" their qualifications to try any such causes: *Provided*,
" that the jury shall be passed upon and accepted in
" panels of four by the parties, commencing with the
" plaintiff."

Sec. 23 of the same act provides:

" The provisions of this act shall apply to proceedings
" in both civil and criminal cases."

In the present case a panel of four jurors were, after
being passed upon and accepted by the state, tendered to
the defense by the state. They were then examined, and
three of them, for instance, were excused for cause, and
one peremptorily. That left the box vacant. The defense then asked the court that another panel of four be
first passed upon and accepted and tendered them by the
state, but the court ruled, against the objection and exception of the defendants, that the defendants must pass upon
and tender the next panel of four jurors to the state. (See
1 A., 39; Vol. A., 71, 72.)

The record discloses that the same point was made in
every instance by the defendants in the course of the empaneling of the jury where the four tendered by the state
were exhausted, either for cause or peremptorily, with the
same ruling on the part of the court, and in every instance
the defendants excepted.

The court stated, upon disposing of the said motion, as
follows (A., 71): " There has never been an instance in
" this court of the state being called upon to tender the
" defendants a second panel before the defendants ten-
" dered them back four."

As to the law on this point, we beg to cite *Braizer* v. *The State*, 34 Ala., 387, and the court there says:

" Where the statute provides a mode of empaneling a " jury, no other mode can be followed."

In *Fitzpatrick* v. *City of Joliet*, 87 Ill., 58, the court (page 62), in delivering its opinion, decides this very point and says: " But the defendant in error held the " affirmative, and was, very properly, in the first instance, " required to pass on the jury first, and this should have " been required as often as new jurymen were placed in " the box to take the place of others who had been ex- " cused, leaving the plaintiff in error an opportunity to " object as often as new jurors were presented, so long as " their rights of peremptory challenge were not ex- " hausted."

CC. IMPROPER REMARKS BY THE COURT.

We respectfully submit that, in addition to the matters hereinbefore considered, plaintiffs in error were aggrieved by the repeated improper remarks made by the court during the progress of the empaneling of the jury and upon the hearing of this case, remarks which were full of hostile suggestion, and, as we view it, could not but have had a tendency to prejudice the minds of the jurors against the plaintiffs in error. We do not propose to prolong our argument by attempting to present to this court all of the remarks made by the presiding judge in the progress of the trial, which are, in our opinion, justly subject to this criticism; but we will proceed to call attention to some illustrations.

Upon the examination of Mr. Shedd, a proposed juror (1 A., 36; Vol. A, 397), after Mr. Shedd had admitted his prejudice against the plaintiffs in error, growing out of what he had heard and read, and also that he had a decided prejudice against the class known as socialists, communists or anarchists, which he believed would prevent him from rendering an impartial verdict if it should appear that the defendants' belonged to that class, this occurred:

" The Court: I know, or the court judicially, what " are the objects of communists, socialists and anarchists. " *   *   * You must presume that I know, be- " cause it has been decided that for a man to say that he " is prejudiced against horse-thieves is no ground for im- " puting to him any misconduct as a juror. Now, you " must assume that I know either that anarchists, social- " ists and communists are a worthy, a praiseworthy class " of people, having worthy objects, or else I cannot say " that a prejudice against them is wrong."

Can it be argued that this remark was not in its nature highly prejudicial to the plaintiffs in error upon the hypothesis of their being socialists, communists or anarchists? Here was a suggestion by the court to the jury that he knew, judicially (of course he did not, but he so stated), what were the objects of socialists, anarchists and communists; and then, by way of illustrating his position, he mentioned prejudice against the class of horse-thieves; the only occasion of such reference being that thereby the court suggested an analogy between the classes. In other words, the expression of the court was exactly equivalent to saying: " I know the purposes of " socialists, anarchists and communists—that they are as " pernicious and unjustifiable as the vocation of horse- " thieves; and therefore Mr. Shedd's prejudice against " this class, even though he admits that it is such that he " could not render a fair verdict where one of them is in-

" volved, is not a disqualifying prejudice." In other words, the court in effect ruled that if a man was a social-ist, anarchist or communist, he was known to the court judicially to be of such evil purposes and so bad a char-acter that he was not entitled to an unprejudiced jury, but was well enough off if he had a jury even of men prejudiced against the class to which he belonged, and that such prejudice was not a disqualification.

No other view of the effect of these remarks can be entertained reasonably in the light of his closing words, when the judge said: " You must assume that I know " that anarchists, socialists and communists are a worthy, " a praiseworthy class of people, having worthy objects, " or else I cannot say that a prejudice against them is " wrong." To so state, after saying that he *did* know their objects, and then to overrule a challenge on the ground of the admitted prejudice, was exactly equivalent to saying that, knowing their objects, and that they were not a worthy class of people, a prejudice against them was not wrong. The constitution provides for an un-prejudiced jury, without regard to the character of the class to which the accused may be supposed to belong.

In connection with the examination of the very next proposed juror, J. K. Misch, after Mr. Misch had ad-mitted a like prejudice to that admitted by Mr. Shedd, and had stated that he thought it would require more testimony if the plaintiffs in error belonged to this class of people to find them not guilty than though they did not belong to this class, and that therefore he did not think that he could make a fair juror, the court asked the question: " Is your prejudice upon this subject based upon " the idea that you suppose this class are in favor of " overturning society by force "? To this remark an ob-jection was at once interposed. That it was improper for

the court to ask a question of this kind we think admits
of no argument, particularly following his former remarks, above quoted. It does not make any difference
upon what the talesman's prejudice was based, if it was
a prejudice that the talesman was conscious of and which,
in the opinion of the talesman, disqualified him to sit in
judgment in the case by destroying his impartiality. It
was not for the court to investigate as to the foundation
of the talesman's prejudice, and particularly not for the
court, in the process of such investigation, to suggest the
idea that the plaintiffs in error were in favor of overturning society by force. Both of these talesmen were challenged peremptorily, Mr. Shedd after the challenge for
cause had been overruled.

In the course of the examination of James H. Walker
(1 A., 105; Vol. F, 41), after the talesman had admitted
that he had an opinion which would *handicap* his judgment, the court said, in the presence of talesmen who
were awaiting examination: " Well, that is a sufficient
" qualification for a juror in the case. Of course, the
" more a man feels he is handicapped, the more he will
" be guarded against it."

This remark of the court is followed in the record by
an exception thus expressed:

" Mr. BLACK: We except to that remark by the court.
" We do not think it is in accordance with observation
" and judgment and experience. We think it is an im-
" proper remark to make in the presence of the jurors,
" and would like to have the record show that the seats
" are full and talesmen present at the time the remark is
" made."

That a man leans against his previous opinion, as here
assumed by the court, is, of course, an utterly mistaken
assumption. If the position here announced by Judge

Gary be correct, then the more prejudiced the jury against the accused—providing only that the jury were men of sufficient intelligence to recognize the prejudice, and men of sufficient honesty to wish to act fairly—the more suitable they would be as jurors, and the more fully they would meet the constitutional requirement of an impartial jury. Can any suggestion be more absurd? But the special objection to the making of the remark at the time and the place was, that it would have a natural tendency to mislead the talesmen awaiting examination. It was, in effect, a statement to them that, no matter what their recognized prejudice in the case, yet that prejudice would not in fact disqualify them from acting as fair and impartial jurors; and it was, therefore, a direct incentive to them to answer to the question whether they believed they could fairly and impartially try the case and render a verdict, that they did so believe, without reference to the prejudice that they recognized as existing in themselves. The remark was clearly improper and highly prejudicial.

The remarks made by the court in connection with the ruling, during the examination of Mr. Waller, we have already presented fully.

A little later, Theodore Fricke was called as a witness for the prosecution. In the course of his examiuation Most's book was presented to him, and he thereupon said that he had seen Most's book in the Arbeiter Zeitung library, and also had seen it sold by Hirschberger at socialistic picnics and mass-meetings, at some of which meetings Spies, Parsons, Fielden, Neebe, Schwab and perhaps Fischer had sometimes been present. Counsel in behalf of the plaintiffs in error objected to this entire line of inquiry, because it was not shown that any of the defendants knew of or participated in the selling, or had anything to do with it, or that they saw the selling. Thereupon, in ruling upon this objection, the following occurred (A., 41, 42; Vol. I, 477):

"The COURT: If men are teaching the public how to "commit murder, it is admissible to prove it, if it can be "proved by items.

"Mr. BLACK. Well, does your Honor know what "this teaches?

"The COURT: I don't know what the contents of the "book are; I asked what the book was and I was told "that it was Herr Most's Science of Revolutionary "Warfare, and taught the preparing of deadly weapons "and missiles, and that was accepted by the other side.

"Mr. BLACK: Does that justify your Honor in the "construction that it teaches how to commit murder, or "stating that in the presence of the jury?"

Defendants thereupon excepted to the language of the court, whereupon the court said:

"I inquired what sort of book it was, and it was stated "by the other side what sort of book it was, and you said "nothing about it; so that in ruling upon the question "whether it may be shown where it was to be found, "where it had been seen, I must take the character of "the book in consideration in determining whether it is "admissible. Whether it is of that character or not, we "will see when it is translated, I suppose. I suppose the "book is not in the English language."

Could any language be more improper than this of the court in passing upon this objection? The language of the court was tantamouut to saying—inasmuch as these plaintiffs in error are teaching the public how to commit murder, this book is admissible to help prove that fact. In other words, the language of the court started on the hypothesis that this was being done. "If," says the court,

" men are teaching the people how to commit murder, it
" is admissible to prove it if it can be proved by items."
And yet, the court was compelled to admit, a little
further on, that he did not know the contents of the
proposed book, but assumed that it was characterized by
teachings to commit murder, and, therefore, ruled that
evidence as to when and where it was disposed of should
be permitted to go to the jury, upon the assumption that
when the translation should afterwards be introduced, it
might have a tendency to establish this hypothesis, suggested by the court, first of all in the rulings in connection
with Waller's testimony, and here repeated in the most
radical form. There was no possible excuse for the suggestion by the court, at that juncture, that Most's book, not
then as yet before the jury, not then as yet translated, did in
fact teach how to commit murder; or making in the presence of the jury the suggestion that was made. The un-
avoidable application which would be made by the jurors
of the remark was to the plaintiffs in error, as the parties
supposed by the court to be engaged in " teaching the
" people how to commit murder."

So, later in the case, when the translations of Most's
book and of the International Workingpeople's Association were offered in evidence (A., 72; Vol. J, 192 *et
seq.*), the court, in allowing the introduction of the docu-
ments, used the following language:

" I have no doubt but what it is competent. The cir-
" cumstances may be significant or not, depending
" upon the surroundings; whether it is significant
" or not it is for the jury to determine from the
" surroundings which come before them. Whether
" the defendants, or any of them, were intending
" to have a mob kill people, and were teaching them how
" to kill people, is a question which this jury is to find out

"from the evidence. And these two translations are ad-
"missible upon the investigation of that question."

Was that question fairly under investigation by this jury? Suppose that the defendants, or some of them, were "intending to have a mob kill people, and were teaching "them how to kill people," what had that to do legitimately with the issue before the jury, which was simply whether or not the plaintiffs in error killed Mathias J. Degan, or advised, assisted, encouraged or abetted that homicide? The suggestion was an improper suggestion to be made. It was an intimation to the jury at an improper time, from an improper source, in an improper manner, that, in the view of the court, it was a question for the determination of the jury, whether the defendants were intending to have a mob kill people, and were teaching them how to kill people.

So, in connection with the ruling upon the motion made in Neebe's behalf, there were highly improper suggestions and remarks made by the court, in our judgment, upon which, however, we have sufficiently commented, and to which we now simply refer.

Finally, under this head, we call attention to the remarks of the court occurring in connection with the examination of Johann Grueneberg, a witness called to the stand by the plaintiffs in error (A., 257, 258; Vol. M, 259, 260.) Mr. Grueneberg had been examined in reference to the occurrences attending the printing of the circular calling the Haymarket meeting, and the ordering out of the line, "Workingmen, arm yourselves and appear in full force!" by Mr. Fischer; the printing of the residue of the circular thereafter without that line, and the distribution thereof. This was all. In the course of cross-examination the representatives of the state were allowed to depart entirely from the direct examination, and to inquire as to the witness' whereabouts, etc., on the days previous to the day of the printing of this circular. The question was asked him as to whether he was at home on Sunday morning, May 2d. To this question an objection was interposed, on the ground that it was not proper cross-examination; whereupon the court ruled in the following language:

" You have put this witness on the stand for the pur-
" pose of showing a thing was taken out of a particular
" circular; whether he has told that thing as it occurred
" depends to some degree upon what his associations,
" feelings, inclinations, biases are in reference to the
" whole business."

Thereupon counsel for plaintiffs, in unfeigned astonishment, responded, " Whether he has told the truth in re-
" gard to that depends upon his biases and inclinations?"

The COURT: " Whether it is to be believed—I don't
" mean whether he has told the truth."

Exception to the ruling and the language of the court was interposed on behalf of plaintiffs in error.

If this same language had been used by counsel instead of by the presiding judge, we would feel warranted in saying it was a deliberate and unjustifiable effort to discredit before the jury an unimpeached witness, testifying in reference to a particular fact as to which there was no attempt to contradict him then or at any time in the progress of the case. It will not be pretended that there is a particle of evidence in this record showing or tending to show that Mr. Grueneberg's testimony as to the taking out of that line in the circular, and as to all the matters connected with it, was not absolutely true. No contradiction of his testimony was in the record up to the time of his testifying and of the court making this ruling, no impeachment had been suggested or attempted. There

was nothing in the record to raise the slightest question,
at that juncture, but that the witness was telling the
exact truth. What justification could there be, then, for
the court to suggest to the jury the question whether the
witness was telling the truth as to the matter testified of,
and that that question was one to be determined at least
measurably by showing the bias, prejudice or associations
of the witness?

We respectfully submit that there can be no excuse
whatever for these various utterances of the presiding
judge to which we have had to call attention, and other
like utterances, and that they were altogether improper,
highly prejudical to the rights and interests of the plaintiffs in error, and therefore materially erroneous.

In support of our position upon this point, and that
such improper remarks afford ground for reversal, we
cite the following authorities:

> *Andrews* v. *Ketcham*, 77 Ill., 377.
> *State* v. *Harkin*, 7 Nev., 382.
> *Hair* v. *Little*, 28 Ala., 236.

DD. THE IMPROPRIETIES OF THE CLOSING ARGUMENT OF THE STATE'S ATTORNEY.

One point made in support of the motion for a new
trial was, that "the closing argument of the state's at-
"torney was improper in its statement of substantive mat-
"ters not in evidence, in its appeals to the prejudices and
"passions of the jury, in its misstatement of the issues,
"and in its abusiveness to the defendants, all having a nat-
"ural tendency to mislead the jury and to prevent a fair
"and impartial verdict." (Vol. O, p. 44.)

In support of this point under the motion for a new

trial, an affidavit was filed setting forth various extracts
taken from the short-hand report of the closing argument
of Mr. Grinnell, which extracts appear in 1 A., 29 *et seq;*
O, 86 *et seq.*, 87 to 94, inclusive. (1 A., 29-33.)

1. THE OBJECTIONABLE REMARKS OF THE STATE'S
ATTORNEY.

From this affidavit it appears the defendants were called
by Mr. Grinnell "loathsome murderers;" also "these
" wretches here;" also " assassins," and a second time on
the same page they are spoken of as " a lot of wretches."
Then shortly followed these words: " There is one step
" from Republicanism to anarchy. Let us never take
" that step. Gentlemen, the great responsibility that is
" devolved upon you in this case is greater than any jury
" in the history of the world ever undertook. This is no
" slight or mean duty that you are called upon to per-
" form. You are to say whether that step shall be
" taken."

The state's attorney further claimed that the jury
were really trying the defendants " for the murder of
" seven officers as well as for the injury to these sixty
" others," and also urged upon the jury, as a reason why
they should find the defendants guilty, that if they were
acquitted that was the end of the case, and there was no
appeal by the State of Illinois, and then used this language: " If, however, in the trial of this case, you should
" find that the defendants are guilty, from the proof in
" this case and under the instruction of the court, you
" then, in rendering your verdict, do what the gentlemen
" upon the other side, from the numerous exceptions they
" have taken, expect you to do, find the defendants guilty,
" they can appeal. If they do not like your verdict they

" can ask this court to set it aside, or the Supreme court
" to review your judgment."

On page 89, the state's attorney, against the objection
and in the face of the contradiction interposed at the time
by defendant's counsel, stated to the jury, in commending
the argument of his associate, Mr. Ingham, as follows:
" As one of the counsel said to me in the hall, his argu-
" ment was unanswerable, and therefore they would not
" undertake it."

On the same page it appears that the state's attorney
used the following language: " Prejudice? Men, organ-
" ized assassins, can preach murder in our city for
" years, you deliberately under your oaths hear the proof,
" and then say you have no prejudice." Thereupon
counsel for defense excepted to the language of the state's
attorney and protested against the continued reference to
the defendants, whose guilt was the question of consideration, as assassins. The court simply replied: " Save
your exceptions."

From the same page it appears that Mr. Grinnell further said: " We stand here, gentlemen, as I told you
" yesterday, already, with the verdict in our favor—I
" mean in favor of the prosecution as to the conduct of
" this case." Counsel for defendants thereupon arose,
took an exception to the statement of the state's attorney,
and denounced the same as outrageous. To which the
court responded, " Save the point upon it."

On page 90 Mr. Grinnell stated as follows: " Gilmer
" told us the story on the 5th or the 6th or the 7th -I
" will not be sure about the date; and he told us all the time
" the same." Thereupon counsel for defendants excepted
to the statement that Gilmer had at all times told the same
story. After some discussion with the court on that
point, the state's attorney stated substantially as follows

(page 91): " When we had Spies under arrest, I confess
" to you then, and after it was developed that a conspiracy
" existed—I confess this weakness—that I did not sup-
" pose that a man living in our community would enter
" into a conspiracy so hellish and damnable as the proof
" showed and our investigations subsequently showed he
" had entered into, and therefore, notwithstanding Gil-
" mer's statement to us so frequently, he was not shown
" and not identified." And thereupon, in reference to his
opening statement as to the bomb-thrower, Mr. Grinnell
stated as follows: " I said in that opening that we
" would show to you who threw that bomb; I said
" in that opening that we would show that the man
" left the wagon, lighted the match and threw the
" bomb.

" That was not absolutely correct. I should have said
" that the man that came from the wagon, as the proof
" shows, and as we knew came from the wagon, was in
" that group, assisted, and that the bomb was thrown by
" the man whom we would show to you. My associates
" found fault with me in the office immediately afterwards
" for not more clearly defining it." To this statement
exception was taken.

Could there be a greater abuse of the privileges of
counsel than this? A part of our attack on Gilmer's
evidence was that to Graham he said he saw the man
light the fuse and throw the bomb—a statement totally at
variance with his evidence. Mr. Grinnell in his opening
had, as he here admitted, stated in effect that the evidence
would show the one man who left the wagon, lighted the
fuse and threw the bomb; a direct confirmation of Graham
and impeachment of Gilmer. Was it allowable to the
state's attorney to attempt in his closing argument to take
back his opening statement, declare what occurred be-

tween himself and his associates and attempt by his assertions to fortify his witness?

Later, Mr. Grinnell stated to the jury as follows (page
92): " Don't try, gentlemen, to shirk the issues. Law
" is on trial. Anarchy is on trial. The defendants are
" on trial *for treason and murder*." And thereupon Mr.
Grinnell proceeded to argue the question of the crime of
treason, and the penalty of treason as death without any
modified punishment, using, with other, the following
language: " Under the laws of this state, if an individual
" is guilty of treason, the punishment is death. There
" is no mitigation, no palliation, no chance for the jury to
" hedge on the offense. For that offense you cannot say
" that this man shall have a few years in the penitentiary,
" and that one a few more, and that one shall suffer the
" extreme penalty of death. No, it is death. And
" treason, gentlemen, can only be committed by a citizen.
" None of these defendants, except Parsons and Neebe,
" are citizens. * * * If they had been citizens, you
" (counsel for defendants) would have proved it. Or else
" there was more design in it than that. You failed to
" prove it, because thinking there might be some possible
" chance or technicality in the upper court. * * *
" The penalty for treason is death, and it is death, in
" treason, whether the individual committing the treason
" kills a man or not." With more language of the same
character.

Farther on in his argument (page 93) he stated as
follows: " But not content, these revolutionists, these
" traitors, these men who have committed treason—I thank
" again the gentleman for the word—these men who have
" committed treason are not content with confining their
" power and influence to the small limits of Cook county,
" but Spies goes to Grand Rapids, and there gives utter-

" ance to these same treasonable sentences," etc. And, again: " Courageous men ! Herr Most gives the plan," etc.

Farther on he called the defendants and others associated with them, "infamous scoundrels," " wretches who " have attempted to betray the law." Thereupon, Mr. Grinnell stated as follows: " Weekly, since the 4th of " May, have bombs been found scattered in the north " and west and south-west parts of the city, and they " will continue to be found." To which statement defendants excepted, as being unsupported by evidence.

Nearing the close of this argument (page 94) he said: " If I had the power I would like to take you all over to " the Haymarket that night, and with you with tears in " your eyes see the dead and mingle with the wounded " and dying, see law violated, and then I could, if I had " the power, paint you a picture that would *steel your* " *hearts against the defendants.*" And then referring to the testimony of the officer who swore that Fielden shot him in the knee, he said: " For the purpose of correcting " myself, I had the officer come to my office and examined " the wound, and I found that the bullet went in there " (indicating) and came out above, going around up " opposite the knee-cap, and was not from behind." Thereupon there was an exception to the statement on the ground that Mr. Grinnell had no right to say that he had seen the wound again, and thereupon Mr. Grinnell repeated his statement, indicating the alleged course of the wound. To all of which defendants excepted.

It will be observed from these statements that, as stated in the point under the motion for a new trial, the closing argument of Mr. Grinnell had in it repeated statements of substantive matter not in evidence, appeals to the prejudices of the jury, distinct misstatements of the issues; and was exceedingly abusive in its expressions towards the defendants.

In other words, in a case where the defendants were on trial charged with murder, and where the counsel for defendants had been prohibited by the court from examining the jurors as to the extent to which their admitted prejudices against anarchists, socialists, etc., might influence them, the counsel for the state called the defendants "loathsome" "murderers," "organized" "assassins," "wretches," "scoundrels" and "anarchists"—claimed to the jury that the law was on trial; that anarchy was on trial—claimed the defendants were being tried, not only for the murder of seven men, instead of the one covered by the indictment, but also for the wounding of sixty others; made positive statements of matters *dehors* the record tending to prejudice the defendants, and appealed to the jury to convict the defendants on the ground that their acquittal was the end of the case, no appeal being allowed to the state, but that upon conviction they could appeal; and urged a conviction as the duty of the jury, in order to save our institutions from overthrow.

We repeat what we have said before herein, that in this case and under this argument and appeal of the state's attorney, the defendants were convicted, not because they were proved guilty of the murder of Mathias J. Degan, but because they were anarchists; and that was the issue which the attorney for the people distinctly stated to the jury was before them.

Such improprieties on the part of the counsel for the state, particularly in a closing argument, have always been held in themselves to entitle the defendants to a new, in order that they may have a fair, trial. This court has had occasion recently severely to reprobate the license of counsel for the state in prosecutions.

2. DECISIONS RELATING TO THE IMPROPRIETY OF
REMARKS OF COUNSEL.

In *Fox* v. *The People*, 95 Ill., 70-79, this court used the following language by Mr. Chief Justice WALKER: " It is complained that the state's attorney was unfair in " his closing argument to the jury; that he assumed facts " that were not proved, and urged them for a conviction. " It is the duty of the Circuit court in such cases to stop " counsel; to effectually prevent such unfairness when " attempted. Its duty is in all cases, and emphatically so " when life or liberty is involved, to prevent such unfair " conduct on the part of counsel. It cannot be sanctioned " to permit the people's attorney to thus treat the accused, " who is restrained of his liberty, and is helpless unless " protected by the court. Nor is it the duty of the state's " attorney to urge an unwarranted conviction, or resort to " unfair means to procure one, when he believes there is " no guilt. The prisoner should in all cases be treated " with fairness, and it is the duty of the court to see that " this right is not infringed.

" Complaints of this character are beginning to be " brought before us, and what is here said refers more to " the rule of practice that should obtain in all cases than " with reference to this case. But in this case we are of " opinion that a portion of the argument on the part of " the people was not fully warranted by the evidence. It " may be that the objectionable portions are not of such a " character as would alone justify a reversal. But when " the unfairness is gross it would be our duty in all doubt- " ful cases to reverse alone for that reason." The judgment in this case was reversed.

See also *Hennies* v. *Vogle*, 87 Ill., 242.

In *Ferguson* v. *The State*, 49 Ind., 43, objection was

made to the expressions of the state's attorney in the closing argument, and in reference thereto the court used the following language:

"The bill of exceptions shows the following facts, "which were also assigned as a cause for a new trial: "'On and during the progress of argument of counsel, "counsel for state commented upon the frequent occur- "rence of murder in the community, and the formation "of vigilance committees and mobs, and that the same "was caused by the laxity of the administration of laws, "stating to the jury that they should make an example "of the defendant. And the defendant, by his counsel, "asked the court to restrain the counsel, and objected to "said comments, because there was no evidence of such "matters before the jury; but the court overruled said "motion, and remarked in the hearing and the presence "of the jury that such matters were proper to be com- "mented upon, to which defendants at the same time "excepted, and still except.'

" The comments and argument of counsel and remarks "of the court during a trial may be within the discretion "of the judge presiding, but it is a judicial discretion, "and if improperly used to the injury of either party, "it may and ought to be revised and controlled by this "court. If it was proper to present these things to "and comment upon them before the jury, it was proper "for the jury to consider them in making up their ver- "dict. These things were outside of the record and the "evidence, and were calculated to prejudice the rights "of the defendant. It was tantamount to saying to the "jury, 'Murders have been committed, vigilance commit- "tees formed and mobs assembled in this county, and you "may take these matters into consideration in making "your verdict; and as you have got a chance now, you

"may make an example of the defendant! The jury
"may have come to a different conclusion from what they
"would if the court had quietly rebuked the counsel, and
"told him to keep his argument within the facts and evi-
"dence in the case. The action of the court was error,
"for which, if for no other cause, the judgment must be
"reversed."

In *State* v. *Smith*, 75 N. C., 306, the judgment was
reversed for misconduct of the state's attorney, consisting
in the following expressions:

"The defendant was such a scoundrel that he was
"compelled to move his trial from Jones county to a
"county where he was not known. * * * The bold,
"brazen-faced rascal had the impudence to write me a
"note yesterday, begging me not to prosecute him, and
"threatening me if I did, that he would get the legisla-
"ture to impeach me." Commenting upon these expressions, after stating the impropriety of their utterance, the
court proceed as follows:

"These charges and invectives were not only allowed
"to go to the jury, but were unexplained and uncor-
"rected by his Honor in his charge to the jury. In
"*Dennis* v. *Haywood*, 63 N. C. Rep., 53, the course here
"pursued by the solicitor is strongly reprobated. 'Sup-
"pose,' said the court, 'a defendant is to be tried for his
"life, and to escape unreasonable prejudices in one
"county, he removes his trial to another. The fact that
"he does so may be used to excite the prejudice that
"he is endeavoring to escape justice; thus he would
"escape the prejudices of one community to find them
"intensified in another. Would the court allow the fact
"to be given in evidence or commented upon by counsel?
"Certainly not.'

"So in *Jenkins* v. *The N. C. Ore-Dressing Co.*, 65

" N. C., 563, it is said, ' Where the counsel clearly abuses
" his privilege to the manifest prejudice of the opposite
" party, it is the duty of the judge to stop him then and
" there.   If he fails to do so, and the impropriety is gross,
" it is good ground for a new trial.'

"And in *The State* v. *Williams*, 65 N. C., 505, a new
" trial was granted in a case where language less harsh
" and violent was allowed by the court, and it was there
" said that it was the duty of the court to intervene for
" the protection of witnesses and parties, especially in
" criminal cases where the state is prosecuting one of its
" citizens.   The defendant was arraigned at the bar of
" the court, mute and helpless, without raising an un-
" seemly controversy with the solicitor.   The court is
" constituted a shield against *all* vituperation and abuse,
" and more especially where it is predicated upon alleged
" facts not in evidence or admissible in evidence. "

In the light of this language, as well as of the language
of our own Supreme court in the 95th Ill., above cited,
where it is said: " It is the duty of the Circuit court to
" stop counsel and effectually prevent such unfairness
" when attempted.   The duty is in all cases, and em-
" phatically so when life or liberty is involved, to prevent
" unfair conduct on the part of counsel.   It cannot be sanc-
" tioned to permit the people's attorney to thus treat the
" accused, who is restrained of his liberty and is helpless
" unless protected by the court.   *   *   *   When the
" unfairness is gross, it would be our duty in all doubtful
" cases to reverse alone for that reason "—in the light of
these expressions, we again call attention to the fact disclosed in this record, that not only was the representative of the state in the case at bar permitted to proceed
with grossly vituperative expressions concerning the defendants, calling them loathsome murderers, organized as-

sassins, scoundrels and wretches, and referring to matters
not in evidence; and, above all, appealing to the patriotic
prejudices of the jury, by claiming that the defendants
had been guilty of treason, for which the penalty was
death, without reference to the commission of the crime
of murder, and asserting that the defendants were not
citizens of this country, save possibly one or two
of them (although there was no evidence in the
record whatever to sustain that assertion—the state's
attorney arguing that they were not citizens, because
had they been we would have proved their citizen-
ship, unless we designedly omitted such proof to escape proceedings against them as traitors), not only
did the court permit the state's attorney to indulge in all
these gross and abusive improprieties in his closing argument, but upon objection and exception being made to
parts of this conduct, the court distinctly refused to interfere, saying to the defendants' counsel that they could
" save the point," and allowing the state's attorney to proceed unchecked and unrestrained. We respectfully submit that a more disgraceful exhibition of the outrageous
and unwarranted abuse of the privilege of counsel has
never blotted the administration of justice in our country.

In further support of our position, we also cite the case
of *Earll* v. *The People*, 99 Ill., 123. And also, without
stopping to quote from the many cases in which this wise,
humane and just rule of conduct has been enforced by
the courts, we cite the following authorities, with the
single observation that they go to the full length of the
cases above quoted from, and that there is no respectable
exception to the rule thus established:

See *Brown* v. *Swineford*, 42 Wis.. 282,
292–294.

Tucker v. *Hennecker*, 41 N. H., 317–322.

Hilliard v. *Beattie*, 59 N. H., 465.

Berry v. *State*, 10 Ga., 522.

Mitchum v. *State*, 11 Ga., 618.

Cobel v. *Cobel*, 79 N. C., 587.

Willis v. *McNeil*, 57 Tex., 465.

State v. *Turnbull*, 86 Mo., 113.

Henry v. *Sioux City*, S. C. Iowa, Dec. 9, 1886; 30 N. W. R., 630.

EE. ERROR IN REFUSING TO ARREST JUDGMENT.

We deem it proper, also, to submit to the consideration of the court the point that there was an error in the court below in overruling our motion in arrest of judgment upon the ground that the verdict of the jury, in view of the indictment, was uncertain.

Here was an indictment containing sixty-nine counts, as before suggested; one series of these counts charged the defendants with jointly committing the murder (a) by throwing a bomb, (b) by a revolver, (c) by an unknown weapon. Then followed ten series of counts of six each, charging the plaintiffs in error as being guilty as accessories to the murder, (a) by the throwing of a bomb by one of their number, (b) by the firing of a revolver by one of their number, and (c) by the use of an unknown weapon by one of their number; and in addition to this, there were six counts, charging the defendants as being accessory to the murder by an unknown party, (a) by throwing a bomb, (b) by the use of a revolver, and (c) by the use of an unknown weapon. Each series of counts charging accessoryship involved three counts, charging that the parties, being present, aided, abetted and assisted the act; and three others that, not being present, they had aided, advised, encouraged or abetted the throwing of the bomb.

The verdict of the jury found the defendants " guilty of " murder in manner and form as charged in the indict- " ment." What does this mean? Does it mean that the jury found the defendants guilty as accessories to the throwing of the bomb by Rudolph Schnaubelt? If that was the finding of the jury and the basis of their verdict, we were entitled to have that appear in the record, to know just what case we were required to meet under this writ of error. Does it mean that the jury found the plaintiffs in error guilty of themselves committing the offense? If so, we were entitled to know that fact, to be prepared in this court to consider that issue. Does it mean that the jury found the plaintiffs in error guilty as accessories to the throwing of the bomb by an unknown party, and not by Schnaubelt? If so, we were entitled to have that fact appear, that in a presentation of this cause to this court we might be disembarrased of the false issue, and might be required to meet alone the finding of the jury, whatever that was.

The indictment charged the commission of the murder in different ways, absolutely irreconcilable with one another. If the plaintiffs in error were guilty of committing the murder, in manner and form as charged in one count, then they were not guilty of the murder in manner and form as charged in another count. In fact, no one murder, in the nature of things, could be committed in manner and form as charged in this indictment, because this indictment charges murder under different and absolutely antagonistic methods, alike as to the party doing the act and the instrument used in the commission of the offense. To find, therefore, that the defendants were guilty of murder in manner and form as charged in the indictment was finding entirely too much. The plaintiffs in error were entitled to have the verdict applied to the particular count or counts in the indictment which the jury found to be supported by the evidence, and to have these counts singled out by the verdict, there being no *nolle pros.* by the state as to any of the counts in the indictment.

We beg the court, by way of testing the soundness of this contention of ours, to select the count in this indictment which is sustained beyond a reasonable doubt by the evidence introduced. It cannot be done!

And here we may call attention, properly, we think, to another error in the charge of the court in reference to the form of the verdict. Such instructions should have directed the jury to designate the count or counts in the indictment under which, if at all, they found the plaintiffs in error guilty.

CONCLUSION.

We confidently submit that material errors obtain in this record as to each and every one of the plaintiffs in error; and as to each and every one of the plaintiffs in error there is an absolute failure to make out a case justifying a conviction by legitimate evidence under the rules of law established by the authorities above considered.

We are not unmindful, however, that the suggestion may be made that while the error may be obvious as to certain of the plaintiffs in error, or while there may be an utter and entire failure to make out a case by legal evidence as to certain of the plaintiffs in error, that the case may stand differently in the judgment of some, either upon the evidence or as to the errors assigned, as to one or more of

the plaintiffs in error; and an affirmance of the judgment
may be urged as to some of them, coupled with a substantial admission that as to others there must be a
reversal.

We are led to suppose that a course of this kind may
be suggested because we find, on inspecting the record,
that there was in this case entered up as against each
plaintiff in error a several judgment. As to this matter of
severing in the judgment, we beg to call attention to the
fact that in our view no weight should be given to this
act of the clerk in the making up of his record, forasmuch
as it appears that the proceedings from the first to the last
were in fact one proceeding so far as the state was concerned. As we have before suggested, our effort to
secure a separate trial for certain of the plaintiffs in error
was opposed by the state, and our application to that end
denied by the court. The indictment is one indictment
against all of the plaintiffs in error, charging them as being
jointly accessories to the above murder. The proceedings from first to last were a unit. The verdict is one
verdict, not finding the plaintiffs in error severally guilty,
save only as to Mr. Neebe, as to whom a different punishment was assigned; but finding the seven plaintiffs in
error other than Neebe guilty and fixing their penalty in
one sentence. The motion for a new trial was interposed
in behalf of them all; and all of the proceedings had
thereunder were as in the case of a single defendant.
Aside from these considerations, however, the law is well
settled that in an action of this character, where parties
are tried jointly as conspirators, and judgment has gone
against them, error as to one reverses as to all.

In support of this position we call attention to the following among other authorities. The rule is stated by

by Mr. Wharton in his work upon criminal pleadings and practice, section 305, as follows:

" From the peculiar character of the pleading in con-
" spiracy, a new trial as to one defendant is a new trial
" as to all," citing in support of the text *Rex* v. *Gompertz*,
9th Queen's Bench, 824; Wharton Cr. Law, 9th Ed., Sec.
1,395; *Com.* v. *McGowan*, 2 Parsons, 341.

In *Com.* v. *McGowan*, 2 Parsons, 365, the law is thus declared on this point:

" But it has been said that although the court shall be
" satisfied the rejection of this evidence might have in-
" fluenced the verdict as to McGowan, still it does not
" apply to Pratt and Pence. If the fallacy of such a po-
" sition has not already been shown, I will refer to one
" case already cited in this opinion, which in my view
" settles the question. It is the case of the *Queen* v.
" *Gompertz*, 6 Penn., L. J., 377, where it is held, in con-
" spiracy, a new trial cannot be granted as to one without
" embracing all. I quote the remark of Lord Ch. J·
" DENMAN. 'I should add, we think that there is no
" ground to disturb the verdict, so far as it affects the de-
" fendant, Gompertz; but where two or more persons have
" been convicted of a conspiracy, it is not possible to
" grant a new trial as to one conspirator and not as to
" the others. Such, in my opinion, is unquestionably the
" law. A different doctrine would subvert the whole
" principle upon which the law of conspiracy is based.
" On trials for this offense, all connected with the trans-
" action are considered as one. The acts of one may be
" viewed as the acts of each of the others. It is the
" union of mind, the concert of action, which creates the
" offense. * * * If, then, it should be admitted there
" was ground foa setting aside the verdict as to one, how

" can the court know the bearing which the evidence of his
" acts, or connection in the affair, might have had in pro-
" ducing the conviction of the others, when, perhaps, if
" such an individual and his transactions were thrown out
" of view, a jury might not have acquitted those on whom
" the reasons for a new trial do not operate so favor-
" ably.' "

The same rule is announced in 3d Russell on Crimes
9th Ed., star page 176. This rule has been recognized and acted upon by this court, so far as we know,
without any exception whatever. These authorities are
controlling; for in the case at bar, the state's sole basis of
conviction, as evidenced by its instructions, was the alleged conspiracy, which, therefore, had to be found by
the jury as the ground-work of their verdict, the conspiracy merged in the felony charged, but a finding of conspiracy being a condition precedent to the verdict in this
case and involved therein, under the theory on which the
cause was tried.

We know of no exception to this rule as to all parties
joining in the writ of error.

We have, perhaps, dwelt upon this case at what may
seem unreasonable length. The importance of the issues
involved, the vast bulk of the record, the variety and
moment of the principles necessarily considered, and the
number of the parties whose lives and liberty are at
stake, must plead excuse if we have offended in this particular; and we are sure will secure for us lenient judgment at the hands of this court.

We repeat that upon a review of the entire evidence
in the case, and under the rules of law, established by the
authorities which we have above presented and considered,
first, that there was no legal evidence in this case to

justify the conviction of any one of the plaintiffs in error;
second, that each and all of the plaintiffs in error have
been, in the language of our statute, "aggrieved by
" manifest and material error appearing of record," against
which they are entitled to be relieved under this writ of
error and pursuant to law.

Respectfully submitted.

W. P. BLACK,
SALOMON & ZEISLER,
Attys. for Plffs. in Error.

NOTE. In further support of our views, we beg to
refer the court to the Brief and Argument filed herein by
HON. LEONARD SWETT, of counsel with us in this cause.

www.ingramcontent.com/pod-product-compliance
Lightning Source LLC
Chambersburg PA
CBHW032304280326
41932CB00009B/694